THE METAPHYSICAL CONFEDERACY

In this portrait of Thornwell, which tradition attributes to William Scarborough,
he is approximately forty years old (ca. 1852-1853) and serving as the president
of the South Carolina College. The engraver was R. Whitechurch, of J. M. But-
ler's establishment, Philadelphia. (Printed by Bell Studio, Lancaster, South Carolina. Used with permission of Florence Earle Roach and Jean Bernhardt,
descendants of Thornwell.)

THE METAPHYSICAL CONFEDERACY

James Henley Thornwell and the Synthesis of Southern Values

The Frank S. and Elizabeth D. Brewer
Prize Essay
of the American Society of Church History

by

JAMES OSCAR FARMER, JR.

MERCER UNIVERSITY PRESS **MP**

ISBN 0-86554-182-5

THE METAPHYSICAL CONFEDERACY
Copyright ©1986
Mercer University Press, Macon GA 31207
All rights reserved
Printed in the United States of America

The paper used in this publication meets
the minimum requirements of American National Standard
for Information Sciences—Permanence of Paper
for Printed Library Materials, ANSI Z39.48-1984. ∞™

Library of Congress Cataloging-in-Publication Data

Farmer, James Oscar, 1943–
The metaphysical confederacy.

Includes index.
1. Thornwell, James Henley, 1812–1862.
2. Presbyterian Church—South Carolina—Clergy—
Biography. 3. Theologians—South Carolina—Biography.
4. South Carolina—Biography. 5. Slavery and the
church—Presbyterian Church. I. Title.
BX9225.T64F37   1986   285'.1'0924 [B]   86-770
ISBN 0-86554-182-5 (alk. paper)

CONTENTS

To my family,
and to the memory of my father

ACKNOWLEDGMENTS

One does not repay the kind of debts one accumulates in the course of writing a book, much less those accrued in the academic career that led to it, except by sharing with others in the way others have shared with oneself. And since this never seems enough, I am happy to be able to express my thanks to some of the people without whose help this book would not exist.

The fine people who are the University of South Carolina at Lancaster have helped with the arrangement of class schedules and clerical assistance, and provided encouragement. I especially want to mention Dean John R. Arnold, Professor Peter Barry, and Cynthia Hampshire. The University of South Carolina helped by offering a summer "faculty exchange" on the Columbia campus when my research was in its final stage.

To Professor George C. Rogers, Jr. of the University of South Carolina I am indebted for patiently guiding this study through its first life as a doctoral dissertation and stimulating me to revise and polish it afterwards. Others whose help I have benefited from include Professors Daniel Hollis and Eugene Long, Allen Stokes and his staff at the South Caroliniana Library, Jerrold Brooks and his staff at the Presbyterian Historical Foundation, Henry Bowden, Theodore D. Bozeman, John Kuykendall, Jack Maddex, Florence Roach, and Louis Weeks.

My wife Judy and my family have helped me in more ways than I can express. Judy has been a constant source of support as well as a typist for the manuscript's several drafts. Beth and Erin have been tolerant of Daddy's odd hours and have kept my spirits high. My parents and parents-in-law have supported me with their interest and resources.

For the moral and monetary support of the Brewer Prize, I thank the American Society of Church History.

INTRODUCTION

For the historian who is interested in the role of religion in society, or the religious person who is attuned to the importance of the past, the American South is a most fruitful subject. Few societies have been more pervaded by religion, or "haunted by God," as James McBride Dabbs put it. Indeed, the region's history is so full of moral questions that "the writing of [it] has often become in itself a religious expression of the author and a moral Rorschach test for the reader."[1] One can hardly write or read about the Southern past, in other words, without becoming involved in speculations on morality, or making value judgments that reveal one's own moral philosophy. The aphorism "history is philosophy taught by examples" is perhaps nowhere more true than in this corner of the field.

Often modern historians have used the South as a metaphor for evil, "playing abolitionist" or attacking the image of the ignorant, prejudiced Southerner. Such uses of the past may be good therapy, and have produced some valuable insights, but sound historical studies are rarely the product of such polemical motivations. The reason for this unwillingness or inability to deal with the values of the Old South in an objective way is not hard to discover. Eric McKitrick perhaps puts it most succinctly when he writes that "nothing is more susceptible to oblivion than an argument, however ingenious, that has been discredited by events." He adds that the works of Southerners have "remained superbly unread," and that "history books refer to them, but with a flicker of impatience, having little time to spend on crackpots."[2] History, McKitrick is reminding us, is written by

---

[1] James McBride Dabbs, *Haunted by God* (Richmond, 1972). Donald G. Mathews, *Religion in the Old South* (Chicago, 1977) xiii.

[2] Eric McKitrick, *Slavery Defended: The Views of the Old South* (Englewood Cliffs NJ, 1963) 1-2. David Donald has written that the proslavery argument "has approximately the same scientific standing as astrology or alchemy." "The Pro-Slavery Argument Reconsidered," *Journal of Southern History* 37 (February 1971): 3. As Carl Becker observed, "All historical writing, even the most honest, is unconsciously subjective, since every age is bound, in spite of itself, to make the dead perform whatever tricks it finds necessary for its own peace of mind." Carl Becker, *The Heavenly City of the Eighteenth-Century Philosophers* (New Haven, 1932) 44.

the winners. Two sets of values have been in opposition to one another through most of our history as a nation; one has cherished dynamism, cosmopolitanism, rationalism, and egalitarianism, while the other has preferred stability, localism, faith, and deference.[3] By the second quarter of the nineteenth century, these opposing value systems were taking on a sectional quality, and politically they expressed themselves most articulately in the debate over slavery. Hence, because this debate was ultimately won by the progressive North, and because the values of the nation have prevailed over those of its minority region, modern historians who share implicitly in these values have found the Old South backward, inferior, and tainted by evil.

The bias that this perspective produces can be blatant and obvious, but it may also be subtle and even unconscious. In the preface to his book *The Inner Civil War*, George Frederickson explains that he is studying the intellectuals of the North not only because their side won the war and shaped the values of the postwar nation, but also because most of this period's major thinkers were Northerners. This is a statement that few students of American thought would oppose. But is it not in part an expression of its author's perspective? Does he not mean that Northern thought was more "respectable"?[4] It would seem that even the large body of Southern thought not directly related to slavery has suffered from a sort of "guilt by association" because it came from the same minds, or the same region, that defended the odious peculiar institution.

Another reason why historians have had difficulty meeting Southern thought on its own terms is that the Cash-Sellers school of Southern historiography has created a conception of the antebellum mind as closed. Plagued by fear and guilt over the dilemma of slavery, the typical Southerner, says this school, adopted an elaborate defense mechanism for his own mind as well as for his society. Closing his mind on the question of slavery, the Southerner thus warped his perspective on all public questions. "If there is one thing you can't think about," said Emerson, "you

---

[3]Richard D. Brown, *Modernization: The Transformation of American Life, 1600-1865* (New York, 1976).

[4]George M. Frederickson, *The Inner Civil War; Northern Intellectuals and the Crisis of the Union* (New York, 1965) viii.

can't really think about anything.''[5] This can lead to the conclusion that Southern intellectuals hardly deserve that name, since they, like everyone else in their society, simply fell into step with the regional orthodoxy. It is not surprising, therefore, that the Southern thinkers who have been most attractive to modern historians were the ''free lances'' who challenged the prevailing ideas of their section and were closer than their neighbors to the liberal mainstream of American thought.[6]

But as admirable and interesting as these shining exceptions are, surely the more typical thinkers of the Old South deserve greater attention than historians have been willing to give them. McKitrick even suggests that the Southern argument ''is intrinsically more interesting than that of the abolitionists because it is more difficult and more complex.'' If this is so, it is because the thinkers of the Old South were confronted with a dilemma, or a complex of dilemmas, that could hardly have produced a less Byzantine response. They labored on a variety of levels to achieve an acceptable resolution of their own and their region's plight; and the tortured writings they often produced in the effort are in themselves good reason why they remain ''superbly unread.'' They failed, at least in the pragmatic sense, but in the process they revealed minds worthy of admiration, and a value system, part of which can be studied with benefit by modern inheritors of the dominant value system.[7] William R. Taylor has suggested that the nostalgia felt by many Americans for the Old South and the romantic appeal of the Civil War are indications of ''our collective anxieties about the kind of civilization we have created'' and ''the kind of social conformity which, it appears, it has been our destiny to exemplify before the world.'' Even the most modern of us, Taylor suspects, occasionally ''allow our thoughts to play over this lingering social image, and to con-

---

[5]Dabbs, *Haunted by God,* 70. The Cash-Sellers thesis may be found in Wilbur J. Cash, *The Mind of the South* (New York, 1941) 92-94, and Charles G. Sellers, Jr., ed., ''The Travail of Slavery,'' in *The Southerner as American* (New York, 1966) 40-71.

[6]See, for example, Clement Eaton, *The Freedom of Thought Struggle in the Old South* (Durham, 1940), and Carl N. Degler, *The Other South: Southern Dissenters in the Nineteenth Century* (New York, 1974).

[7]McKitrick, *Slavery Defended,* 2. Conservatives like Clinton Rossiter have long been telling us that the thinkers of the Old South ''deserve to be better known and understood by modern Americans.'' Rossiter, *Conservatism in America* (New York, 1955) 128.

cede with mingled pride and wonderment: 'Once it was *different* down there.' "[8]

The materialist and collectivist tendencies of modern life have produced a growing ambivalence and equivocation in the world of political and social thought. The political "liberal" is not as sure of himself as he was a few years ago. Also, and perhaps not coincidently, the image of the South is currently being upgraded, with the new label "Sun Belt" becoming prominent. As one might expect, this new mood is producing, among its other offspring, a revision of our image of the Southern past.

The scholarship that has dominated Old South historiography in the mid-twentieth century, including the field of the Southern mind, has been focused primarily on the plight of a minority region whose economy and social values ran contrary to the prevailing national norms. Themes stressed within this framework have included Southern defensiveness, anti-intellectualism, ideological orthodoxy and, of course, the drift toward secession. However, in the last few years a new school has appeared, especially in the area of antebellum thought, which seeks to go beyond these valuable but ultimately unsatisfying studies. These scholars have asked more probing questions about their subject and have generally taken a more sympathetic view of the people whose works reveal the outlines of the antebellum mind. As a result of this development, Old South thinkers are no longer dismissed as archaic relics of a dead world, whose efforts to shore up a fatally flawed society are not worth serious examination. The conclusions that this new scholarship eventually produces about the values championed by these thinkers may be little different from those of the last generation. Nonetheless, the result will be a more complete understanding of the world from which this thought came.[9]

---

[8]William R. Taylor, *Cavalier and Yankee; The Old South and the American National Character* (New York, 1957) 341. Taylor reminds us that the society symbolized by the aristocratic planter was a myth. He also analyzes the creation of that myth. Myth-making was no doubt one of the by-products of Southern thought in the antebellum era. But the efforts of Old South intellectuals were directed not at the making of myths, but rather at establishing and defending a Southern ethic. That they fell short of success in making reality match the ideal is the common fate of all such efforts.

[9]Among these studies are several that have given direction or reinforcement to this project, particularly Theodore D. Bozeman, *Protestants in an Age of Science* (Chapel Hill, 1977); E. Brooks Holifield, *The Gentlemen Theologians* (Durham, 1978); Drew G. Faust, *A Sacred Circle: The Dilemma of the Intellectual in the Old South, 1840-1860* (Baltimore, 1978); Robert J. Brugger, "The Mind of the Old South: New Views," *Virginia Quarterly Review* 56 (Spring 1980): 277-95; and Michael O'Brien, ed., *All Clever Men Who Make Their Way; Critical Discourse in the Old South* (Fayetteville AK, 1982) intro.

These recent works produce a substantially different image of the antebellum intellectual than that which has generally been portrayed. He was deeply conscious of his mental gifts and the consequent obligation to contribute to his society, or to mankind. He was often critical, especially before the 1850s, of his home region, in an effort to perform a proper function. He was an individual and did not fit easily into a mold of social conformity. His domination of the region's educational, public-information, and religious institutions enabled him to exert significant influence on his time and place. Yet whether his perspective was that of science, arts and letters, theology or politics, his thought pointed to a social consensus that would undergird the besieged region as it moved toward its climactic moment.

The nineteenth century witnessed a crisis of values throughout Western civilization, as the industrial revolution worked its way into the intellectual and spiritual as well as the material world. Tantalized though many of them were by modern life, Southern thinkers chose a stance of opposition and reaction. At first plagued by self-doubt, they struggled to convince themselves, their region, and the outside world of the worth of their society and the superiority of their values. Some have noted in their efforts an attitude of defensiveness, even paranoia. They *were* defensive, because they were weaker than the forces that opposed them. But increasingly, during the years leading to secession, they presented their case with confidence. And in articulating their traditional values on a high intellectual plain, they provided a counterweight to the fear and self-doubt that—as recent studies have shown—were central to the Southern condition of those (as well as later) times.[10] To the extent that they were successful, secession was the product not of fear, but of confidence and even certitude.

A major facet of this traditional value system was orthodox Christian theology. By examining the career and thought of James Henley Thornwell of South Carolina, one may see in microcosm the religious perspective of the Old South and the efforts to build a sectional defense on this foundation. Thornwell seems an appropriate subject, as he was widely considered to be the leading figure not only in Southern but also in American Presbyterianism during the generation preceding the Civil War. Educated at the South Carolina College, he joined its faculty in 1837 and was chosen its president in 1851. While filling the pulpit of Columbia's First

---

[10]Steven Channing, *Crisis of Fear* (New York, 1970); Numan P. Bartley, *The Rise of Massive Resistance; Race and Politics in the South in the 1950s* (Baton Rouge, 1969).

Presbyterian Church, he also helped found and edit the *Southern Presbyterian Review,* perhaps the leading religious publication in the South. He also edited the *Southern Quarterly Review* in its last year of publication (1855-1856) and, after retiring from the college, taught theology at Columbia Theological Seminary from 1855 to 1862. This crowded career was climaxed by his role as the guiding light in the formation of the Southern Presbyterian Church in December 1861. He died the following year. Thornwell, though, was more than an active participant in the religious life of the South. His mind epitomized the Calvinist outlook and the conservative sociopolitical position of his region. And as the center of a circle of like-minded men, he formed a crucial link in the network of Southern thinkers who planted the seeds that the politicians would cultivate and harvest.

Thornwell was a thorough South Carolinian and spent almost all of his life in his native state. While this may reduce his claim as a figure of regional or national importance in some eyes, historians have long recognized South Carolina as the spawning ground of the Deep South. So it may be suggested that this leading Palmetto preacher can be seen as the prototype of Deep South religious thought.[11]

A study such as the one attempted here is a difficult one for at least two reasons. Writing about the religion of another time or place has been compared to "writing a diary for someone else." By its very nature religion is a part of man's private inner world and not easily communicated from one to another, especially across barriers of time and distance.[12] This particular exercise in religious history is further complicated by focusing on the career of one whose written work was formidable even to his colleagues. As one of them wrote to another, "one can't sleep over it and understand it."[13]

---

[11]South Carolina, wrote William Schaper at the beginning of this century, is "one of the fertile sources from which have spread many of the characteristic ideas and institutions of the [South]. Much that is typical of the South is here found in its purest and most accentuated form; whence it comes that a study of her local history often suggests the clew [*sic*] of the proper understanding of the South as a section." William Schaper, "Sectionalism and Representation in South Carolina," *Annual Report* of the American Historical Association, 1 (1900): 257.

[12]Edwin McNeill Poteat, Jr., "Religion in the South," in W. T. Couch, ed., *Culture in the South* (Chapel Hill, 1935) 248.

[13]John L. Girardeau to John Adger, 23 March 1870, James Henley Thornwell Papers, South Caroliniana Library, University of South Carolina.

Confronted by a mass of such material, the sensible historian turns his attention elsewhere, especially if he lacks theological training. This is no doubt the reason Thornwell is often mentioned as an important figure, but seldom studied in much detail. Yet, as J. Franklin Jameson wrote many years ago, religious history is unsurpassed as a "means of estimating the American character."[14] What is true of the national character is, some have suggested, even more true of the Southern mind. "One cannot rethink the thoughts of antebellum Southerners," writes Robert Brugger, "without coming to terms with their piety."[15] James Henley Thornwell would therefore seem to be an excellent subject through which to seek a better understanding of the mind of the Old South.

---

[14]Presidential Address to the American Historical Association, *American Historical Review* 13 (January 1908): 286-302, quoted in William W. Sweet, *Religion in the Development of American Culture, 1765-1840* (Gloucester MA, 1963) vii.

[15]Brugger, "The Mind of the Old South," 288.

CHAPTER 1

The Moral Octave

On 23 November 1860, as the American people pondered the meaning of Abraham Lincoln's victory in the presidential election, Charlestonian Henry William Ravenel read in his *Courier* a sermon preached at St. Michael's Church by the Reverend J. H. Elliott. Entitled "Our Christian Duties in the Present Emergency," it was for Ravenel consoling proof of the "entire unanimity which pervades all classes of our people, and the spirit which prevails for prudence and wisdom in our actions."[1] If Ravenel had any anxiety regarding the position of the Southern clergy in the coming crisis, he need not have. Sermons like the one he read were being delivered and printed all over the South that autumn and would continue to provide moral certainty for the Confederacy in the months and years ahead.[2] They were the centerpieces of the mind-conforming and conscience-easing service rendered to the South by its intellectuals, and most particularly by its clergy.

Although the Southern apologia has been studied extensively, its breadth and depth have yet to be fully comprehended. Reflecting on the generation of debate that had preceded secession, one Southerner con-

---

[1]Henry William Ravenel, Journal, 23 November 1860, South Caroliniana Library, University of South Carolina.

[2]*Fast Day Sermons, or the Pulpit on the State of the Country, 1860-1861* (New York, 1861); James W. Silver, *Confederate Morale and Church Propaganda* (Tuscaloosa AL, 1957). For similar Northern pronouncements, see Sidney E. Ahlstrom, *A Religious History of the American People* (New Haven, 1972) 670-73.

cluded that no stone had been left unturned as his region sought to defend itself against the rising tide of outside criticism. In the mass of paper and ink that had been generated in response to the call for defense, the South's case had been presented "theologically, geologically, oryctologically, paleontologically, archaeologically, chronologically, genealogically, orismologically, philologically, etymologically, zoologically, herpitologically, ophiologically, mazologically, physiologically, osteologically, myologically, ethnologically, psychologically, sociologically, and often quite illogically."[3]

While noting, perhaps with some surprise, that so serious a topic could be handled with humor at that hour, the modern reader may also be struck by the first category in the list. Whether placed there deliberately or not, the theological facet of Southern thought had played a leading role in the battle of minds that preceded the battle of bullets. Not only had the clergy more than held its own among the contributors to the Southern apologia, but laymen had joined with them in couching the sectional struggle in terms reminiscent of the Old Testament. Indeed, as the final crisis neared, the entire region seemed to take on an aura of tribal religiosity, of chosenness.

The passage of Donati's comet in 1857 was seen from many pulpits and pews as "a herald of the imminent outpouring of divine wrath," which would fall on the infidel North. From many clergymen came the "dark suggestion that the God of the Yankees was not God at all but the Antichrist loosed at last from the pit."[4] From his pulpit in New Orleans' First Presbyterian Church, Benjamin Morgan Palmer assured his flock that "in this struggle we defend the cause of God and religion."[5] Episcopal Bishop Steven Elliott of Savannah followed suit: "We are fighting for great principles, for sacred objects-principles which must not be compromised, objects which must not be abandoned. . . . We are fighting to drive away . . . the infidel rationalistic principles which are sweeping over the land."[6]

---

[3]R. B. Mays, "The Divine Legation of Thomas Jefferson," *DeBow's Review* 30 (May/June 1861): 529.

[4]Wilbur J. Cash, *The Mind of the South* (New York, 1941) 82-83.

[5]Sermon of 28 November 1860, in Frank Moore, ed., *Spirit of the Pulpit* (New York, 1861) 56. Probably no Southern clergyman outdid Palmer, who was James Henley Thornwell's protégé, in bellicosity from the pulpit in the early months of 1861 and throughout the next four years. See Thomas C. Johnson, *The Life and Letters of Benjamin Morgan Palmer* (Richmond, 1906) 237-39.

[6]Sermon of 13 June 1861, in Moore, *Spirit of the Pulpit*, 137-38.

Ministers reassured their congregations—if reassurance was needed—that the South was morally clean and ready to withstand any test. "We are willing to meet our adversaries, not only on Constitutional grounds, but on reason, on religion, on expediency," said another clergyman, "and dare them to their face to dislodge us from our position."[7] Yet if great suffering was to be the South's lot, her clergy would stand with her. "Whatever be the fortunes of the South," wrote one, "I accept them for my own. . . . She is in every sense my mother. I shall die upon her bosom; she shall know no peril, but it is my peril—no conflict, but it is my conflict—and no abyss of ruin into which I shall not share her fall. May the Lord God cover her head in this her day of battle!"[8]

This crusading imagery was nowhere better exemplified than in the words of James Henley Thornwell. "The parties to this conflict," he wrote, "are not merely abolitionists and slaveholders—they are atheists, socialists, communists, red republicans, jacobins on the one side, and the friends of order and regulated freedom on the other. In one word, the world is the battleground—Christianity and atheism the combatants; and the progress of humanity the stake."[9] The imagery extended to the act of secession itself. As the new Confederacy began to coalesce during the winter of 1861, Virginia's George William Bagby urged the readers of his *Southern Literary Messenger,* "Let us tear from the national flag the fifteen stars which the despots of the North have attempted to sully with the imputation of barbarism. Let us give these stars a double brilliance by forming them into a cross—the Southern Cross—emblem of that pure and holy religion which has been reviled, trampled and spit upon in the interest of abolitionism.

---

[7] W. T. Leacock, "Thanksgiving, 1860," ibid., 52. Those who were less certain also spoke in religious terms. Wrote South Carolina historian-diplomat William Henry Trescot, "If we are indeed carrying out God's plans, the hour of our triumph will come." Trescot, "South Carolina, Colony and State," *DeBow's Review* 27 (1859): 687. North Carolina planter James Anderson cautioned that only "inscrutable Providence" knew what was in store for the South, but that it would "doubtless be for his own glory." James Anderson to a friend, 26 November 1858, in Anderson-Thornwell Papers, Southern Historical Collection, University of North Carolina. (Anderson's son Robert married one of Thornwell's daughters.)

[8] John D. Wade, *Augustus Baldwin Longstreet; A Study in the Development of Culture in the South* (New York, 1924) 343. There were, of course, Southern clergymen who did not share this view. See W. Harrison Daniel, "Protestant Clergy and Union Sentiment in the Confederacy," *Tennessee Historical Quarterly* 23 (1964): 284-90.

[9] Cash, *Mind of the South,* 83.

. . . ''[10] With sentiments such as these as part of the backdrop, it was entirely fitting that the first scene of the secession drama should have been acted out in Columbia's First Baptist Church.

The importance of religion in antebellum American life has been widely noted. From its beginning this nation's fabric was interwoven with Christianity, and during the first half of the nineteenth century waves of evangelical faith swept across the land with a force that left few lives untouched. The growth in church membership and the establishment of church colleges attest to rising interest in religion and its concerns. In the South Atlantic states alone between 1830 and 1854, Baptists grew from 99,083 to 246,225 members, while the corresponding numbers for Methodists were 92,740 and 232,715, and for Presbyterians 23,120 and 41,750. Prior to 1830 there were only three church colleges in the South, all founded by Presbyterians. Between 1830 and 1844 Methodists and Baptists joined the Presbyterians in establishing a total of thirteen colleges in the region, and eight more were opened before the Civil War, climaxing with the University of the South (Episcopal) at Sewanee, Tennessee, in 1860.[11]

While there were still many "unchurched" Southerners at mid-century, the Census of 1850 listed 7,514 clergymen in the Southern states, in a free population of 4,464,651. This meant that there was one preacher for every 594 free people in the region.[12] "In the middle of the nineteenth century," writes James W. Silver, "it was generally conceded that the great influences in life were of a religious nature. The primary purpose of existence with most people was eternal salvation. Therefore it was deemed essential that the individual should conduct his everyday affairs in harmony with the wishes of a just and stern God."[13]

---

[10]*Southern Literary Messenger* 32 (January 1861): 71, quoted in Joseph L. King, Jr., *Dr. George William Bagby* (New York, 1927) 90-91.

[11]Henry S. Stroup, "The Religious Press in the South Atlantic States, 1802-1865" (Dissertation, Duke University, 1942) 71-72. John McCardell, *The Idea of a Southern Nation: Southern Nationalists and Southern Nationalism, 1830-1860* (New York, 1979) 179-80, 202.

[12]*Seventh Census of the United States: 1850* (Washington, 1853) lxvii, 82, quoted in E. Brooks Holifield, *The Gentlemen Theologians: American Theology in Southern Culture, 1795-1860* (Durham, 1978) 25.

[13]Silver, *Confederate Morale,* 25. Charles Reagan Wilson argues that "the ties between religion and culture in the South have actually been even closer than has so far been

Given the religious tone of Southern life, it was natural that the re-gion's clergy played a major role in shaping its values and attitudes. Per-haps Professor Silver has stated this point more forcefully than anyone else. "As no other group," he writes, "Southern clergymen were responsible for the state of mind which made secession possible, and as no other group they sustained the people in their long, costly and futile war for Southern Independence."[14] Others have suggested that the schisms in the churches paved the way for the final break.[15] This may seem strong, but when one considers that in addition to their regular duties the Old South clergy pub-lished a large share of the region's literary output, edited many of its pe-riodicals, and administered and taught in most of its schools and colleges, the full extent of the church's power in Southern life becomes evident.[16]

The relationship between religious thought and the rest of the intellec-tual milieu was also much more intimate in the antebellum era than is true today. A look at the periodicals of the Old South reveals the overlapping of the sacred and the secular. The religious press devoted considerable space to nontheological topics, and the political and literary publications were

suggested," and concludes that "by 1860 . . . a religious culture had been established, wherein a religious outlook and tone permeated Southern society." Wilson, "The Religion of the Lost Cause: Ritual and Organization in the Southern Civil Religion, 1865-1920," *Journal of Southern History* 46:2 (May 1980): 219, 220. For a good illustration of the hum-ble piety of the late antebellum mind, see the Diary of John McLees, especially January 1857, South Caroliniana Library, University of South Carolina.

[14]Silver, *Confederate Morale*, 101. E. T. Thompson, *Presbyterians in the South, 1607-1861*, vol. 2 (Richmond, 1913) 84.

[15]William W. Sweet, *The Story of Religion in America* (New York, 1950) 312. This view was first expressed as a prediction by John C. Calhoun and by the Charleston *Mercury* of 14 June 1844. See McCardell, *The Idea of a Southern Nation*, 200, 201. The idea was first treated historically in Robert L. Stanton, *The Church and the Rebellion* (New York, 1864). Several recent students of the topic voice similar opinions. See, for example, Wil-liam H. Barnes, *The Southern Baptist Convention, 1845-1953* (Nashville, 1954); Donald G. Mathews, *Slavery and Methodism* (Princeton, 1965); Sydney Ahlstrom, *A Religious History of the American People*, 670-73; McCardell, 184-200; and, most recently and most significantly in C. C. Goen, *Broken Churches, Broken Nation: Denominational Schisms and the Coming of the American Civil War* (Macon GA, 1985).

[16]Henry S. Stroup, *The Religious Press in the South Atlantic States, 1802-1865: An An-notated Bibliography with Historical Introduction and Notes* (Durham, 1956). Stroup lists 159 journals and finds their circulation steadily increasing throughout the antebellum pe-riod (26). See also McCardell, *The Idea of a Southern Nation*, 177-80, 202-25, and John S. Ezell, "A Southern Education for Southrons," *Journal of Southern History* 17 (August 1951): 303-27.

full of religious material.[17] The gap between science and theology that would soon become so wide was, as of 1860, still being bridged in the thought and writings of American intellectuals generally. The Darwinian revolution, with its polarizing impact on modern thought, waited in the wings.

This can be seen more personally, and perhaps more effectively, in the many close relationships that existed between Southern religious leaders and the region's thinkers in general.[18] Perhaps a few examples will suffice. Virginian George Fitzhugh was not an overtly religious thinker; but one of his closest friends was his pastor, William Friend, of Port Royal's Episcopal Church. William Elliott, conservative and influential Beaufort, South Carolina planter-author, was the good friend of John Bachman, perhaps the South's leading Lutheran clergyman. Maryland's leading literary light, John Pendleton Kennedy, received the bulk of his formal education from two Presbyterian ministers, and later, despite his diverse interests, reserved Sundays for reading theology. Low Country South Carolina's radical congressman William Porcher Miles was an active Episcopalian who saw the church as "the divinely appointed instrument of intellectual and social as well as spiritual progression." While "not a blind follower of ecclesiasticism or theological dogma," James Louis Petigru, leader of the South Carolina Bar, was "a constant worshiper in the Episcopal Church" and a close friend of the elder Benjamin M. Palmer, pastor of Charleston's Congregational Church. Henry Timrod, a fixture of Charleston's intellectual circle and later "poet-laureate of the Confederacy," called his craft "the next sacred thing to the great chart of salvation." South Carolina physician and botanist Henry William Ravenel was chairman of the vestry of St. Thaddeus Church (Episcopal) of Aiken; in his journal he reveals a deeply religious mind, as do the papers of Nathaniel Russell Middleton of Charleston.[19]

---

[17]See, for examples, the *Southern Presbyterian Review, Southern Quarterly Review, Russell's Magazine,* and *The Southern Literary Messenger.*

[18]See also Richard M. Weaver, "Older Religiousness in the South," *Sewanee Review* 51 (April 1943).

[19]Harvey Wish, *George Fitzhugh, Propagandist of the Old South* (Gloucester MA, 1962) 18. Elliott to James Louis Petigru, 27 April 1862, Elliott-Gonzales Papers, Southern Historical Collection. Charles H. Bohner, *John Pendleton Kennedy: Gentleman from Balti-*

Yet while the religiosity of antebellum America gave a strong spiritual tone to the sectional clash of values, scholars have yet to explain fully the nature of the church's impact and the role played by her leaders in the shaping of a Southern cosmology. In general, the secondary literature has contented itself with references to the socially conservative and theologically orthodox traits of Southern religion. Historians have dealt more fully with the secular features of that clash. William R. Taylor's *Cavalier and Yankee* has no parallel as a study of the opposing images the two sections came to represent. Taylor reminds us, as Wilbur J. Cash did earlier, that the "cavalier" was only partly real at best. But mythmaking tends to create a self-fulfilling effect, and for some Southern thinkers there was a conscious effort to make reality conform to myth.[20] Our fascination with the South, old and new, may be due in part to our suspicion that the region illustrates the power of myth to shape reality, when aided by the efforts of Southerners themselves.[21]

The success of this image building can be measured in at least one way, for before the idea of secession and separate nationhood could become viable, a degree of self-consciousness and self-confidence had to be produced in the Southern mind. Paradoxically, this confidence coexisted with

---

more (Baltimore, 1961) 11, 13, 211. William Porcher Miles, *Annual Address Delivered before the Clariosophic Society* [of South Carolina College] (Charleston, 1847) 8. James P. Carson, *James Louis Petigru, The Union Man of South Carolina* (Washington, 1920) 239, 61. Edd W. Parks, *The Essays of Henry Timrod* (Athens GA, 1942) 48. Henry William Ravenel Journal, 5 August, 19 May 1860; Nathaniel Russell Middleton Papers, Southern Historical Collection. In her study of a small network of Southern intellectuals, Drew Faust shows that even men not generally thought of as religious might be deeply influenced by the religious tone of their culture. Her subjects, William Gilmore Simms, James Henry Hammond, Nathaniel Beverly Tucker, George Frederick Holmes, and Edmund Ruffin, all revealed in their letters and public writings the impact of religion on the Southern mind. These men frequently used biblical metaphors and compared themselves to Old Testament prophets such as Samuel, Daniel, and Job. Drew Faust, *A Sacred Circle: The Dilemma of the Intellectual in the Old South, 1840-1860* (Baltimore, 1978). These men and others shared what Charles C. Cole has called the propensity of their age to transport all issues into the "moralistic octave." Cole, *The Social Ideas of Northern Evangelists, 1826-1860* (New York, 1954) 189.

[20]William R. Taylor, *Cavalier and Yankee; The Old South and the American National Character* (New York, 1957). For an example of the religious perspective on this crisis, see C. Gregg Singer, *A Theological Interpretation of American History* (Nutley NJ, 1969) 82-84.

[21]William C. Havard, ed., "The South: A Shifting Perspective," in *The Changing Politics of the South* (Baton Rouge, 1972) 3.

a fear of black insurgency, as has been effectively shown by Steven Channing.[22] But nations, even nations built on a foundation of slavery, are not born out of fear alone. The concept of nationhood involves a *zeitgeist* around which a people can cohere. A metaphysical confederacy, in other words, had to precede the physical Confederacy.

The architects of this metaphysical confederacy were the Old South's intellectuals: writers, scientists, clergymen, professional men, and thoughtful amateurs. Their message, aimed both at fellow Southerners and the outside world, and articulated with increasing clarity as the climax approached, was one of reassuring self-righteousness. It was not always thus. Prior to 1850, as recent scholarship demonstrates, there was a self-critical tone to much of the thought and writing of the South.[23] After that date the voice of the region's internal critics would join ranks with its defenders in the production of an impressive apologia. Before examining this transformation, a brief look at the general intellectual milieu of the Old South may be helpful.

I

The antebellum Southern mind was shaped by two fundamental conditions. One was the simple, rural setting dictated by the Southern economy. The other was the aberrant social system that placed the region in an increasingly hostile environment as the nineteenth century progressed. So powerful were these influences that efforts to improve the region's intellectual vigor were, on the whole, disappointing. The Old South was not the cultural wasteland some have described. She was the home of the majority of the nation's colleges; accordingly, a larger proportion of her white population attended college than the North's. She could boast of several impressive collections of books and art. Newspapers and magazines proliferated within her bounds. The 1850s saw a fivefold increase in the number of volumes in her public libraries, and new library buildings were going up through the region. In South Carolina, for example, their number grew from 16 to 361 during the decade. The Palmetto State, which had in

---

[22]Steven Channing, *Crisis of Fear; Secession in South Carolina* (New York, 1970). Channing does recognize that the "radical mind of 1860" displayed "confidence in the justice of their cause" (163).

[23]Drew Faust, *A Sacred Circle*. Michael O'Brien, ed., *All Clever Men Who Make Their Way; Critical Discourse in the Old South* (Fayetteville AK, 1982).

Charleston a cultural center of the first rank, claimed one and one-half volumes per white person, while Massachusetts had one-half volume per person. Societies to promote art, science, and history were founded in the state during this decade. One scholar has concluded that "the Southern gentry possessed an average of intelligence and an ability to think, write and talk which has seldom been equaled on so extensive a scale among any other people."[24]

Yet all of this is somewhat misleading. Many Southern "colleges" were little more than finishing schools for the sons of the upper class. Indeed, even with the growing sectional tensions and the push for a "Southern education for Southrons," many of the region's young men finished their educations at Northern colleges such as Harvard, Yale, The College of New Jersey (Princeton) and the University of Pennsylvania until almost the eve of secession. Southern periodicals generally failed financially for the simple reason that they were not read. South Carolinian William John Grayson said that the main reasons for the failure of so many Southern literary reviews were the absence of a large publishing house in the region, the small size of the reading public, and the fact that so little literature was produced in the South that was worthy of being reviewed. A Southern review, he concluded, was "a head without a body, a portico without a temple."[25] But the proud Southerner would reject criticism based on a quantitative yardstick and insist that his region's cultural attainments were more a matter of style and attitude. The Yankee, he might say, knew a great deal, especially about making money, but the Southerner knew how to *live*. This difference was often traced to deeply rooted ethnic qualities. The chivalrous Norman cavalier had placed his stamp upon the South, while the cul-

---

[24]One scholar has identified more than thirty periodicals from the 1850s with "Southern" in their titles, but even the healthiest of them, the *Southern Literary Messenger*, endured a borderline existence. King, *Dr. George W. Bagby*, 36. For figures on colleges and other institutions, see Clement Eaton, *A History of the Old South* (New York, 1964) 59-60; Cash, *Mind of the South*, 91. On the formation of the Carolina Art Association in 1857, see *Russell's Magazine* 1 (January 1857). On the South Carolina Historical Society, see *Collections of the South Carolina Historical Society*, vol. 1 (Charleston, 1857) v-vi. The laudatory evaluation of the Southern gentry is in Avery Craven, *Edmund Ruffin, Southerner* (New York, 1938) 13-14.

[25]Samuel G. Stoney, ed., "The Autobiography of William John Grayson," *South Carolina Historical Magazine* 49 (1948): 98.

ture of the North was that of the Saxons, dissenters, and commercial classes of England.[26]

Whatever the validity of this popular myth, the chivalrous gentility it so proudly pointed to was, to the extent it existed, as much a product of the Southern economy as of "racial stock." It was this plantation economy with its simple, rural setting that dictated the nature of Southern culture. As Cash explained it, "Complexity in man is inevitably the child of complexity in environment." In the Old South most energies were channeled into the activity of planting, and for the successful, into the social world that went with planter status. If this was not enough, there was the arena of politics. By comparison, "the life of the mind seemed an anemic and despicable business, fit only for eunochs [sic]."[27]

The most active of minds could be stifled by the loneliness and routine of a planter's life. The young James Petigru described the life of a typical Low Country South Carolina planter: "He is fairly within the vulgar pale, lording it over the farm, talking of venison, drum-fish, cotton-seed and politics. . . . This is the state in which a man quietly vegetates, and like other vegetables is governed by steady principles, and is led to dissolution by regular gradations, without the annoyance of passion or eccentricity of mind." Later in life, on his own plantation, he complained: "My time is spent reading Michaux and botanizing a little and sleeping a great deal."[28] Gilmore Simms was bothered by several afflictions that were brought on

---

[26]See, for example, "The Difference of Race between Northern and Southern People," *Southern Literary Messenger* 30 (June 1860): 401-409. Also, "A Contest for the Supremacy of Race, as between the Saxon Puritans of the North, and the Normans of the South," ibid. 33 (1861): 19-27. On the issue of the proper education for a Southerner, see Ezell, "A Southern Education for Southrons," 303-27.

[27]Cash, *Mind of the South*, 99. William Gilmore Simms made this point in 1858. Simms to James Hammond, 28 January 1858, in Mary C. Oliphant et al., eds., *Letters of William Gilmore Simms*, vol. 4 (Columbia, 1955) 15. Simms reminded Hammond that an agricultural people "are not accustomed to that constant attrition of minds and interests which sharpens the wits, and makes daring and eager the enterprize of all commerical people" (15).

[28]Petigru to Susan Petigru, 26 August 1851, Petigru Transcripts, Library of Congress. Quoted in Robert N. Olsberg, "A Government of Class and Race; William Henry Trescot and the South Carolina Chivalry, 1860-1865" (Ph.D. dissertation, University of South Carolina, 1972) 161. See also William J. Grayson, *James Louis Petigru* (New York, 1866) 51-52.

or aggravated by loneliness—depression, hypochondria, and excessive sentimentality—all of which were magnified by the diseases and early deaths of several family members. He vacillated between periods of pathetic idleness and the prolific productivity of a man trying to escape the enervating effects of life on his plantation, "Woodlands."[29] His friend James Hammond tried to occupy himself with "scholarly accomplishments," ordering histories from England, experimenting with grape vines, and preparing papers for the South Carolina Agriculture Society. But in his own words, he "slipped into a life of sexual dissipation and spent many days crippled by nervous indigestion."[30] Even the energetic Maryland author John Pendleton Kennedy was lulled into indolence by the plantation. From his family home in Virginia he wrote his wife, "I have written nothing at my book since I came to the country, for with all the apparent leisure of my life here, it is true that I am really too busy in idleness."[31]

Even those who could resist the seductive ease of plantation life might recognize its effects on others and on Southern culture. William Henry Trescot told a friend that his historical works were "written to avoid being idle . . . and published to avoid the reputation of idleness." Generalizing on the experience of those around him, Trescot concluded that "the development of the highest scholastic attainment requires a centralized civilization which our institutions are not calculated to create." The life of the planter "may be happiness," he observed, "but it surely is not civilization." His own plantation Trescot called his "social St. Helena."[32] Mary Boykin Chesnut, wife of the wealthy South Carolina planter-politician James Chesnut, despaired at being bottled up at "Mulberry" or the other family estates near Camden. For her the stimulation of Columbia or Richmond was infinitely preferable to "the dread stillness and torpor of our Sahara at Sandy Hill." She was often "ill" at home, but rarely so away from

---

[29]Simms to Hammond, 12 April 1858, in Oliphant, *Letters of Simms,* 4:50.

[30]Hammond to Milledge L. Bohnam, 4 March 1857, Bohnam Papers, South Caroliniana Library. Carol R. Bleser, *The Hammonds of Redcliff* (New York, 1981).

[31]Bohner, *Kennedy,* 225.

[32]Trescot, *Annual Address before the Calleiopean and Polytechnic Societies of the Citadel Academy* (Charleston, 1856) 8, 17; Trescot to William Porcher Miles, 20 August 1853, Miles Papers, Southern Historical Collection; Trescot to Hammond, 5 December 1858, Hammond Papers, Library of Congress, quoted in Olsberg dissertation, 165.

it.[33] George Fitzhugh aptly summed up these sentiments when he wrote, "Farming is the recreation of great men; the proper pursuit of dull men."[34]

One should not conclude from the foregoing that the dominance of the farm and plantation rendered the South intellectually barren, for most of the region's leading thinkers were not planters, and those who were experienced such isolation only for limited periods. They had ample opportunity as ministers, lawyers, or teachers to enjoy each other's stimulating company in the towns and cities. Michael O'Brien overstates only slightly when he notes that "most Southern intellectuals had as little to do with planting cotton as the *New York Times* book reviewer has with the sweatshops of Wall Street."[35] Yet Southerners with artistic and intellectual interests faced another handicap. Far from being encouraged in their efforts, they had to cope with the attitude expressed by a friend of Virginian Philip Pendleton Cooke, author of the popular lyric *Florence Vane*. "Why do you waste your time on a damned thing like poetry? A man of your position could be a useful man."[36] As a young man, James Thornwell was cautioned about the limited role played by the scholar in his culture. While a student at the South Carolina College, he wrote to his mentor and patron, William Robbins, that he was considering a career in letters. Robbins, while praising him for setting his aspirations on "higher, nobler objects," warned him not to disparage those who followed humbler paths. Then he added, "An accomplished and elegant scholar, and a profound one too, if you please, is a *white swan* in our land, I admit; but his fame is confined, after all, to a very limited sphere; and though he may work out for himself a name of celebrity, yet he is of little real use in life." Robbins hoped that

---

[33]C. Vann Woodward, ed., *Mary Chesnut's Civil War* (New Haven, 1981) 78, 182, 183; Bell I. Wiley, "Diarist from Dixie: Mary Boykin Chesnut," *Civil War Times Illustrated* 6:1 (April 1977): 26.

[34]C. Vann Woodward, ed., *Cannibals All!* (Cambridge MA, 1960) intro. Extensive treatments of this theme are David Bertelson, *The Lazy South* (New York, 1967), and Vann Woodward, "The Southern Ethic in a Puritan World," *William and Mary Quarterly* 30 (1968): 343-70.

[35]O'Brien, *All Clever Men*, 20. On the influence of urban life in the region, see David R. Goldfield, "Pursuing the American Urban Dream: Cities in the Old South," in Blaine A. Brownell and David R. Goldfield, eds., *The City in Southern History: The Growth of Urban Civilization in the South* (Port Washington, 1977) 52-91.

[36]Cash, *Mind of the South*, 99-100.

Thornwell would become a lawyer like himself.[37] This attitude reveals what Clement Eaton calls the "curious combination of romanticism and practicality" in the Southern mind.[38] Others had similar experiences. Even as successful a literary figure as Maryland's John Pendleton Kennedy, author of the novels *Horseshoe Robinson* and *Swallow Barn,* turned to business, law, and politics to gain respect.[39] Virginia's Nathaniel Beverly Tucker abandoned novels for political tracts, with the same result. Philip Cooke's brother, John Esten Cooke, felt constrained to conceal his authorship of the novel *Leatherstocking and Silk* to avoid injuring his legal practice.[40] And William Gilmore Simms, the Old South's leading man of letters, reflected bitterly on the lukewarm reception he received from Southern readers, comparing his efforts to "drawing water in a sieve."[41] As if to sum up the plight of the Southern literary man, editor John Reuben Thompson of the *Southern Literary Messenger* warned the students at Washington College in 1850, "Anyone who would choose the making of books as a means of support in this day, with his eyes open to the bankruptcy of thousands before him might well, in my judgment, be made the subject of a commission of lunacy."[42]

All of these people were sensitive to the life of the mind and sensed in themselves a drive that they felt set them apart. Perhaps it was because their surroundings were so ill-suited to a life of intellectual vigor that they were so aware of their peculiarity. This, plus the social and political dilemma that confronted the late antebellum South, seems to have made these people more introspective than most. William Gilmore Simms believed that

---

[37]William Robbins to James Henley Thornwell, 23 May 1831, quoted in Benjamin M. Palmer, *The Life and Letters of James Henley Thornwell, D.D., LL.D* (Richmond, 1875) 75-76. Hereafter referred to as Palmer.

[38]Clement Eaton, *The Growth of Southern Civilization, 1790-1860* (New York, 1963) 320-21.

[39]Bohner, *Kennedy,* 32, 215.

[40]Eaton, *Growth of Southern Civilization,* 320-21.

[41]Simms to James Hammond, December 1847, in Oliphant, *Letters of Simms,* 2:385-86. See also Simms to Hammond, 10 May 1845, ibid., 61.

[42]Benjamin B. Minor, *The Southern Literary Messenger* (New York, 1905). For an analysis of the problems of the writer in the Old South by one with first-hand experience, see Henry Timrod, "Literature in the South," *Russell's Magazine* 5 (August 1859): 385-95.

he and his friends had a spiritual kinship because of their "genius" and their "peculiar moral constitution."[43] It seems that these two traits went hand in hand in the minds of many Southern thinkers. Possessing high intelligence, they also shared a strong moral perspective. Their values, as well as their interests, occupied a higher plane. As a result, they sometimes felt a sense of alienation. The young George Frederick Holmes put such feelings to verse:

> To think is but to learn to groan
> To scorn what all besides adore
> To feel amid the world alone
> An alien on a desert shore.[44]

Such feelings took their toll on many personalities. Edmund Ruffin, whose agricultural research went largely unappreciated, developed a greater hunger for compliments and became deeply sensitive to criticism. He drank heavily until the realization of imminent alcoholism led him to total abstinence.[45] Simms and James Hammond wrote each other often of their depressions, and both vacillated between great ambition and a professed disgust for popular acclaim. The following passage in a letter from Simms to Hammond at the close of 1847 is illustrative.

I am greatly behind hand with my publishers. I have numerous tasks before me which I cannot neglect. On the performance of these tasks depend my resources, which, to deal with you frankly, are small and diminishing. My residence in South Carolina, is unfavorable to me as an author. I lose $2000 per annum by it. Our planting interests barely pay expenses and my income from literature which in 1835 was $6000 per annum, is scarce $1500 now, owing to the operation of cheap reprints which pay publishers & printers profits only & yield the author little or nothing. To earn this $1500 I have to labor constantly, and being absent from the field, I labor at a venture, not being able to seize upon the occasion. I think, accordingly, to remove from the State to New York. . . . Here I am nothing & can be & do nothing. The South don't care a d—m for literature or art. Your best

---

[43]Simms, "A New Spirit of the Age," *Southern Quarterly Review* 8 (April 1845): 319; Simms, "Year of Consolation," ibid., 12 (July 1847): 294.

[44]George Frederick Holmes, "Miscellaneous Notes," MS, 1842, 106, Holmes Papers, Perkins Library, Duke University.

[45]Craven, *Ruffin*, 10-11, 7.

neighbor & kindred never think to buy books. They will borrow from you & beg but the same man who will always have his wine, has no idea of a library. You will write for and defend their institutions in vain. They will not pay the expense of printing your essays. . . . At the North, the usual gift to a young lady is a book—in the South, a ring, a chain, or a bottle of Eau de Cologne![46]

There is an element here of what Richard Hofstadter called "status anxiety." That is, concern about one's own inadequate social standing can lead to frustration and a drive to elevate oneself by reforming society.[47] Even "well-placed" Southerners might feel intellectually isolated. John Pendleton Kennedy, while remembered best for his novels, also enjoyed a successful political career, which included service in Congress and as Secretary of the Navy under President Millard Fillmore. In his Baltimore home he hosted such notables as Daniel Webster, John Quincy Adams, Henry Clay, and William Henry Harrison. He was acquainted with Charles Dickens and was a friend of William Makepeace Thackeray; in short, by the 1850s he enjoyed the position of literary elder statesman of Maryland. Yet he was disappointed over the dearth of mentally stimulating companions. After one exasperating evening at a party, he wrote in his journal, "I must write an essay on Bores." A feeling of intellectual isolation led him to despair, "I have nobody in the world to talk to. All my acquaintances . . . weary me with prices and values and current news. . . . A spiritual man is unknown to me."[48]

This longing for the fellowship of a kindred spirit was felt by many. "If I could travel as my heart can, I would be with you . . . at any time on a moment's notice," wrote James Hammond to Edmund Ruffin.[49] Being,

---

[46]Simms to Hammond, December 1847, in Oliphant, *Letters of Simms,* 2:385-86. Other examples are Simms to Hammond, 18 August 1852, ibid., 3:196; Simms to James Lawson, 19 July 1834, ibid., 1:59. For a classic example of the ambitious Southern intellectual thwarted by his environment, see the sketch of Henry Hughes of Mississippi in Ronald Takaki, *A Pro-Slavery Crusade: The Agitation to Reopen the African Slave Trade* (New York, 1971) 89-94.

[47]Richard Hofstadter, *The Age of Reform* (New York, 1960).

[48]Bohner, *Kennedy,* 218-19.

[49]James Hammond to Edmund Ruffin, 15 June 1846, quoted in Faust, *A Sacred Circle,* 20. Hammond met Ruffin in 1843 when, as governor of South Carolina, he hired him to do a study of the state's land and resources. Ruffin came to consider South Carolina his spiritual home, but declined Hammond's urgings that he move his residence there.

in his own words, "of a contemplative, solitary caste," Hammond complained that "even in the bosom of my family, . . . I am without real sympathy—isolated—unknown."[50]

So the plight of the Old South intellectual, and the state of the Southern mind generally, were to a large extent products of the region's rural setting. But the state of mind in the mid-nineteenth century was also profoundly influenced by the South's relationship with the North and the outside world generally, a relationship that hinged upon the South's "peculiar institution." The stress on the nation's intellectual and emotional bonds, no less than its political bonds, mounted during the second quarter of the nineteenth century as slavery became a public issue. Reacting defensively to the growing abolitionist assault, Southern thought underwent a process that has been described as "the decline of Jeffersonianism."[51] The republican philosophy of Jefferson was not exactly abandoned in the South; what was being rejected in the 1830s was the perfectionist branch of Jefferson's thought that had taken root in the North. It may, of course, be argued that this was not Jeffersonianism at all. A historically more valid strain might be traced through the thought of John Randolph of Roanoke and John Taylor of Caroline, to that of John C. Calhoun.[52] But the romantic reform movement in the North had so successfully linked itself to the Sage of Monticello that by mid-century some Southerners were openly disavowing their region's greatest son.[53]

It was not the particular issues of the day, no matter how momentous, that determined which region of the country was truer to the spirit of Jefferson. The South was losing touch with that spirit not because of its defense of slavery. After all, Jefferson had been unable to abandon that institution. But Jeffersonianism was dealt a severe wound in the South by the methods employed in the region's defense and the effects of those

---

[50]Hammond, "Thoughts and Recollections," MS bound volume, South Caroliniana Library.

[51]Vernon L. Parrington, *Main Currents in American Thought,* vol. 2 (New York, 1927) 63-67.

[52]Arthur M. Schlesinger, Jr., *The Age of Jackson* (New York, 1945) ch. 3, "The Keepers of the Jeffersonian Conscience," 18-30.

[53]Harvey Wish, *George Fitzhugh, Propagandist of the Old South* (Gloucester MA, 1962) 43-44, 53.

methods on the intellectual atmosphere. In this regard the 1832 Virginia legislative debates about slavery are often pointed to as a benchmark, for this was the last time that the central dilemma of Southern life was subjected to formal debate. The growing menace of abolitionism, reinforced by fears of slave unrest, gave rise, on this subject at least, to a besieged mentality. How damaging this was to freedom of thought generally is a matter of some dispute. The older view, represented by Clement Eaton, held that the liberal mind of the region was hobbled by the knee-jerk reaction to abolitionism and that a rigid orthodoxy was imposed in all areas of thought.[54] A closer examination of the Old South's literary output suggests that Eaton and company overstated their case. The range of subject matter and variety of points of view in the region's periodicals indicate that even though they stood together against the abolitionists, Southerners could still differ with each other on other topics.[55]

Yet the more eccentric of the region's intellectuals did note with regret the increasing homogenization of Southern minds. Ten years before the final crisis John Pendleton Kennedy complained to his friend William Gilmore Simms, "An observer can not fail to note that the manners of our Country [the South] have been tending toward a uniformity which is visibly effacing all local differences."[56] As a non-native, South Carolina College professor Francis Lieber felt the pressure more directly. "The time is fast approaching here," wrote Lieber to a friend during the Nullification Crisis, "when every man, especially in my position, will be stigmatized if he does not openly, positively and loudly come out for disunion—a time like the reformation when a man was called and treated like a heretic unless he loudly pronounced himself for pope and cardinals. A time may come, perhaps soon, when I may no longer feel perfectly at ease to write

---

[54]Clement Eaton, *The Freedom of Thought Struggle in the Old South* (New York, 1964) passim; Charles G. Sellers, ed., "The Travail of Slavery," in *The Southerner as American* (Chapel Hill, 1960) 40-71; Joseph C. Robert, *The Road from Monticello: A Study in the Virginia Slave Debates of 1832* (Durham, 1941). For an excellent discussion of the impact of this constricting process on Southern writers, see Louis D. Rubin, Jr., ed., "The Literary Community in the Old South," in *The Writer in the South* (Athens GA, 1972) 1-33.

[55]O'Brien, *All Clever Men*, 21-22.

[56]Bohner, *Kennedy*, 187.

frankly from my heart in any letter.''[57] Lieber was not typical in that he would eventually leave the South. But others who would stay were strongly tempted. Gilmore Simms often considered moving to New York, where he would have a larger audience (see n. 46). And James Louis Petigru's long-simmering frustrations surfaced bitterly as he watched his native state secede politically from a union she had long since left psychologically. ''I made a great mistake in 1832,'' he told his sister, ''when I might have quit the country [South Carolina] myself, with the prospect of doing something.'' Petigru had indeed done something in South Carolina. He had remained a staunch unionist to the end. But as such, he had so isolated himself that he had been assigned the role of admired eccentric—the exception who was so singular that he could be tolerated without fear.[58]

A more widespread consequence of slavery and its defense is seen in the career of Robert Woodward Barnwell. Scion of an old South Carolina family, Barnwell was born to a former United States congressman in 1801. He graduated at the top of his Harvard class in 1821, after serving as commander of the Harvard Military Company. Classmate Ralph Waldo Emerson spoke of ''the high, affectionate, exceptional regard in which I, in common I believe with all your contemporaries of 1817-21, have firmly held you as our avowed chief. . . . '' Blessed with poise and grace, Barnwell returned to his family's plantations and moved easily into the pattern of public service expected of such men. He was elected without opposition to the state legislature and then moved on to the Congress. In 1835 he was chosen president of the South Carolina College, where he became a close friend of the young professor James Thornwell. He served one year of Calhoun's unexpired Senate term in 1850 and served in both houses of the Confederate Congress. Yet he seems to have been ''going through the motions'' and left no distinctive record. Clement Eaton, while calling him one of the most attractive of the Old South patricians, suggests that he ''never

---

[57]Lieber to ''My Dear Ruggles'' [Samuel], 23 August 1830, quoted in Steven Channing, *Crisis of Fear*, 36. Lieber remained at the South Carolina College until 1857, when he resigned after being bypassed for the presidency. The willingness of Southern thinkers to criticize their region has not been widely noted, but see, for example, Carl N. Degler, *The Other South: Southern Dissenters in the Nineteenth Century* (New York, 1974); Drew Faust, *A Sacred Circle;* and John R. Welsh, ''William Gilmore Simms, Critic of the South,'' *Journal of Southern History* 26 (May 1960): 201-14.

[58]Carson, *Petigru*, 363.

fulfilled the promise of his youth.'' Perhaps the life of inherited wealth and status stifled his early drive. In accepting the status quo under which he so easily prospered, he relinquished the drive that might have brought him to great heights, or, as he may have sensed, to a position at variance with that of his region.[59]

Other men of Barnwell's generation were more troubled than he by the conflict between regional and national values. William Campbell Preston was deeply torn by the slavery dilemma. Born in 1794, he was the son of a congressman from Virginia. He graduated from the South Carolina College in 1812, read law in the office of William Wirt in Richmond, and finished his education with two years of study and travel in Britain and Europe. Rejecting the invitation of his Boston friend George Ticknor to settle in the North, he returned to South Carolina for a career in law and politics, which he called ''the object of a Southern man's life.'' He gained a wide reputation as an orator and held seats in the state legislature and the United States Senate. In 1845 he was chosen president of his alma mater. A man of secure status and generally orthodox views, Preston was nonetheless troubled. In two letters, written less than two weeks apart, he revealed that even as late as 1857 he remained disturbed over slavery. Recommending Reverend Thornton Stringfellow's pamphlet in defense of slavery to his friend Waddy Thompson, he said it had ''wrought a change in my views which have been worrying me all my life.'' Yet only twelve days later, while asserting that ''no foreign panacea can be allowed to meddle with it,'' he admitted that in his mind slavery was ''unfortunate.''[60]

With that one word, Preston revealed the tension and ambiguity that plagued Southern thought at mid-century. The failure of the secession

[59]Clement Eaton, *The Mind of the Old South,* rev. ed. (Baton Rouge, 1967) vii, 65-67; Emerson to Barnwell, 6 July 1866. Typed copy in the Southern Historical Collection, Miscellaneous Letters. Benjamin F. Perry, *Reminiscences of Public Men* (Philadelphia, 1833) 124; Linda T. Prior, ''Ralph Waldo Emerson and South Carolina,'' *South Carolina Historical Magazine* 79 (October 1978): 254, 262; Palmer, 147. On Barnwell, see also Daniel W. Hollis, ''Robert W. Barnwell,'' *South Carolina Historical Magazine* 56 (1955): 131-37. Hollis concludes that Barnwell was overly modest, and therefore less prominent than he could have been. He died in 1882, after several years as librarian at the University of South Carolina.

[60]*Cyclopedia of Eminent and Representative Men of the Carolinas,* vol. 1 (Madison WI, 1892) 249-50; Preston to Thompson, 10 August 1857, quoted in Eaton, *Freedom of Thought,* v; Preston to David Campbell, 22 August 1857, quoted in Channing, *Crisis of Fear,* 77.

movement of 1850-1851, and the success of the same movement ten years later, point to the 1850s as the decade in which the Southern mind crystallized. In 1850, South Carolina, not to mention the rest of the South, was not yet single-minded enough to follow the quixotic lead of its radicals. Aided by events both within and without the region, Southern thinkers would, during the next ten years, create a metaphysical confederacy on whose ears the radical arguments of 1850 would fall more receptively. But before this could happen, the Southern thinker himself would have to clarify his understanding of the Southern condition and his relationship with his society. In so doing, he would move from a position of critic to that of defender.

II

The ideal of the intellectual's place in his society was captured by Robert Barnwell Rhett in his eulogy of James Louis Petigru: "Certainly no man has lived in our day who possessed so much moral and so little official authority."[61] Devoid of all power but that of persuasion, the intellectual can, this ideal suggests, exert a great influence on his time and beyond. Petigru, no doubt, would have dismissed this compliment as hyperbole, for his relationship with his society was a frustrating one. His experience, though perhaps extreme, was typical of that of intellectuals generally. The intellectual usually finds himself, indeed often places himself, in an adversary relationship with the state and society. His desire for influence is therefore thwarted unless he can either exercise it in the role of critic or abandon this role and become an articulator of his society's values. The ambiguity that many Southern thinkers felt toward their region's values led them to vacillate between these two roles. But as the Southern mind hardened, the latter role became more comfortable.

The Southern thinker, like intellectuals generally, was frustrated because the values of his society denied him the status to which he felt entitled. These men, or the nonpolitical among them, were engaged in pursuits that could bring them only limited honor in their neighbors' eyes. As a result, at least some of them seem to have suffered from a mixture of guilt and shame. Robert Coles, the psychologist who spent several years studying the South and her children in the 1960s, concluded that consciously or

---

[61]*Memorial of the Late James L. Petigru, Proceedings of the Bar of Charleston, South Carolina, March 25, 1863* (New York, 1866) 22.

unconsciously, most Southerners feel a sense of shame when they fall short of expectations.[62] Many writers—among them William Faulkner, Robert Penn Warren, and C. Vann Woodward—have described the role of guilt in Southern life. Shame, a social as opposed to private force, is more likely to be the "primary sanction" in "pre-modern" societies, where the community is still strong and individualism has not eroded the power of social pressure.[63] Living in such a society, the Old South intellectual must have felt doubly insignificant as sectional tensions increased, because a community in crisis tends to pay less attention to those who represent careful thought and more to those who represent action. Had he remained aloof from the mainstream, he would have been considered virtually irrelevant at the moment when he most wanted to be heard.[64]

The frustration and ambiguity that this relationship produced are clearly visible. Speaking of his good friend Gilmore Simms, Alfred P. Aldrich said, "I have heard him again and again discourse of [sic] his beloved South Carolina, so affectionately, with such tender earnestness, that it sounded more like the praise of a lover speaking of his lady love. And again I have heard him inveigh so violently that it sounded like an indignant rebuke of a father to a disobedient child."[65] Simms could write of his native Charleston "to which I owe no favor, having never received an office, or a compliment, or a dollar at her hands," and moan, "Great God! what is the sort of slavery which brings me hither!"[66] And yet after Appomattox he would announce to a Northern visitor, John T. Trowbridge, that

> Charleston, sir, was the finest city in the world; not a large city, but the finest. South Carolina, sir, was the flower of modern civilization. Our people were the most hospitable, the most accomplished, having the highest degree of culture and the highest sense of honor, of any people, I will

---

[62]Robert Coles, *Children of Crisis: A Story of Courage and Fear* (Boston, 1964) 27, 322.

[63]James McBride Dabbs, *Haunted by God* (Richmond, 1972) 114.

[64]Edward Shils, *The Intellectuals and the Powers, and Other Essays* (Chicago, 1972) ch. 1.

[65]Oliphant, *The Letters of Simms*, 1:lxxxiii-lxxxiv.

[66]William P. Trent, *William Gilmore Simms* (Boston, 1892) 239. This is from a letter of 30 October 1858.

not say of America, sir, but of any country on the globe. And they are so still, even in their temporary destitution.[67]

Is there a better example of the oft-noted love-hate relationship between the Southern intellectual and his region?

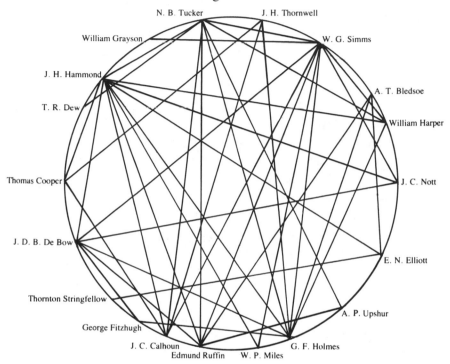

PERSONAL INTERACTIONS AMONG SLAVERY'S DEFENDERS

The diagram is courtesy of Drew Faust, whose article ''A Southern Stewardship: The Intellectual and the Proslavery Argument'' appeared in *American Quarterly* 31 (Spring 1979). Copyright © 1979, American Studies Association (publisher).

Perhaps the one positive result of this state of affairs was the tendency of many Southern thinkers to turn to each other. The formation of ''sacred circles'' of like minds helped to create a sense of community in lieu of the more formal associations that would develop in the twentieth century. Of course, people generally tend to associate in small groups. But in the Old

---

[67]Quoted in Jay Hubbell, *The South in American Literature, 1607-1900* (Durham, 1954) 584-85. See also John T. Trowbridge, *My Own Story, with Recollections of Noted Persons* (Boston, 1903) 310.

South, with its focus on the plantation and the family as the primary social units, such groups may have been even more important.[68] The small size of the South's intellectual class meant that the membership of these groups overlapped, and the colleges and periodicals of the region acted as clearinghouses through which various groups related to each other.[69] Add to these the associations of marriage and church, and the result was a complex network of individuals from almost every field of thought.

Several well-known proslavery writers, for example, were linked through such ties. Nathaniel Beverly Tucker, George Frederick Holmes, and Thomas R. Dew were colleagues at William and Mary. Tucker was close to Gilmore Simms and James Hammond in South Carolina. Holmes was a cousin of Chancellor Harper and part of a circle that included Simms, Albert Taylor Bledsoe, James Henley Thornwell, and Edmund Ruffin. Holmes was also acquainted with James D. B. DeBow and George Fitzhugh. Hammond was close to Simms and Harper. Each of these men had associations that linked him to other networks as well.[70]

Such circles were not new to the late antebellum period. Similar groups have been identified in socially conscious Charleston in the eighteenth

---

[68]Faust, *A Sacred Circle,* passim. Dabbs, *Haunted by God,* 111. Professional associations, such as medical, scientific, and historical societies, were forming in the South in the late antebellum period. Regarding the small group as a social phenomenon, see Robert Golembiewski, *The Small Group* (Chicago, 1962); Michael Olmstead, *The Small Group* (New York, 1959); Gerald M. Phillips, *Communication and the Small Group* (Indianapolis, 1966).

[69]As editor of the *Southern Quarterly Review,* Simms was able to call on many friends and acquaintances for contributions. South Carolinians among them included James Hammond and Marcus Hammond, Joel Poinsett, Judge Mitchell King, Francis Lieber, William J. Grayson, James D. B. DeBow, David F. Jamison, David J. McCord and Louisa McCord, Father Patrick N. Lynch, Rev. James Warley Miles, William H. Trescot, William Elliott, and Dr. Robert W. Gibbes. From Virginia came contributions from Simms's good friends Nathaniel Beverly Tucker and George Frederick Holmes, and from Matthew Fontaine Maury. Trent, *Simms,* 165.

[70]Faust, *Sacred Circle,* 6, 15, 147. For examples of their work on slavery, see *The Pro-Slavery Argument; as Maintained by . . . Chancellor Harper, Dr. Simms, and Professor Dew* (Charleston, 1852); E. N. Elliott, ed., *Cotton Is King, and the Pro-Slavery Arguments, Comprising the Writings of Hammond, Christy, Stringfellow, Hodge, Bledsoe, and Cartright . . .* (Augusta, 1860); Edmund Ruffin, *The Political Economy of Slavery . . .* (Washington, 1853); George Frederick Holmes, review of *Uncle Tom's Cabin* in the *Southern Literary Messenger* 18 (December 1852): 721-31. The interactions of the South Carolina intellectual network can be studied in the papers of William Porcher Miles, located in the Southern Historical Collection, University of North Carolina.

century: the Monday Club, the Friday Club, the Ugly Club, the Beefsteak Club, and others.[71] James L. Petigru's Charleston house was the headquarters for a brilliant circle in the 1820s that included Hugh Swinton Legare, William Harper, William Martin, and others.[72] John Pendleton Kennedy founded the Monday Club in Baltimore in the 1830s.[73] A stimulating group in Columbia drew members from the South Carolina College, the Presbyterian Seminary, and the Arsenal Hill Military Academy. These institutions included, in the 1850s, William Campbell Preston, Benjamin M. Palmer, James Thornwell, Wade Hampton, and Joseph Le-Conte.[74]

Perhaps the best-known intellectual circle in the Old South was the Russell's Bookstore group of Charleston. John Russell's establishment on King Street became in the 1850s the gathering place for a group including William Gilmore Simms, James Louis Petigru, Alfred Huger, Judge Mitchell King, Benjamin Gildersleeve, Dr. Samuel Henry Dickson, and Bishop Patrick N. Lynch. Around these men hovered several admiring young literary aspirants, most of whom had a hand in producing *Russell's Magazine*, the short-lived but notable literary publication that operated from 1857 to 1860. These younger men included Paul Hamilton Hayne and W. B. Carlyle, the magazine's editors, and Henry Timrod, John Dickson Bruns, Samuel Lord, Jr., Frederick Peyre Porcher, Middleton Michel (Hayne's brother-in-law), Samuel Y. Tupper, and Benjamin J. Whaley.[75]

Interestingly, the network to which a Southern thinker belonged was rarely limited to the area below the Mason-Dixon Line. Further, while the growing tensions of the 1850s often tended to restrict the subject matter of the letters they wrote, it did not, in most cases, curtail these intersectional associations. This seems to have been particularly true of men with scientific interests, as the journal of Henry William Ravenel of Charleston

---

[71]Eugene Sirmans, *Colonial South Carolina, a Political History* (Chapel Hill, 1960) 230.

[72]William Jackson Grayson, *James Louis Petigru, a Biographical Sketch* (New York, 1866) 113.

[73]Bohner, *Kennedy*, 29.

[74]William Armes, ed., *Autobiography of Joseph LeConte* (New York, 1903) 172-73.

[75]Trent, *Simms*, 227. Also Sidney J. Cohen, "Three Notable Ante-Bellum Magazines of South Carolina," *University of South Carolina Bulletin*, no. 42, pt. 2 (1915); Paul H. Hayne, "Antebellum Charleston," *Southern Bivouac* 1 (September-November 1885): 328.

reveals.[76] However, other South Carolinians with wide-ranging interests also struck lasting friendships with Northerners. These include Simms and James Lawson of New York; Thornwell and Edward Everett of Boston; James L. Petigru and Everett; Paul H. Hayne and Bayard Taylor, John Greenleaf Whittier and William Cullen Bryant; and James Mathews Legare and Henry Wadsworth Longfellow.[77]

The importance placed on these networks by those who belonged to them can be seen in the voluminous correspondence of many Southern thinkers. "Rarely do I send fewer than two or three letters to the P. O. daily," Gilmore Simms wrote Mary Lawson, daughter of his friend James Lawson, and "once or twice every week, I send a dozen."[78] The nature of these relationships varied, of course, but one cannot read the correspondence without recognizing that sharing interests of the mind created ties of the heart. The sympathy and encouragement that were exchanged along with personal news and intellectual discourse reveal the emotional depth of these associations.

Perhaps nowhere are these feelings better summed up than in a letter from Simms to a young friend in literature, John Esten Cooke of Virginia. Simms had been touched by the warmth and admiration of a recent letter from Cooke, and was reminded of his friendship with Nathaniel Beverly Tucker, which ended prematurely with Tucker's death in 1851. He wrote to Cooke, "I once wrote a letter to old B. Tucker . . . and closed it with 'Yours *lovingly*.' . . . [His reply] showed that his heart was touched by the use of a word which men employ femininely only. . . . Surely . . . in a

---

[76]Henry William Ravenel Journal, 14 November 1860, lists his correspondents for the past year. See also William H. Longton, "Some Aspects of Intellectual Activity in Antebellum South Carolina, 1830-1860: An Introductory Study" (Dissertation, University of North Carolina, 1969) 154-57.

[77]Simms to James Lawson, 4 July 1861, in Oliphant, *Letters of Simms,* 4:369; Palmer, 361; Everett to Thornwell, 15 November 1854, Thornwell Papers, South Caroliniana Library, University of South Carolina; Max L. Griffin, "Whittier and Hayne: A Record of Friendship," *American Literature* 19 (March 1947): 41-58; Charles Duffy, ed., *Correspondence of Bayard Taylor and Paul Hamilton Hayne* (Baton Rouge, 1945); E. G. Bernard, "Northern Bryant and Southern Hayne," *Colophon,* n.s. 1 (Spring 1936): 536-40; Petigru to Everett, 28 October 1860, quoted in Carson, *Petigru,* 359-60; see also ibid., 325-26, 337; Curtis C. Davis, *That Ambitious Mr. Legare: The Life of James Matthews Legare of South Carolina* (Columbia, 1971) 116, 118-19.

[78]Simms to Mary Lawson, no date, but probably February 1859, in Oliphant, *Letters of Simms,* 4:126. Simms's prolific correspondence was not matched by many, of course.

guild like ours, which the world never welcomes to *its* love . . . there should be much more love among ourselves! *We,* at least, will try to love one another, at once as men and brothers.''[79] The depth of Simms's commitment to two of his friendships was revealed when he named a son Beverly Hammond. He had grown very close to Beverly Tucker in the brief time of their correspondence, and his relationship with Hammond, which spanned three decades, was certainly one of the most influential in Simms's life. Each man found the other among the few acquaintances he could admire intellectually. They shared the same basic political and social philosophy, as well as the view that Hammond was the logical heir to Calhoun's position in South Carolina and the South. Their voluminous and rich correspondence and their many visits provided a continual opportunity for mutual reinforcement and the crystallization of their views. Simms wrote to Hammond once of ''our mutual career.'' And after Hammond's death Simms would write, ''We had few or no secrets from each other—we took few steps in life without mutual consultation. . . . I felt that there was something akin in our intellectual nature.''[80]

Such close relationships were naturally common among members of the clergy, though they were usually limited by denominational barriers. Seminary contacts, denominational publications, and ecclesiastical duties formed the basis for both strong individual ties and the growth of networks of ministers. While the division of the two largest Protestant denominations, the Baptists and Methodists, into Northern and Southern bodies in the 1840s reduced the geographical scope of these friendships, intersectional contacts of an informal nature did continue. In the Presbyterian church the ties were not broken until after 1861, and therefore the networks of clergymen remained more national in these denominations.[81] James Thornwell's clerical circle included Robert J. Breckinridge, John Adger, Thomas Smyth, Benjamin Morgan Palmer, and John Girardeau.

So the Old South intellectual was sustained, despite his frequent physical and psychological isolation, by a community of kindred spirits that both encouraged him in his own efforts and reminded him of his membership in a peculiar class—set apart from the society he both loved and resented.

---

[79]Simms to Cooke, 26 July 1859, ibid., 164-65.

[80]Ibid., 3:210; 4:469.

[81]Holifield, *The Gentlemen Theologians*, 44-46.

His desire for recognition, for honor, would drive him to make a positive contribution to this society. For the better-educated clergy, who had many contacts with community leaders, the approbation of others was often a major concern. As one of them wrote, one should never expose "the cloth" to "the contempt and derision of the intelligent and discerning."[82] Good conduct was not necessarily sufficient to earn them the respect they wanted. Thornwell told his Columbia Seminary students that as followers of Christ, they could expect a life of ridicule and abuse from "sophists and buffoons." "It requires uncommon moral courage," he added, "to resist the sneers of contempt." In a time when religion was being put on the defensive by association with narrow fanaticism, there was, Thornwell warned, "a strong temptation to be ashamed of its doctrines, its promises, and its

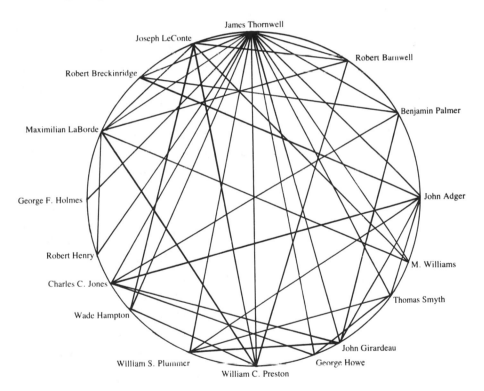

---

[82]Ibid., 37.

hopes.''[83] The publication of sermons, a far more common practice in antebellum America than later, was one way for the clergy to gain respect and prestige.[84] Another, especially for the more intellectual ministers, was the campaign to present Christianity in a rational setting and to submit its teachings to close intellectual examination. By so doing they could provide a ''useful'' service.

Clearly, the most useful service the South's clergy, and its intellectuals in general, could provide was a defense of the peculiar institution, and, ultimately, of secession and war. This position, as I have noted, was the one most of them took. Why? Many modern scholars, using the mixed blessing of hindsight, have inferred that the conservative, proslavery position was the natural and obvious one for the region's thinkers to take, and further, that the conservative thought of the Old South was nothing more than a convenient ground from which to reject the criticisms of the abolitionists. No doubt many Southerners were led to the conservative philosophy for no more profound reason than that it suited their prejudices and their self-interest. Nevertheless, the conclusion that the region's intellectual and spiritual leaders were merely lending a veneer of respectability to this self-interest is a hasty one and needs reexamination.

A closer look at the thought of the Old South reveals that it evolved as historical forces worked a change in Southern life. In general, between 1840 and the early 1850s the Southern thinker moved from the position of critic to defender of his society. Yet it is important to see these seemingly contradictory roles as two sides of the same coin. The role of critic and reformer was adopted in some cases in an effort to move the society toward the ideal to which these thinkers aspired, so they could then more easily defend it to the outside world. The role of critic came naturally. As Simms put it, ''The man of real genius'' is always a critic of the world in which he lives, since his superiority inevitably alienates him from others and his ''discontent'' manifests itself as a ''commentary upon . . . his social condition.''[85] Richard Hofstadter could hardly have stated more cogently the notion of ''status anxiety'' as a motivation behind reform efforts. For to

---

[83]James Henley Thornwell, Seminary Lecture, n.d., Thornwell Papers, South Caroliniana Library.

[84]Holifield, *The Gentlemen Theologians*, 44-45.

[85]Simms, ''Bulwer's Genius and Writings,'' *Magnolia*, n.s. 1 (December 1842): 331.

the degree that his efforts succeeded, the Southern intellectual would find himself in a more congenial society, one that appreciated him more and therefore would allow him to play his desired role.[86]

High on the list of targets for these native critics were the size and tastes of the South's reading audience. The failure of many Southern magazines and the low status of writers of poetry and fiction have already been noted. While lamenting this, Southern writers often focused more directly on the region's seeming obsession with things political. "No periodical can well succeed in the South, which does not include the *political* constituent," wrote Simms. "The mind of the South is active chiefly in the direction of politics. . . . The only reading people in the South are those to whom politics is the bread of life."[87] Later observers have often concurred with this assessment. Allen Tate described the Old South as "hag-ridden with politics" and offered as an explanation the view that "all aristocracies are obsessed politically, so that the best intellectual energy goes into politics. . . ."[88] Some Southern writers were disturbed by the hypersensitivity of their region to what they considered constructive criticism. "There is a certain class of minds," wrote the editor of the *Southern Literary Messenger*, "who see in every effort [of criticism] some imaginary thrust at the 'peculiar institution.'" This, he said, was "foolish."[89]

Another focus of criticism were the quantitative values that the South, following the example of the North and Europe in the nineteenth century, was increasingly embracing. The materialism of the age was having what many saw as a detrimental effect on the quality of thought and morals. As George Frederick Holmes put it, "The age of steam in things mechanical has produced an age of steam in things intellectual."[90] The wasteful exploitation of the Southern soil provided Simms an apt analogy for describing this materialism and its effects. Referring to the depletion of the soil in his native state, he wrote that it had been stricken by a "growing and

---

[86]Faust, *Sacred Circle*, 114.

[87]Quoted in Hubbell, *The South in American Literature*, 367.

[88]Allen Tate, "The Profession of Letters in the South," in Tate, *Essays of Four Decades* (Chicago, 1968) 523.

[89]*Southern Literary Messenger*, April 1856, quoted in Hubbell, *The South in American Literature*, 341.

[90]George Frederick Holmes, "The Present Condition of Letters," *Southern Literary Messenger* 11 (March 1845): 172.

wasting process which in the moral as in the physical culture has left us to the possession of such bald and sterile fields."[91]

Yet despite such criticism, few of the Old South's intellectuals left the region for the more hospitable climate outside. Indeed, that outside world was for them no real option. Perhaps James Louis Petigru, one of the few who maintained his credentials as critic until the end of the antcbellum era, explained this best. On 25 April 1861, *London Times* correspondent William H. Russell was honored at a party held at Petigru's home on Charleston's Broad Street. Russell was impressed by his host and remarked on the uniqueness of his views in that city. Petigru replied, "When a similar remark was made to my friend Plutarch he said, 'I live in a small town and I choose to live there lest it should become still smaller.' "[92] In these words Petigru captured the deep sense of community and belonging that has so often been spoken of by Southerners down through the years. A natural identification with place and kin was being augmented during the late antebellum years by a growing sense of membership in a family under siege. Fraternal criticism tended to give way, therefore, to fraternal solidarity. The image of the older brother turning from pest to defender of his sibling is perhaps apt. Certainly the attack on slavery was central to this shift of the intellectual from critic to defender, as I will show later in the case of Thornwell. The typical Southern intellectual, who probably never considered leaving the South as Petigru had, would increasingly eschew criticism and "choose to live there" emotionally and ideologically as well as physically.

Perhaps the classic example of this drift from critic and would-be reformer to defender, at least among intellectuals, is that of George Frederick Holmes. Like his fellow Virginian Edmund Ruffin and his South Carolina friends Gilmore Simms and James Hammond, Holmes was, in his early career, a rather outspoken critic of many aspects of Southern life. A man seemingly devoid of ability in practical affairs, the young Holmes lived on the edge of poverty while reading in the great works of the Enlightenment and absorbing their progressive philosophy. He attracted attention as a writer of histories and philosophical essays, and he held brief

---

[91]Simms, "Southern Agriculture," *Magnolia* 4 (March 1842): 131; see also Edmund Ruffin's essays in *The Farmer's Register* 12 (1836).

[92]Carson, *Petigru*, 379.

and unhappy tenures on the faculty of William and Mary and as president of the newly founded University of Mississippi. Then marriage into a wealthy and prominent family (his father-in-law, Henry Wise, was governor of Virginia) gave him the leisure to devote himself more fully to scholarship, and as a result he was appointed to a chair in History at the University of Virginia. Meanwhile, Holmes had begun to despair at the trends of the nineteenth century and to distrust the materialistic concept of progress. By the 1850s he was exploring the new field of sociology and concluding from its teachings that the South's way of life offered the best hope for the traditional values he had by now embraced. Now for the first time in his life, Holmes was at peace. He found his final philosophical home in the Roman Catholic Church. During the waning years of the antebellum era, he provided the South with defenses of a highly philosophical and moral tone.[93]

One measure of the decline of Southern self-criticism is the changing views of some South Carolina thinkers on that state's leading figure, John C. Calhoun. During his lifetime the senator was certainly not free from criticism at home. It came from the pens and mouths of such well-known public figures as Gilmore Simms, James L. Petigru, and James H. Thornwell.[94] But with Calhoun's death in 1850, the criticism dwindled and eventually stopped. Even to his former enemies he became the Great Man of the South who symbolized the region's ideology and integrity.[95] Here one sees an important feature of the Southern intellectual's defense of his society and its leaders. It was the mythical figure of Calhoun that they praised. It was an ideal that they defended, rather than the flawed reality they knew too well. The man became a saint. The society became almost a heaven. These defenders were not only delivering counterpunches to the Northern

---

[93]Regarding Edmund Ruffin's early criticism, see Craven, *Edmund Ruffin, Southerner*, 27, 108. Regarding Simms and Hammond as critics, see Faust, *A Sacred Circle*, ch. 5, esp. 87-89, 96-98. Regarding Holmes, see Neal Gillespie, *The Collapse of Orthodoxy; The Intellectual Ordeal of George Frederick Holmes* (Charlottesville, 1972). For a more dramatic "about-face," see Davis, *That Ambitious Mr. Legare*, 114-23.

[94]Simms to Hammond, 1 May 1847, in Oliphant, *Letters of Simms*, 2:310. Hammond even criticized Calhoun in his eulogy. See *An Oration on . . . John C. Calhoun* (Charleston, 1850) 17, 66-67. Petigru once compared South Carolina to a "rich, fat, lazy old planter" who employed an overseer to manage his estates. "One morning the planter woke up and found the overseer [Calhoun] master of the plantation." Carson, *Petigru*, 237.

[95]Palmer, 390.

critics of the South; they were also holding up for their fellow Southerners an ideal worthy of emulation.

In embracing an idealized conception of their own society, Southern thinkers did not abandon the role of critic. Rather, they focused that criticism on the world outside. The agrarian strain of Jeffersonian thought, which had dimmed during the 1820s and 1830s, reasserted itself at mid-century in a reactionary rejection of "free society" and its materialistic progressivism. "Anti-reform," Louis Filler has observed, "has often been a species of reform, concerned for the state of society, urgent in its demands to return to allegedly better conditions."[96] So it was for the typical Southern intellectual in the prewar decade. As the possessor of a strong moral consciousness, he was engaged in an effort to understand the human condition and to fit the institutions of society to it. Whatever misgivings he may have had about Southern society, he found it increasingly preferable to the outside world, whose tendencies he read as frightening. Spurred on by these fears, he resolved the dilemma of his place in his world. He would articulate the values of his region for itself and the outside world. He would offer as his gift to the South a defensible ideology. In so doing he would engage in a symbolic form of action, thus satisfying his desire for power by performing a function his region would accept, and indeed one without which it could not have moved beyond defensive postures to the assertion of nationhood. Theological thought formed a central facet of this Southern apologia, and perhaps no one contributed more significantly in this regard than James Henley Thornwell.

---

[96]C. S. Griffin, *The Ferment of Reform, 1830-1860* (New York, 1967) 30.

CHAPTER **2**

The Pastor-Professor as Polemicist

James Henley Thornwell, who was acclaimed during his own lifetime as "our Southern giant" and "the Calhoun of the Church," and whose theology, one leading religious historian contends, "has dominated most of the history of Southern Presbyterianism," was born on a plantation in Marlboro District, South Carolina, on 9 December 1812.[1] He was the second of six children of an English-born plantation overseer and a staunch Calvinist Baptist mother. Little is known of his boyhood, except that the family was poor, and the father's death shortly after the boy's eighth birthday drove both his widow and the children to work.[2] James's early education came from a succession

---

[1]The reference to "our Southern giant" was made by W. F. DeSaussure, and is in Benjamin M. Palmer, *The Life and Letters of James Henley Thornwell, D.D., LL.D.* (Richmond, 1875) 123. The "Calhoun of the Church" label is referred to as Thornwell's popular title in L. G. VanderVelde, *The Presbyterian Church in the Federal Union, 1860-1869* (Cambridge MA, 1932) 30. The other reference to Thornwell's stature is in H. Shelton Smith, "The Church and the Social Order as Interpreted by James Henley Thornwell," *Church History* 7 (June 1938): 116. Thornwell's birthplace is given as Chesterfield District in an unsigned biographical sketch in the Thornwell Papers, South Caroliniana Library, University of South Carolina.

[2]Palmer, 16. In his obituary of Thornwell, Theodore Tilton of New York wrote that John C. Calhoun had once called Thornwell "the greatest of living Americans." Tilton emphasized the great man's lowly origins among the "white trash" of the South. This, he added, was no discredit to him, but the positions he held on public issues in later life indicated that he had forgotten "the rock from whence he was hewn." Theodore Tilton, "The Second Son of Carolina," *The Independent*, 1 September 1862; reprinted in *Sanctum Sanctorum, or Proofsheets from an Editor's Table*, ed. Tilton (New York, 1870) 64-65.

of teachers at a "field school" near his home. Being rather frail and caring little for play, he studied late into the evenings and gained a reputation locally as something of a prodigy. Word of his abilities reached General James Gillespie, a wealthy planter who, with young Cheraw attorney William Henry Robbins, underwrote James's schooling until he was graduated from the South Carolina College.

The boy's appreciation for his patrons' generosity and their admiration of him led to ties that would be broken only by death.[3] They fostered an ambition that seems to have needed very little encouragement, while his mother instilled in him her strict Calvinism. He tested her will, and was punished often and severely, but her efforts had their intended effect. His only "bad habit" as a youth was tobacco, which he began chewing at age eleven and smoking a little later. Both habits would stay with him all his life. Deeply sensitive, Thornwell as a boy and young man was easily moved to tears and generally preferred to avoid a situation that might bring out his strong emotions. He wrote rather than said words that he feared would displease others. On at least one occasion he avoided a parting scene with Henry Robbins rather than risk the embarrassment of tears.[4]

While living with Robbins in Cheraw, he developed an interest in law and acted as an apprentice to his patron. Yet the attorney encouraged a broad intellectual interest, and by the time he was sixteen the boy had read deeply in the classics and could talk intelligently about Locke's *Essay Concerning Human Understanding*—a work that would provide a point of departure for much of his philosophical and theological writing. The delight he took in pleasing his elders is evident in the few letters to them that survive. In one, however, written when he was sixteen, he sadly informed Henry

---

[3]Palmer, 27-37. See also Thornwell to Mrs. Robbins, 4 April 1843; quoted in Palmer, 247-49. Palmer was Thornwell's protégé and a leading Presbyterian clergyman in his own right. He makes no effort in his biography to hide his adulation of his subject, and said elsewhere that "in this case, my heart held the pen." Henry A. White, *Southern Presbyterian Leaders* (New York, 1911) 378. The biography was published while many of Thornwell's associates were still living, and this accounts for the many liberties Palmer takes with his sources, both omitting and changing parts of what Thornwell and others wrote. He does not always use the ellipsis when deleting material, so his account must be used with caution. Nonetheless, it is an indispensable source, since it is based on recollections of Thornwell's contemporaries as well as written material. Robbins died on 26 March 1843, while Gillespie outlived Thornwell (Palmer, 247, 29).

[4]Palmer, 47-50.

Robbins that since he had decided to abandon the law for theology, he could no longer accept Robbins' patronage. Robbins replied that although he thought James ideally suited for the law, he wanted the boy to choose his own field of study, and so the relationship continued.[5] His letters of this period reveal a mind developed well beyond its years, though one senses in the complex vocabulary and highly formal style the effort of a budding adolescent to impress his elders.[6] In the summer of his sixteenth year he wrote to Robbins, who was then in New England, of his views on dueling. "Is it not to be lamented," he asked, "that a squeamish sense of false honour is so prevalent?" Later that summer he sent another letter to Robbins in the form of an essay on the theme, "discontent is not criminal."[7]

Therefore, it came as a shock both to the boy and to those who knew him that he failed the examination for entrance into the Junior Class of South Carolina College in 1829. Although only seventeen, he had obviously expected little difficulty in the examination and was, in his own words, "overwhelmed with confusion, and ashamed to show my face." He determined to stay in seclusion until "I redeem my reputation."[8] This he did on his second try, entering the school in January 1830.

The new student received a mixed reaction from his fellows in Columbia. One of them later recalled him as "perhaps the most unpromising specimen of humanity that ever entered such an institution. Very short in stature, shorter by a head than he became in later life, very lean in flesh, with a skin the colour of old parchment, his hands and face as thickly studded with black freckles as the Milky Way with stars, and an eye rendered dull in repose by a drooping lid, he looked, to use an Irishism, as if he was twenty years old when he was born."[9] Another college friend, J. Marion

---

[5]Ibid., 44-48. See especially Thornwell to Robbins, January 1829. Writing later of the law, Thornwell said, "It is a good profession to contract the mind and freeze the heart." Surely he could not have had the generous and broad-minded Robbins in mind in saying this, however. Thornwell to W. M. Hutson, 18 February 1832; quoted in Palmer, 84.

[6]His letter on his choice of theology as a career, for example, states, "The relation which has hitherto subsisted between us is now to be dissolved."

[7]Palmer, 50-51. Perhaps the fullest primary source on Thornwell's early education is a letter from James Gillespie to Nancy Thornwell, James's wife, 10 February 1864, in the Thornwell Papers.

[8]Thornwell to Robbins, 5 December 1829; quoted in Palmer, 55.

[9]Ibid., 53. This description, like much of Palmer's information, was given to him after Thornwell's death.

Sims, later described him as "small, frail and malarial-looking." Eighteen years later Thornwell would still describe himself as "hopelessly lean." Apparently referring to his skin, his admiring fellow clergyman Benjamin M. Palmer once told an engraver, "he has one of those unfortunate faces that can not be deguerotyped [*sic*]. Every attempt . . . has produced only a queer and grotesque characterature [*sic*]."[10]

Yet references to Thornwell during his college years, as thereafter, rarely concentrate on his physical appearance: his intellect and personality made the major impression. He had indicated his scholarly bent while living with Robbins, and as he prepared for his second entrance examination, he wrote to Robbins, "There is no being on earth more happy than the student."[11] This remark was not made casually, for there have been few harder-working college students. He spent fourteen hours a day in "severe study" during the week and relaxed on Saturdays by reading history.[12] He was an avid reader of the *Southern Review,* a notable literary publication of the 1830s, and criticized its articles in long letters to his patrons. Feeling a weakness in language usage, he read and memorized long passages from the Bible, Shakespeare, Milton, Vergil, and Edmund Burke. His excellent memory would enable him to flavor his lectures, sermons, and conversations with quotations from these writers for the rest of his life. The same classmate who had spoken so disparagingly of his appearance also commented that though his "manners were unpolished . . . his air was self-reliant; and though free from boasting, he was evidently conscious of the mental power within him, which would make him more than a match for most men, and would throw into the shade his physical defects."[13]

While he spent too much time in study to get into much trouble, another classmate recalled three instances when James took part in college frivolity: a "College treat" when virtually the entire student body imbibed a quantity of wine and cordials, and "our friend was not in the minority"; a prolonged hot-punch party on a day when snow forced the suspension of

---

[10]J. Marion Sims, *The Story of My Life* (New York, 1884) 107. Thornwell to Matthew J. Williams, 17 July 1848, Thornwell Papers. Williams, a mathematics professor at the South Carolina College, was a good friend of Thornwell. Palmer to J. M. Wilson, 17 May 1855, Benjamin M. Palmer Papers, Perkins Library, Duke University.

[11]Thornwell to Robbins, 19 December 1829; quoted in Palmer, 55.

[12]Ibid., 62; and Thornwell to Robbins, 30 November 1830, ibid., 73.

[13]Ibid., 63, 53.

classes; and a nocturnal visit to the strawberry patch of a nearby resident. Thornwell, he added, ''was not a professor of religion while at College.''[14] Yet, these exceptions aside, he was not generally ''one of the boys.'' His intelligence and his substantial ego made him a natural debater, and perhaps as compensation for his physical shortcomings, he had an admitted tendency to sarcasm. ''His words burned like fire,'' recalled one fellow student, ''his sarcasm was absolutely withering.'' Another remembered him as ''severe in retort.'' ''His eloquence was unequalled,'' said another, ''and his argumentative powers the most amazing. He could detect and expose a fallacy with more dispatch and completeness than I ever witnessed in any other man.'' For his fellow student Marion Sims, later to become internationally famous as a pioneer gynecologist, Thornwell's command of language and his ability to play upon the emotions of his audience were only slightly inferior to the gifts of John C. Calhoun.[15]

As a result he was ''admired for his transcendent qualities, but not loved'' by his classmates. Writing to his mentor during his first term in Columbia, he admitted, ''There are seven in one hundred and twenty with whom I sometimes associate,'' and only one of them intimately.[16] Yet he was, by his own account, the leader of his literary society, the Euphradean, within one month after joining it. He ''won the gown'' as orator of the month on his second attempt at debate in the club. And there is perhaps an indication of his developing political views here. On the question, ''Whether it is probable that the nations of Europe will advance further in refinement than they have done,'' he argued and ''proved'' the negative.[17] A natural tendency toward elitism would undergird his conservative views;

---

[14]Ibid., 77. This refers to the fact that he was not a member of any church. The fellow student was W. M. Hutson, whose letter of 24 September 1872 to Palmer is in the Palmer Papers, Duke University.

[15]Palmer, 63-65; Seale Harris, *Woman's Surgeon: The Life Story of J. Marion Sims* (New York, 1950) 16. Regarding his ego, Thornwell would soon write that people at Harvard ''give me credit for a virtue which I was never suspected of possessing by my friends at home, and that is *modesty*.'' Thornwell to James Gillespie, 15 September 1834, Thornwell Papers.

[16]Palmer, 64 and 67, quoting Thornwell to Robbins, 12 February 1830. He did not name the intimate.

[17]Thornwell to Gillespie, 24 January 1830, in Palmer, 66. The gown itself posed a problem for the small-framed orator, since it was large enough to fit a six-footer. ''Some method must be contrived to obviate this difficulty,'' he wrote Gillespie.

in this case, he was presumably arguing that Europe's increasingly egalitarian social climate was not conducive to high cultural achievements. Such political views were tested and clarified during Thornwell's college days by the reading and study of Berkeley, Hume, Shaftesbury, and Cicero, as well as Jonathan Edwards and the Scottish philosopher-theologian Dugald Steward, whom he said he loved as a brother.[18]

Whatever young Thornwell's relationship with his fellow students, he made what professor Maximilian LaBorde called ''an extraordinary impression'' on the faculty. He was, says LaBorde, ''particularly a favorite with [College President Thomas] Cooper and [Professor of philosophy Dr. Robert] Henry, who predicted with confidence his future distinction.''[19] It is interesting that Thornwell should have won favor with two such diverse men, for Cooper was a controversialist by nature, a deist and freethinker in philosophy, while Henry was a mild-mannered orthodox Christian. Thornwell seems to have borrowed from both of them, becoming a storm center of controversy himself, but in the role of defender of the faith against the forces represented by Cooper. During his student days Thornwell, like most of the young men who came to Columbia in those years, was much taken with President Cooper. Mr. Robbins, in a letter to his protégé, referred to Cooper as ''your idol.''[20] Thornwell went through the usual period of examining various schools of thought while in college, and Cooper's influence no doubt accounts for his brief interest in deism and Socinianism.[21] Cooper's powers did not, however, seem to affect young Thornwell's politics. The president was among the leading figures in the nullification movement, which was brewing while Thornwell was at the school, but he sided with the Unionists in that portentous fight.[22] As for

---

[18]Ibid., 66, 68, 82. He also read and admired the works of Thomas Reid and Thomas Brown, Scottish Common Sense philosophers (ibid., 76).

[19]Maximilian LaBorde, *History of the South Carolina College* (Columbia, 1859) 331.

[20]Palmer, 61. The letter is quoted without a date.

[21]Socinianism is named for Faustus Socinus (1530-1604), who denied the doctrine of the trinity and divinity of Christ, and offered rationalistic explanations for many Christian precepts. Socinianism considers the supernatural aspects of the Bible to be allegories, or natural phenomena unexplainable to primitive minds. Thornwell later wrote to Palmer that he ''found it a system that would not hold water.'' He called it a ''Christless Christianity'' (Palmer, 79).

[22]Daniel W. Hollis, *The University of South Carolina*, vol. 1. (Columbia, 1951) 162. For references to Cooper's views on politics, see William W. Freehling, *Prelude to Civil War* (New York, 1965) 128-31, 216, 236, 255.

Dr. Henry, Thornwell felt a great debt to his teaching and paid respect to his memory in an article in the *Southern Quarterly Review* many years later.

A few days after his nineteenth birthday, in December 1831, Thornwell graduated at the top of his class and entered a period of drifting and searching. It is clear that he had yet to feel the pull that Christianity would soon exert upon him. In fact, it seems that at this point he had given little consideration to following a religious career, except for the youthful flirtation with theology mentioned above. A Calvinist upbringing had collided with skepticism during his college years to produce a conflicting array of thoughts and emotions in the young man. "I can take you to the very spot," he would later write, "where I stood and gnashed my teeth, and raised my hand, and said, 'Well, I shall be damned, but . . . I am not to blame. God made me as I am, [a doubter] and I can't help my wickedness.' "[23]

Still undecided about his future, Thornwell applied, shortly before his graduation, for the College librarianship. When he did not receive the position, he accepted an invitation to remain at the College as a tutor for the spring 1832 term, so he could continue to read in the Greek and Latin classics.[24] But by that May he had taken a teaching position in Sumterville, where he joined the nearby Concord Presbyterian Church. Looking back on this event in later years, Thornwell not only made much of it, but also attributed it to the workings of Providence. Most of those who have written about him, being Presbyterian ministers themselves, have done the same. For earlier that spring, while browsing through a Columbia bookstore, he had come across a copy of the *Westminster Confession of Faith*. He bought it, and in the words of one of his seminary students, "was so fascinated by the logical unfolding of Scripture truth that he read it through that night." Benjamin Palmer stresses the importance of this little book as an influence on Thornwell's mind, noting that its attraction for him at this point was its logic, but also says that Thornwell could not yet give it his "heart and soul."[25]

---

[23]Palmer, 97.

[24]Ibid., 87, 84.

[25]Ibid., 80-81; Thomas H. Law, "Dr. Thornwell as Preacher and Teacher," essay in *Centennial Addresses Delivered before the Synod of South Carolina in the First Presbyterian Church, Columbia, October 23, 1912, Commemorating the Birth of the Rev. James Henley Thornwell* (Spartanburg, 1913) 7.

Perhaps not, but he had not taken this step of affiliating with the church lightly. He had wrestled mightily with the essential questions of the Christian faith and with the matter of his own vocation.[26] Feeling an increasing burden of sinfulness during his senior year in college, he had at first rebelled, protesting that he had not made himself this way. ''I am not to blame,'' he later recalled himself saying. Then he came to see this as the unpardonable sin, and for three months he went through a tortuous ordeal, rarely sleeping, and at times trying to escape in alcohol. The loneliness and poverty of his situation in Sumterville added to this crisis, and in this state he evidently found in the *Confession of Faith* an intellectually satisfying resolution of tension. On the day he united with the Concord Church, he wrote, ''I feel myself a weak, fallen, depraved and helpless creature, and utterly unable to do one righteous deed without Thy gracious assistance.''[27] By late June he could write to his childhood friend Alexander Pegues that he was thinking seriously about the ministry. But, perhaps feeling the need to reassure him, he added, ''I am still as warmly as ever devoted to the Classics and Metaphysics. I look upon them both as absolutely essential in the education of a minister.''[28]

So the young man had chosen the path he would follow and the perspective from which he would make his impact on the world. The youth whose patrons and fellow students had imagined him as a lawyer and perhaps a politician, and who had once envisioned for himself a career in letters, would embark on a career that, some have suggested, afforded him less opportunity for direct influence on his time than his talents might have deserved.[29]

---

[26]Thornwell to Alexander Pegues, 2 February 1832; quoted in Palmer, 87-90.

[27]Ibid., 95-97. It is significant that during this period he was corresponding with Professor Henry, who influenced him greatly (Palmer, 92). In his ''Memoir of Dr. Henry,'' Thornwell contrasted him with Thomas Cooper. ''Dr. Cooper was an avowed materialist; Dr. Henry's tendencies were all to idealism. Dr. Cooper looked upon utility as the criterion of right; Dr. Henry looked upon right as the criterion of utility. Moral rules, according to Dr. Cooper, were flexible and variable; according to Dr. Henry, eternal and immutable. Dr. Cooper was . . . a Deist; Dr. Henry a thoroughgoing advocate of the Nicene Creed. . . . There was but one subject upon which they thoroughly agreed, and that was politics '' (Thornwell, ''Memoir of Dr. Henry,'' *Southern Quarterly Review* n.s. 1 [1856]: 200).

[28]Thornwell to Alexander Pegues, 25 June 1832; quoted in Palmer, 100-101.

[29]Paul L. Garber, ''James Henley Thornwell, Presbyterian Defender of the Old South,''

Certainly putting this decision behind him did not solve all his problems; the next two years were a difficult time for Thornwell. After several months in Sumterville, he went to Cheraw as principal and teacher at the Cheraw Academy, where he had studied as a boy. One spiritual crisis had been resolved, but another was building, and in the meantime he was often gloomy and despondent, as his letters reveal. His "blues" [Thornwell's word] abated somewhat during a revival that came to Cheraw at that time, but he clearly had not yet found the sense of purpose and strength he would later possess. A friend wrote that his religion was "too much a matter of the intellect," and Palmer agrees that as a man of great logical powers, Thornwell found it very difficult to give himself over to a force so heavily emotional in its perspective.[30]

Compounding his spiritual unease was a thwarted love affair, probably his first. He had fallen deeply in love, but the relationship was blocked by elders who saw no promise in him. Palmer, the only source on this episode, provides no specific information, seeing it as a subject that required "all the delicacy possible." He reveals only that Thornwell's "affections had been seriously entangled . . . but the stern prudence of older heads could see little that was promising in the poverty of the ardent wooer, nor in his unsettled plans, his soaring visions, and his somewhat fitfull temper." Parental opposition did not prevent the "attachment" from running through "the whole of this period" of his life, however.[31] Also, teaching, at least teaching young boys, proved a difficult and unsatisfying task for him. He seems to have had too high a standard of performance for most of his students, and his opinion of them, once formed, became rigid. He was dogmatic in a way that won him few supporters and he was sensitive to criticism.[32]

Some eighteen months after his affiliation with the Presbyterian Church, Thornwell applied, in November 1833, to the Harmony Presbytery as a

---

published essay in South Caroliniana Library. (This is the introduction to Garber's thesis, "The Religious Thought of James Henley Thornwell," Duke University School of Theology.) The view that his clerical career prevented the full development of Thornwell's potential is found in Colyer Meriwether, *History of Higher Education in South Carolina* (Washington, 1889) 167.

[30]Palmer, 112.

[31]Ibid., 108-109.

[32]Ibid., 109-11. As Palmer candidly admits, this trying time took its toll on Thornwell's personality.

candidate for the ministry. His testimony as to his personal religious experience and his reasons for seeking the ministry did not satisfy the examining committee. But one of its members interceded, saying he saw something in the young man that suggested great potential, and he was accepted as a candidate.[33] Now came the choice of a place to train for the pulpit. The most convenient one, Columbia Theological Seminary in the state capitol, was still quite new, having opened its doors in 1831. It had only two professors at this time, and according to one who would later study there under Thornwell, it was judged "inadequate." Specifically, James needed several languages that were not yet available at Columbia. Princeton Seminary would seem the logical choice, but it is not known whether he sought admission there. In any event, he was still in Cheraw in the spring of 1834 when a professor at Andover Seminary, Dr. Ebenezer Porter, stopped there on his way north from Columbia and offered James a place at this school and a scholarship. He was off to Massachusetts that summer.[34]

Andover, a Congregationalist institution, was a disappointment in several respects. It did not then offer the courses he had been told he could study there: "German, Syriac, Chaldee, nor Arabic." "Nothing, in short, is taught here which is not taught equally well at Columbia," he wrote General Gillespie that August. Further, the theology taught at Andover was "awfully New School" and "the habits of the people are disagreeable to me."[35] The young Thornwell's opinion of the Andover theology is chal-

---

[33]Ibid., 112-13.

[34]Law, *Centennial Addresses,* 8; Palmer, 113; Thomas C. Johnson, *Life and Letters of Benjamin M. Palmer* (Richmond, 1906) 64-65.

[35]Thornwell to James Gillespie, 13 August 1834; quoted in Palmer, 115. The term "New School" refers to the element of the Presbyterian Church that tended to both simplify and democratize the faith. It was strongest in the old Northwest, but was by the 1830s quite popular in New England as well. To orthodox Calvinists, the New School seemed too soft on the doctrine of original sin and election. New Schoolers were found both in the evangelical and the more conservative sectors of the church. See Sydney Ahlstrom, *A Religious History of the American People* (New Haven, 1972) 465-68. As for Thornwell, he cared neither for their theology nor them. To Gillespie he wrote that Andover was "peopled with a sad mixture of gentlemen and plough-boys. I use the term gentlemen in its vulgar sense, having reference merely to manners and not to the heart." There seems to be here a note of class bias as well as ideology. For an extended discussion by Thornwell of the theology of the Harvard divinity students, whom he considered to be all Unitarians, see his letter to Alexander Pegues, 14 August 1834; quoted in Palmer, 117-18.

lenged by most modern scholars. Its faculty was anti-Unitarian, one scholar notes, and indeed its periodicals were moderate "Protestant theology at its best." Thornwell's comments, then, seem to be an early indication of the theological point of view he would champion and the somewhat intolerant attitude he would hold in matters both personal and theological.[36]

While its theology was far less to his liking, Harvard Divinity School, a short distance from Andover, did offer most of the courses he wanted, so he enrolled there in the fall of 1834 to study German and Hebrew, and attend other lectures as well. He intended to remain there only until January and saw his Harvard studies as preparatory to entering the senior class at Columbia Seminary.[37] Following the advice of his mentors, he moved into his new field of endeavor with uncharacteristic caution and even gained a reputation, as he took delight in telling them, for modesty.[38] However, while at Harvard he wrote several essays, including one on the study of the classics that he submitted to the *North American Review*. He also planned "an elaborate work" on the philosophy of the Greek language, "on which I hope to found a reputation." He confided to General Gillespie, "I have an eye on a professorship in the Theological Seminary at Columbia [a position he would attain twenty-two years later]. That institution is destined to take the lead in this country."[39] One wonders what prompted this rather rash prediction. Was Thornwell already thinking about the sectional crisis and the theological struggle that he and other Southern religionists would see as central to it?

His stay in Cambridge was even shorter than he had planned, for he left Harvard on 4 October 1834, explaining that a physician had told him the Boston winter might kill him.[40] His health was poor that fall, no doubt the result of prolonged study and reading. But his distaste for these strange surroundings must have added weight to the doctor's advice. Of his fellow

---

[36]Herbert Hovenkamp, *Science and Religion in America, 1800-1860* (Philadelphia, 1979) 217.

[37]Thornwell to Gillespie, 13 August 1834; quoted in Palmer, 116.

[38]Henry Robbins to Thornwell, 23 August 1834; quoted ibid., 116-17. Thornwell to Gillespie, 15 September 1834, Thornwell Papers.

[39]Thornwell to Gillespie, 27 August 1834; quoted in Palmer, 120. Palmer notes that the work referred to here, though left incomplete at Thornwell's death, was the main basis for his reputation as a scholar.

[40]Ibid., and Thornwell to Alexander Pegues, 1 October 1834; quoted ibid., 126.

students he once wrote, "The peculiarity of their belief consists in *not be-lieving* . . . the system of the Orthodox." From his point of view, they were all Unitarians, and for him the tenets of this sect were "little better than downright infidelity. . . . " Clearly he felt out of place, for even to his logical mind the religion of Boston was cold and sterile. "There is no fanaticism, no enthusiasm here; it is all sober truth; and those who laugh at these things now, will weep bitterly in a coming day." He admitted that the Harvard library was excellent, but thought that the students' mediocrity contrasted sharply with its caliber.[41] Although as the weeks went by he began to write of friendships and exciting experiences such as a lecture by Edward Everett, he concluded shortly before his departure, "I had just as soon send a son to Columbia as to Cambridge."[42]

Within less than two months after his return to South Carolina, Thornwell, not yet twenty-two years old, was licensed to preach by the Harmony Presbytery. Whether or not his Massachusetts experience deserves the credit, he evidently had made considerable progress since his earlier examination for candidacy. After hearing his licensing examination, a professor at Columbia Seminary is reported to have said, "Brethren, I feel like sitting at this young man's feet, as a learner." Among those present for the examination were some men from the town of Lancasterville, where a Presbyterian church was in the process of being established. Their impressions of Thornwell led, the following spring, to a call from that newly formed church.[43] Another sign of the young man's "towering ambition" is his reaction to this call. He hoped for rejection by the Bethel Presbytery rather than confinement to so humble a setting. But he was approved; and still plagued by doubts as to his divine ordination, he came to Lancasterville in May 1835.[44]

It was then, according to Thornwell and those who later heard him speak of his gradually deepening faith, that he first sensed the assurance of hav-

---

[41]Thornwell to Alexander Pegues, 14 August 1834, ibid., 117-18; Thornwell to Gillespie, 27 August 1834; quoted ibid., 120.

[42]Thornwell to Gillespie, 6 September 1834, 121-22; Thornwell to Pegues, 1 October 1834; quoted ibid., 126.

[43]Ibid., 127. The Seminary professor was probably George Howe.

[44]Ibid., 128-29; and Law, *Centennial Addresses*, 8-9. See also John B. Adger, ed., *Collected Writings of James Henley Thornwell*, vol. 4 (Richmond, 1871) 32-33. The phrase "towering ambition" is Palmer's.

ing chosen the right path. As he rose to preach his first sermon in the new church, he felt a powerful sense of divine acceptance, and he carried his new congregation with him. Says Palmer, "[S]ome gathered unconsciously near the pulpit, in breathless suspense upon the young prophet's lips."[45] As Thornwell wrote to his mentor, General Gillespie, describing his ordination service, "I felt that a new era had commenced in my life in that I was no longer a citizen of the world, but an ambassador of God, standing in the stead of Jesus Christ and beseeching men to turn from the unsatisfying vanities of a fleeting life and to fix their hopes on the enduring sources of beatitude which surrounds [sic] the throne of God." The service, he added, impressed upon him "the tremendous weight of ministerial responsibility" and made him painfully aware of his inadequacy.

This letter also reveals both the strong Calvinist theology and the powerful verbal gifts of the young minister. "No man can bring himself to feel the sinfulness of his own nature—the thunders of the sacred desk—although they may alarm for a season[,] cannot unfold in their true light, the hideous features of depravity and guilt. The minister is but a sword in the hands of God to cut the guilty down . . . and is altogether useless [without God's power]. . . . God and God alone can arm truth with barbed arrows to pierce the sinner's heart." He added that he knew he was totally dependent on divine grace for a successful ministry, and asked for Gillespie's prayers "when you kneel in humility at the footstool of mercy." He expected very little leisure, for he had "laid down a regular course of study" in addition to his pastoral duties. This was good, however, for "it is hard to preserve our virtue from the rust of idleness. Few men can be unoccupied and innocent at the same time."[46]

One sees revealed here the mind and spirit of the typical nineteenth-century, evangelical Protestant clergyman. The sentiments so fervently expressed in this letter would later be defended against both "New School" Presbyterianism and the progressive rationalism that was then laying the

---

[45]Palmer, 129-30. Palmer writes that he has told this episode as it was related to him.

[46]Thornwell to Gillespie, 13 June 1835, Thornwell Papers. This was written on the day following Thornwell's ordination and installation in Lancasterville. He would soon assume the pulpits of Waxhaw and Six Mile Creek Churches as well. For a discussion of the concept of the ministry shared by most Southern evangelicals, see Anne C. Loveland, *Southern Evangelicals and the Social Order* (Baton Rouge, 1980) ch. 2.

foundation for deep intellectual and political divisions in American culture.

The young minister seems to have required little time to gain the respect of his new congregation and community. His preaching, contrary to what some had predicted, was effective with general audiences. His sermons in the early years rarely exceeded thirty minutes. (Later they would run sixty or longer.) A regular attender reported that "his sermons created great enthusiasm among the people of all denominations, who crowded into the little church until it overflowed." On one such occasion, after "preaching for an hour and a half, he took out his watch, stopped suddenly, and apologized to the congregation, saying he had no idea he had been speaking so long. The cry rose at once from all parts of the house, 'Go on! go on!' And he did go on for nearly an hour more." Such an episode is rare indeed in a Presbyterian church, notes Palmer. He added that in his view Thornwell's greatest, and most unique, ability as a preacher was in synthesizing several elements of Christian doctrine that his hearers knew in their distinct settings, but had not unified in their own minds. He could, as Palmer put it, take the various elements and "build up the grand temple before the eyes of his audience, laying beam upon beam, and stone upon stone" until the edifice was complete.[47] He became a familiar figure in Lancaster District as he rode between the three churches in his charge on his horse, Red Rover. His weekday exuberance provided an appealing contrast to his Sunday-morning solemnity. He romped with children and traded jests with grown-ups.[48] Clearly he was more at ease than he had been in some time.

An interesting illustration of Thornwell's status in his new community comes from the life of his college friend, J. Marion Sims. A native of the Hanging Rock area of Lancaster County, Sims returned home to practice medicine in the same month that Thornwell arrived there. His childhood sweetheart, Theresa Jones, was the daughter of one of Lancasterville's most prominent families, which also happened to be among the pillars of Thornwell's church. Her grandmother, according to local tradition, had been Andrew Jackson's first love, and now that Old Hickory was in the White

---

[47]Palmer, 130-34. His "Inaugural Discourse" as professor at Columbia Seminary is a good example of this. See *Collected Writings of Thornwell*, 1:573-82.

[48]Palmer, 134-46.

House, that connection loomed large indeed. In the Jones' parlor was a silver snuff box given her by the president. Theresa's father, recently deceased, had been one of the largest landowners in the area and the town physician as well. His widow was now determined to block any romantic attachments between Theresa and young Dr. Sims, whose family was not socially prominent and whose prospects were unpromising. Despairing of making any progress with this awe-inspiring woman, Sims turned to Thornwell, who invoked his pastoral authority and forensic gifts in his friend's behalf. Ten days after being visited by her young pastor, Mrs. Jones relented and gave her blessing to the engagement. Thornwell, of course, conducted the wedding.[49]

Before long Thornwell found himself in a situation comparable to that faced by Sims. For the object of his affections was Nancy White Witherspoon, Theresa's cousin and the daughter of Lancasterville's leading citizen, Colonel James Witherspoon. The colonel was a former lieutenant governor of South Carolina and a candidate for Congress. He was also the nephew of John Witherspoon, who had been president of The College of New Jersey and the only clergyman to sign the Declaration of Independence. Though not happy at the prospect of his daughter being supported on a preacher's salary of six hundred dollars a year, Witherspoon could hardly refuse the young man he considered the intellectual equal of George McDuffie and John C. Calhoun. James and Nancy were married on 3 December 1835.[50] Harriet Martineau observed that it was common for Southern clergymen to marry above their economic status: "Not a few planters in the South began life as poor clergymen, and obtained by marriage the means of becoming planters."[51] At the time of their marriage, Nancy was twenty-seven and James not quite twenty-three. She was "tall, and of a large frame, with unusual force of character . . . firm as a rock and yet kind and loving." Though their life together was saddened by the deaths of four of their nine children, the marriage, by all accounts, was a happy one. Nancy was later described by one of Thornwell's colleagues as "simple, kind, and yet highly refined in her manner."[52]

[49]Harris, *Woman's Surgeon,* 13-14, 35-39.

[50]Palmer, 137.

[51]Harriet Martineau, *Society in America,* vol. 2 (London, 1837) 351; quoted in Holifield, *The Gentlemen Theologians,* 31.

[52]Joseph G. Wardlaw, *Genealogy of the Witherspoon Family* (Yorkville SC, 1910) 132-

Thornwell's ministry in Lancasterville was to last less than three years; at the close of 1837 he accepted the chair of Belles Lettres and Logic at his alma mater.[53] He was willing to make this change because although successful in the eyes of others, he had fallen short of the high aspirations he had for himself as a pastor. The journal he kept during the Lancasterville years reveals his continued sense of failure to *feel*, as well as he *understood*, the message of Jesus. "I can see very clearly how I ought to be affected," he wrote, "but then I am not so affected." He frequently rebuked himself and despaired at the recollection of many sins, especially those of vanity. "I see nothing about myself that is right," he wrote once. One senses in these outpourings of anguish that, though gratified in many ways, Thornwell is too anxious about failure to remain for long in this station.[54]

Thornwell would later admit that he much preferred a city pastorate to one in a small village; and Columbia, which in the late 1830s was barely more than a village itself, was described by another newcomer as "a very neat little city [which] affords many facilities of a religious, literary and commercial character." The South Carolina College was "a popular and prosperous institution. The buildings are I suppose the best and most expensive in the Southern country. Indeed I have never seen their equal. The Theological Seminary is also fine and well endowed by the Synod to which it belongs."[55] So it must have been with some relief that Thornwell accepted the opportunity to return to an academic setting. Nonetheless, there were some, just as before, who questioned his fitness for the new position. He lacked the proper appreciation of aesthetics, they felt. His biographer is at pains to disprove this, pointing to his love for, and meticulous care in

---

33. For an illustration of their relationship, see James to Nancy, 3 July 1841, Thornwell Papers. See also excerpts of a letter from Alexander T. McGill to his wife, 31 March 1853, in Margaret DesChamps Moore, "A Northern Professor Winters in Columbia," *South Carolina Historical Magazine* 60 (1959): 191. The Thornwells lost their first child at the age of three months, and others at two years, eight years, and twenty years, all before James's death. A fifth child, Gillespie Robbins, died at age eighteen—in 1863—as a result of battle wounds (*Witherspoon Family*, 132-33; Palmer, 137).

[53]Hollis, *University of South Carolina*, 1:163.

[54]Thornwell Journal, 2 April, 14 May, 4 June, 19 July, 30 July, 5 September 1836, in Palmer, 139-42.

[55]Ibid., 556; Zelotus Holmes to his family, 27 November 1839, Zelotus Holmes Papers, South Caroliniana Library. Holmes had recently arrived from Ohio to study at Columbia Seminary when he wrote this description. His opinion was not shared by all.

the use of, the English language; his powers as an orator; and his enraptured response to the wonderful scenery of the Swiss Alps. Yet, as even he recognized, his admired subject was "a reasoner, and not a dreamer," and he notes with approval that he was soon shifted to the chair of Metaphysics.[56]

But metaphysics alone failed to satisfy Thornwell's sense of spiritual obligation, and after three semesters at the College he resigned to become the minister of Columbia's First Presbyterian Church, succeeding his brother-in-law, John Witherspoon. He held this pastorate only for the year 1840, however; at the end of that year his friend Stephen Elliott resigned the chair of Sacred Literature and the Evidences of Christianity, and the chaplaincy of the South Carolina College, to become bishop of the Episcopal Diocese of Georgia. Thornwell filled these vacancies. He had first declined, and urged his friend and ministerial colleague Thomas Smyth of Charleston to apply for the position. "The truth is," he confided to Smyth, "I am anxious to avoid the responsibility of either accepting or declining. My church will protest warmly against my going to the College. . . . I take you to be the man for the place." Smyth responded that his leaving Charleston would be taken by the New Schoolers there as a victory and his church would be weakened. After urging him in a second letter to look to God on the subject, and receiving Smyth's second demurrer, Thornwell accepted the dual post in the fall of 1840.[57] He had finally found his niche, for now he was "entrusted with the care of souls, and those of a most important class in society," as well as the intellectual training of plastic minds. Now twenty-eight years old, he would remain in this post for ten years.[58]

The decade of the 1840s saw Thornwell's rise to prominence in the Presbyterian Church as well as his increasing influence at the South Carolina College and, indirectly, in the state as a whole. In all matters his in-

---

[56]Palmer, 147-49.

[57]Thomas Smyth, *Autobiographical Notes, Letters and Reflections,* ed. Louisa Cheves Stoney (Charleston, 1914) 177-79. Thornwell and Smyth were "always intimate friends" and theological brothers. Smyth preached the sermon at Thornwell's installation as professor at Columbia Seminary (ibid).

[58]During his brief service in the First Presbyterian Church, the size of that congregation almost doubled. Thornwell to Gillespie, 2 October 1840, Thornwell Papers; Palmer, 153-56. Palmer considered Thornwell's return to the College "the great turning point of his career" (217).

fluence was, on the whole, conservative. He had sided with the "Old School" during the schism in American Presbyterianism in 1837, opposing both the liberalization of doctrine and the bureaucratization of the Church's structure. He attacked "Papism" and became involved in running battles with the Roman Catholic press. He contributed pieces to numerous religious periodicals and in 1847 helped to found the *Southern Presbyterian Review,* which became a leading voice for orthodoxy. In that year, at age thirty-four, he became the youngest moderator of the General Assembly in the history of the American Presbyterian Church.

Meanwhile, his mere presence at the College served to boost the forces of orthodox religion, which had been in decline during the administration of President Cooper. Thornwell, though, contributed more than his presence. He actively engaged the liberal forces at the school, winning greater support for the institution from the Baptists and Methodists as well as the Presbyterians and, incidentally, alienating at least a few Episcopalians. After ten years on the faculty of the College, during which he was called by several churches (and almost took one pulpit, only to be circumvented by the combined efforts of the College's Board and the Charleston Presbytery, of which he was a member), Thornwell left Columbia for Charleston's Glebe Street Presbyterian Church in May of 1851. Here he enjoyed a welcome respite from the toils of academia, but it was to be brief: that December he was offered the presidency of the college he had so recently left. By the 1840s the South Carolina College presidency was "one of the most prominent and sought-after positions in the State. In prestige it ranked just behind the United States Senatorships and the governorship."[59] Flattered but ambivalent, Thornwell left the decision to his new congregation, and they reluctantly released him. So for the next four years he would direct the affairs of his alma mater. These years were highlighted by the articulation of his views on public higher education and his efforts to buttress the classical curriculum that was the College's trademark.[60]

He left the presidency at the end of 1855 to take the chair of Didactic and Polemic Theology at Columbia Theological Seminary, though he would influence the life of the College as a trustee until his death. Early in 1856

---

[59]Hollis, *University of South Carolina,* 1:142.

[60]Ibid., 162-76. See Thornwell's *Letter to Governor Manning* (Charleston, 1853), and Palmer, 334-38.

Thornwell added to his seminary and church duties the editorship of the *Southern Quarterly Review*. This journal, which over the last two decades had published some important work, was now in decline due to insufficient subscription. Unfortunately, the new editor would prove unable to reverse this process. The *Review* folded the following year, despite his strenuous efforts to attract an array of luminaries to its pages. By now he, like most Southerners, was increasingly preoccupied with the growing tensions between the sections.[61]

Though a unionist in 1830 and 1850, and though opposed to separate secession for South Carolina until late in 1860, Thornwell had little difficulty in casting his lot with the Confederacy. Political separation merely formalized the intellectual, and for him, spiritual separation that had been building during his adult life. So it was a natural, if painful, climax for him to lead Southern Presbyterians in the formation of a separate General Assembly in December 1861. He died the following August, four months before his fiftieth birthday, still hopeful of his new nation's victory and the values that—for him as for many others—it cherished and symbolized to the world.

The public career of James Henley Thornwell was confined within rather narrow limits. Chronologically it spanned only twenty-seven years. Geographically it was bounded by the state of his birth and his lifelong residence. Topically it focused upon religion and closely related matters. Yet these limitations belie the impact he exerted on his time. A closer look at the man, considering his personality and mental gifts, will reveal more about his significance than this brief biographical sketch has done.

I have noted that he was highly regarded by both faculty and fellow students at the South Carolina College in the early 1830s. By mid-century their regard had broadened and deepened, but he had acquired some enemies as well. Physically he was still an unlikely candidate for greatness. Small and frail, he weighed barely one hundred pounds. Friends expressed concern over his "fleshless frame" and urged him to "nurse [his body] a little." His shoulders drooped, as did his eyelids.[62] But intellectually he felt himself the match for any man, and his ego seems not to have suffered

---

[61]Palmer, 397, 418-19.

[62]Law, "Dr. Thornwell as Preacher and Teacher," in *Centennial Addresses,* 12. Matthew J. Williams to Thornwell, 19 August 1853, Thornwell Papers.

on account of his physical appearance. On the verge of manhood, he had written to childhood friend Alexander Pegues, "My . . . visions of fame are as airy as they used to be. . . . To die unknown, unhonoured, and unsung, like the wild beasts of the field, I hope in God may never be my gloomy fate." Yet, he had added, "by fame I mean the esteem of the wise and good, not . . . the noisy acclamation of the crowd." He added that his walks in churchyards had impressed on him the number of people who merely lived out their allotted time, whose gravestones could say only that they were born and had died. For him there would have to be more.[63] Aware of this desire for the admiration of others, he continually cautioned himself against letting this subvert the noble aims he had set.

He also had, in spite of his physical shortcomings, more than a little vanity.[64] Perhaps a manifestation of this was his expensive taste. Though frugal with the funds given him as a student by Robbins and Gillespie, he soon demonstrated a love of fine things, and in Palmer's words, insisted that "the best was always the cheapest." And he always bought the best, whether in books, clothing, horses, or cigars. His usual garb was a black swallow-tail coat, thick-heeled boots, and a beaver hat.[65] Palmer once offered him a cigar that was "as good in quality as he felt he could afford," only to have him puff on it for a moment and pitch it through an open window, declaring that "any man who will smoke such cigars will steal!"[66] While his personal habits were generally beyond exception, he indulged in one that could be upsetting to his friends. He was an inveterate "night-owl" who loved to sleep until late in the morning. With half-seriousness he would contend that the night was meant for work and the day for rest, and that one of man's many errors was to reverse this natural order.[67]

It was with his voice and his pen, but mainly the former, that Thornwell made his reputation. Addressing the South Carolina College's Euphradean and Clariosophic Societies on their fiftieth birthday in 1856, he

---

[63]Thornwell to Alexander Pegues, 29 April 1832; quoted in Palmer, 94. Ironically, Thornwell's headstone in Columbia's Elmwood Cemetery bears only his name.

[64]Palmer to J. M. Wilson, 17 May 1855, Benjamin M. Palmer Papers. Regarding an engraving of Thornwell being planned, he wrote that to please its subject, "it must be done in the highest style of the art."

[65]Law, "Thornwell as Preacher and Teacher," 12.

[66]Palmer, 135. Palmer says that Thornwell was "addicted" to tobacco (23).

[67]Thornwell to Nancy Thornwell, 11 May 1841, Thornwell Papers.

revealed his high regard for the value of eloquence. "Speech is the Alpha and Omega . . . of every enterprize," he told the students. "Among a people of such itching ears, it is manifestly of the last importance that glib tongues should be cultivated." As to what makes a good speaker, he listed patient study first, noting that Demosthenes copied Thucydides eight times. He then spoke of the proper choice of subjects, pointing to the Bible, Shakespeare, Milton, and Pope, and finally advocated practice.[68]

His own speaking style was, to Palmer, the very definition of eloquence—"logic on fire." Though neither the sound of his voice nor his mannerisms were in themselves appealing, he had a powerful effect on his hearers.[69] Recalling the first time he heard Thornwell preach, in Columbia's First Presbyterian Church in 1839, Palmer wrote many years later, "A thin, spare form, with a slight stoop in the shoulders, stood in the desk, with soft black hair falling obliquely over the forehead, and a small eye, with a powerful gleam when it was lighted by the inspiration of its theme." The scripture reading was "perhaps a trifle monotonous" and the prayer lacked "fervour," but the discourse was overpowering. Palmer remembered a "conscious resistance" to its aggressive tone, "and then, as link after link was added to the chain of a consistent argument . . . the effect at the close was to overwhelm and subdue."[70] In his eulogy of Thornwell, Palmer remarked that "he wove garlands of beauty around discussions the most thorny and abstruse."[71]

While perhaps not quite as enthusiastic, others attested to his pulpit prowess. He was "not a preacher for the masses," wrote Thomas Law, another younger Presbyterian clergyman who had studied under Thornwell. His "language was too academic and his arguments were too closely knit in Aristotelian logic for them." "I have heard him try to preach to children" without much success, Law added. "Not that his preaching was cold and unemotional," however. Once when he preached on the Last Judgment in Charleston, "the whole congregation appeared terror-stricken and unconsciously seized the back of the pews." A young man who was

---

[68]MS of Thornwell's address to Euphradean and Clariosophic societies, December 1856, Thornwell Papers.

[69]Law, "Dr. Thornwell as Preacher and Teacher," 12.

[70]Johnson, *Life and Letters of Palmer*, 67. Palmer, *Life and Letters of Thornwell*, 154.

[71]Johnson, *Life and Letters of Palmer*, 265-66.

present testified "that he was never so frightened in all his life."[72] Shortly after arriving in Columbia in 1839 to attend the Seminary, a young Ohioan named Zelotus Holmes wrote his parents, "I had never been priviledged [*sic*] to meet the clergyman who corresponded to the idea I had formed of that office until I came to this place. I am now pleased to have such an [*sic*] one before me. One who while he exhibits the Piety and Energy of the Gospel, together with a remarkable power of intellect, is at the same time *sound* in the Christian faith. Such a man is Dr. Thornwell, who fills the Presbyterian pulpit in this place."[73]

The young seminarian's opinion was shared by others whose judgments on the subject of oratory, pulpit or otherwise, would carry more weight. After hearing Thornwell preach on "Popery" to the Presbyterian General Assembly of 1847, Dr. J. W. Alexander, another leading divine, wrote, "Dr. Thornwell is the great [Church?] man of the South, and I do not think his learning or powers of mind overrated." "His sermon was ill delivered, but nevertheless a model of what is rare, viz.: burning hot argument, logic in ignition, and glowing more and more to the end: it was a *memoriter,* and with terrific *contentio laterum.*"[74] Daniel Webster, something of an authority on oratory, told William Campbell Preston that a Thornwell sermon in the South Carolina College Chapel was "one of the finest exhibitions of pulpit eloquence I ever heard." Edward Everett held Thornwell's argumentative powers and intellect in high regard.[75] John C. Calhoun compared him to Timothy Dwight, his teacher at Yale. Other admirers included George Bancroft and Henry Ward Beecher, two men who could hardly have been further removed from Thornwell ideologically. At a New York City dinner party in May 1856, Bancroft, then a professor at Harvard, presented Thornwell with two volumes of Aristotle's works, and inscribed the flyleaf of one in Latin. It read: "A testimony of regard to the

---

[72]Law, "Dr. Thornwell as Preacher and Teacher," 16, 13.

[73]Zelotus Holmes to his family, 27 November 1839, Zelotus Holmes Papers.

[74]Palmer, 300.

[75]Quoted in *The State* (Columbia SC), 11 March 1925. Photocopy in Thornwell Papers. When Everett was visiting in Columbia in 1857, he and Thornwell enjoyed a conversation in which they exchanged quotations from Thucydides, Everett in English and Thornwell in Greek. Witnessing this exchange, William DeSaussure later called Thornwell "our Southern Giant" (Palmer, 123).

Rev. J. H. Thornwell, the most learned of the learned.''[76] Henry Ward Beecher wrote, after Thornwell's death in the midst of the Civil War, that ''by common fame, Dr. Thornwell was the most brilliant minister in the Old School Presbyterian Church, and the most brilliant debater in the General Assembly. This reputation he early gained and never lost. Whenever he was present in the Assembly, he was always the first person pointed out to a stranger.''[77]

Thornwell's powers were displayed in the classroom as well as the pulpit. Fellow professor Maximilian LaBorde commented,

> As a teacher, few, if any, have equalled, and certainly none have surpassed him. Never was there in our walls a clearer head, a more acute mind. . . . The most complex problems, the most abstract questions, furnished the occasions for the display of his highest powers. . . . His mind was ever in search of law and principle; errors, like straws, he knew, floated upon the surface, and truth, like the pearl, was only to be found below.

Agreeing with the assessment of others, LaBorde found him unappreciative of beauty. ''He is essentially a man of truth,'' who ''revolts at the imaginative, the ficticious [sic]. . . . Of the world of fancy he knows but little, . . . [though] he has a love for ancient thought and speculation amounting almost to reverence, and his chosen companionship is with the great masters, Plato and Aristotle.'' Their impact on his mind was clearly visible, for ''who,'' asked LaBorde, ''can resist the power of his logic?''

---

[76]The volumes were *Rhetoric, Poetry and Natural Philosophy,* and *Organon,* both in German. This story may be found in a letter from W. S. Patterson, clerk of the King's Mountain Presbytery, Davidson NC, to the librarian, University of South Carolina, 4 November 1948, in Thornwell Papers, Box 6.

[77]Joseph M. Wilson, ed., *The Presbyterian Almanac, 1863,* 211-12. In the Thornwell Collection at the University of South Carolina is a file of seventy-three letters attesting to his standing among his contemporaries as a scholar, theologian, and preacher; see file 7878. By the end of his life, word of his reputation had crossed the Atlantic. See Thornwell to Nancy Thornwell, 19 July 1860, and to James Gillespie, 21 July 1860, from Belfast, Thornwell Papers. Scattered throughout his papers are letters from around the United States soliciting essays, inviting him to lecture and preach, and calling him to other pulpits, all of which give evidence of Thornwell's wide reputation. See, for example, Mrs. Catherine V. Devens to Thornwell, from Millbury MA, 12 September 1854, and the Thalian Society of Oglethorpe University to Thornwell, 26 April 1853, asking him to give the commencement address at that school.

LaBorde probably came as close as anyone to capturing the essence of Thornwell's mind when he said, "He luxuriates in the profound."[78]

Thornwell's influence at the College was summarized by President William Campbell Preston in 1846, when the professor was considering a call to the pulpit of the Second Presbyterian Church of Baltimore.

> We cannot afford to lose Dr. Thornwell from the College. In the first place, he is the representative of the Presbyterian Church, which embraces the bone and sinew of the State, without whose support the institution cannot exist. In the second place, he has acquired that moral influence over the students, which is superior even to law; and his removal will take away the very buttresses on which the Administration of the College rests.[79]

As the College's president in the 1850s, Thornwell "united more of the qualities which give fitness for the high office, than anyone who has filled it."[80] When a friend urged Charleston intellectual James Warley Miles to seek the faculty position vacated by Thornwell upon his appointment as president, Miles demurred, in part "because I shrink from the comparison of succeeding a man of such undoubted intellectual ability as Thornwell."[81] A Northern visitor to Columbia in the early 1850s wrote that Thornwell was "the most important personage in town, not excepting the Governor himself. The brilliancy of his talents, his great learning, and his position [the College presidency] all combine to give him ascendancy of influence."[82] His resignation as president in 1855 produced so much editorial regret in the state press that the Charleston *Mercury* asked, "Is he the only man" capable of filling the post?[83]

----

[78]LaBorde, *South Carolina College,* 332-34. Others substantiated LaBorde's appraisal. "All in all he completely towered above any other I have known as a teacher," wrote Law, "Thornwell as Preacher and Teacher," 18. In John M. Wells's *Southern Presbyterian Worthies* (Richmond, 1936), the chapter on Thornwell, which comes first, is entitled "The Scholar." Although he had no earned degrees beyond the Bachelor of Arts, he received honorary doctorates of divinity from Jefferson College in Pennsylvania, Hampden-Sydney in Virginia, and Centre College in Kentucky (Palmer, 269).

[79]Palmer, 281.

[80]LaBorde, *South Carolina College,* 350-51.

[81]James Warley Miles to David McCord, 24 April 1851; quoted in *South Carolina Historical Magazine* 43 (1942): 188.

[82]Alexander McGill to his wife, 10 February 1853; quoted in Moore, "A Northern Professor Winters in Columbia," 183-92, esp. 188.

[83]Hollis, *University of South Carolina,* 177.

As a respected man of God, Thornwell exerted spiritual force over any community of which he was a part. In February 1856, two months after he had left the College presidency for the Seminary a few blocks away, a virtual battle between more than 200 students and the town militia appeared imminent. The students, angered over the beating and arrest by Columbia police of one of their own, had armed themselves with guns from the cadet arsenal and were met at the guardhouse by some 200 citizens, with weapons loaded. The new College president, Charles McCay, and the mayor were trying without success to calm the young men when someone called Thornwell from his seminary lecture room.

> The former president raced from his lecture to the scene of the conflict and moved rapidly among the students, urging them to retire to the campus. He assured them that he would investigate the situation, and if they were in the right, and no other means of redress were possible other than fighting, that he himself would lead them. He then marched toward the campus shouting, "College! College!" and was followed by the entire assembly of students. Probably nobody else in the State could have done it.[84]

This episode suggests William R. Taylor's portrait of the cavalier as the heroic figure who brought order to all he surveyed. "Only the Cavalier possessed the heroic force of character which was required to hold back the restless flood of savagery that threatened to overflow the country."[85]

Not all of Thornwell's contemporaries held him in such high esteem. No one with so combative a personality or so narrow a vision of the truth could escape his share of criticism. Francis Lieber seems to have been on good terms with his colleague at the South Carolina College until he concluded that Thornwell had led the effort to defeat his bid for the College presidency in 1855. Assuming that religious bigotry was back of this (Thornwell had supported Charles McCay, a Presbyterian, for the post), Lieber, an Episcopalian and much too liberal in his religious views to suit Thornwell, turned against him. He called Thornwell a "nineteenth century Jonathan Edwards" (a reference Thornwell no doubt prized if he knew of it) and he also remarked that Thornwell "seems to forget that Savior means healer and religion ought to be a balm" rather than a source of friction.

---

[84]Ibid., 199. Palmer, 396.

[85]William R. Taylor, *Cavalier and Yankee; The Old South and the American National Character* (New York, 1957) 301-302.

Writes Lieber's biographer, "When an enthusiast declared that there had been no men like Thornwell since Calvin, Lieber replied, 'I hope so.' "[86] Another College colleague, William Hooper, once wrote Thornwell that he had always thought he was too belligerent a man to be a servant of the Prince of Peace.[87]

So polemical did Thornwell become in arguments with his various adversaries that he later regretted the tone of much of his controversial writing. He was typical of nineteenth-century Protestants in his anti-Catholic bigotry, and nowhere is this abrasive side of his personality more visible than in his exchanges with Roman Catholic Bishop Patrick Lynch of Charleston. However, even when engaging other Presbyterians in debate, he often exceeded the bounds of charity, evoking fear and resentment in his opponents and dismay in his allies. As to why he became so bellicose on such occasions, he was certainly a man passionately committed to his beliefs, which he had not arrived at casually, but only after deep study. Hence his style in debate was that of a man who is on familiar ground and certain of the truth. Second, Thornwell's life was full of personal sorrow because of the illnesses and deaths of four of his children, and some of his polemical work was produced under the strain of these tragedies. Much of his most biting and bigoted writing was done while he was still a young man (he was twenty-nine when he wrote his attack on the *Apocrypha,* for example); he mellowed considerably as he got older.[88]

---

[86]Frank Freidel, *Francis Lieber, Nineteenth-Century Liberal* (Baton Rouge, 1948) 133, 285. Lieber, born in Berlin in 1800, was an internationally respected political scientist who taught political economy at the South Carolina College from 1835 to 1855, and later at Columbia University. He once called the South Carolina College faculty a "conclave of mummies" (140).

[87]William Hooper to Thornwell, 28 February 1850, Thornwell Papers.

[88]Thornwell, *Arguments of Romanists from the Infallibility of the Church and the Testimony of the Fathers in Behalf of the Apocrypha, Discussed and Refuted* (New York, 1845) esp. 12, 21, 23, 25; Smyth, *Autobiographical Notes,* 192. John B. Adger, prefatory note to Thornwell's writings on Roman Catholicism, in Adger, ed., *Collected Writings of James Henley Thornwell,* vol. 3 (Richmond, 1871) 281. Here Adger quotes Thornwell as pointing out that some of this material was written "in the chamber of the sick, and by the bed of the dying." Adger also notes that in some of these replies to the Catholic writers, Thornwell employed "very strong language" in dealing with the errors of that faith, and "also considerable asperity of language toward his assailant personally. Having heard him express the intention, if he should live to republish, of modifying these expressions, the Editor has considered it his duty to carry out, according to his best judgment, the known wishes of the author." In spite of these deletions, the modern reader of these exchanges must recognize that Thornwell's attacks were more pugnacious than those of his adversary, Bishop Lynch. See also Palmer, 226, 569.

Thornwell's pugnacity was not reserved for combat with sectarian foes, however, nor was it confined to his earlier years. In 1857 he wrote a review of a new algebra book by Professor Daniel H. Hill of Davidson College. The review so pained Hill that he wrote a plaintive letter in reply. Thornwell had indicated his low opinion of science as a subject for well-rounded scholars, suggesting that its utility was limited to the training of engineers and soldiers. Hill replied:

> I do not object to your particular views. I am willing that you should pronounce Newton and Pascal . . . ninnies and fools. I am willing that you should assert that *creatures* (you will not allow me to call them men) can calculate the movements of the heavenly bodies *without thought*. I am willing that you should regard as a "necessary evil" the study that gives us the loftiest conceptions of the power and glory of the omnipotent God. But I am not willing that you should use my name in the connection that you have employed. . . . Had you believed the book of no real value . . . and said this in your Review, I would . . . not have complained. It is a very different matter when with one breath you say that you are incompetent to form a judgment of its merits, and in the very next breath, pronounce it unfit for colleges where *Men* are in training, and fit only for military schools where senseless soldiers and engineers are made.

Returning some of the sarcasm for which Thornwell was known, Hill continued,

> For ten years I followed the unmanly, stupid profession of arms. [He would serve as lieutenant general in the Confederate army.] For ten more I have been "dwarfing and stunting" my mind with mathematical studies. I hope to be improved by the "Critical Notices" in the Southern Presbyterian [Review]. If that remedy fails, I will try to read some of the articles, though I die in the attempt. First. I complain that our Great Southern Teacher whose opinion I most valued, has been entirely indifferent to this first Southern book of science. Second. That the review of my book has been made the occasion of most unkind reflections upon mathematical studies—reflections calculated to do immense mischief in regard to the circulation of the work. Third. That while professing to be unable to judge of the merits of the book . . . you have pronounced it unfit for college purposes. . . . A poor stupid fool who has been a soldier and is still an engineer has no claims upon your notice. But God has given him the feelings of a man, notwithstanding his unmanly avocation[,] and even the worm will writhe when trampled upon. For past kindness I have not been ungrateful. All who know me will say that I have been your most consistent admirer. Yours truly, D. H. Hill.

There is no copy of Thornwell's reply in his papers; but he surely did write one, for Palmer notes that on more than one occasion Thornwell was sorry to learn that his words had hurt another.[89]

Even close friends had to bear the brunt of Thornwell's verbal attacks when they took the other side in debates with him. Once in the heat of a synod debate he referred to Thomas Smyth as "a vessel putting to sea without ballast." He later apologized for the remark, and evidently no permanent harm was done to their relationship.[90] Chancellor Job Johnston perhaps had such a comment in mind when he wrote Smyth a few years later that Thornwell's "severely analytical mind carries him to positions and holds him there and makes him regardless of all consequences—*fiat justitia et veritas ruat caelum*. ['Let justice and truth be served though the heavens should fall.'] But wherever his head is, his heart is right and his charity warm and . . . I have always loved him as a man, admired him as profound, able and eloquent, and reverenced him as a Christian."[91]

Another criticism often leveled at Thornwell involved his combativeness. His sometimes-difficult preaching style has already been mentioned. This was partly due to his tendency to approach the sermon as he did all oratorical and literary exercises, as a form of debate. Even on his deathbed the old fondness for debate did not leave him. His close friend and fellow clergyman John Adger recalled that during Thornwell's last day, as he drifted in and out of consciousness, he mumbled something that Adger had heard many times before, and that for him captured Thornwell's personality: "Well, you have stated your position, now prove it."[92] One of Thornwell's admirers, who approved of this combative style, praised him for a piece he had published in the *Southern Quarterly Review*, but added: "I do not recognize your usual amount of bellicose pugnacity. . . . I do not desire to see an unrivaled logician and peerless intellectual gladiator spoilt. The military posture is precisely the proper attitude for your mind.

---

[89]David H. Hill to Thornwell, 13 December 1857, Thornwell Papers. Palmer, 568-69.

[90]Smyth, *Autobiographical Notes*, 192. One wonders if Thornwell was not his own worst enemy because of his combative personality. Smyth notes, for example, that in the debate referred to here, his side won by "an overwhelming majority" (ibid).

[91]Ibid., 257, quoting Job Johnston to Thomas Smyth, 27 September 1849.

[92]John B. Adger, memorial to Thornwell in *Memorial Volume of the Semi-Centennial of the Theological Seminary at Columbia, South Carolina* (Richmond, 1881) 188.

It is your peculiar mission to charge full into the enemy; to seize, like Sampson, *the jaw of the first ass,* and slay the uncircumcised Philistines.''[93] One imagines Thornwell nodding accordingly as he read this. In any case, this was the posture for which he was generally known, and this was to be the challenge he would hurl at the Northern critics of the South: "You have stated your position, now prove it." Facts and logic were his weapons—the only ones he respected.

Could such a man, intellectual, single-minded, devout, have a sense of humor? Surprisingly, friends and colleagues concur that Thornwell did. Maximilian LaBorde noted that "he exhibits no peculiarities in his manners; there is nothing eccentric, nothing different from other men. . . . He is fond of a joke, tells a good one himself, and laughs heartily.''[94] Nor was he above "bending the rules" or playing jokes. While at Harvard he and a friend had gotten good seats for Edward Everett's eulogy of Lafayette by posing as visiting dignitaries. "We did the thing with such grace," he wrote General Gillespie, "that the claim was admitted, and we joined the line with John Quincy Adams, Daniel Webster, and that whole tribe, chuckling all the while over our new bought dignity. [I] could hardly persuade myself that I was simply James H. Thornwell, once pedagogue in the Cheraw Academy. . . . A little impudence is a great help in this world.''[95]

Years later he was still putting this axiom to use. Thanking his wife's brother-in-law for a gift of some "exquisite cigars," he added that they had only one fault, which "modesty forbids me to mention." He then proceeded to express regret that "it is becoming fashionable to put up such cigars in such *small* boxes." Recalling Walpole's definition of gratitude as "the expectation of future favours," he added:

> We love our friends so much, that we rejoice in everything which gives them an opportunity of showing how much they deserve to be loved. . . . If you should come across another box of cigars, and should be doubtful whether they are better than the ones sent or not, you need not scruple [*sic*] about sending them to me for my judgment, as I assure you it will put

---

[93]Benjamin R. Stuart to Thornwell, 5 June 1856, Thornwell Papers.

[94]LaBorde, *South Carolina College,* 351-52.

[95]Thornwell to James Gillespie, 6 September 1834; quoted in Palmer, 122.

me to no sort of inconvenience, and I will take great pleasure in resolving your doubts.[96]

There are numerous examples in Thornwell's writing of the delight he took in injecting humor into even "serious" topics. In a review of Frederick A. P. Barnard's *Improvements Practicable in American Colleges,* he applauded the book's argument that the purpose of a college is "to educate, and not to inform," and noted only one objection. "We might raise a question as to the right of the mathematics to be put upon a footing of equality with the classics [Barnard was a mathematician], but the ointment, in other respects, is so sweet, that we shall not throw away the box for the sake of a single dead fly. Something may be pardoned to professional prejudice."[97] Enjoying humor himself, he also appreciated it in the work of fellow clergymen, although, as the following illustrates, he was never far from the seriousness that was due spiritual matters. Charleston Unitarian minister Samuel Gilman earned Thornwell's praise for being "among the few clergymen in this country" who would branch out into the field of letters. Reviewing Gilman's *Contributions to Literature,* he applauded the reverend's "keen sense of the ridiculous" and his use of satire. Yet a moment later he faulted Gilman for not rebuking the practice of praying seated. Standing or kneeling were, for Thornwell, the only proper postures for communing with God. In the same review Thornwell opined that "religion would be no loser, if both organs and organ-lofts were banished from all our meeting-houses."[98]

With this brief look at Thornwell's personality, and at his contemporaries' assessment of him, one may wonder what was the proper role for such a man to play, the ideal niche for him to fill. Historians have granted him due respect. "More than any other he molded and reflected the mind of Southern Presbyterianism in the decades preceding the Civil War," writes one. He was the Old "South's most sophisticated theorist," says another. A third has called him "one of the most eloquent spokesmen for

---

[96]Thornwell to Dr. Joseph G. Wardlaw, 13 December 1852; quoted in Palmer, 371-72. Wardlaw was Nancy Thornwell's sister's husband.

[97]Thornwell, review of *Improvements Practicable in American Colleges* (Hartford CT, 1856), in *Southern Quarterly Review,* n.s. 1, no. 1 (April 1856): 168-88.

[98]Thornwell, "Critical Notice of Rev. Gilman's *Contributions to Literature,*" *Southern Quarterly Review,* n.s. 1, no. 2 (August 1856): 430-36. For other examples of Thornwell's wit, see Palmer, 374, 376-78.

the Southern viewpoint.'' Clement Eaton calls him ''the intellectual inter-
preter of the religion of the [Southern] upper middle class,'' and says that
he ''exercized [*sic*] great power in South Carolina and throughout the
Southern Presbyterian Church.'' Perhaps the most expansive appraisal of
Thornwell in the secondary literature is Alice Felt Tyler's. She concludes
that as a result of growing Southern dominance of church courts, Thornwell ''became the real leader of American Presbyterianism'' before the war.
More recently, Michael O'Brien acknowledges him as ''the leading Presbyterian theologian of his day in the South and among its most influential
educators.''[99]

Yet his admiring biographer seems at pains to explain why he did not
achieve more. It must be remembered, of course, that he died in his fiftieth
year. ''Alas,'' wrote Palmer, ''death came too soon for the church to realize the high legacy her heart was coveting. These things she was expecting at his hands: a system of theology from his own point of view,
exhibiting the nexus between all its parts and blending those in a perfect
unity; a rediscussion of the Christian Evidences, with reference to the subtle, rationalistic philosophy by which they have been impugned; and a book
on Morals, in which the foundation of the true philosophy of human obligation should be laid bare.'' Only a part of the first task was done in finished form, though aspects of the second and third were treated extensively
in Thornwell's class lectures, some of which later found their way into
print.[100]

The disappointment that some felt with Thornwell went beyond his
failure to leave behind a systematic record of thought. Some contemporaries believed that his abilities were wasted in the pulpit and in academia.

---

[99]Ernest T. Thompson, *Presbyterians in the South, 1607-1861* (Richmond, 1963) 497-
98. Donald Mathews, *Religion in the Old South* (Chicago, 1977) 176. Robert T. Handy,
ed., *Religion in the American Experience* (Columbia SC, 1972) 382. Clement Eaton, *The
Mind of the Old South*, rev. ed. (Baton Rouge, 1967) 205. Alice Felt Tyler, *Freedom's
Ferment* (Minneapolis, 1944) 520. Other assessments are in Clifton E. Olmstead, *Religion
in America, Past and Present* (Englewood Cliffs NJ, 1961) 95-96; Margaret B. Des-
Champs, ''Union of Disunion? South Atlantic Presbyterians and Southern Nationalism,
1820-1861,'' *Journal of Southern History* 20 (November 1954): 484-98. Michael O'Brien,
ed., *All Clever Men Who Make Their Way; Critical Discourse in the Old South* (Fayetteville AK, 1982) 420.

[100]LaBorde, *South Carolina College*, 372-73. The task of selecting and editing Thornwell's works was made more difficult by his failure to put much of his writing in finished
form. See Adger's preface to vol. 1 of *The Collected Writings of Thornwell*.

Putting the case most directly, one historian has suggested that his failure to meet ''the high expectations of his friends . . . may be due to the fact that he deliberately turned away from almost the only field for the proper exercise of great gifts at that time in the South.'' In other words, by eschewing politics, he minimized the impact of his talents. Given the emphasis upon politics and public service in antebellum culture, there seems to be an implicit suggestion here that any man of Thornwell's gifts who avoided politics was failing to fulfill a public obligation. This could especially be said of the crisis years of the 1850s when the beleaguered South needed the aid of all her sons. From this point of view, Thornwell was closest to his proper place when he held the College presidency. By accepting the Seminary professorship, which he saw as the will of God, he was not only sacrificing two thousand dollars a year in salary, but also doing a disservice to his state and region.[101]

How did Thornwell feel about this question? The best answer is that he vacillated between different feelings, as most of us do about such things. After ten years on the College faculty, he could tell a close friend,

> I am satisfied that the possibilities of usefullness [*sic*] in such a situation are largely overrated. The influence which a good man can exert is rather negative than positive; it consists more in preventing evil than in directly doing good. . . . But Providence seems to have cast my lot where my labour is drudgery, and my reward is disappointment. My time is so frittered away by the constant intervention of external duties, that I can pursue no consecutive plans of study. . . . But here I am, mysteriously shut up to a position which is not the object of my choice, discouraged, mortified, distressed at the fruitlessness of my efforts, toiling day after day without hope, worn down by constant pressure of responsibilities, and unsustained, for the most part, by sympathy, co-operation, or approval . . . of those around me . . . I have faithfully preached the gospel here . . . but what has been the result? In only one aspect of the case, do I feel that I have done a valuable work; and that is, in breaking down the spirit of infidelity, which had largely taken possession of the State. Under God's blessing, I have succeeded beyond what I could hope, in changing the whole current of association upon the speculative question of the truth of Christianity. This is

---

[101]Meriwether, *Higher Education in South Carolina*, 167.

something, but it is not *salvation;* and the salvation of souls is the object of my toil.[102]

These are not the words of a contented man of God, and Palmer tells us that these were Thornwell's "habitual feelings" with regard to his work at the College, though he underestimated the effects of his labors there.[103] Thornwell seems never to have been fully satisfied with his circumstances, and elsewhere Palmer grants that he experienced the occasional "lapses" that are the result of frustrations felt by all clergymen, and of his being "constituted for action rather than repose."[104] So perhaps he was brought by divine influence to a series of positions that denied him the full opportunity of exploiting his talents.

Yet a short time after writing the unhappy words quoted above, he could reject an opportunity to move, saying, "The position which I occupy here I cannot relinquish; it opens a wide and increasing field of usefulness and is, in many respects, the most desirable in the Southern country."[105] Less than a month later he would write to another friend, "My mode of life here [at the College] is all that I could desire, as to physical comfort. I sit up all night, reading, musing, and smoking; and just before the sun, with its orient beams, dispells ghosts, goblins, and infernal spirits to their respective jails, I stretch my limbs upon an ample couch, continue my cogitations till my soul is locked in the silent embrace of slumber sweet; and I abide in the land of dreams until it becomes a man to refresh in a more active way."[106] If academic life was always this easy, he could receive satisfaction from his work as chaplain in ministering to the souls of the students, for whom he had deep feelings and high hopes.[107] The many letters he received from parents, indicating that they were placing their sons in his

---

[102]Thornwell to Robert Breckinridge, 12 March 1847; quoted in Palmer, 300-301. See also Palmer, 223-24.

[103]Ibid., 300-301.

[104]Ibid., 339-40.

[105]Thornwell to Alexander Pegues, 17 June 1848; quoted ibid., 308.

[106]Thornwell to Matthew J. Williams, 17 July 1848; quoted in Palmer, 310. Williams was professor of mathematics at the South Carolina College and a close friend. Thornwell's family was probably in Lancasterville when he wrote this from the College.

[107]See, for example, his commencement sermon of 6 December 1852, in Thornwell Papers.

care—spiritually as well as intellectually—no doubt added to the sense of mission that he brought to his work at the College, both as professor and as president.[108]

The College was no stranger to the infighting that is common to bureaucracies. Tensions within the faculty and between faculty and students often approached the breaking point, and once in 1850, the entire junior class was suspended for "rebellion against the authorities."[109] Such irritants, in addition to "other causes of a more personal and private nature," which Palmer preferred not to divulge, led him eventually to accept the call of Charleston's Glebe Street Presbyterian Church in March 1851. The previous summer he had written his good friend Matthew Williams, who taught mathematics at the College, of the joys of the family plantation near Lancasterville and his dread at returning "to the walls of our prison. College to me is like a dungeon; and I go to its duties like a slave whipped to his burden [an interesting commentary perhaps on his reaction to plantation life]. Nothing keeps me there but the fact that God's providence has put me there, and I am afraid to leave without some intimation of Divine will. Perhaps a day of greater usefulness may come."[110]

That "greater usefulness," some felt, could only come in politics. It would have been an almost perfect scenario for Thornwell, after putting South Carolina College on the "right path," to have moved on to the forum of the United States Senate, where his oratorical powers would have had their proper setting. This prospect raises an interesting question: what would have been the effect of Thornwell's presence in the Senate? Would he— assuming he could have made any difference at all—have provided the kind of clear and rational eloquence to the Southern argument that could have bolstered the forces for sectional compromise? Or would his intellectual purity and ignorance of political ways have only added to the lofty moral refusal to compromise, which already was a large part of the South's problem as the minority section? In short, would he have helped or hindered the chances of avoiding civil war? Such a question is purely speculative,

---

[108]See, for example, Joseph Martin to Thornwell, 7 December 1852, Thornwell Papers.

[109]Palmer, 347; Matthew Williams to Thornwell, 22 July 1853, Thornwell Papers. Hollis, *University of South Carolina*, 1:87-93, 155-58.

[110]Thornwell to Matthew Williams, 22 August 1850; quoted in Palmer, 343. He ends this letter with an apology for boring Williams with a subject he has spoken of many times before.

since as far as we know he was never seriously approached on this matter, probably because his views on the issues of the 1850s were at variance with the position of the South Carolina leadership. But Thornwell's distaste for politics, and especially the vulgarity of politicians who had adopted the Jacksonian approach to office seeking, made it most unlikely that he would have accepted such an opportunity.[111] Further, one must assume that for Thornwell any position lacking a clear divine ordination would have been unacceptable. He could not have felt comfortable in such circumstances, and would not have given such a position his best. So, no matter how attractive the political arena was for talented Southerners of his generation, it was not for Thornwell the ideal environment. His contribution, the political aspect of which was far from negligible, was primarily within the spiritual realm.

---

[111]Palmer, 469. A typical Thornwell comment on politics is in Palmer, 169. An excellent illustration of the intellectual's distaste for politics may be found in *Russell's Magazine* 1 (April 1857): 88-89, where the author, probably Paul Hamilton Hayne, urges ''young men of talent'' not to ''defile themselves'' in politics.

CHAPTER **3**

Thornwell's Intellectual Milieu*

Among the many significant events in the life of James Henley Thornwell, two stand out as symbolic milestones in the life of nineteenth-century America and of the Old South in particular. The first was his supplanting of Thomas Cooper as the guiding light of the South Carolina College in the 1840s, and the second was the establishment of the Perkins Chair in the Natural Sci-

---

* Several recent studies have informed this chapter. Theodore Dwight Bozeman's *Protestants in an Age of Science: The Baconian Ideal and Antebellum Religious Thought* (Chapel Hill, 1977), is an excellent study of the influence of the Scottish Common Sense philosophy on nineteenth-century Presbyterian thought, and of its emphasis on limiting scientific speculation within the bounds of inductive thought. Also very useful are his "Inductive and Deductive Politics: Science and Society in Antebellum Presbyterian Thought," *Journal of American History* 64:3 (December 1977): 704-22; and "Nature, Science and Society: A New Approach to James Henley Thornwell," *Journal of Presbyterian History* 50 (1972): 307-25. E. Brooks Holifield's *The Gentlemen Theologians; American Theology in Southern Culture, 1795-1860* (Durham, 1978) is a study of the well-educated town clergy in the Old South and their insistence that rational thought was the friend, not the enemy, of revealed religion. Anne C. Loveland, *Southern Evangelicals and the Social Order, 1800-1860* (Baton Rouge, 1980), studies the common experiences and attitudes of this group, and places them in the context of their world.

Other helpful sources include Sydney Ahlstrom, "The Scottish Philosophy and American Theology," *Church History* 24 (September 1955): 257-72; idem, *A Religious History of the American People* (New Haven, 1972); Franklin L. Baumer, *Religion and the Rise of Skepticism* (New York, 1960); John Bodo, *Protestant Clergy and Public Issues, 1812-1848* (Princeton, 1954); George H. Daniels, *American Science in the Age of Jackson* (New York,

ences as Connected with Revealed Religion at Columbia Theological Seminary in 1859.[1] These episodes not only coincide with the boundaries of the Old South's climactic era, but also dramatize two powerful and often antagonistic forces in nineteenth-century society—religion and science. The essence of Thornwell's thought was an effort to build a synthesis between these two rivals for the mind of modern man. It was perhaps not accidental that in attempting this, he also provided an intellectual perspective from which the values of Southern society could be defended. Between the two episodes mentioned above, Southern thought underwent a major transformation, and Thornwell provides as good a vantage point for viewing it as any of his contemporaries.

The passing of Thomas Cooper from the South Carolina scene was an event fraught with meaning. Cooper symbolized better than anyone in America, after the death of Thomas Jefferson, the mind of the eighteenth-century Enlightenment. That movement, centered in Europe but finding a naturally hospitable climate in America, had challenged centuries-old social and intellectual structures, including the church. As a "free thinker" and an intellectual gadfly, Cooper had tangled with the forces of orthodoxy prior to coming to South Carolina. His international reputation as a scientist could not offset the danger he represented in the minds of Virginia Presbyterians when Jefferson—who called him "the greatest man in America in the powers of his mind"—urged his appointment as professor of science and law at his new university. Denied that position, Cooper accepted the presidency of the South Carolina College in 1819. Although his

---

1968); Erskine Clark, *Wrestlin' Jacob: A Portrait of Religion in the Old South* (Atlanta, 1979); R. Hookyaas, *Religion and the Rise of Modern Science* (Grand Rapids MI, 1972); Herbert Hovenkamp, *Science and Religion in America, 1800-1860* (Philadelphia, 1979); Thomas C. Johnson, *Scientific Interests in the Old South* (New York, 1936); William H. Longton, "The Carolina Ideal World: Natural Science and Social Thought in Ante-Bellum South Carolina," *Civil War History* 20 (June 1974): 118-34; Donald G. Mathews, *Religion in the Old South* (Chicago, 1977); Elwyn Allen Smith, *The Presbyterian Ministry in American Culture: A Study in Changing Concepts, 1700-1900* (Philadelphia, 1962); Ernest Trice Thompson, *Presbyterians in the South, 1607-1861* (Richmond, 1963); Major Wilson, "Paradox Lost: Order and Progress in Evangelical Thought of Mid-Nineteenth Century America," *Church History* 44 (1975): 352-66.

[1]Regarding the chair of natural science and revealed religion, see James A. Lyon, "The New Theological Professorship," *Southern Presbyterian Review* 12:1 (April 1859): 182; James Woodrow, "Inaugural Address," ibid., 14:4 (January 1862): 505-31; Clement Eaton, *The Mind of the Old South* (Baton Rouge, 1967) 237.

violently antitariff and pronullification views won him wide popularity in the Palmetto State in the 1820s, his religious skepticism cost him much of it and led him into continual clashes with the state's orthodox churchmen and legislators. His reference to the Bible as "an absurd collection of frivolous tales" is an example of the public statements that made him anathema to the state's religious community.[2]

Thornwell, who had been drawn to Cooper while a student at the College, would later write,

> His religious opinions had rendered him so offensive to the religious people of the State, that it became clearly impossible for the College to answer the ends of its establishment, if he continued at the head of it. He was a man of eminent abilities, and of extensive and varied attainments. The benevolence of his nature, the frankness of his temper, and the natural simplicity of his manners, joined to his widespread fame as a man of science, and a sufferer in the cause of liberty, gave, in his person, the fairest opportunity to liberal opinions to illustrate their boasted power of good. The result, according to the popular verdict, was a miserable failure. Public sentiment demanded a change.

Thornwell would come to view Cooper and his other favorite teacher, Dr. Robert Henry, as epitomes of the two opposing forces in nineteenth-century thought; indeed, he used the occasion of Dr. Henry's death in 1856 to dramatize their contrasting positions. "Dr. Cooper was an avowed materialist; Dr. Henry's tendencies were all to idealism. Dr. Cooper looked upon utility as the criterion of right; Dr. Henry looked upon right as the criterion of utility. Moral rules, according to Dr. Cooper, were flexible and variable; according to Dr. Henry, eternal and immutable." In a line that spoke volumes about the South, he concluded, "There was but one subject upon which they thoroughly agreed, and that was politics."[3]

Responding to growing public pressure, the legislature removed Cooper from the College presidency in 1834, thus ending antebellum South Car-

---

[2]Dumas Malone, *The Public Life of Thomas Cooper, 1783-1839* (New Haven, 1926); Eaton, *Mind of the Old South*, 27-28, 236. Thomas C. Johnson notes that the young Benjamin M. Palmer was among many South Carolinians who were sent out of state to college rather than to Columbia, because of their parents' opposition to Cooper's views. Johnson, *The Life and Letters of Benjamin Morgan Palmer* (Richmond, 1906) 47. Palmer went to Amherst.

[3]Thornwell, "Memoir of Dr. Henry," *Southern Quarterly Review* (1856): 200-202.

olina's brief flirtation with modern thought. The void left by his departure was soon filled by Thornwell. Arriving in Columbia in 1838 as Professor of Belles Lettres and Logic, he soon shifted to the more appropriate Chair of Sacred Literature and the Evidences of Christianity; and long before being elevated to the presidency in 1851, he had achieved actual, if unofficial, hegemony over the institution. He was, in the words of the university's modern historian, "perhaps the most important person connected with the institution during the twenty five years following his arrival."[4]

While Thornwell's meteoric rise in the College spoke well for his personal gifts, it was also indicative of a major trend in Southern thought in the first half of the nineteenth century. This was a religious awakening that, when measured by the inefficient yardstick of church membership, could be called revolutionary. The Baptists and Methodists of the South more than doubled their numbers between 1830 and 1860, and the other Protestant denominations showed impressive growth as well. The main impetus for this success was provided by the evangelical spirit that had gripped much of America in the early 1800s. Driven by a zealous and emotional faith, which in this century has been called Fundamentalism, this movement would provide Southern religion with the distinguishing features that persist to the present day.[5]

Yet Southern religion then, as now, was not homogenous. Excluding the Roman Catholics, whose numbers, especially outside of the cities, were very small, Southern Christianity can be divided into three elements: the genteel (Episcopalians), the Calvinistic (Presbyterians), and the evangelical (Baptists and Methodists).[6] Insofar as their differences were minimal, their combined strength in antebellum society warranted attention, and the removal of Cooper was a recognition of this fact. Thornwell's rise, then,

---

[4]Daniel W. Hollis, "James Henley Thornwell and the South Carolina College," *Proceedings of the South Carolina Historical Association,* 1953, 17-36. See also Hollis, *The University of South Carolina,* vol. 1 (Columbia, 1951) 161-62. For another reference to Thornwell's status at the college, by a contemporary, see Maximilian LaBorde, *History of the South Carolina College* (Charleston, 1874) 347-72.

[5]Charles Sydnor, *The Development of Southern Sectionalism, 1819-1848* (Baton Rouge, 1948) 294; Donald G. Mathews, *Religion in the Old South* (Chicago, 1977), is especially good on Evangelicalism. Also see Ernest R. Sandeen, "Towards a Historical Interpretation of the Origins of Fundamentalism," *Church History* 36 (1965): 66-83.

[6]Eaton, *Mind of the Old South,* 222-23. Chapter ten of this book, "The Religious Experience," is a good introduction to this topic.

might be seen as indicative of the growing influence of the religious constituency in general. But the view that denominational differences in the Old South were insignificant is that of a cultural outsider. For Thornwell's contemporaries the differences were very real, and he was very much the symbol of Presbyterianism. So his position as the outstanding religious personality in South Carolina at mid-century takes on a more specific meaning.[7] Indeed, it would seem indicative of the Presbyterians' confidence in Thornwell and his influence at the College that while South Carolina Methodists, Baptists, and Lutherans were establishing colleges in the 1850s (Wofford, Furman, and Newberry), they did not join this movement.[8]

In any case, Thornwell's triumph over his old "idol" Cooper was prophetic. His polemical spirit found a worthy challenge in debating the men of modern science, of which Cooper was a leading harbinger. Few of his contemporaries would have taken issue with the observation of Scottish Presbyterian James McCosh in 1851 that "we live in an age when the reflecting portion of mankind are [sic] much addicted to the contemplation of the works of nature."[9] Amateur collectors and experimenters were everywhere gathering, recording, and analyzing data, and a growing number of professionals were emerging in colleges and societies. The American Association for the Advancement of Science was founded in 1848.

In South Carolina alone, the number of men making significant contributions to the sciences was proof that nature had indeed captivated the mind of the age.[10] When the British geologist Sir Charles Lyell visited

[7]Paul Leslie Garber, *James Henley Thornwell, Presbyterian Defender of the Old South* (Richmond, 1943) 1.

[8]Hollis, *University of South Carolina,* 161-62, 166, 173. A different explanation of Thornwell's rise, emphasizing his role as the upcountry voice in the intrastate sectionalism of South Carolina, is given in Avery Craven, *The Coming of the Civil War* (Chicago, 1942) 14. Craven's point is well taken, but it is significant that three of the four men who followed Cooper in the College presidency (Robert Henry, Robert Barnwell, and Thornwell) were Presbyterians.

[9]James McCosh, *The Method of Divine Government* (New York, 1851) 11. McCosh would become president of the College of New Jersey in 1868.

[10]South Carolinians who contributed to the growth of scientific knowledge in the generation prior to the Civil War included John Bachman, John Barrett, Richard T. Brumby, Henry M. Bruns, Langdon Cheves, Samuel Henry Dickson, William Elliott, Louis R. Gibbes, Robert W. Gibbes, William J. Grayson, James Henry Hammond, John Edwards Holbrook, Francis S. Holmes, William Hume, Mitchell King, Maximilian LaBorde, John LeConte, Joseph LeConte, William M. Michel, James Moultrie, Francis Peyre Porcher,

Charleston in December of 1841, he noted with pleasure the work of several naturalists whom he found "zealously engaged" in their studies.[11] Modern historians have given South Carolina, and the Charleston area in particular, high status among American scientific communities. William Stanton lists Charleston along with Boston, New Haven, and Philadelphia as the three centers of scientific interest in antebellum America.[12] And Clement Eaton has observed that "South Carolina was pre-eminent in the cultivation of scientific studies, probably because of the presence of the cultural center of Charleston and because the aristocratic organization of society provided leisure."[13] It has sometimes been asserted that the Old South was not a hospitable climate for the objective research of the scientist; Eaton suggests that this was certainly the case after 1830. Yet he contradicts himself when he notes that the volumes of the *American Journal of Science* for the 1850s show the South represented in "proper proportion."[14] William Longton and William Stanton have demonstrated that this index is indeed correct; for if Southerners' interest in science changed as the century progressed, that interest became more intense as the questions science was raising came to bear more directly upon the interests of the South.[15]

Frederick Augustus Porcher, Edmund Ravenel, Henry William Ravenel, Thomas Smyth, and William Charles Wells. The acknowledgments in Francis Holmes's *Post-Pleistocene Fossils of South Carolina* (1860) are an index to Charleston's intellectual community. Also, see circular dated 4 October 1853, announcing the formation of the Elliott Society of Natural History and listing the names of the officers. Bachman was the first president. Seven men are listed as vice-presidents and eight as curators. Edmund Ravenel Collection, microfilm, South Caroliniana Library. See also Clark A. Elliott, *Biographical Dictionary of American Science* (Westport CT, 1979).

[11]Charles Lyell, *Travels in North America in the Years 1841-1842*, 2 vols. (New York, 1845) 1:138-39.

[12]William Stanton, *The Leopard's Spots: Scientific Attitudes toward Race in America, 1815-1859* (Chicago, 1960) 123.

[13]Eaton, *Mind of the Old South*, 242. Charleston had the nation's oldest municipal college, on whose faculty the sciences were well represented; a medical college; a museum of natural history that Louis Agassiz called second only to that in Philadelphia; and several societies and clubs whose members contributed original research to the various fields of science.

[14]Ibid., 243, 232.

[15]Stanton, *The Leopard's Spots*, 123; William H. Longton, "Some Aspects of Intel-

Perhaps no segment of Southern society better demonstrates this continuing interest in science than the clergy. As Theodore Bozeman and Brooks Holifield have amply shown, the better-educated ministers of the Old South, especially the Presbyterians, were in step with the tradition of rational thought. From Justin Martyr in the second century A.D., through Thomas Aquinas and John Calvin, to Jonathan Edwards and James Henley Thornwell, a strong, if not always dominant, theme of rationalism ran through Christian thought. A cornerstone of this tradition was Francis Turretin (1623-1687), whose *Institutio Theologiae Elencticae* was a basic text at Princeton, Union, Columbia, and Danville seminaries. Presbyterians were not alone in their interest in science. The *Columbian Star*, the leading Baptist paper of the upper South, carried on its masthead a star, flanked by "Religion" and "Science." In 1824 the Lutheran Synod of South Carolina required its ministers to study moral and natural theology.[16] Courses in the sciences were mainstays in the curricula of Southern, as well as Northern, colleges—the church-supported as well as public ones. Men who were products of this tradition saw science and religion as complements to each other, and they struggled in the mid-nineteenth century to accommodate these apparently divergent systems of thought.[17]

In the early decades of the nineteenth century, the relatively static "world as machine" view of the Enlightenment was being modified by the more evolutionary concept of life that would dominate the romantic period. This change came out of the work of Charles Lyell and others in geology and biology, which emphasized the great age of the earth, and the bewildering multitude of life forms that had existed and did exist. These revelations caused the neoclassical conceptions of the eighteenth century

---

lectual Activity in Ante-Bellum South Carolina, 1830-1860: An Introductory Study" (Ph.D. dissertation, University of North Carolina, 1969) 173. See also Daniels, *American Science in the Age of Jackson*, 201-30; Robert V. Bruce, "A Statistical Profile of American Scientists, 1846-1876," in *Nineteenth-Century American Science: A Reappraisal*, ed. George H. Daniels (Evanston, 1972) 74, 79. See also Ronald Numbers and Janet Numbers, "Science in the Old South: A Reappraisal," *Journal of Southern History* 48 (May 1982): 163-84.

[16]Holifield, *The Gentlemen Theologians*, 74, 81-83. See also John B. Adger, ed., *Collected Writings of James Henley Thornwell*, vol. 1 (Richmond, 1871) 32; Johnson, *Life and Letters of Palmer*, 591-92.

[17]Holifield, *The Gentlemen Theologians*, ch. 4, esp. 74, 81-82.

about nature and God to be transformed into "romantic" ones. Things were slowly but constantly changing for the better, in accordance with immutable natural laws.[18] For South Carolina intellectuals this shift threatened to upset a long and comfortable association with the classical view. Eighteenth-century South Carolina was a society at rest: its static social and political structure melded perfectly with its favorite intellectual concepts of order and permanence. For this society, God (though perhaps now in retirement) was in His heaven and all was right with the world. The Old South said with Alexander Pope, "One truth is clear, *Whatever is, is right.*" The tenacity of this neoclassical construct is seen in the continuing popularity of the heroic couplet, the Addisonian essay form, and the Horatian ode down through the antebellum period. As late as 1862 William John Grayson expressed a firm preference for Dryden and Pope over the modern romantics Keats and Southey.[19]

Yet Grayson was of the older generation by the time he expressed that view, and in his masterpiece *The Hireling and the Slave* (1856) he used the heroic couplet to offer "some variety to the poetic forms that are almost universally prevalent."[20] The younger men had made their accommodation with romanticism, although strictly on their terms. It had begun in the 1820s when the burgeoning of the natural sciences gave rise to geological surveys, sponsored by state governments. Those who made these surveys often went on to become amateur collectors and cataloguers of species and scientific data in general. Among the most significant fruits of this labor was "Views of Nature," an article that appeared in the *Southern Review* in November 1828. Its author was Stephen Elliott (1771-1830), a South Carolinian who had begun collecting species of plants on and near his Beaufort plantations as early as 1800. He had published his research in

---

[18]Daniels, *American Science in the Age of Jackson*, passim, and Johnson, *Scientific Interests in the Old South.*

[19]Longton, "The Carolina Ideal World," 118-34; William R. Taylor, *Cavalier and Yankee: The Old South and the American National Character* (New York, 1957) 57; Jay Hubbell, *The South in American Literature, 1610-1900* (Durham, 1954) 442; Guy M. Cardwell, "The Influence of Addison on Charleston Periodicals, 1795-1860," *Studies in Philology* 35 (July 1938): 456-70. Pope's epigram was the motto of eighteenth-century Charleston merchant Henry Laurens.

[20]William John Grayson, *The Hireling and the Slave*, preface, quoted in Vernon L. Parrington, *Main Currents in American Thought*, vol. 2 (New York, 1927) 99.

A Sketch of the Botany of South Carolina and Georgia, in two volumes, and was now ready to interpret the larger significance of his findings.[21]

Elliott's article paid respect to the new knowledge and concluded that it reaffirmed the old South Carolina assumptions. The forms of life now observed on earth were, he said, essentially the forms of creation. Some changes must have occurred, since species did vary as he had observed, but organisms remain essentially similar to their predecessors. Those changes that do occur are not the result of chance, but of a master plan. The age of the earth, he recognized, is much greater than previously thought, but the Bible is not discredited by this.[22] Elliott died in 1830, yet there were plenty of others to carry on his investigations and his careful accommodation of the old and new. In 1834 the young Charleston doctor Edmund Ravenel (1797-1871) published a catalogue of North Atlantic shells, and in the same year John Bachman (1790-1874) published a catalogue of Low Country flora.[23]

Both Ravenel and Bachman followed the conservative, reverent approach of Elliott in their interpretations of nature and nature's God. But others, generally outside the South, were already advancing interpretations that challenged the comfortable orthodoxy of these pious naturalists. Geology was already upsetting venerable assumptions, and data were being gathered that would give birth to a new field of study with radical possibilities: anthropology, and ultimately to its even more potent offspring, sociology. These new disciplines would soon pose potentially lethal challenges to much of traditional Western thought, and to the Judeo-Chris-

---

[21]Stephen Elliott, ''Views of Nature,'' *Southern Review* 2 (November 1828): 408-31; idem, *A Sketch of the Botany of South Carolina and Georgia* (Charleston, 1821 and 1824).

[22]Elliott, ''Views of Nature.'' For background, see John Dillenberger, *Protestant Thought and Natural Science* (New York, 1960).

[23]Regarding Edmund Ravenel, see Longton, ''Intellectual Activity in Ante-Bellum South Carolina,'' 65. John Bachman, *Catalogue of Phaenogamous Plants and Ferns Native and Naturalized, Found Growing in the Vicinity of Charleston, South Carolina* (Charleston, 1834). Ravenel, a graduate of the University of Pennsylvania Medical School, was for many years professor of chemistry at the Medical College of South Carolina. His plantation was a center of scientific studies and was visited by John J. Audubon, Louis Agassiz, and others. His brother, Henry William Ravenel (1814-1887), was a leading botanist of his day. Bachman was born and educated in New York, but for fifty-nine years, beginning in 1816, he was pastor of St. John's Lutheran Church in Charleston.

tian mentality that dominated the Old South in particular.[24] Anthropology began as an inquiry into the racial differences within the human family. America, with its mixture of red, white, and black people provided a natural laboratory for this.

In their investigations into the origins of these differences, scientists of the eighteenth century operated within the Enlightenment view of an orderly cosmos with fixed components. All animals designated as "man," said Swedish naturalist Linnaeus in his *Systema Naturae* (1735), are of one species, and as such are members of an unchanging category created by God. But Lord Kames, a Scottish judge and student of science and metaphysics, suggested that racial differences were too great for all of mankind to be embraced by one species. Thus was opened the question of how, if all men are descended from Adam and Eve, racial differences came about. The first authoritative American answer came from Dr. Samuel Stanhope Smith, president and professor of moral philosophy at Princeton. For Smith racial differences were the result of man's ability to adapt to environmental conditions in different parts of the world. Descended from the same original parents, the human species had developed many varieties. Thus was begun a movement, centered at Princeton and led by Presbyterian clergymen, to adapt scientific thought to Christian teachings. When he came to Columbia Seminary to take its new chair in science in 1861, Professor James Woodrow was inheriting a tradition almost a century old.

But what a turbulent century it was, for Dr. Smith's was far from the last word on this subject. Indeed, by the time of the Civil War, an "American School" of anthropology had sprung up to challenge him. Its pioneer figure was Dr. Samuel G. Morton, a widely respected Philadelphia physician and professor of anatomy. In *Crania Americana* (1839) Morton developed the concept of distinctive racial differences, not explainable by climatic variations, which were measurable in terms of cranial size and shape. The study of his large collection of skulls led Morton to conclude that the five races he identified occupied distinct ranges on the scale of cranial capacity, though they did overlap. (The popularity of Morton's work led to the phrenology fad of the 1830s and 1840s.) Morton traced the origin of these differences to the time of the "dispersion of our species"

---

[24]This section is taken largely from Stanton, *The Leopard's Spots,* 3-14, 65-81, 100-109, 113-21. This may be compared with George M. Frederickson, *The Black Image in the White Mind* (New York, 1971) 71-78, 83-90.

throughout the earth, after the flood described in Genesis. An all-wise Creator had adapted each race "from the beginning to its peculiar local destination," Morton concluded.

The devout and cautious Morton had opened the door, and others, unhampered by such restraints, would venture more boldly into this delicate subject. Among them was Dr. Josiah Clark Nott. Born in Columbia, South Carolina, in 1804, he graduated from the South Carolina College in 1824 and received the M.D. degree from the University of Pennsylvania Medical School in 1827. After practicing briefly in Columbia and traveling to Europe for further study, Nott settled in Mobile, Alabama, where he gained a wide reputation as a surgeon. He became interested in the correlation between race and health, and in 1843 he produced a study which concluded that the mulatto is generally physically inferior to both races in the South because he is a hybrid—the product of "two distinct species." Nott added that racial mixing would therefore be suicidal to the white race. None of this, of course, disturbed most of Nott's fellow Southerners. But he did not stop there. He soon ventured the opinion that the white and black races were the products of separate creations. It was ironic that the logical climax of the course pursued by the American School of anthropology would first be reached by a Southern gentleman. For in suggesting the theory of multiple creations, Nott had hit the orthodox South in its heart of hearts, by challenging the authenticity of Genesis. He had no intention of allowing "those worn out legends to obstruct the path of science."[25]

Nott's challenge to biblical authority was quickly met by the league of clergymen-scientists who formed so important a part of the South's intellectual community. In a field not yet dominated by professionals, many, perhaps most, of the eager amateurs were clergymen.[26] Their response to the challenge represented by Dr. Nott was often predictable enough. Much of it was simple, orthodox biblicism, betraying very little thought. The Southern church rallied around the Bible in the 1850s in much the same

---

[25]Stanton, *The Leopard's Spots*, 68-69. Nott would soon team with George W. Glidden to write *Types of Mankind* (1854), the then-definitive study of racial differences.

[26]Prominent examples include John Bachman; Moses Ashley Curtis, North Carolina Episcopalian; Stephen Elliott, South Carolina and Georgia Episcopalian; Francis Lister Hawks, North Carolina Episcopalian; James Warley Miles, South Carolina Episcopalian; Elisha Mitchell, North Carolina Presbyterian; Thomas Smyth, South Carolina Presbyterian; James Woodrow; and James Henley Thornwell.

way as later Southern spokesmen would rally against evolution, socialism, and racial integration. The region's periodicals, secular and religious, were filled for the fifteen years preceding the Civil War with diatribes from both sides of this emotional battleline.[27] The editor of *The Southern Presbyterian* traced the "gross heresies" of Nott and Glidden to "that Arch-infidel, Rousseau," and concluded, "If the bold and unblushing infidelity of Nott and Glidden is science, then we prefer to be unscientific."[28]

Yet it is significant that many of the defenders of revealed religion chose not simply to cling to their traditional faith and ignore all else, but to meet science on its own ground. Sharing the popular interest in science, the liberally educated clergy needed a subject matter suited to their particular perspective and a method of inquiry that would insure their not threatening the integrity of God's Word. They found both. Natural theology became their subject, and the inductive method—"Baconianism," as elaborated by Scottish Common Sense philosophy—became their method.

Simply defined, natural theology is the quest for God through the medium of his handiwork. Subscribers to natural theology reverenced nature as a "second book" of revelation. Far from seeing conflict between revealed religion and nature, they insisted upon the mutual dependence of the two. The order and beauty so manifest in nature pointed, for them, to a supernatural wisdom and directed the observer to a divine cause, thereby confirming and reinforcing the teachings of Scripture. Science, therefore, as long as it was properly understood and used, sustained Christianity.[29] For the educated clergy, and especially the Presbyterians, the idea of being apathetic or fearful about the study of nature was simply unacceptable. To reject the study of God's handiwork was to close one avenue through which

---

[27]See, for example, the running debate of Nott and the Reverend Moses A. Curtis in the *Southern Quarterly Review* for 1845 and 1846. Also see *SQR* 10 (October 1854): 281; *Southern Literary Messenger* 21 (January 1855): 30; and Frederickson, *The Black Image in the White Mind*, 71-96.

[28]*The Southern Presbyterian* (Columbia SC), 9 November 1854, 14.

[29]The major sources on natural theology used by Southern colleges and seminaries were William Paley, *Natural Theology* (1802) and Joseph Butler, *Analogy of Religion, Natural and Revealed, to the Constitution and Course of Nature* (1736). The volumes of the *Southern Presbyterian Review*, beginning in 1847, contain a mine of articles developing the basic themes of natural theology. See, for example, E. F. Rockwell, "The Alphabet of Natural Theology," *SPR* 10 (1857-1858): 411-36. Butler remained a widely used text in the 1850s. See also Holifield, *The Gentlemen Theologians*, 90.

man might approach the Almighty. To fear the consequences of rational inquiry into nature was to separate the Creator from his creation. To deny oneself the proper use of his God-given mind was a sin.

Thornwell absorbed this view in his intellectual training and became its ardent defender throughout his life.[30] Indeed he, as well as anyone, personified the nineteenth-century American linking of orthodox Christian theology with rational inquiry into nature.[31] Unwilling, nay unable, to ignore the phenomena that the scientific world was revealing to the mind of man, and yet convinced of the guiding hand of divine power in the universe, men like Thornwell (chiefly the liberally educated clergy) took a middle ground between rational deism and agnosticism on one hand, and the anti-intellectualism of evangelical orthodox Christianity on the other. Typical was an article in *The Southern Presbyterian* entitled "Science Confirming the Bible." "We are amazed at the boasting of infidels and the trepidation of Christians on the threat posed by science," wrote the editor. "Every discovery, every advancement in true science, confirms more and more [the Bible's] truth."[32] In Thornwell's words, "External nature, to reason, . . . becomes an august temple of the Most High." Since mortal man was not capable of rising to the full contemplation of God through His Word, he "must study God in his works, as children who cannot look the sun in the face behold its image in the limpid stream."[33]

As convinced as Thornwell and the other "gentlemen theologians" of the Old South were of the need to join theology and science, the clergy as a whole was far from united on this point. For many, science seemed bent on cutting the anchor of faith and setting man adrift in a vast and deep sea of doubt. The scientist, for these fearful souls, was virtually the Anti-Christ. His skeptical outlook and his speculative methods made the gulf between

---

[30]Theodore D. Bozeman, "Science, Nature and Society: A New Approach to James Henley Thornwell," *Journal of Presbyterian History* 50 (1972): 307, 25; idem, *Protestants in an Age of Science;* Holifield, *The Gentlemen Theologians.*

[31]Thornwell to Robert Breckinridge, 27 January 1841; quoted in Benjamin M. Palmer, *The Life and Letters of James Henley Thornwell, D.D., LL.D.* (Richmond, 1875) 223-24. Another model is Edward Hitchcock; see Stanley Guralnick, "Geology and Religion before Darwin: The Case of Edward Hitchcock, Theologian and Geologist," in Nathan Reingold, ed., *Science in America since 1820* (New York, 1976) 116-30.

[32]*The Southern Presbyterian,* 9 September 1852, 2.

[33]Thornwell, "The Being of God," in *Collected Writings of James Henley Thornwell,* ed. John B. Adger, vol. 1 (Richmond, 1871) 63.

his world and that of the Church impossible to bridge, because science was aggressively rational, skeptical, and empirical, while Christianity was intuitive, submissive, and sentimental. Science was founded upon doubt, Christianity upon faith. Nowhere was this view more widely or strongly held than in the South, where romanticism exerted its influence so pervasively. Despite the demonstrable interest in science among Southerners of the mid-nineteenth century, Richard Weaver was at least partly right when he wrote that while the rest of the West was eagerly questing after the god of science and materialism, the American South "has persisted in regarding science as a false messiah." There has been among Southerners, Weaver feels, a belief that "beyond a certain point, victories over nature are pyrrhic."[34]

In the late twentieth century, disenchantment with "social engineering" and worries about DNA research are elevating this long-held Southern suspicion to the status of dogma with many.[35] They may well identify with the thinkers of the Old South who so distrusted the "isms" of the North. One quickly finds, when reading the works of the mid-nineteenth-century Southern clergy, that even the most intellectual of them disliked the word *rationalism* and shunned the label *rationalist*. For them, these terms applied to the "free-thinkers" and skeptics whose work even the most rational of these men found shockingly atheistic. Typical was Augustus Baldwin Longstreet, Methodist minister, humorist, and college administrator, whose brother James was a major figure in the Civil War. While not a brilliant man, Longstreet was no anti-intellectual either. Yet he disliked the name *Nineteenth Century* for a magazine because it was "dangerously suggestive in this age of science and reform." Longstreet, who held the presidency of the South Carolina College from 1857 to 1861, would later view the Civil War as a contest between a "Christ-taught band" of the South and a "science-taught band" of the North.[36]

Aware that the concerns expressed by Longstreet were shared across the South, Southern scientists took care to emphasize their orthodoxy. Vir-

---

[34]Richard Weaver, *The Southern Tradition at Bay* (New York, 1968) 31-32.

[35]Roy Reed, "Revisiting the Southern Mind," *New York Times Magazine*, 5 December 1976, 109.

[36]John D. Wade, *Augustus Baldwin Longstreet; A Study in the Development of Culture in the South* (New York, 1924) 267-68. Holifield, *The Gentlemen Theologians*, 87.

ginian Matthew Fontaine Maury, a leading pioneer in oceanography, told the University of Virginia class of 1855 that in any conflict between science and religious orthodoxy, the latter must prevail.[37] Expressing an implicit assumption behind natural theology, Maury told the students that his rule of thumb was

> never to forget who is the Author of the great volume which nature spreads out before us, and always to remember that the same being is also the author of the book which Revelation holds up to us; and though the two works are entirely different, their records are equally true; and when they bear upon the same point . . . it is as impossible that they should contradict each other as it is that either should contradict itself. If the two cannot be reconciled, the fault is ours, and it is because, in our blindness and weakness, we have not been able to interpret aright, either the one or the other or both.[38]

Human "blindness and weakness," then, were major obstacles in the path that led to truth, both theological and scientific. Though man's fallibility might forever bar him from the inner sanctum of understanding, he could perhaps approach it if he used the right methods and tools—those that took his limitations into account. For many, perhaps most, orthodox Protestants in the nineteenth century, these methods and tools were those of Baconianism and Scottish Common Sense philosophy.[39] The notion, widely accepted among historians, that Old South thinkers rejected the modernist outlook of Northern and European progressive thought, along with the "new science" that produced it, is derived from a somewhat superficial look at the writings of Southerners who were influenced by this

---

[37]Diana Fontaine Maury Corbin, *A Life of Matthew Fontaine Maury* (London, 1888) 160. For a general discussion of Southern attitudes toward science and reform, see Clement Eaton, "The Resistance of the South to Northern Radicalism," *New England Quarterly* 8 (1935): 215-31.

[38]Maury to "My Dear Sir," 22 January 1855, Matthew Fontaine Maury Collection, Library of Congress; quoted in John C. Greene, "Objectives and Methods in Intellectual History," *Mississippi Valley Historical Review* 44:1 (June 1957): 70. See also George H. Daniels, *Science and American Society: A Social History* (New York, 1971) 220.

[39]Helpful introductions to the Scottish philosophy can be found in Bozeman, *Protestants in the Age of Science;* Holifield, *The Gentlemen Theologians*, ch. 5; Sydney E. Ahlstrom, "The Scottish Philosophy and American Theology," *Church History* 24 (September 1955): 257-72; Herbert Hovenkamp, *Science and Religion in America, 1800-1860* (Philadelphia, 1978) esp. 4-24.

Baconian-Scottish school. Take, for example, the statement that appeared in the *Southern Presbyterian* in 1857: "Abused or misguided intellect has ruined our world."[40] The writings of Southerners in the late antebellum period abound with such quotable remarks, and generally historians have been content to display them as indications of the shallow reactionary spirit that, they suppose, dominated Southern thought on the eve of secession. A closer look at such statements, however, reveals a good deal more than the ostrichlike posture suggested in many histories of Southern life and thought. An impressive array of Southern thinkers, led by the liberally educated clergy, pursued a course vis-à-vis science that attempted to blend the new knowledge with revealed truth as they understood it. "We must meet rationalists on their own chosen ground," wrote Thornwell.[41] In this effort Baconianism and Common Sense philosophy proved to be valuable allies.

The Scottish philosophy, in the words of one scholar, "was not so much a set of conclusions as it was a way of thinking that could commend itself to a variety of thinkers."[42] The breadth of influence of this school of thought has only recently been appreciated (see n. 39). It was used by Harvard professor Levi Hedge to buttress liberal theology, by Nathanial William Taylor of Yale to "ameliorate the harsher features of Calvinism," and by Charles Hodge of Princeton Seminary to fortify Protestant orthodoxy.[43] "It became," says one author, "an evangelical world-view that permeated every classroom and which eventually influenced hundreds of ministers, countless schoolmasters, and dozens of practicing scientists and physicians."[44] What was this ubiquitous creature with the humble name Common Sense? Also known as Scottish Realism, Common Sense philosophy was a product of the Scottish enlightenment of the eighteenth century. This

---

[40]*The Southern Presbyterian*, 7 February 1857, 1.

[41]Holifield, *The Gentlemen Theologians*, 111.

[42]Ibid.

[43]Ibid., and Ahlstrom, "The Scottish Philosophy and American Theology," 262-64. See also Ahlstrom, "The Romantic Religious Revolution and the Dilemma of Religious History," *Church History* 46 (June 1977): 150. With the publication of *A History of Philosophy in America* (New York, 1977), by Elizabeth Flower and Murray G. Murphy, the importance of the Scottish philosophy may be said to have been given its proper recognition.

[44]Hovenkamp, *Science and Religion in America*, 5.

"Scottish Renaissance," as it has been called, was a cultural flowering that centered in the four universities of that country: Glasgow, Aberdeen, St. Andrews, and primarily Edinburgh. This intellectual movement took place amidst religious controversy that was triggered by the new science and the deistic philosophy it engendered. Reacting to this menace, Scottish Christianity became divided into an "Evangelical," or "Popular," party and a "Moderate" party. The former leaned toward the English revivalists, epitomized by George Whitefield, while the latter preferred the path of careful scholarship, eloquent preaching, and natural theology. While the Moderates were formally orthodox, the Popular camp was more rigidly Calvinistic. By the middle of the eighteenth century, the Moderates had gained control of the Church of Scotland and ushered in an era of revitalized theology and rigorous scholarship, which yielded Common Sense philosophy as an important component.[45]

This philosophy was the answer of the orthodox Christian mind to the views of John Locke, David Hume, and Bishop George Berkeley. Locke's concept of *tabula rasa* held that man's knowledge is gained exclusively through the senses. He can know nothing about the physical world apart from sensory data and his reflection on them. Further, his knowledge of the spiritual world would come only through the same empirical process, or through divine revelation, as found in the Bible. For Locke there was no universal seed of religious consciousness in men. Hume built his epistemology on the foundation laid down by Locke. He went on to assert that since man's knowledge about any subject is limited to what his senses tell him, and since his senses can tell him nothing about the fundamental questions pertaining to religion, he cannot know the answers to these questions. The spiritual dilemma Hume raised was responded to by Berkeley. Perhaps, said the Anglican bishop, ideas are the only real things. If this were so, and if man's knowledge consisted entirely of ideas received through the senses, then one could say that man does perceive reality. Suppose nothing exists except in the minds of perceiving beings. But God, Berkeley insisted, perceives everything continually. The world is God's Idea. Man, therefore, through sharing God's ideas, has accurate knowledge about the world.[46]

---

[45]Ahlstrom, *A Religious History*, 257-59.

[46]Ibid., 260, and Hovenkamp, *Science and Religion in America*, 6-7.

For most people, this skeptical philosophy was either impossibly obscure or ludicrous. It seemed obvious that the objects in the physical universe are real and our perceptions of them essentially reliable. Out of Scotland, Hume's homeland, came the "common sense" reaction to the skeptics.

The antecedents of this philosophy may be traced as far back as Aristotle, but its own spokesmen could not agree upon a modern father. James McCosh, a leading mid-nineteenth-century disciple, credited George Turnbull of Aberdeen University as "the first metaphysician . . . to announce unambiguously and categorically that we ought to proceed in the method of induction in investigating the human mind."[47] The philosophy was developed most fully by Turnbull's student, Thomas Reid (1710-1796), and then popularized by his disciple, Dugald Stewart. Reid, a Presbyterian minister who succeeded Adam Smith in the Chair of Moral Philosophy at Glasgow in 1763, may be said to have launched the Common Sense school with his *Inquiry into the Human Mind on the Principles of Common Sense* (1764). He advanced four points that comprise the essence of Scottish Common Sense philosophy: (1) Philosophy depends on scientific observation, with the primary object of this observation being not the external world but self-consciousness. (2) Principles may be established, based on this observation of consciousness, which are independent of experience. (3) Matter cannot be the cause of anything. It is only an instrument in the hand of the real cause, which is an intelligent being. (4) The basic principles of morality are self-evident intuitions.[48]

Essentially, Reid was defining the mind as an instrument that performs processes, not just a repository for the collection of empirical data. He agreed with Hume that empirical data alone are not sufficient basis for proving the reality of the external world. But rather than following Hume into skepticism, he argued that one must at some point accept some unverifiable notion—for instance, the notion that one's senses are providing reliable information. Since such intuitive assumptions are universal, in Reid's view, he called them "Common Sense." However, Reid stopped far short of rejecting empiricism completely. We must rely on the senses

---

[47]Ahlstrom, 260.

[48]Ibid., 261; Sir William Hamilton, ed., *The Works of Thomas Reid*, vol. 1 (Edinburgh, 1846-1863) 131; Holifield, *The Gentlemen Theologians*, 112-13.

as the source of knowledge, he said, but the mind's rational powers perform the additional function of assimilating the countless bits of empirical data they receive. By discovering the presuppositions implicit in this assimilation, men arrive at "self-evident principles." Although unprovable, these principles are essential to the mental process; among them are "those things did really happen which I distinctly remember," and "in the phenomena of nature what is to be will probably be like to what has been in similar circumstances."[49]

Reid's best-known disciple, Dugald Stewart (1753-1838), elaborated Reid's ideas and linked them to the scientific method of Francis Bacon. Emphasizing the limitations of human reason as well as its essentialness, Stewart taught that the proper use of Reid's system would be through the inductive method. Philosophy could become a science, he suggested, if its practitioners would gather all available data on a question first, and only then, with a clear sense of the limitations of rational powers, advance to speculation. Reid himself had suggested that when he said, "If we would know the works of God, we must consult themselves [*sic*] with attention and humility, without daring to add anything of ours to what they declare."[50] The subsequent development of Scottish Realism leads to Sir William Hamilton, a Scottish contemporary of Thornwell, who tied Immanuel Kant's thought into that of Reid and Stewart and built a theology on this basis. For Hamilton the nexus of this progression from Reid through Kant was this: "A learned ignorance is . . . the end of philosophy, as it is the beginning of theology."[51]

Common Sense philosophy arrived in America when John Witherspoon emigrated from Scotland in 1768 to take the presidency of the College of New Jersey. As an orthodox Protestant, Witherspoon (who was distantly related to Nancy Witherspoon Thornwell) was most interested in this philosophy as a weapon against the deism and materialism that had

---

[49]Hovenkamp, *Science and Religion in America,* 9; Holifield, *The Gentlemen Theologians,* 114.

[50]Holifield, *The Gentlemen Theologians,* 117-18; Hovenkamp, *Science and Religion in America,* 11.

[51]Holifield, *The Gentlemen Theologians,* 118; William Hamilton, *Lectures in Metaphysics,* 2 vols. (Boston, 1859) 1:34; 2:530.

arisen out of Enlightenment thought.[52] It would be difficult to exaggerate the influence of Witherspoon on the mind of late-eighteenth- and early-nineteenth-century America. He lectured on moral philosophy for twenty-five years at Princeton, and among his students were 13 college presidents, 114 clergymen, 6 members of the Continental Congress, 23 United States senators, 24 members of the House of Representatives, 13 governors, and 3 Supreme Court justices.[53]

Among the earliest native Americans influenced by the Scottish School were Benjamin Franklin and Thomas Jefferson. Franklin admired Lord Kames, a leading proponent of the school, and liked the philosophy for its positive effect on moral conduct. The young Jefferson studied the words of Kames and Dugald Stewart, whom he met in Paris in the 1780s. His favorite professor at William and Mary was William Small, a Scot. Garry Wills has suggested that the Scottish philosopher Francis Hutchinson was more important than John Locke in shaping Jefferson's philosophy, but this view has been challenged by Ronald Hamowy.[54] In any case, as one student of the school's influence has concluded, "there is a consensus of opinion among scholars that the Scottish philosophy of Common Sense had a crucial function in the establishing of 'the American mind.' "[55] Perry Miller wrote that the philosophy "constituted what must be called the official metaphysics of America" for more than fifty years, and Howard Mumford Jones called it "the official academic belief" of the first half of the nineteenth century.[56] Clearly, then, its appeal was not limited to the rather narrow field of Princetonian Calvinism.

-----

[52]L. H. Butterfield, *John Witherspoon Comes to America* (Princeton, 1953); Terence Martin, *The Instructed Vision: Scottish Common Sense Philosophy and the Origins of American Fiction* (Bloomington IN, 1961) 6.

[53]Martin, *The Instructed Vision*, 6.

[54]Garry Wills, *Inventing America: Jefferson's Declaration of Independence* (New York, 1979); Ronald Hamowy, "Jefferson and the Scottish Enlightenment: A Critique of Garry Wills' *Inventing America: Jefferson's Declaration of Independence*," *William and Mary Quarterly* 36 (October 1979): 503-23. The discussion was continued by other scholars in *William and Mary Quarterly* 37 (July 1980): 529-40.

[55]Martin, *The Instructed Vision*, vii.

[56]Ibid. Miller considered the demise of the philosophy in the years following the Civil War as the great but unspoken intellectual event of the Gilded Age. Perry Miller, *American Thought from the Civil War to World War One* (New York, 1954) ix.

As Sydney Ahlstrom notes, it became the dominant philosophy at Harvard, Yale, and Andover—three institutions that, with Princeton, had long been the leading centers of theological training in America. Harvard, which by 1810 "was for all purposes a Unitarian institution," was under the influence of "an unbroken succession of emphatic Scottish advocacy down to 1889." Yale, which remained at least moderately orthodox, felt the Scottish influence through Timothy Dwight, the grandson of Jonathan Edwards who became its president in 1795, and his greatest pupil, Nathaniel William Taylor, who taught theology at Yale's new divinity school. At the more-orthodox Andover, the Common Sense school was represented by Leonard Woods and his successor, Edwards Amasa Park. These men and their institutions range across the spectrum of Christian thought in the early nineteenth century, thus demonstrating the variety of branches that sprang from Scottish Realism.[57] Their influence, added to that of Witherspoon and his Princeton successor and son-in-law Samuel Stanhope Smith, produced an American clerical establishment that, whatever its differences, shared a common philosophical view. "For sixty years," concludes one scholar, "the men who taught the most popular courses in moral and analytic philosophy, who questioned and licensed ministerial candidates, who . . . wrote the college textbooks, were disciples of the Scottish Enlightenment."[58]

The message that was handed down to three generations of young seminarians, and carried by them to the four corners of the land, was that the chief enemy of Christianity was the unbridled speculation of rationalism. The church had nothing to fear from science properly pursued through the Baconian method. The threat came from men who preferred "sitting in front of their fires and thinking about the problems of knowledge, causation, free will, and divine providence. These men were not physicists but metaphysicians; their conclusions were not 'evidences' but 'mere hypotheses.' " The result of such speculation too often was infidelity.[59] Princeton's Charles Hodge took this view to its extreme when he boasted that "a new idea never originated in this seminary."[60] Infidelity, however, was not the only pos-

---

[57]Ahlstrom, A Religious History, 262-66.

[58]Hovenkamp, Science and Religion in America, 20.

[59]Ahlstrom, A Religious History, 262; Hovenkamp, Science and Religion in America, 10.

[60]Ahlstrom, A Religious History, 265.

sible consequence of such thinking. It could also lead to social and political upheaval. Had not the French Revolution been fed by the rationalism of the Paris salons? Was not the end result of such rationalism seen in such radical works as Thomas Paine's *The Age of Reason*? If such results were to be avoided here, an intellectually respectable defense of Christian orthodoxy was needed. Baconianism would serve as that defense.

The Scottish philosophy enjoyed a broad appeal in the United States, but it was particularly popular among the Southern clergy. Its influence can be traced in the careers of Presbyterians John Holt Rice at Hampden-Sydney, David Caldwell at the University of North Carolina, Moses Waddel at Willington Academy in South Carolina and the University of Georgia, Jonathan Maxcy and James Thornwell at the South Carolina College and Columbia Seminary, Robert Lewis Dabney at Union Seminary in Richmond, and Robert J. Breckinridge at Danville (Kentucky) Seminary. Common Sense was also widely adopted by the Methodists. Nathan Bangs recommended the philosophy as an antidote to "the errors of Locke," and in 1857 the Southern *Methodist Quarterly Review* called Sir William Hamilton "the most illustrious philosopher of the age." Thomas Cooper had complained in 1831 that the Scottish philosophers "are favorites with the clergy (and of course wrong)."[61]

The Scottish philosophy was not a perfect partner for orthodox Christian theology in the modern world, and eventually, by the end of the nineteenth century, it would be widely abandoned in a yearning for something spiritually fresh. For the orthodox mind of Hodge and his Presbyterian colleagues had embraced a doctrine that, in Sydney Ahlstrom's words, "became less a living language of piety than a complex burden to be borne." Ahlstrom believes this is at least partly because in adopting Common Sense, the Calvinist tradition lost something vital—"the fervent theocentricity of Calvin." The emphasis upon self-consciousness as the oracle of religious truth made man's need, rather than God's Word, the guiding light. So, then, it is not surprising that early-twentieth-century American theology would embrace "evolutionary idealism, the social gospel, and the 'religion of feeling.' "[62] Christianity, many would conclude, can not be made scien-

---

[61]*Methodist Quarterly Review* 2 (1857): 619. Thomas Cooper to Benjamin Gildersleeve, 2 July 1831, Gildersleeve-Cooper Letters, Southern Historical Collection; quoted in Holifield, *The Gentlemen Theologians,* 118-20.

[62]Ahlstrom, *A Religious History,* 268-69.

tific; the effort to do so was injurious to it. But all this is, of course, another story.

Taking their cue from the reverent epistemology of the Scottish school, Southern thinkers explored natural theology from several perspectives, among them biology, sociology, geology, and history.

John Bachman, who for most of his life was pastor of St. John's Lutheran Church in Charleston, was an internationally known naturalist.[63] To his neighbors he was a pious but genial little man who campaigned formidably against alcohol and loose living, advocated improvements in agriculture and education, and exposed P. T. Barnum's "Mermaid" as a hoax. The Bachman home, which included almost a dozen children, was further enlivened by the presence of dogs, cats, squirrels, and other creatures running about. Despite numerous family illnesses and deaths, Bachman led a generally happy life, collecting specimens, corresponding, campaigning for science, and ministering to his own and a black congregation.[64] His national reputation was based mainly on his collaboration with John James Audubon. The two began a somewhat unlikely friendship in 1831 when Audubon visited Charleston while gathering material for his *Birds of America*. Bachman chided Audubon for his drinking and profanity, but defended him against the attacks of other naturalists. Two of Bachman's daughters married Audubon sons. The two men coauthored the four-volume study of *The Viviparous Quadrupeds of North America,* published between 1845 and 1854. Bachman was awarded a Ph.D. by the University of Berlin in 1838.[65]

Bachman was typical of the religiously oriented naturalists of his day. He was fond, for example, of drawing comparisons between nature and religion. The metamorphosis of the caterpillar into the butterfly he compared to the exchange of man's earth-bound life for the spiritual glory of

---

[63]Dumas Malone and Allen Johnson, eds., *Dictionary of American Biography,* 20 vols. (1928-1947) 1:466-67. Stanton, *The Leopard's Spots,* 123; Catherine L. Bachman, *John Bachman, the Pastor of St. John's Church, Charleston, South Carolina; Letters and Memories of His Life* (Charleston, 1888); Claude H. Neuffer, ed., *The Christopher Happholdt Journal* (Charleston, 1960), contains a ninety-page biography of Bachman, with whom Happholdt toured Europe in 1836.

[64]Longton, "Intellectual Activity in Ante-Bellum South Carolina," 66-67.

[65]Alexander Sprunt, Jr., "Audubon and Bachman—Naturalist and Clergyman," *Audubon Magazine* 53 (1951): 76-83ff.

the Hereafter.[66] He also subscribed, as did most of his colleagues, to the doctrine of the "great chain of being." Although a strong advocate of human inquiry into the secrets of nature, Bachman again typified Southern scientists of his day in insisting that scientific speculation must be conducted within the bounds of the inductive process. He warned the members of the American Philosophical Society in 1837, "In our investigations of nature, we are perhaps too prone to build our theories first, and afterwards seek for the facts which are to support them."[67] If the scientist keeps his ego in check and allows nature to reveal herself to him, then science could pose no threat to any religion, morals, or social institutions that are sound.

For Bachman, the theory that the family of man contained several species and that these species were the products of separate creations was a prime example of the unwarranted and dangerous deductive speculation against which he had warned the members of the American Philosophical Society. By the mid-1840s this view was gaining support in Bachman's neighborhood as well as nationally. Dr. Josiah Clark Nott spoke in Charleston in 1847 and converted many to the concept of human pluralism. Bachman had little respect for Nott, discounting his ideas as those of a man driven by ambition. But when Louis Agassiz arrived in Charleston in December of that year, Bachman eagerly awaited his comments on the subject, for he prized Agassiz's opinion "more than any man's in America."[68] He was to be disappointed. For the great Harvard naturalist, who had arrived in America the previous year, was undergoing a change in his own anthropological beliefs. His first exposure to blacks in the American North had filled him with horrible fascination and convinced him that, though human, they were not members of his species. Believing that species are fixed, and not essentially altered by environmental adaptation, he was inching toward the theory of multiple creations. This view did not, to Agassiz, fly in the face of the Bible: though Genesis makes no mention of

---

[66]Bachman, "On the Habits of Insects," *Southern Literary Journal* 2 (August 1836): 410.

[67]Bachman, "Observations on the Changes of Color in Birds and Quadrupeds," *Transactions of the American Philosophical Society Held at Philadelphia, for Promoting Useful Knowledge*, n.s. 5 (1839): 197-239. Quotation is found on page 198.

[68]Bachman to Louis Agassiz, 31 December 1847; quoted in Bachman, *John Bachman*, 251-52.

races that differed from Adam and Eve, neither does it deny the possibility. Agassiz did believe in the brotherhood of man under the fatherhood of God, so he tried to reassemble humankind by stressing the arbitrary nature of the species concept and arguing that human unity need not rest exclusively on mere physical similarity. Having thus guarded himself against infidelity, he could announce to his Charleston audience the dramatic conclusion that "the brain of the Negro is that of the imperfect brain of a seven month's infant in the womb of the white."[69]

Bachman's first response to this heresy came in the meetings of the Conversation Club of Charleston, where he was joined in the minority by Reverend Thomas Smyth of the Second Presbyterian Church. This was followed in 1850 by the publication of *The Doctrine of the Unity of the Human Race Examined on the Principles of Science* (Charleston, 1850). In the same year he engaged Dr. Samuel Morton, leading advocate of multiple creations, in a running debate in the pages of the *Charleston Medical Journal and Review*.[70] Bachman and Smyth agreed that the Bible is truth; that Adam and Eve were the parents of us all; and that although we cannot know the mysterious way God produced the races of man in six thousand years, He did. Bachman agreed with Morton that species are fixed and without dimension in time or space. But he argued, as had eighteenth-century naturalists, that animals do change when they migrate to a new climate, and this satisfied him as an explanation for the races of man. Here Bachman was on the path that Charles Darwin would pursue to its climax, but he lacked Darwin's imagination.

Yet for Bachman, common ancestors and a common Creator did not make the races equal. He was a thorough Southerner in his social and political views, and in defending religious orthodoxy he would not commit political heresy. There had been an "original type," he argued, and from this original type the Caucasian had "improved" while the Negro had "degenerated" through climatic influences. "We have been irresistibly drawn to the conviction," he concluded, "that in intellectual powers the

---

[69]Stanton, *The Leopard's Spots*, 100-109; Edward Lurie, "Louis Agassiz and the Races of Man," *Isis* 45 (1954): 227-42.

[70]For examples of this debate, see Stanton, *The Leopard's Spots*, 126. Thomas Smyth's views on the subject are found in Smyth, *The Unity of the Human Race Proved to Be the Doctrine of Scripture, Reason and Science* . . . (Charleston, 1850). See, in particular, J. W. Flinn, ed., *Complete Works of Rev. Thomas Smyth*, 8 vols. (Columbia, 1910) 8:31.

African is an inferior member of our species.''[71] When defenders of slavery suggested that Bachman's views provided ammunition for the abolitionists by implying that as a human the black man possessed natural rights, he found it necessary to respond by reminding them that he had always "openly and fearlessly" defended "the institutions of South Carolina." Whatever the dangers of the single-creation view, for Bachman they paled in comparison to those that arose when the authority of the Bible was rejected. The abolitionists of the North had "openly renounced" the Bible when it got in their way, he recalled, and had been rendered "more rabid" in the process. If the South followed their example, it would not only be a strategic error "more dangerous" than all their ravings, but would threaten the moral fabric of Southern society and the souls of its members.[72]

The South Carolina intellectual community followed these debates closely, and several of its members participated. Henry William Ravenel produced an article for the *Southern Quarterly Review* in which he attempted to harmonize the diverse views of Bachman and the American School of Anthropology. To Ravenel, the variations within a species found in different places and at different times simply proved the genius of the Master Planner of the universe.[73] Carolinians had a golden opportunity to demonstrate their scientific interest in March of 1850, when the American Association for the Advancement of Science held its annual convention in Charleston. Numerically, at least, they dominated the proceedings. Three Carolinians were elected officers of the association, and fourteen of the forty-odd papers were by residents of the Palmetto State.[74] Throughout the

---

[71]Bachman, *The Doctrine of the Unity of the Human Race Examined on the Principles of Science* (Charleston, 1850) 158, 212.

[72]Bachman, "An Examination of Professor Agassiz's Sketch of the Natural and of the Animal World and Their Relation to the Different Types of Man, . . . " *Charleston Medical Journal* 10 (1855): 482-534.

[73]Henry William Ravenel, "Physical Science in Its Relation to Natural and Revealed Religion," *Southern Quarterly Review*, n.s. 3 (April 1851): 42.

[74]The South Carolina participants: John Edward Holbrook, John Bachman, Robert W. Gibbes, Richard Yeadon, Mitchell King, Elias Geddings, Henry R. Frost, Thomas Genron Prioleau, John Bellinger, Thomas Ogeir, Thomas Burden, William Hawkesworth. See the *Proceedings of the American Association for the Advancement of Science* 3 (March 1850): v, xviii, 1-2.

coming decade Southerners, and Carolinians especially, would publish a spate of scientific articles in the medical, literary, and religious press.[75]

The great strides made in the scientific study of nature since the beginning of the "scientific revolution" in the seventeenth century reached what many saw as a climax in the mid-nineteenth century with the birth of the scientific study of human society. The term *sociology* is credited to the Frenchman Auguste Comte (1798-1857), but Virginian George Frederick Holmes had suggested as early as 1840 that the next stage of scientific study should focus on human society.[76] Among the first Americans to respond to Comte's idea, and the first to use the term sociology in a book title, were Southerners Henry Hughes and George Fitzhugh.[77] For both of these men, the study of human society vindicated the sociopolitical system of the South, and their written work betrays a propagandistic motive.

Fitzhugh developed an anticapitalistic philosophy that enabled him to attack the "free" society of the North and to defend slavery as a benign form of socialism that was greatly to be preferred to the social and economic anarchy he saw in the North.[78] At first Fitzhugh rejected the multiple-creation theory of the American School of Anthropology. "We abhor the doctrine of 'Types of Mankind,' " he said, "first, because it is at war with scripture, and secondly, because it encourages brutal masters to treat negroes . . . as wicked beasts."[79] However, by the eve of the Civil War, he was telling the readers of *DeBow's Review* that the white and black races were separate species and arguing—on what he saw as the same ground— that Southerners and Northerners were biologically distinct since the for

---

[75]A sampling of their work may be found in nn. 73-99. See also the files of *Journal of the Elliott Society* (Charleston), *Charleston Medical Journal and Review, Southern Quarterly Review,* and *Southern Presbyterian Review.* The most outstanding example is Henry William Ravenel, *The Fungi of Carolina,* 5 vols. (Charleston, 1852-1860).

[76]George F. Holmes, "Notes on Theology," MS vol., 1840, Holmes Papers, Perkins Library, Duke University.

[77]Henry Hughes, *A Treatise on Sociology* (Philadelphia, 1854); George Fitzhugh, *Sociology for the South* (New York, 1965). H. G. Duncan and W. L. Duncan, "The Development of Sociology in the Old South," *American Journal of Sociology* 39 (1933-1934): 649-56.

[78]Harvey Wish, *George Fitzhugh: Propagandist of the Old South* (Baton Rouge, 1943).

[79]Fitzhugh, *Sociology for the South,* 95.

mer were descended from Norman and Roman stock while the latter's ancestors were Anglo-Saxon.[80]

Henry Hughes, while not as well known as Fitzhugh, was equally important as a pioneer in the new field of sociology. Born in Port Gibson, Mississippi, in 1829, he received a broad classical education and developed a deep interest in science as a boy. In 1853 he was elected a fellow of the New Orleans Academy of Arts and Sciences. In the same year he studied in Paris, where he may have met Auguste Comte. His *Treatise on Sociology* was published the following year. In it he contrasts what he calls the "free sovereign" society, exemplified by the Northern states, with the "ordered sovereign" society of the South. In the former, the interests of the capitalist and worker are antagonistic, and there is a constant threat of social strife. In the latter Hughes finds an institutionalized relationship between capital and labor, or the "warrantor" and the "warrantee," as he calls them. This system is superior, he argues, because the interests of the two components are the same. It is not chattel slavery, he insists. "Property in man is absurd. Men cannot be owned. In warranteeism what is owned is the labor obligation, not the obligee." Poverty and social unrest, unavoidable problems in free society, are nonexistent in an ordered society. Hughes even embraced the movement to reopen the African slave trade as an affirmation of the morality of the Southern social system.[81]

The work of Fitzhugh and Hughes illustrated the willingness of Southerners to marshal the new discipline of sociology in defense of native institutions. Yet in the 1850s and for some time to come, sociology bore the stigma of immaturity and lacked wide recognition as a sound academic discipline. The study of human society needed a link with the older and more respected sciences. This link was provided by men who expanded their bases in biology, geology, and other fields in the direction of sociology. Perhaps the most important of these was Joseph LeConte. "One of the half dozen most capable professional scientists in the Old South," LeConte was born on a Liberty County, Georgia, plantation in 1823. With a chemistry laboratory and a botanical garden on the plantation, his father, a Northern-born planter and amateur scientist, easily interested Joseph and

---

[80]Wish, *Fitzhugh*, 298-99.

[81]Ronald Takaki, *A Pro-Slavery Crusade; The Agitation to Reopen the African Slave Trade* (New York, 1971) 84-101.

his brother John in scientific investigations. After receiving a sound, if haphazard, education at home (he had nine tutors in as many years), Joseph attended Franklin College and then received the M.D. degree from the College of Physicians and Surgeons in New York City in 1845. After five years of medical practice in Georgia, he journeyed to Massachusetts, looking for more stimulation in the classes of Louis Agassiz at Harvard. Agassiz would later recommend him to his alma mater, now the University of Georgia, with the statement that he had never known a better student. LeConte remained on the faculty in Athens until 1857, when a dispute over student discipline led him and his brother John to resign in favor of positions at the South Carolina College. There he became a close friend of Thornwell. He remained, except for wartime service, until 1869. At that time, again with his brother, he accepted a position on the faculty of the newly opened University of California.[82]

Typical of Southern scientists of his day, LeConte was vitally interested in the current controversies between science and religion. Also like most of them, he considered science an adjunct to, indeed the strong right arm of, Christianity. In his inaugural address at the South Carolina College in 1857 (delivered, according to tradition, in the chamber of the House of Representatives), LeConte assured his audience, as geologist Richard Brumby had done nine years earlier, of his sound views in this area. He hailed the advances made in the sciences in the last decade, comparing the current stage of scientific development with the last days of the Israelites' sojourn in the wilderness. With science's greatest achievements still in the future, he predicted that the day would come when human society itself would be reduced to scientific manageability. As for the clash between science and theology, "There was a time," he said, "when the battleground of Faith and Infidelity was situated in the domain of the metaphysical science(s)—the attacks of Voltaire and Hume." But that time was almost past. "The athiest [sic] is nearly extinct—is a fossil not an enemy." Geology was soon to become "the chief handmaid of religion among the sciences."[83]

---

[82]Malone and Johnson, *Dictionary of American Biography*, 6:90-91. Eaton, *Mind of the Old South*, 229-31; Theodore D. Bozeman, "Joseph LeConte: Organic Science and a 'Sociology for the South,' " *Journal of Southern History* 39:4 (November 1973): 565-82. The appraisal of LeConte's ability is Bozeman's; see 566.

[83]Eaton, *Mind of the Old South*, 237.

LeConte was not just pacifying a potentially critical audience with these remarks. They are consistent with his approach to all of his work. One student of LeConte's career has noted that "even his most technical writings, such as a series of lectures on coal delivered before the Smithsonian Institution in 1857 or an essay 'On the Agency of the Gulf Stream in the Formation of the Peninsula of Florida,' published in a national scientific journal in the same year, were presented as contributions to natural theology as well as to empirical knowledge." In the "Lecture on Coal," LeConte begins, "Nature is a book in which are revealed the divine character and mind. Science is the interpretation of this divine work."[84] Just as astronomy had illustrated God's "unchangeableness in space," he added, geology would now illustrate "His . . . unchangeableness in time."[85]

Such an attitude well fitted LeConte for participation in a notable trend, which was both national and especially representative of the Southern mind, away from the mechanistic view of the eighteenth century and toward an organic conception of life. Whereas the Enlightenment had emphasized the machinelike precision of the universe, the romantic period focused on the universe as the organism writ large. Aided by the growing popularity of natural history, intellectuals increasingly likened society to a giant and complex organism. Conservatives found such images quite attractive, since they suggested a clear parallel between the ponderously slow and fragile growth of a living organism and the "ideal" pattern of development in human society. Reformers beware, they could argue, you are violating a law of nature. The analogy was not lost on Southern apologists in the late antebellum period. Not only was it used by sociologists Fitzhugh and Hughes, but also by other Southern thinkers, including James Thornwell.[86]

Joseph LeConte brought his scientific expertise to this school of thought. Though he was trained in all of the sciences, and much of his early work was in geology, he recognized the life sciences as holding a superior position. Here the influence of his mentor Agassiz is apparent, since Agassiz held that the history of the earth was a series of "Preparations" for the

---

[84]Bozeman, "LeConte," 569; Joseph LeConte, "Lectures on Coal," Smithsonian Institution *Annual Report,* 1857 (Washington, 1858).

[85]LeConte, "Lectures on Coal," 120.

[86]Harvey Wish, *Ante-Bellum: Writings of George Fitzhugh and Hinton Rowan Helper on Slavery* (New York, 1967) 57, 139; Adger, *Collected Writings of Thornwell,* 4:428.

arrival of the highest form of life—man. Thus was man's place at the center of God's universe affirmed by geology. For example, in his "Lectures on Coal," LeConte argued that God had formed coal in the earth in anticipation of man's development of the steam engine. Further, America's superior coal supply was God's preparation for the "glorious destiny" of this nation. (He evidently did not draw any conclusions from the fact that most of our coal was in the North.)[87] If living matter is more important than inert matter, and if man is the highest form of life, then the ultimate science is the study of man—sociology. All others are but its foundations.[88]

The first presentations of the full implication of this organic concept appeared in the pages of the *Southern Presbyterian Review* in the late 1850s and the early 1860s. As has been noted, James Thornwell was the head of the group of Columbia Seminary men who published this influential journal. The articles were the product of long discussions between LeConte and his fellow intellectuals in Columbia during the late 1850s while he was teaching there. In his autobiography LeConte writes that the faculties of the South Carolina College, the Columbia Theological Seminary, and the Arsenal Hill Military Academy "formed the nucleus about which gathered many intellectual men and women." It was this company, which included William Campbell Preston, Benjamin Morgan Palmer, Wade Hampton, and James Thornwell, that stimulated his thinking on the sectional crisis and on the service sociology could render to the Southern cause. Thornwell, because he was especially interested in LeConte's thoughts on a new sociology for the South, solicited the essay mentioned above.[89]

What was this organic concept of society that LeConte developed? If, as he argued, human society was an "organism," it was therefore "subject . . . to the same laws of development as other organisms."[90] It followed, then, that individuals were like cells in the animal or plant. They could be traced from their undifferentiated condition in the embryonic stage

----

[87]LeConte, "Lectures on Coal," 131.

[88]LeConte, "Scientific Relation of Sociology to Biology," *Popular Science Monthly* 14 (January 1879): 325; quoted in Bozeman, "LeConte," 572.

[89]William D. Armes, ed., *The Autobiography of Joseph LeConte* (New York, 1903) 172-73; LeConte, "The Relationship of Organic Science to Sociology," *Southern Presbyterian Review* 13 (April 1860): 40.

[90]LeConte, "The Principles of a Liberal Education," *Southern Presbyterian Review* 12 (July 1859): 312.

of development, to their mature state in the fully developed organism. The more primitive the society, the more identical its human components. The more mature the society, the more specialized and interdependent will be its elements. Further, in a mature society, as in a mature organism, each component must perform its peculiar function if the body is to operate properly. LeConte developed this analogy in great detail, and concluded that tampering—especially naive, misguided tampering—with the social body will have the same result as interfering with the functioning of the biological organism. This was all the more true for him because society's organic structure, like all of nature, was the work of God's hand.[91]

How was this social organism to be studied? It would not be right to perform experiments with human society as we do with lower animals. As it happened, God had provided an alternative by displaying life in a variety of conditions and at different levels of development. Therefore, the method of study would be simple observation and comparison. But that could be fruitful only after the "lower" sciences had been mastered. Having done this, LeConte could proceed to draw some analogies. The most telling of these, he seems to have felt, was the comparison of social reform with blind genetic tinkering. (LeConte did not use this phrase, and certainly had no conception of the literal sense in which it is used today.) The great danger he saw was that the human desire to improve society had outstripped our understanding of the organism with which we were eagerly experimenting. The rash and impatient reformers of the North were creating a crisis by disrupting, or threatening to disrupt, normal social progress, which is very slow. First, we must develop our knowledge of this new science, sociology. Then, perhaps, we will be able to manipulate human society.[92] Again the inductive approach to science was held to be the only proper and safe one.

LeConte was heartened, in his reading of Southern proslavery arguments, to find a growing interest in and respect for scientific processes in the areas of social and political thought. By calling history to her aid, and pointing out that such "healthy" societies as ancient Greece had practiced slavery, the South might soon expose the error of "the dogmas of univer-

---

[91]LeConte, "Lectures on Coal," 165-66. LeConte, "The Relation of Organic Science to Sociology," 43, 52.

[92]LeConte, "The Principles of a Liberal Education," 328-29.

sal liberty and equality'' and place slavery ''on a scientific basis which is absolutely invulnerable.''[93] The reformer would ask why we should have slavery just because the Greeks did. LeConte would respond that society is not subject to the imposition of man's philosophy upon it. Reason must be content to sit at the feet of Nature and humbly learn.[94]

LeConte's organic model was not static. Change, he conceded, was healthy for any organism; but it must be allowed to come at its natural pace. The lesson of sociology is that ''too rapid change creates a fevered unhealthy condition in the organism.'' The removal of any institution from the social body was dangerous at best. When that removal was done by an amateur, as to LeConte most reformers were, the action could harm the health of society. Amateurism was dangerous in any science, but in the most complex of all, sociology, it was pernicious and possibly fatal.[95]

In providing a comforting sense of order in human society, the new science of sociology, LeConte hoped, would both preserve the Southern way of life and prevent violent sectional conflict. His organic model had been able to provide an intelligent explanation of the process of social growth. It had also, in providing a case for the sluggish pace of social change, buttressed respect for existing institutions. A proper education in sociology might be the balm that would cool the reformers' zeal and heal the fraternal wound in the organism that was the United States. Though LeConte was not to be such a miracle worker, his work clearly indicates that in the Old South scientists—as well as politicians, clergymen, and other intellectuals—felt a vital stake in the region's ideologies. It also suggests that the scientist, perhaps more than anyone else, possessed a vocabulary and a set of procedures that enabled him effectively to express the viewpoint of the Southern mind.[96]

Thus the natural sciences could point the way toward a proper application of behavioral science. But behind both, in the minds of men like LeConte, lay the comforting foundation of natural theology. There would be change, but there was always order within change, for God was at the

---

[93]LeConte, ''The Relation of Organic Science to Sociology,'' 56, 58-59.

[94]LeConte, *Inaugural Address Delivered in the State House, December 8, 1857* (Columbia, 1858) 5.

[95]LeConte, ''The Relation of Organic Science to Sociology,'' 52.

[96]Bozeman, ''LeConte,'' 582.

helm of history. It was possible, then, even in the midst of rising sectional tension, to retain an optimism about the present *and* future. As Charleston Episcopalian James Warley Miles wrote to a friend, "As to the ultimate result of the grand struggle in which the South is engaged, it would be impiety to doubt our triumph, because we are working out the great thought of GOD."[97]

While many Old South thinkers gained confidence from the natural sciences and sociology in the ultimate vindication of their society, others reached the same conclusions from the study of history. The flowering of local and state historical societies, and of historical writing, in the late antebellum period testifies to the importance the region's intellectuals placed on the study of the past. One such group was the South Carolina Historical Society. At its third annual meeting on 27 May 1858, the society's president, James Louis Petigru, delivered an address that is a model expression of history's value to the antebellum mind. Taking his cue from the Baconians, Petigru opened his address with an attack on the excesses of rationalism, which to many conservatives was the chief heresy, spiritual and intellectual, of the age. Reason, critical as it is, is fallible, he argued, and must be tempered with experience. Two opposing viewpoints may be equally secure in the application of reason to their defense. "It is history that comes to the relief of conscience when perplexed by the conflict of opinion; and furnishes a guide for conduct and judgement, when reason is at fault. . . . The questions which Reason could not solve, are silently settled by Time."[98] If this were literally true, five thousand years of recorded time may well be expected to have resolved all controversies. But, as Petigru conceded, the record of the past is imperfect, both in its omissions and in its susceptibility to prejudice and vanity. He did note with confidence, however, that the chronology of Moses, "which assigns a comparatively recent date to the first appearance of man on this globe, is corroborated by the investigations of science, and that the unity of the human race, a dogma consecrated by his authority, . . . cannot be disproved by reason."[99] Here

---

[97]James Warley Miles to "My dear Friend" [Anna Rebecca Young], n.d., James Warley Miles Papers, Perkins Library, Duke University.

[98]James Louis Petigru, "Oration Delivered on the Third Anniversary of the South Carolina Historical Society, May 27, 1858," *Collections of the South Carolina Historical Society* 2 (Charleston, 1858) 10. The address covers pages 9-21.

[99]Ibid., 12.

Petigru invoked the aid of both nature and revealed religion in the defense of what is, against the fanciful notions of reformers about what might be.

History is being called upon here to play a crucial utilitarian role of offering the authority of experience as a counterweight to the authority of idealistic reason. Still, for history to be accepted as such an authority, Petigru recognized, it must be elevated above the petty uses to which it was (and is) sometimes put. As one of the few outspoken unionists in South Carolina at that time, Petigru could appreciate better than most of his listeners the notion that every question has two sides, and he could sense the danger in blind patriotism. "History is false to her trust," he continued,

> when she betrays the cause of truth, even under the influences of patriotic impulses. It is not true that [during the Revolution] all the virtue was in the Whig camp, or that all the Tories were a band of ruffians. They were conservatives, and their error was in carrying to excess the sentiment of loyalty, which is founded in virtue. . . . Their cause deserved to fail; but their sufferings are entitled to respect. . . . History will . . . show towards them the indulgence due to the unfortunate.[100]

Time alone, he suggests, provides the perspective from which the true state of affairs can be seen.

There is, and one suspects it is intentional, an ingenious double-edged sword hidden in these remarks by a troubled friend of the South to his like-minded audience in the twilight of the antebellum era. One can picture heads nodding in agreement as Petigru cautioned against ignoring the lessons of the past, for history reveals that the Old South, with its stratified society and slave-labor system, was closer to the norm of human experience than was the free society of the North and of Western Europe. And yet the particular lesson he points to must have unnerved at least some of his hearers, for was he not hinting that loyalty to tradition can blind good men to the truth and lead them to defend the status quo foolishly? Was he not warning them against the danger of the course of Southern nationalism? Does not modern history, when practiced with intelligence, show to the defenders of the Old South "the indulgence due to the unfortunate"? Yet his message, if received, would soon be lost in the hue and cry that would follow John Brown's raid some eighteen months later. History could disturb, but more often for the Southern mind, it consoled. Just as the study of nature

---

[100]Ibid., 20.

provided Southern thinkers with a rational basis for defending their society, so the study of man's past provided empirical evidence as to which social and political systems are sound and which are not. The systems that have stood the test of time and have produced the most successful societies become normative for the present and the future, Southerners would argue.[101]

Southerners were not alone in the mid-nineteenth century in their interest in the past. As the pace of change accelerated with the industrial revolution, many in the Western world looked longingly back to a seemingly simpler, more stable, and for the upper classes, more natural way of life. This nostalgia, easily understandable to late-twentieth-century man, was, one suspects, stronger in the Old South because these people could find so few contemporary societies with which to identify. The more romantic among them felt at home in the world of Sir Walter Scott's Waverly novels, with its stratified society and aristocratic values. Others longed for the selfless dedication they saw in their ancestors of the revolutionary generation; indeed, they decried the materialism that seemed to be eroding this dedication among their contemporaries.[102] Still others fixed their backward gaze on ancient Greece and Rome, societies much like their own in some ways, and therefore sources of some comfort in a world so far removed from those elitist communities.

This interest in the distant past is not surprising considering that these records of ancient life could provide much-needed reassurance to Southerners who saw the rest of Western society embracing ideals and institutions alien to theirs. The ancient societies were based on slavery, were elitist, and esteemed freedom and individualism only for those at the top. Their literature was superior to that of the moderns, it was argued, because without the printing press it catered only to the tastes of the literate few.[103]

Many Southerners found kindred spirits among the ancients. George Fitzhugh admitted to his friend George Frederick Holmes, ''All the [ideas]

---

[101]George Fitzhugh, ''Oliver Goldsmith and Dr. Johnson,'' *DeBow's Review* 28 (1860): 505.

[102]An example is William Gilmore Simms. See Mary C. Oliphant et al., eds., *Letters of William Gilmore Simms,* vol. 3 (Columbia, 1955) 523.

[103]This view was expressed by George Fitzhugh. Harvey Wish, *George Fitzhugh, Propagandist of the Old South* (Gloucester MA, 1962) 263.

which I thought original with me, I find in Aristotle."[104] Aristotle, for example, supported slavery. "Nature," he wrote, "has clearly designed some men for freedom and others for slavery; and with respect to the latter, slavery is both just and beneficial."[105] Fitzhugh also saw a congenial mind in the conservative Greek dramatist Aristophanes and noted the similarities between the evils he satirized and those of modern civilization.[106] These discoveries led Fitzhugh to a greater appreciation of the value of history, since its perspective revealed "that Southern society is *normal*, Northern society *exceptional* and *experimental*."[107]

What was the value, then, of being in step with the times if the modern world was losing its moral moorings and jettisoning much of what was redemptive in traditional society? Writing in *Russell's Magazine* in 1857, Frederick Adolphus Porcher summed up the attitude of many Southern thinkers toward the Northern avant garde. Noting the Northern (one might say national) emphasis on making money, he asked,

> Is this the life for a people to live under the eye of God, and in full development of civilization? Is all of life to be an unceasing struggle after more? Is the heart of man never to expand to the warm influences of home, and all its associations of family, of kindred, and of friendly affections? Is man to become a money-making, cotton-spinning, iron-founding, machine? . . . Is man never to stop, and . . . enjoy the fruits of his intelligent activity? If these things are so, . . . then forever be banished from our thoughts all aspirations after such progress; let us cherish our conservatism; be content to advance cautiously and safely in wealth, and gratefully meanwhile . . . enjoy that life which God has alloted [*sic*] us in this beautiful world.

When Porcher compared the recent history of the Northern states with his native South Carolina, he saw ferment on the one hand and tranquility on the other, and lauded the respect for tradition that, in his mind, was responsible for the virtual homogeneity of his society.[108]

---

[104]Fitzhugh to Holmes, 11 April 1855; quoted in Wish, *George Fitzhugh*, 20.

[105]George F. Holmes, "Observations on a Passage in the Politics of Aristotle Relative to Slavery," *Southern Literary Messenger* 16 (1850): 193-205.

[106]George Fitzhugh, "Black Republicans in Athens," *DeBow's Review* 23 (1857): 20-26.

[107]Wish, *Fitzhugh*, 118-19.

[108]Frederick A. Porcher, "Southern and Northern Civilization Contrasted," *Russell's Magazine* 1 (May 1857): 104-105.

For William Gilmore Simms and many others, the Revolution provided an excellent laboratory in which to explore the lessons of history. The elucidation of the past, Simms believed, enabled the historian to lead the "people out of the bondage of the present."[109] More to the point, the Revolution was for Simms an intellectual movement. Its driving force was the idea of American nationalism. It could therefore instruct Simms's contemporaries, who were also involved in a war of ideas.[110] Others agreed. One writer regarded the republication of Simms's revolutionary romance, *The Cassique of Kiawah,* in 1859 "as something very nearly amounting to a national benefit."[111] For Virginia's Nathaniel Beverly Tucker, the past revealed insights that could be used in predicting the future, as he did in his 1836 book, *The Partisan Leader,* which foretold Southern secession. South Carolina's William Henry Trescot looked to the Revolution as an example of moderation. His state's founding fathers "sheltered no wild sentiment, fostered no mischievous principle of universal democracy. . . . They conducted a revolution with the caution of a lawsuit."[112] Southerners of the late antebellum era had indeed found a usable past.

Since they placed such a high value on history, it is not surprising that as the nineteenth century reached its midpoint, many Southerners were increasingly alarmed at the ease with which their neighbors accepted their written history from Northern pens. In forfeiting to the North the writing of the nation's history, they warned, the South was permitting its children to receive their heritage from those who held it in scorn. The American history text used at The Citadel, Marcius Willson's *American History* (New York, 1856), denigrated the morals of the colonial South, and Samuel Whelpley's *Compend of History* (New York, 1846), which was used at

---

[109]Quoted from the *Southern Literary Messenger* of 10 May 1859; in Simms's *Letters,* 1:lxxvii.

[110]William Gilmore Simms, *The Partisan: A Tale of the Revolution* (New York, 1835) viii.

[111]William Gilmore Simms, *The Sources of American Independence* (Aiken SC, 1844) 9-10. See also "South Carolina and the Revolution," in Simms's *Letters,* 3:523.

[112]William H. Trescot, *The Diplomacy of the Revolution: A Historical Study* (New York, 1852) 153-55; quoted in Nicholas Olsberg, "A Government of Class and Race; William Henry Trescot and the South Carolina Chivalry, 1860-1865" (Ph.D. dissertation, University of South Carolina, 1972) 102.

several Southern colleges, was critical of slavery.[113] The dangers of this condition were obvious and must be remedied. "What child has not been taught to believe religiously, that all that is good, all that is noble, all that is venerable in our country is derived from the Puritan?" Frederick Porcher asked the members of the South Carolina Historical Society in June 1857. By way of illustration he noted that the battle of Fort Moultrie, as great an event as the battle of Bunker Hill, was ignored in the list of Revolutionary War battles published in *Harper's Gazetteer*. Porcher urged the society's members to make the rectification of such wrongs one of their main tasks.[114]

Porcher was not alone. A contributor to *Russell's Magazine* was appalled to read in the *Edinburgh Review* an article announcing that the founding fathers, North and South, were opposed to the expansion of slavery. Hastening to correct this "gigantic roguery," he reminded *Russell's* readers that five of the first seven presidents had been slaveholders. A close examination of the words of the founding fathers in debate reveals none of the current rantings about slavery, he added. Even Jefferson's reference to the slave trade was expunged from the final draft of the Declaration, and the antislavery provision of the Northwest Ordinance was balanced by the tacit understanding that slavery would expand into the Southwest, he said. The essay concludes with a dire warning that such reinterpretation of the nation's past cannot be allowed to go uncorrected. As for the source of the *Edinburgh Review* piece, he traced it to "Boston and New York." Such "crimes" deserved "the pillory," he concluded.[115]

The liberal trend in American historiography disturbed George Fitzhugh, who wrote a "scorching" review of George Bancroft's popular history of the United States. Fitzhugh criticized Bancroft's theme of progress and his "inner light" doctrines. We need, he said, "an historian who shall show that the serfs of Europe, in the days of Cressy [*sic*], Agincourt, and

---

[113]John Ezell, "A Southern Education for Southrons," *Journal of Southern History* 17 (August 1951): 315.

[114]Frederick A. Porcher, "Inaugural Address," *Collections of the South Carolina Historical Society* 1 (Charleston, 1857) 15-16. Porcher, a Yale graduate, held the Chair of History and Belles Lettres at the College of Charleston. His specialty was South Carolina, and he advocated broadening the concept of history to include social and economic topics as well as political. See his edited memoirs in the *South Carolina Historical and Genealogical Magazine* 44-48 (1943-1947). The South Carolina Historical Society was organized on 2 June 1855. Porcher, ibid.

[115]"The Edinburgh Review Reviewed," *Russell's Magazine* 1 (April 1857): 1-14.

Poictiers, were brave, wholesouled men who had homes, position, and place, in the world, but that now, the hireling class, the majority of mankind, have neither masters, nor homes, nor certain means of support."[116] Recognizing the need to shore up the historical consciousness of young South Carolinians, William Gilmore Simms revised his history of the state for republication in 1860, making it more relevant to the times. He suggested to his congressman-friend William Porcher Miles that the book would be useful for politicians as well, and urged him to keep a copy with him in Washington for ammunition against his Northern enemies.[117]

The pressures of the sectional debate in the 1850s seem to have driven many Southerners back to their roots, personal as well as corporate. Ancestor worship was becoming a fetish with some that produced what at least one contemporary saw as unhealthy consequences. "Forced . . . to think of ourselves much more than was profitable," wrote William Henry Trescot, "we . . . learned to talk about ourselves much more than was needful. We seem, somehow, to have become uncertain of our old position, and boast of our birthright in language we never inherited from our fathers." Patriotism became "so intensely local that it was a positive hinderance [sic] to breadth and freedom of thought."[118]

Yet there is more here than the narrow provincialism and paranoia that many historians have detected in the minds of antebellum Southerners. Men like Petigru, Fitzhugh, Holmes, Porcher, and Trescot recognized the power of the historian to influence the present and future by his interpretation of the past. Moreover, their concern for the state of history in their society parallels the concern of other Southern thinkers for the inductive study of nature as an aid in the defense of their institutions. Here, too, the clergy played an active role. For just as religion could guide the hand of science toward a reverent appreciation for the natural order of the universe, so could it impart to the study of the past the needed moral perspective. Indeed, Petigru provides an example of the connection between the historian and the

---

[116]George Fitzhugh, "Mr. Bancroft's History and the Inner Light," *DeBow's Review* 29 (1860): 598-613; quoted in Wish, *Fitzhugh*, 267-68.

[117]Jon Wakelyn, *The Politics of a Literary Man: William Gilmore Simms* (Westport CT, 1973) 230.

[118]William H. Trescot, *Oration Delivered before the Alumni of the College of Charleston, June 25, 1889* (Charleston, 1889) 12. Quoted in Olsberg, "A Government of Class and Race," 170.

preacher. On 4 July 1844, he delivered an oration on the heroic role of South Carolina in the American Revolution. His "old friend" Dr. Benjamin Palmer, pastor of the Congregational Church of Charleston, paid him what he considered his highest compliment on it, saying that with a little alteration it would make a fine sermon.[119] Palmer's nephew—also named Benjamin, and a protégé of Thornwell—would later raise the function of the clergy as ennobler and defender of Southern traditions to perhaps its highest level in sermons from the pulpit of the First Presbyterian Church of New Orleans.

This chapter began with the suggestion that the removal of Thomas Cooper from the South Carolina College presidency revealed a shift in the intellectual perspective of that state and the region in general, and that this shift was climaxed at the end of the antebellum era with the creation of a new Chair in the Natural Sciences and Revealed Religion at the Columbia Theological Seminary. It is, of course, convenient for the purposes of this study that both of these events happened in Columbia and that James Thornwell played a role in both. Although other pairs of related events might be found to suggest the essential change that the South experienced between 1830 and 1860, these two do seem particularly symbolic. Cooper had been the most-visible spokesman in the South for the modernist, "free thinker" view of religion. This view held that religion was a relic of the pre-Enlightenment era when the human mind needed its consolations, and that the scientific achievements of the eighteenth and nineteenth centuries had discredited it and made it unnecessary. It is impossible to say how many Southerners agreed with him. Though they were surely in the minority, their numbers, especially among the more literate, may have been larger than is generally assumed. James Henry Hammond may have spoken for many when he said that religion had an important social function of upholding order, but that as for religion as it was generally preached, "who believes it?"[120]

It was perhaps with a disturbing awareness of such attitudes that the more-orthodox leadership in Southern institutions began around the middle of the nineteenth century to shore up the intellectual credentials of the

---

[119]James P. Carson, *James Louis Petigru, The Union Man of South Carolina* (Washington, 1920) 239.

[120]Untitled thoughts, Hammond-Bryan-Cummings Papers, South Caroliniana Library.

faith. Thornwell had been on the job in this capacity at the South Carolina College since 1838, but since the ouster of Cooper there had been no one at that institution to teach the controversial science of geology. This void was filled in 1848 by the arrival of Richard Trapier Brumby from the University of Alabama. Whatever his scientific credentials, Brumby was a good choice insofar as his religious views were concerned. He would soon be elected an elder in Columbia's First Presbyterian Church. As if to demonstrate his orthodoxy, he was asked by the trustees to deliver a public address in the State House. He complied with *An Address on the Sphere, Interests and Importance of Geology.* He argued for the great age of the earth. To his mind, this did not reveal any conflict with Genesis. During its vast lifetime, he added, the planet has undergone massive changes. There was convincing evidence, he suggested, that the land where the State House stood was once under the Atlantic, along with much of Eastern and Southern North America. Brumby was, in short, one of the many scientists who are now seen as precursors of Darwin. Yet he couched his remarks in reverent references to the Creator and His wonderful works, and concluded that the universe was created and continues to function in accordance with divine law.[121]

The confidence expressed in this lecture and the many similar essays in the religious press during the 1850s is perhaps belied by the continuing repetition of the assurance that faith ultimately has nothing to fear from science.[122] As noted above, Baconianism was the refuge orthodoxy used to defend itself against the new science; but at mid-century the onslaught of science was building momentum. Hence the forces of faith must have felt that silence from their camp would be interpreted as confusion and doubt. It might be suggested that this outpouring of defense amounted to

---

[121]Richard T. Brumby, *An Address on the Sphere, Interests and Importance of Geology, Delivered December 8, 1849, in the Hall of the House of Representatives* (Columbia, 1849). See also Brumby's review of Hugh Miller, *Footprints of the Creator,* in the *Southern Presbyterian Review* 4 (July 1851).

[122]An excellent example is the article on geology by Hugh Miller, reprinted on the front page of the *Southern Presbyterian* for 23 March 1854. Miller, editor of the *Edinburgh Witness,* took the position that would be adopted by most "liberal Christians" of the late nineteenth century: that both Genesis and the new science were true, each in its own way, and that one did not have to choose between them. The editor of the *Southern Presbyterian,* Reverend Washington Baird, recommended Miller's essay especially to "the *youth* of the present day." Ibid., 2.

an overreaction indicative of inner doubts. In any case, the religious and literary press would not, some felt, be sufficient for the battle. Well-trained forces were needed in the pulpits. Ministers must be conversant with the new science and able to repel its assault.

So it was perhaps with a mixture of fear and confidence that the Presbyterians established the "Perkins Professorship of Natural Science in Connection with Revelation" at Columbia Seminary. This novelty in theological education was designed, says the historian of Southern Presbyterianism, to "evince the harmony of science with the records of our faith."[123] "It is with an earnest purpose," wrote B. M. Palmer, that "we labor to establish the harmony of scripture and science. For if . . . you shake my faith in [the Bible] . . . you launch me upon a sea of doubt which has neither bottom nor shore."[124]

The proposal to establish the seminary chair was first made in the form of a resolution adopted by the Tombeckbee Presbytery of Mississippi in 1857. The resolution spoke of the need "to have men capable of defending the faith once delivered to the saints." Soon thereafter, a Judge Perkins of Columbus, Mississippi, donated thirty thousand dollars toward the endowment of the chair, which was subsequently established in Columbia and named in his honor.[125] In reporting and encouraging support for this dramatic development, an article in the *Southern Presbyterian Review* candidly noted that the professorship was needed to help curb the counterproductive efforts at defense of Scripture by men whose zeal surpassed their knowledge. There was considerable division within the ranks, as men who "have taken it for granted that their interpretation of the Bible was

---

[123]Thompson, *Presbyterians in the South,* 1:505. Clement Eaton suggests that the professorship is evidence of fear of science as an enemy of Christianity. Eaton, *The Mind of the Old South,* 237. Holifield sees it as a sign of some distress on this subject (*The Gentlemen Theologians,* 84-85). He calls it the end of the era of clerical optimism regarding science. Although those involved treated the professorship as the first of its kind, Amherst College had appointed Edward Hitchcock professor of "natural Theology and geology" around 1850. Hovenkamp, *Science and Religion in America,* 47.

[124]Benjamin M. Palmer, "Baconianism and the Bible," *Southern Presbyterian Review* 4 (October 1852): 252. This was originally given as an address to the Eumenean and Philanthropic Societies of Davidson College earlier that year and then reprinted (Columbia, 1852).

[125]James A. Lyon, "The New Theological Professorship," *Southern Presbyterian Review* 12 (April 1859): 182.

the only true interpretation . . . have charged men equally as pious, and far their superiors in ability, with betraying the cause of religion.''[126]

After some three years of raising the necessary funds and surveying the field for the right man, Professor James Woodrow was called to the chair from Oglethorpe University in 1861. The son of a Presbyterian minister, Woodrow was born in Carlisle, England, in 1828. Soon after his birth the family emigrated to America and settled in Ohio. James graduated from Jefferson College in Pennsylvania, studied with Louis Agassiz at Harvard, and received the Ph.D. summa cum laude from the University of Heidelburg in 1856. To these two degrees would later be added the M.D., D.D., LL.D., and J.U.D.[127] In his inaugural address he noted that there were no models for his position "either in America or Europe." He affirmed his belief in the literal truth of the Scriptures and his confidence that nothing produced by science could be inconsistent with the Bible. Secure in this position, he called for freedom of inquiry among both scientists and theologians in pursuit of the common truth. He made no reference to Charles Darwin, whose writings would lead him to a position that would cost him the Perkins professorship.[128]

Woodrow's career at the seminary is significant as a measure of the tenacity of the Baconian-Scottish school of thought among the orthodox clergy of the South. While his eventual antagonists, such as Robert Lewis Dabney of Union Seminary and John Girardeau of Columbia Seminary, were also in this tradition, Woodrow was its more faithful disciple. In his 1863 essay, "Theology and Its Assailants," he questioned who the true friends of the Bible were. Noting that geology and its kindred sciences had been widely assaulted because they threatened to revise some long-held and cherished notions, he suggested two reasons for this attack on science. "It must often be the result of weak faith, and a secret dread that, after all,

---

[126]Richard S. Gladney, "Natural Science and Revealed Religion," *Southern Presbyterian Review* 12 (October 1859): 461.

[127]Clement Eaton, "Professor James Woodrow and the Freedom of Teaching in the South," *Journal of Southern History* 28 (February 1962): 4.

[128]James Woodrow, "Inaugural Address," *Southern Presbyterian Review* 14 (January 1862): 505-30. Woodrow was fired by the seminary in 1884 after a church trial in which he explained his qualified acceptance of Darwin's theories on evolution. He was not, however, defrocked, nor was he removed from the editorship of the *Southern Presbyterian Review* or the *Southern Presbyterian*. He resigned from the former post in 1885 and from the latter in 1893. Eaton, "Professor James Woodrow," 5, 12.

something may be found out, that will compel an abandonment of belief in the Bible." Second, it may be that "while we have undoubting faith in the word of God, we have equal confidence in our ability to interpret it, and are influenced by that intolerance toward all who believe either less or more than ourselves, which is the disgrace of our kind." We who love the Bible, he suggested, should act in "the spirit of forebearance and love taught in its pages." Most of the clerical critics of geology, he observed, did not follow the Baconian way of gathering sufficient evidence before reaching conclusions as to its danger to the faith. As an example, he referred his readers to a review of the antigeological writings of David N. Lord, which had appeared in the *Southern Presbyterian Review* two years before. This kind of pedantry, Woodrow suggested, Christianity would be better off without.[129]

To the end of the antebellum period and beyond, the orthodox thinkers of the South, lay and clergy, kept the faith in the ultimate harmony of God's works and His Word. In seeking to come to terms with this threatening aspect of modern thought, they were asserting, perhaps more forcefully than their less-intellectual brethren, the integrity of Southern thought and values. These thinkers would gradually come to view secession as the means of preserving those values which for them were embodied in the phrase "orthodox Christianity," and which, subconsciously at least, they identified with the Old South.

---

[129]James Woodrow, "Theology and Its Assailants," *Southern Presbyterian Review* 15 (April 1863): 549-69. See especially 550, 552. In one of his last pieces for the *Review*, in 1884, entitled "Evolution," Woodrow revealed that the era of synthesizing science and Christian theology was ending. "We hear much about the harmony of science and Scripture," he wrote, "but is it likely that there can be total harmony between two such different fields?" To him, "their contents are so entirely different that it is in vain and misleading to be searching for harmonies." "The Bible does not teach science," he added. Yet he saw no challenge to its teachings, for "what difference can it make with regard to any relation between ourselves . . . and God and the Lord Jesus Christ, whether the earth came into existence six thousand years ago, or six thousand million years ago." *Southern Presbyterian Review* 35 (1884): 341-68. Quotations are on 342, 344, and 347.

CHAPTER 4

Thornwell's Philosophy and Theology

"**W**e have separated from our brethren in the North as Abraham separated from Lot." Thus did James Thornwell describe the formation of the Presbyterian Church in the Confederate States of America in December 1861.[1] In turning to the Bible to explain the most political act of his career, Thornwell revealed the theological perspective that pervaded his life and thought. In all of the avenues his career followed—clergyman, college professor, college administrator, editor, ecclesiastical leader, and seminary professor—he was first and foremost a Christian and a student of Christian theology.

That he would be called, indeed implored, to leave the lofty perch of the South Carolina College presidency and assume the chair in theology at a small and struggling seminary indicates that his fellow clergymen saw him primarily in this light. While granting that the move would be a loss to the college and the state, the *Southern Presbyterian* stressed the importance of the role he would play at the seminary. Referring to the new science with its attendant threat to faith, and to the decline in public morals

---

[1]James Henley Thornwell, *Address to All the Churches of Jesus Christ throughout the Earth* (Columbia, 1861); quoted in Henry A. White, *Southern Presbyterian Leaders* (New York, 1911) 326.

that, in the paper's view, was closely related to the modernism produced by science, the editor advised: "In this day, when the battleground is shifted by the enemies of our faith, when the attack is from a new quarter, and the defense requires new learning . . . when the Evidences of Christianity have to be studied from new points of view, Dr. Thornwell, whose studies have for years been shaped to meet these very attacks from our Protean foe, can, as Professor of Theology, do a work for his church and his country, and his age, such as he can do in no other position."[2]

Whatever one's view as to what he might have accomplished in politics had he chosen that path, one is forced by an examination of Thornwell's life to conclude that he found his niche in theology. If he did not receive the recognition he might have in this discipline, it is still, one suspects, the area in which he would most want to be remembered. In any case, it was the role that his colleagues virtually insisted that he play, and he seems to have confirmed their feelings when, in his inaugural address at Columbia Seminary, he said he felt that his whole life had been a preface to that appointment.[3]

"Southern theology in the nineteenth century was the product of a dual impulse: it reflected both intellectual commitments and social compulsions."[4] This characterization by a modern scholar could probably be applied to the theology of any time and place; it certainly applies to the theology of Thornwell. Indeed, the spiritual and intellectual commitments that he affirmed blended so smoothly with the perspective of his society that there was only a minimal tension between the two in his thought. Thornwell was a man whose philosophy was so well suited to his time and

---

[2]*Southern Presbyterian,* 6 July 1854, 2. While Thornwell's decision to leave the College the following year was not an easy one, he reached it, one suspects, because he agreed with the view expressed by the *Southern Presbyterian.* As for his impact on the Seminary, one statistic at least indicates that it was positive. During the 1850s the average graduating class numbered about twelve. By 1859, the year that the students who entered the school along with Thornwell finished, the graduates numbered eighteen. In 1862, the year of his death, the Seminary graduated thirty-one new ministers. Louis La Motte, *Colored Light; The Story of the Influence of Columbia Theological Seminary, 1828-1936* (Richmond, 1937) 302-308.

[3]Thornwell, "Inaugural Discourse as Professor of Theology, Columbia Seminary, Delivered October 13, 1857," in John B. Adger, ed., *Collected Writings of James Henley Thornwell,* vol. 1 (Richmond, 1871) 379.

[4]Brooks Holifield, *The Gentlemen Theologians; American Theology in Southern Culture, 1795-1860* (Durham, 1978) 6-7.

place that he could give himself to it with virtually no reservation. This could also be said of most Old South clergymen as well. One study of leading Old South theologians has found only two who did not fit the mold of "rational orthodoxy": Samuel Gilman (1791-1858), a Harvard-trained Unitarian who came to Charleston from Massachusetts, and James Warley Miles (1818-1876), a Charleston Episcopalian who was deeply influenced by European romanticism and by Transcendentalism.[5] To this short list might be added Virginian Moncure Daniel Conway (1832-1907), although most of his adult life was spent north of the Potomac.[6]

Thornwell's great aim as a theologian can be compared with that of Thomas Aquinas in medieval Europe, Jonathan Edwards in colonial America, and the twentieth-century theologian Ronald Gregor-Smith. All of these men tried to come to grips with new ideas and to reconcile the disparate values of their day. While others held firmly to the old or eagerly embraced the new, these men looked for ways to synthesize the old and new, and thus preserve an intellectual and spiritual continuity in a world of change.[7]

Thornwell's theological views were grounded in his upbringing, confirmed in his early training, and never wavered throughout his career. His ministry began just as the Old School-New School controversy within American Presbyterianism was coming to a head, and he immediately identified with the firm Calvinism of the former. Writing to his wife Nancy from the November 1836 meeting of the Synod of South Carolina and

---

[5]Ibid., 62-71. Regarding Gilman, see Daniel Howe, "A Massachusetts Yankee in Senator Calhoun's Court: Samuel Gilman in South Carolina," *New England Quarterly* 44 (June 1971): 197-220. Regarding Miles, see Ralph Luker, "God, Man and the World of James Warley Miles, Charleston's Transcendentalist," *Historical Magazine of the Protestant Episcopal Church* 39 (June 1970): 101-36.

[6]Conway, the product of a prominent slaveholding family and a pious Methodist upbringing, read Emerson, attended Harvard Divinity School, and became a Unitarian and an abolitionist. See Mary E. Burtis, *Moncure Conway, 1832-1907* (New Brunswick NJ, 1952). Clement Eaton calls him "perhaps the boldest thinker that the Southern church produced in antebellum days." Clement Eaton, *The Freedom of Thought Struggle in the Old South* (New York, 1964) 293.

[7]Regarding Aquinas, see A. Whitacre et al., *St. Thomas Aquinas* (Manchester, England, 1925). Regarding Edwards, see O. E. Winslow, *Jonathan Edwards* (New York, 1940), and Sydney Ahlstrom, *A Religious History of the American People* (New Haven, 1972) ch. 19. Regarding Gregor-Smith, see Eugene T. Long, ed., *God, Secularization and History; Essays in Memory of Ronald Gregor-Smith* (Columbia, 1974).

Georgia, the youthful delegate predicted a "stormy session" as the two schools contended, and added, "You know, my dearest, where your husband will be found."[8] The following year he attended his first General Assembly and witnessed the schism of the church. Henceforth the Old School would be the arena in which he would carry on his battles for Calvinism.

His identification with the Great Reformer of Geneva was recognized both by himself and by his colleagues, all of whom were Calvinists. When some students at Columbia Seminary good-naturedly caricatured the professors in 1861, Thornwell was shown grasping the naked Adam by the shoulder and scolding him for his sin, which made humankind so miserable.[9] Speaking of his lectures on theology at the seminary, one student complained, "That man, Jimmie Thornwell, finds in Calvin's *Institutes* what John Calvin himself never thought of."[10] In a memorial volume celebrating the fiftieth anniversary of Columbia Seminary, his colleague John Adger, in bemoaning Thornwell's short life, compared him to Calvin. Both men were "cut off in the noon of life," Adger said, and both made their greatest contributions as ecclesiastics. "I am by no means sure," added Adger, "that, all things considered, Thornwell did not make a contribution to ecclesiastical reformation in itself of as much value as Calvin's."[11] He meant Thornwell's role as defender of traditional Calvinism in the face of nineteenth-century modernism. Granting the natural tendency toward hyperbole that such occasions foster, one may dismiss Adger's lofty evaluation of his friend. But the view of Thornwell as the nineteenth century's Calvin is not unreasonable. Perhaps only Princeton's Charles Hodge and Robert L. Dabney of Union Seminary in Richmond deserve equal billing in this role.

Thornwell was a Calvinist in his attitude toward theological study. He had a conservative's reverence for the great minds of the past and recognized the importance of grounding modern scholarship on their founda-

---

[8]Thornwell to Nancy Thornwell, 24 November 1836, Anderson-Thornwell Papers, Southern Historical Collection.

[9]Augustine Smyth to Thomas Smyth, 29 January 1861, in Thomas Smyth, *Autobiographical Notes, Letters and Reflections,* ed. Louisa Cheves Stoney (Charleston, 1914) 584.

[10]James S. Cosby, quoted in Thomas Law, *Centennial Addresses in Honor of James Henley Thornwell* (Columbia, 1912) 19.

[11]*Memorial Volume of the Semi-Centennial of the Theological Seminary at Columbia, South Carolina* (Columbia, 1884) 188-91.

tions. Yet he was "progressive" based on his belief that divine revelation was an ongoing process. In this, he was a product of the reformed tradition.[12] In his conception of worship, he also followed Calvin. In Thornwell's church the sermon was always the centerpiece of the service. The order of worship was austere. Prayer, he held, should only be engaged in when standing or kneeling. Sitting while praying denoted a presumptuous informality in God's presence. Music was kept to a minimum; and he personally viewed the use of instrumental music in worship as unscriptural and distracting.[13]

A fuller picture of Thornwell's Calvinism must come from his own words. His accounts of the spiritual struggle and conversion he experienced while working briefly as a teacher in Sumterville in 1832 have already been noted (see ch. 2). The sense of release that he experienced at the end of this period of tension did not free him forever from feelings of guilt and unworthiness, however. In a letter to his mentor, General James Gillespie, shortly after arriving in Lancasterville to begin his first pastorate, he said that at his ordination he felt "a new era had commenced in [his] life—that [he] was no longer a citizen of the world, but an ambassador of God." He added that he had "trembled" at the "tremendous weight of ministerial responsibility" and called on the Holy Ghost to make his humble efforts effective in the saving of souls. His task would be impossible otherwise, for

> no man can bring himself to feel the sinfulness of his own nature. The thunders of the sacred desk, although they may alarm for a season, cannot unfold in their true light, the hideous features of depravity and guilt. The minister is but a sword in the hands of God to cut the guilty down, and as a sword is utterly inefficient without a [hand?] to wield it, so the minister of the Gospel is altogether useless without the [illegible] power of God. . . . God and God alone can arm truth with barbed arrows to pierce the sinner's heart.

---

[12]Thornton Whaling, "Dr. Thornwell as a Theologian," in Law, *Centennial Addresses,* 24. See also John Leith, *Introduction to the Reformed Tradition* (Atlanta, 1977).

[13]Ernest T. Thompson, *Presbyterians in the South, 1607-1861,* vol. 1 (Richmond, 1963) 463. Thompson says Thornwell was joined in these views by such leading churchmen as Robert Breckinridge, Robert Dabney, John Adger, and John Girardeau. Organs, he adds, did not become common in Southern Presbyterian churches until the beginning of this century.

Confidently he asserted the truth of the message he had been called to preach. "We preach a revelation—this is our distinctive character. We have nothing to do with plausible conjectures or probable opinions—we do not proclaim doctrines which appear to be true—but we are bound to preach just what we have received, and we preach it as beyond all doubt or cavil, absolutely true, because we have absolutely the best light upon the subject." The Baconianism that he had by then already adopted would be mitigated by his implicit assumption, given explicitly here, that the Scriptures are divine revelation and therefore the ultimate truth. He closed this letter with an additional indication of his Calvinism, this one regarding his attitude toward work. Describing the many hours he was devoting to study, visiting, and other pastoral duties, he added, "I shall have but few hours of leisure, and I want but few, for it is hard to preserve our virtue from the rust of idleness. Few men can be unoccupied and innocent at the same time."[14]

There is, in the postscript to this letter, an indication that Thornwell's views on the relationship between the Christian church and moral questions were not yet set in the form they would later so forcefully take. "Have you seen Wardlaw's Christian Ethics?" he asked Gillespie. "It is an excellent book and I think settles the question of moral obligation upon an unmovable foundation. It exposes powerfully *the unnatural separation of morality and religion* and explains clearly the exact nature and precise elements of love to God"[15] (emphasis mine).

In the journal Thornwell kept while in Lancasterville, one sees further signs of Calvinistic piety. He intended it, he wrote, to trace "my growth in grace." Feeling that he had a long way to go in this regard, he noted regularly the evidences of his need. He was too infrequently concerned, he said, with "eternal things." Nancy's brief illness made him realize that he failed to appreciate the gifts of God and to thank him sufficiently for them. He confessed to feelings of selfishness, pride, and vanity, and at times doubted "whether I am a child of God." Even his sermons were occasions for pride, rather than joy in sharing God's work. He was disturbed by temptations. "I have lately been terribly beset with the dark and horrible suggestions of the great adversary of souls. . . . My soul has been in thick

---

[14]Thornwell to James Gillespie, 13 June 1835, Thornwell Papers.

[15]Ibid.

darkness." His religion was not as satisfying as he felt it should be, and he felt responsible for this as well. While condemning the Arminianism of local Methodists from his pulpit so harshly that he later repented of offending them with his unruly tongue, he bemoaned his own lack of emotion. "My understanding assents, but my feelings are dead. My religion seems to be all in the head. Would to God it were otherwise!"[16]

It was evidently at this time that Thornwell wrote a personal "Confession of Sin," some excerpts from which will reveal just how plagued he was by the sense of depravity that was at the heart of his Calvinism.

> I. "Thou shalt have no other gods before Me."
>
> I have broken this commandment, and do continually break it, by not knowing and acknowledging God to be the only true God, and *my* God. I have been guilty of *atheism,* in ascribing to chance, or luck, or fortune, what has been brought about by the dispensations of His providence. I have been guilty of *idolatry* in several respects. 1. In worshiping self . . . 2. In worshiping *fame* . . . 3. My love of self and of fame has given rise . . . to . . . ambition. . . . I have been anxious, burningly anxious, to be regarded as the *greatest* scholar and most talented man that ever lived. Think, O my soul, upon thine atheism and idolatry!
>
> I have looked upon Him as a hard master. . . . I have broken this commandment [through] unbelief, heresy, . . . carnal delights . . . and deadness in the things of God. . . . I have also consulted the silly practice of fortune-telling.
>
> II. "Thou shalt not make unto thyself any graven image."
>
> This law requires a *spiritual* worshiper. I have made images of God in my mind, . . . and have often made light of the solemnities of worship. These two commandments present me in the awful and hell-deserving light of an atheist, an idolater, a sensualist.
>
> III. "Thou shalt not take the name of the Lord thy God in vain."
>
> I have broken this commandment by swearing; by making light of God's word. . . . This commandment requires a consistent profession of religion. Mine has not been so. I have been light, and giddy, and vain. . . . I have, for purposes of argument, and showing my own wit, misapplied and

---

[16]Thornwell, manuscript journal, quoted in Palmer, *The Life and Letters of James Henley Thornwell, D.D., LL.D.* (Richmond, 1875) 139-42, from 2 April, 14 May, 2, 4 June, 19, 30 July, and 5 September 1836. The journal is at the Presbyterian Historical Foundation in Montreat, North Carolina. Arminianism is named for Jacobus Arminius (1560-1609), who criticized Calvin's doctrine of election, arguing that all men have a chance of salvation through God's grace, and that man is not the vile being Calvin describes him to be.

perverted the word . . . of God . . . and too often, at table, my request for
a blessing is a mere mockery.
IV. "Remember the Sabbath day to keep it holy."
Every Sabbath finds me in violation of this law. My thoughts are prone
to be away from God.

Summarizing these shortcomings in a prayer at the end of his confession,
the young minister acknowledged that his heart was "rotten" and he deserved hell. "O Lord, give me a new heart; a heart to hate sin and self, to
love Thy glory in the face of Jesus Christ, and to serve Thee continually,"
he prayed.[17]

The depth of urgency that his journal and "Confession" reveal about
his own soul Thornwell transferred to the souls of his children and his congregation. To his young daughters he wrote, "You ought to beg God to
show you and make you feel that you are sinners and . . . lead you into the
way of salvation through his son." "You must begin early to fear God,"
he urged them.[18] His pulpit manner was intense. "He was very earnest,"
recalled one parishioner. "His eye kindled with intense excitement; his
whole frame quivered."[19] What he may have lacked in oratorical ability,
he gained in the presence that his deep convictions gave him. The consensus of those who commented upon his preaching was that its most notable
feature was the blending of "vigorous logic with strong emotion. He reasoned always, but never coldly."[20]

He would carry these qualities with him when, in 1837, he accepted
the position of professor and chaplain at the South Carolina College. His
sermons in the College chapel, many of which have survived, reveal perhaps an even greater solicitude for the malleable souls of his student congregation. In the classroom he was ever the logician, but in the College
pulpit he was wholly the preacher. His love and concern for his youthful
charges come through most clearly in his Commencement sermons, when
he seemed to reach out one last time with the message of saving grace.

---

[17]Thornwell's "Confession of Sin" and "Prayer," n.d., quoted in Palmer, 142-44.

[18]Thornwell to his daughters, 17 August and 12 September 1846, Anderson-Thornwell
Papers.

[19]Quoted in Palmer, 130.

[20]Thomas H. Law, in *Centennial Addresses,* 16-17. For other references to Thornwell's
pulpit style, see Palmer, *Life and Letters of Thornwell,* 131, 132, 154, 155, 424, 431, 438,
547-52.

"Think, as you go out into the world, on the things I have said as your pastor," he urged the class of 1852. May we meet "in the great day, at the right hand of God." One senses that his message to them was delivered so earnestly because it was the one he felt so in need of himself: do not let your intellectual attainments and pride stand in the way of your yielding to God's power. "Never be ashamed of the Gospel," he pleaded on another such occasion. "Let me beg you not to leave these walls without seeking that union with Christ which is the source of evangelic power."[21]

The world his students would soon enter was, for Thornwell as for Calvin, an evil place. The blend of fascination and repulsion familiar in the writings of pious Christians runs through his observations on the material world. One sees this most clearly in the letters he wrote to Nancy and others from Europe, and in his comments about Charleston while he briefly held the pastorate at the Glebe Street Church there in 1851. Even the religious community of the port city shocked him in its worldliness. "Fine houses, splendid organs, fashionable congregations, these seem to be the rage. It is not asked *what* a man preaches, but *where* he preaches, and to *whom*. . . . This state of feeling I am anxious to see thoroughly undermined." A moment later, however, he was noting the need for a larger building to house his growing congregation.[22]

The mysteries of God's providence would, Thornwell held, remain mysterious to fallen man. Consoling General Gillespie about the epidemic that had swept his plantation and infected several of his slaves, he wrote that God's judgments, "though they may be confined to individuals, . . . are equally intended for all, and the individuals immediately affected may be the wiser and better than those whom the hand of the Lord has mysteriously spared." The spiritual state of men cannot be determined by their outward condition. Yet "lessons may be extracted from every visitation of the Divine rod."[23]

There is also in Thornwell something—one might say too much—of the fanatic, and the fanatic's bigotry. Perhaps the conviction of his own guilt and inadequacy, and the resulting intensity of his religious life led

---

[21]Commencement Sermon, 6 December 1852, MS, Thornwell Papers; Commencement Sermon, n.d., Thornwell Papers.

[22]Thornwell to Thomas E. Peck, 1 July 1851, Thornwell Papers.

[23]Thornwell to James Gillespie, 6 November 1845, Thornwell Papers.

him unconsciously to a narrowness of mind where questions of faith and salvation were concerned. One scholar who is not chary of treating such matters concludes that he had a "nearly incomprehensible fear of personal damnation" that made the attainment of salvation his first priority. His convictions thus "hardened into an eerie fanaticism defensively directed against anyone who disagreed with him."[24] Another states that although "by nature as well as by training, he had a distinctly philosophical mind, . . . his strictly orthodox religious convictions gripped him so intensely as to preclude his attainment of world renown in the field of philosophy."[25] James Warley Miles, a contemporary with distinctly different religious beliefs, listed Thornwell among the "narrow-minded" men who "would brand the Apostles themselves . . . as apostates, if they did not subscribe to the Westminster Catechism or some newfangled Confession of Faith."[26] Thornwell himself recognized this aspect of his religion and that of his colleagues when he jokingly asked to be remembered to "the sour race" of Columbia Presbyterians.[27]

Certainly Thornwell was not a man to shy away from controversy, or to mince words when referring to his adversaries. The entire third volume and part of the fourth of his *Collected Writings*, as edited by his friend John Adger, are devoted to his "controversial" works, which are largely directed at various aspects of Roman Catholic theology and polity. To his fellow Presbyterian clergyman Robert Breckinridge, he explained that Catholicism was the reason for the social problems of France: "Liberty and Protestantism are the only things that can give dignity, stability and real glory to the French people. As long as they continue to be cursed with Popery, their efforts to establish free institutions must be abortive."[28] His at-

[24]William Longton, "Some Aspects of Intellectual Activity in Ante-Bellum South Carolina, 1830-1860, an Introductory Study" (Ph.D. dissertation, University of North Carolina, 1969) 248.

[25]Walter P. Brandenburg, "The Place of James Henley Thornwell in the History of Education in South Carolina" (M.A. thesis, University of South Carolina, 1939) 21.

[26]James W. Miles to David McCord, n.d., quoted in James H. Easterby, "Letters of James Warley Miles to David James McCord," *South Carolina Historical and Genealogical Magazine* 43 (1942): 190.

[27]Thornwell to F. P. Mullally, pastor of First Presbyterian Church, Columbia, 10 July 1861, Thornwell Papers.

[28]Thornwell to Robert Breckinridge, 22 August 1842; quoted in Palmer, 234. This view was confirmed, for Thornwell, by the revolutions of 1848.

tacks on Catholicism became so ferocious as to cause Bishop Patrick Lynch of Charleston to remind him that Catholics had feelings as well as Presbyterians.[29] So vitriolic did Thornwell become in commenting on his religious enemies that many references to him in the secondary literature confine themselves to these inflammatory statements. On one occasion, when addressing the Euphradean and Clariosophic societies of the South Carolina College, he described Transcendentalism as "a monster that should never have seen the light," and dismissed Kant, Fichte, and Schelling as "miserable tools in the hand of the fiend of darkness for consumating [*sic*] his black designs of malice and hate upon our wretched race!"[30]

While he was not always this exercised, one finds throughout Thornwell's published writings a mood of certainty. If read without reference to the intellectual currents of that day, these works would reveal little of the inner struggle that orthodox churchmen must have experienced as their beliefs and values were challenged. In these pieces Thornwell seems oblivious to the notion that he is dealing with questions about which good and wise men may disagree. In reflecting on the dogmatism of so much of his work, one wonders how Thornwell would have reacted to the Darwinian controversies of the postwar period, where he would have stood in the heresy trial of James Woodrow, for instance. Speculation may be fueled by knowing that those who led the fight against Woodrow's accommodation with Darwin, including John Girardeau of Columbia Seminary and Robert Dabney of Union Seminary, considered themselves to be theological disciples of Thornwell. Woodrow had perhaps equal claim to that role, however, in his insistence upon scientific inquiry as the friend of Christianity.

Perhaps no more appropriate capsule of Thornwell's Calvinism can be found than the table of contents to volumes 1 and 2 of Thornwell's *Collected Writings*. Volume 1 contains sixteen of his theological lectures. The titles of these lectures epitomize Calvinist theology:

The Being of God
Man's Natural Ignorance of God
The Nature and Limits of Our Knowledge of God
The Names of God

---

[29]Bishop Patrick N. Lynch to Thornwell, in Adger, *Collected Writings,* 3:753.

[30]Thornwell, "Address Delivered to the Euphradean and Clariosophic Societies, 1839," Thornwell Papers.

The Nature and Attributes of God
Spirituality of God
The Incommunicable Attributes of God
Creation
Man
Moral Government
The Covenant of Works
Original Sin
The State and Nature of Sin
The Pollution and Guilt of Sin
Degrees of Guilt[31]

The second volume of the *Writings,* entitled *Theological and Ethical,* includes several essays and sermons that carry the Calvinistic doctrines beyond the topics of volume 1: "Outline of the Covenant of Grace and Testimony to Sublapsarianism; Election and Reprobation; The Necessity of Atonement; The Priesthood of Christ; The Gospel, God's Power and Wisdom; The Personality of the Holy Ghost; and The Nature of Salvation."[32] One may conclude, by this, that Thornwell's theology was informed by his intense spiritual focus and by a Calvinistic viewpoint untempered by the liberalizing forces of the nineteenth century.

At the same time, however, he approached theology using the same rational mind with which he studied any other subject. Religion, he told his audience in his inaugural address as Seminary professor, "has no sanctity to protect it from the torch of a searching inquiry into its principles." There were, he cautioned, two errors that should be avoided in such inquiries. The first is that of thinking "that Theology is to be construed from consciousness—that the Divine life within us is the rule and measure of it. This is a radical mistake; it is the rule and measure of that Divine life. We must try our hearts by it, and not it by our hearts." The second error is that of bringing to theology a preconceived system and trying to harmonize the Scriptures with it. This, said Thornwell, was the error of the "New England theologians." "They have made it an appendix to their shallow and sophistical psychology, and to their still shallower and more sophistical ethics." Instead, we must "accept the facts of revelation as we

---

[31]Adger, *Collected Writings,* vol. 1, table of contents.

[32]Ibid., vol. 2, table of contents.

accept the facts of nature." By "enlightened interpretation" we "ascertain the dicta." Then we proceed to the "laws" that explain them. "But we must never forget that all cannot be explained. Our knowledge is a point, our ignorance immense. But we can know enough to glorify God, and to save our souls."[33] These statements embody Thornwell's understanding of the Scottish philosophy of Common Sense as applied to theological study.

Thornwell's confident application of man's God-given, though sin-flawed, reason to the study of nature and Scripture inevitably led him, with others, to question the verbal accuracy of holy writ. Was the Bible literally inerrant? Was every part of it equally the product of divine inspiration? Did the humanity of its authors mean that its message had been filtered through their limited minds? How far may geological data be allowed to modify our interpretation of Scripture without fatally weakening its power as the bulwark of morality, the primary source of our knowledge of God, and hence the key to salvation? These and other such questions would lead to crises in Christianity in the decades following the Civil War, but they were already troubling many thinkers by the early nineteenth century.

The problem was not new. The Protestant Reformation had set the stage for it by asserting the individual Christian's obligation, and ability, to read and arrive at his understanding of the Bible. John Calvin had labored over the above questions and concluded that the doctrine of the literal infallibility of Scripture was not true. The Bible's message had to be accessible to all, and therefore it must have been written in the vernacular, or in such a way as to be understandable to laymen. So, Calvin reasoned, the astronomical concepts of Joshua and Genesis need not disturb us by their conflict with those of Galileo. The Bible does contain various errors, Calvin noted. As a trivial example, in Deuteronomy 10:22 it states that seventy people went with Jacob into Egypt, but in Acts 7:14 the number is given as seventy-five. Calvin attributed the inconsistency to the use of faulty Greek transcriptions of the Old Testament by Luke, the author of Acts.[34] While he noted other examples of this type of inaccuracy, Calvin emphasized the importance of focusing on the profound message of the Bible and

---

[33]Ibid., 1:579, 82.

[34]John Calvin, Commentary on Acts 7:14, in Corp. Ref. 75; cited in R. Hooykaas, *Religion and the Rise of Modern Science* (Grand Rapids MI, 1972) 117-22.

not becoming pedantic where details are concerned. Yet the thrust of Calvin's teaching was in conflict with this view, for he wrote so forcefully on the power and omniscience of God that his followers concluded that His Word must be infallible.

Thornwell was thus a typical Calvinist in his own uncertainty on this question. He asserted his belief in the plenary inspiration of the Bible. In 1849 he described his view of the Bible's genesis with the phrase "verbal dictation," adding that this is the only conception that "makes the Bible what it professes to be—the Word of God." Take away this principle and everything is in jeopardy, he insisted.

> Any hypothesis which sets aside Divine testimony to every statement and doctrine of the Bible is inconsistent with the exercise of that faith which the Scriptures exact. . . . If [the Bible's] contents, in any instances, however insignificant, rest only upon the testimony of the human agents employed in writing it, in those instances we can only believe in man; the statements may be true, but they cease to be Divine and infallible, and the assent which we yield to them becomes opinion and not faith.[35]

The biblical authors, in this view, were simply human conduits through which the divine message was delivered to man. Yet Thornwell's rational mind could not hold consistently to this position. His reading of Scripture and of the works of other theologians led him to accept the use of textual criticism, or "lower criticism," which is concerned with the authenticity of biblical texts and thus with the problems of translation and the evolution of word meanings.[36] In his lectures at Columbia Seminary in the late 1850s, Thornwell took the position that the fullest possible understanding of Scripture involved not only the careful study of the words themselves, but also the rational investigation of their evolution through various texts. In company with such conservative Southern theologians as George Howe and Robert L. Dabney, he argued that the pursuit of the original text was a necessary part of biblical exegesis. All three men, for example, recognized

---

[35]Adger, *Collected Writings*, 3:9-77; quotation is on 51. Thornwell, "The Standard and Nature of Religion; a Review of Morrell's Philosophy of Religion, Section 1, an External Standard Vindicated," *Southern Presbyterian Review* 3:2 (September 1849): 249-321.

[36]Thornwell, "Cannon" and "Inspiration," Thornwell Collection, Presbyterian Historical Foundation; cited in Holifield, *The Gentlemen Theologians*, 96. Thornwell, "Revelation and Inspiration," *Southern Presbyterian Review* 9:4 (April 1856): 555-81.

that the last line of the Lord's Prayer, in Matthew 6:13, is a later addition to the original.[37]

Such recognition inevitably led Thornwell to the questions that new geological studies were raising about Scripture, especially the creation story in Genesis. Influenced by the work of the Scottish theologian Thomas Chalmers (1780-1847), Thornwell and other Southern Presbyterians gradually came to the view that the six days of Genesis were the conclusion of a process stretching over eons and climaxing with the creation of man.[38] Having accepted this proto-Darwinian concept, would Thornwell have proceeded to investigate and make an accommodation with Darwin himself? I cannot do more than guess here, but clearly Thornwell's rationality was restricted by his faith in the Bible; hence it seems likely that Thornwell would have stood with the conservatives had he lived long enough to take part in their debate. Had he stood by his own words in his inaugural address at the Seminary, he would have at least remained open to new thought. He told that audience that we can never have "an adequate knowledge of God," and for this reason theology cannot be a pure science. Likewise, "Our science can never transcend our faculties. All our knowledge is relative and phenomenal, measured by our faculties and confined to appearances. But as far as it goes it is real—phenomena are not a sham; they are the indications of realities which transcend themselves and are enhanced by faith."[39]

---

[37]Holifield, *The Gentlemen Theologians*, 98. Thornwell, MS lecture on Colossians, ch. 1, Thornwell Papers.

[38]Holifield, *The Gentlemen Theologians*, 99. "The Late Dr. Chalmers," *Southern Presbyterian Review* 1:3 (December 1847): 56-89. "The Six Days of Creation," *Southern Quarterly Review* n.s. 1, no. 1 (April 1856), probably by George Holmes. See Thornwell to Holmes, 17 June 1856, Holmes Letterbook, Perkins Library, Duke University.

[39]Thornwell, "Inaugural Address," in Adger, *Collected Writings*, 577-78. A list of discussion questions Thornwell used in teaching his classes at the seminary demonstrates the thorough examination of the conflict between Scripture and geology to which his students were subjected. MS of class questions, n.d., Thornwell Papers. For a glimpse at the evolving view of a leading nineteenth-century clergyman-scientist, see Stanley M. Guralnick, "Geology and Religion before Darwin: The Case of Edward Hitchcock, Theologian and Geologist (1793-1864)," in Nathan Reingold, ed., *Science in America since 1820* (New York, 1976) 116-130. Hitchcock began his career as a confident synthesizer of science and Scripture, but retreated, by the late 1850s, to the view that religion need not stand or fall on its compatibility with geology. In this he pointed to the view that would eventually dominate Protestant thought. See esp. 129-30.

The views expressed above, and Thornwell's theology in general, betray the influence of Scottish Common Sense philosophy. He had first encountered this school at about the age of sixteen when he came across a copy of Dugald Stewart's *Elements of the Philosophy of the Human Mind* in General Gillespie's library. He would later tell Benjamin Palmer that as he read it, he "felt that his fortune was now made." Palmer called the book "the pivot upon which his whole intellectual history subsequently hinged."[40] Late in life Thornwell told George Frederick Holmes that his interest in philosophy had been kindled by reading Stewart and that he still admired him.[41] Within a month after arriving at the South Carolina College, he encountered the works of Berkeley and Hume, and wrote his mentor that he was exploring the "train of reasoning by which matter and spirit are proved to be nonentities." He found it "ingenious enough, although it depends entirely upon a hypothesis which philosophers have assumed without the slightest evidence, viz, that the mind does not perceive anything but its own ideas." This leads to the conclusion that nothing exists but ideas. "The absurdity of the conclusion should have led them to suspect their premises." "It is amusing to observe into what a labyrinth of perplexities men may involve themselves," the seventeen-year-old Thornwell submitted.[42] He would soon conclude that such views were not only absurd, but dangerous, and would find in the Scottish philosophy an effective antidote to them.

By the time Thornwell enrolled in college in 1829, this philosophy had spread far beyond its American hub, Princeton. While one of his two favorite professors, Thomas Cooper, ridiculed it, the other, Robert Henry, became its firm proponent and introduced his classes to the works of Thomas Reid, Dugald Stewart, and company.[43] Young Thornwell's respect for Henry was great and would grow with the passing time and the crystallization of his own philosophy. Many years later he would memorialize his old professor as "the most eminent scholar in this State . . . to whom, more than any other man, living or dead, we are indebted for the

---

[40]Palmer, 45.

[41]Thornwell to George Frederick Holmes, 7 July 1857; quoted ibid., 411.

[42]Thornwell to James Gillespie, 24 January 1830; quoted ibid., 66.

[43]Holifield, *The Gentlemen Theologians,* 120.

direction of our own studies, and for whatsoever culture . . . our mind has received.''

Henry was born in Charleston in 1792, the year his parents arrived from the West Indies. His father was Scottish and his mother English. Robert was tutored by the Reverend Buist, a University of Edinburgh graduate who assumed the pulpit of Charleston's First (Scotch) Presbyterian Church about 1800. He later received the M.A. degree from Edinburgh himself, in 1814. There he studied under Thomas Brown, a student of Dugald Stewart who had succeeded him in the chair of moral philosophy. While in Scotland, Henry met William Hamilton, who would become the leading spokesman for the Scottish school in Thornwell's time. He was ordained a minister by the Charleston Presbytery in 1817, and the next year he joined the faculty of the South Carolina College as professor of moral philosophy and logic. His emphasis on the primacy of logic in the curriculum bore fruit, said Thornwell, in the ''general tendencies of mind which the statesmen and scholars of the commonwealth [of South Carolina] have confessedly exhibited.''[44] The seed planted by Henry was nurtured at Andover, especially in the classes of Moses Stuart and Leonard Woods, Jr.[45] Though Thornwell had thought Andover's theology ''awfully New School,'' he did admire Stuart, whom he called ''the only able man in the institution.''[46] Stuart, a student of Timothy Dwight at Yale, ''spent his life defending the Bible from every kind of critic.'' He taught that man's rational nature and hermeneutical skills are God-given, and that God expects man to use these skills in interpreting His revelation.[47] Stuart took what, for Thornwell, was too liberal a view in arguing that geology and Genesis could possibly contradict one another. Stuart believed that Moses, the supposed author of the

---

[44]Thornwell, ''Memoir of Dr. Henry,'' *Southern Quarterly Review* n.s. 1, no. 1 (April 1856): 189-206. The quotation is on 196.

[45]Herbert Hovenkamp, *Science and Religion in America, 1800-1860* (Philadelphia, 1979) 20, 28-29.

[46]Thornwell to Gillespie, 13 August 1834; quoted in Palmer, 115.

[47]Hovenkamp, *Science and Religion in America,* 62-63. Moses Stuart, ''Are the Same Principles of Interpretation to Be Applied to Scripture as to Other Books?'' *American Biblical Repository* 2 (1832): 124-37. Stuart's answer was ''yes.'' See also Edward Hitchcock, ''The Connection between Geology and Natural Religion,'' *American Biblical Repository* 5 (1835): 113-38.

Pentateuch, was not writing science. "Inspiration," he said, "does not make men omnicient [*sic*]."[48]

While rejecting this idea, Thornwell did find Stuart's cautious approval of man's rationalism in the study of God's world and Word compatible with his own rational mind. For him, as Brooks Holifield has said, Scottish Realism provided a way of demonstrating both the possibility, and the necessity, of natural theology.[49] In Thornwell's words, "The man who has pondered, and is prepared to answer aright the question, what can we know? is the only man who is furnished against the temptations" of rational skepticism.[50] To employ the language of philosophy, Thornwell liked Scottish Realism because it provided a middle way between the equally dangerous extremes of sensationalism and idealism. Idealists believed that reason could solve all mysteries and thus render revelation unnecessary, or prove it fraudulent. Sensationalists, following Locke, became skeptical of anything not perceived by the senses, including the supernatural.[51]

In the mind of Thornwell, philosophy and theology shared almost equal appeal. He loved the one and was so grounded in the other that he was compelled to view life through its perspective. As the philosopher he could say, in an essay entitled "The Love of Truth," "There is no principle which needs to be more strenuously inculcated, than that evidence alone should be the measure of assent." "Whatever opinions we hold that are not the offspring of evidence . . . are not held by us in the spirit of truth." "They are helps to our faith, but should never be made the props for it."[52] As the theologian, he opened his course on the Evidences of Christianity at the South Carolina College by cautioning his students that it was not the purpose of this course to prove the teachings of the faith. "We accept our re-

---

[48]Quoted in Hovenkamp, *Science and Religion in America*, 81. This is the view that Columbia Seminary professor James Woodrow would eventually arrive at in the 1880s.

[49]Holifield, *The Gentlemen Theologians*, 120.

[50]Thornwell to Matthew J. Williams, 26 August 1850; quoted in Palmer, 344. See also Maximilian LaBorde, *History of the South Carolina College* (Columbia, 1859) 335-36, 340-43.

[51]Thornwell, "The Office of Reason in Regard to Revelation," *Southern Presbyterian Review* 1 (1847): 33. Thornwell found much to admire in Immanuel Kant's *Critique of Pure Reason*. Holifield, *The Gentlemen Theologians*, 121.

[52]Thornwell, "The Love of Truth," *The Library of Southern Literature*, vol. 12 (Atlanta, 1907) 5311-12.

ligion,'' he told his classes, ''not as the result of speculation or philosophical thought. We have not reasoned it out for ourselves.'' ''We receive it upon the authority of God. We accept it as a Divine Revelation. The design of [the course] is to show that it is justly accepted in that character.''[53] The common ground between these two positions is that man has been given a powerful intellect and is expected to use it in testing the truth of what he is asked to believe; yet such tests must, because of man's flawed nature, be conducted within carefully constructed rules of inquiry, with experience and evidence taking precedence over abstract speculation. His thought, like that of the Scottish school, recognized the possibility, the necessity, and the ultimate insufficiency of natural theology. It was a valuable adjunct to revelation, but only that; human limitations prevented it from being more. The theologian stood on divine revelation, while philosophy helped him maintain his balance. Thornwell summarized this middle way when he wrote, ''Of the infinite, we know that it is, though we do not know what it is.''[54]

It was both fitting, and indicative of antebellum Presbyterian thought, that the lead article in the first issue of the *Southern Presbyterian Review* was Thornwell's exploration of ''The Office of Reason in Regard to Revelation.''[55] For ten years he had been presenting his views on this question to classes at the College, and here he set them forth for a wider audience. The essay reveals not only Thornwell's middle-ground position regarding faith and reason, but also his firm confidence in the compatibility of the teachings of natural and revealed theology. John Adger would later summarize Thornwell's argument this way: Reason, when applied to the supernatural, ''may prove but cannot refute—in the Natural, she may refute, but cannot establish.''[56] No Christian should fear the power of science or true reason, Thornwell asserted, for

Not a single contradiction to any principle of science and philosophy can

---

[53]Thornwell, ''Opening Lecture to the Junior Class in the Evidences of Christianity,'' MS, n.d., Thornwell Papers.

[54]Adger, *Collected Writings*, 2:609. See also ''On the Being of God,'' 4, notes on a lecture by Thornwell, MS in Thornwell Papers.

[55]Thornwell, ''The Office of Reason in Regard to Revelation,'' *Southern Presbyterian Review* 1 (June 1847): 1-33.

[56]Adger, *Collected Writings*, 3:183.

be justly imputed to the Records of Christianity. Time was when infidelity exulted in the prospect of reading the doom of the Gospel in the mysteries of the stars; but astronomy now is made subservient to its glory. . . . Then the bowels of the earth were ransacked, and some secret voice was invoked from the monuments of faded races and past generations to give the lie to the narrative of Moses, but Nature, in all her caverns, answered back to the testimony of inspiration.[57]

These views were aired for a generation of students at the South Carolina College, and indeed at most other Southern schools as well. For the course in the Evidences of Christianity was a standard part of the antebellum curriculum. Stephen Elliott introduced the course in Columbia in 1831, and Thornwell succeeded him as its professor in 1837. The textbooks for the course, also standard throughout the South, were Joseph Butler, *Analogy of Religion, Natural and Revealed, to the Constitution and Courses of Nature* (1736), and William Paley, *Evidences of Christianity* (1794). Butler's book, whose theme was that biblical revelation was consistent with God's manifestation in nature, was a standard text as late as the mid-1850s. Thornwell used it in spite of what he saw as its "glaring defects."[58] Paley's book, which Thornwell thought more highly of, was a response to Hume's skepticism. It built a voluminous case for the reliability of the biblical authors and the logical consistency of the Scriptures with each other.[59]

One gets the impression from Thornwell's admiration for the Scottish school that he was simply another of its many mouthpieces in antebellum America. But when one looks further into his writings, and especially into his lectures and essays on metaphysics, it is clear that this is not the case. Indeed, it may be argued that Thornwell was the first, or among the first American orthodox theologians to break, at least partially, with the Baconianism of the Scottish school. Theodore D. Bozeman has noted that in 1855 Sir David Brewster challenged the notion that only inductive investigation could lead to sound scientific knowledge. Successful hypotheses may have any origin, "fancy" included, he argued. The important thing is not where they originate, but whether they can stand up to empirical ex-

---

[57]Ibid., 219-20.

[58]Thornwell to Robert J. Breckinridge, 27 January 1841; quoted in Palmer, 223-24.

[59]Holifield, *The Gentlemen Theologians,* 90-95. Thornwell, "Historical Evidences," a lecture on Paley, in "Notes on Lectures by Thornwell and Palmer," MS, Thornwell Papers.

amination. According to Bozeman, it was not until the latter 1860s that Harvard's Chauncey Wright brought this view into the American orthodox theological debate.[60] However, the same caveat on the inductive method was made by Thornwell in lectures to his South Carolina College classes in metaphysics, probably in the early 1840s.[61]

While beginning this course with the usual (for orthodox Christians) emphasis on the critical importance of Bacon's method, he quickly moved beyond this point. The first lecture informed the students: "It was not until the influence of the true principles of philosophical investigation began to be felt and carried out, in consequence of the impetus given by Lord Bacon to the world, that any real advances were made." As a result of Bacon's work, and the subsequent efforts of the Scots, "It is now universally conceded," he continued, "that the same laws of investigation which are essential to success in . . . physical science are equally necessary in . . . the study of the mind."[62] In the second lecture, however, he went beyond this, arguing that "in addition to observation and experience, valuable assistance may be derived from hypothesis and analogical conjecture. They give our observations an aim and a purpose." He quickly added that "no hypothesis should be rested in or received as true until it has been confirmed by a large and copious induction." We must be careful, he cautioned, not to confuse "the ingenious with the profound."

Thornwell found several examples of the proper use of hypothesis buttressed by evidence. "The theory of gravity took rise from a fortunate conjecture suggested by analogy. The Copernican system . . . was only a hypothesis until confirmed by subsequent experiment. Franklin's discovery of the identity of lightning and electricity" grew out of his conjectures, as did Harvey's "discovery of the circulation of the blood." He added that the view of the complementary roles of hypothesis and induction was common in the latest philosophical thought. He, though, was evidently among the few orthodox theologians of the antebellum era who were willing to concede even this much to the speculative German thinkers whose flights of fancy could be so dangerous to orthodox teachings.[63]

---

[60]Theodore Dwight Bozeman, *Protestants in an Age of Science: The Baconian Ideal and Antebellum Religious Thought* (Chapel Hill, 1977) 166-67.

[61]"Lectures on Metaphysics," MS, n.d., Thornwell Papers.

[62]Ibid., "Lecture First."

[63]Ibid., "Lecture Second."

Finding that all modern thinkers have their ancient counterparts, Thornwell saw nineteenth-century German metaphysics as a restatement of elements of Plato's thought. Aware of his incompatibility with these contemporary rationalists, he naturally identified himself with the more empirical Aristotle. Yet even Plato, if studied with one eye on the limits of human reason, could be edifying to the Christian thinker, he conceded. In his "Plato's Phaedon," written while he edited the *Southern Quarterly Review* and published in that journal in 1856, he explores some of the teachings of the great philosopher. This work, which is subtitled "Concerning the Soul," he found to be "an important contribution to natural theology." In it Socrates is near death and tries to explain to his students why he is so serene about it. The theme is that death is a blessing to the good man, because through it he enters the purer life of the soul. Why does he believe this? To the argument that the soul may perish with the body, Socrates replies that what existed before birth will logically survive death. Why does he believe the soul existed before the body? "We have the idea of equality [an odd choice of quotation by Thornwell]—an idea which never fluctuates nor changes." Such an idea has no true example in nature, nor do the good, the beautiful, and the just. "They were in the mind before . . . and experience does nothing but furnish the occasions on which they are revived. . . . Man, consequently, must have existed in a previous state, and all true knowledge is reminiscence."[64] Thornwell concurred.

> We believe that there is a necessary connection between immortality and knowledge, when knowledge is taken in that high sense in which it is discussed by Plato. We would use the connection as a proof of the existence of God. . . . Eternal truth implies an Eternal Mind. . . . If knowledge of God is necessarily connected with immortality, it is extremely credible that in giving man one, He designs for him the other also.[65]

Man's goal, Socrates told his students, is to reach a harmony with Truth. "Real truth," explained Thornwell, "that which alone was worthy of the name, and which could be dignified as knowledge, was conversant only with the permanent, the unchanging, the eternal." It could be approached only by going beyond the world of appearances, and this can be done only

---

[64]Thornwell, "Plato's Phaedon," *Southern Quarterly Review*, n.s. 1 (August 1856): 416, 417, 419, 423-25.

[65]Ibid., 426.

by living a philosophical life. In this view Thornwell finds a pagan harbinger of the teachings of Jesus. "Socrates insists, as the indespensible [*sic*] condition of philosophy, upon what in a wider, though analogous sense, our Savior makes the indespensible condition of salvation—the crucifixion of the flesh." Plato's world of senses and world of truth find their Christian analogies in the world of depravity and the world of God. Self-denial is the path from the former to the latter. "We can trace in this philosophy a yearning after, and a preintimation of the wisdom which descended in Jesus," Thornwell concluded.[66]

Thornwell's Seminary lectures on theology shed more light on his view of reason. Here he chooses to place himself between what he sees as the equally misguided poles of Roman Catholic and "Rationalist" theology. The former he finds unacceptable because it requires that the individual relinquish his rational freedom and adopt the views of the Church hierarchy, while the latter errs by relying totally upon human reason and thus making theology a branch of philosophy. For orthodox Protestant theology, he argues, the Bible is the ultimate authority, but human reason is employed in its interpretation.[67] As for the relationship between reason and revelation, he poses a rhetorical question:

> Can there be an accredited revelation which contains things which are contradictory to reason? If by reason we are here to understand the complement of those primitive truths and cognitions, with the legitimate deductions from them, which enter into the universal consciousness of the race, spontaneously considered, there is and can be but one answer. These fundamental facts of consciousness cannot be set aside without annihilating all intelligence. To deny them, or to question them, is to reduce all knowledge to zero, or to skepticism. No revelation, therefore, can contradict them, without committing an act of suicide; it would destroy the very condition under which alone it can be known and received as a revelation.

But when basic laws of intelligence are not violated, reason alone is not competent to judge a revelation false. Being flawed by sin, human reason is finite. We do not reject everything we cannot explain.[68]

---

[66]Ibid., 421, 422, 423.

[67]Thornwell, "Lecture One," "Preliminary Observations" (lectures on theology), in Adger, *Collected Writings*, 1:43-45, 48.

[68]Ibid., 50-52; quotation is on 50.

In his third lecture on metaphysics, Thornwell came to grips with the Scottish school directly. The first difficulty he found was that they were unnecessarily confusing on some of their points, not the least of which was the term that gave them their name. ''The pure reason of Kant is only another name for the common sense of Dr. Reid,'' he suggested. On a more substantial level, he contended that if reason, or common sense, is as universal and infallible as Reid implies, then ''every man is under the constant and infallible guidance of Heaven.'' Hence reason being infallible, man can answer all questions. Such logic had already produced its subversive fruits in the writings of Cousin, Thornwell noted. Cousin held that intuition is the highest degree of knowledge. This idea could result in every man resorting to his own intuition for obtaining ''truth'' or for rejecting someone else's ''truth,'' and thus lead to philosophical chaos. Thornwell joked that this put too much faith in reason, but quickly returned to the seriousness that this matter demanded. This notion of reason as God's visitation of the individual creates ''what we call enthusiasm,'' or ''the breath of God within us; it is immediate intuition [as] opposed to induction and demonstration. . . . It is impossible to express in any adequate names the extent to which I conceive these principles to be dangerous. They hoist the floodgates of fanaticism, licentiousness and crime, and sanctify the most outrageous abominations of human fancy and conceit under the hallowed name of inspiration.''[69]

Turning from Reid to his disciple Dugald Stewart, Thornwell found a philosopher with whom he was much more comfortable. First, he improved on the awkward term ''common sense'' by referring to ''the fundamental laws of human belief.'' These, said Stewart, ''are tacitly acknowledged by all men learned or ignorant without any formal enunciation in words or even any conscious exercise of reflection.'' These laws ''are not the first principles . . . from which all our knowledge is derived,'' said Thornwell, paraphrasing Stewart. Seeking a metaphor with which to make the point to his class, he suggested that these ''intuitive truths . . . are to our faculties exactly what light is to the eye—they do not create the objects, but enable us to see them—they do not supply us with ideas, but enable us to judge them.'' What, then, are these self-evident truths?

---

[69]''Third Lecture,'' ibid. Another example of Thornwell's criticism of the Scottish philosophy is in ''Lecture Two'' on theology, in Adger, *Collected Writings,* 1:57.

"We believe intuitively in the informations of our consciousness, and the facts of memory. These confirm belief in existence. We believe our faculties and therefore we believe all their disclosures." Coming to the view that coincided with his own, he continued, "All truth resolves itself ultimately into a matter of faith. We believe, because we feel determined to believe by the laws of our own nature—the constitution of our minds." In our thinking and investigation, "If we did not [eventually] stop at a matter of faith . . . there would be an infinite series in all our deductions and consequently there would be no possibility of ever arriving at a conviction of certainty." Finally, we "believe because we cannot help believing."[70] Rising to the climax of his lecture, the professor expostulated,

> In reviewing this subject we cannot avoid the conviction so humbling to the pride of human reason and so mortifying to the vanity of the skeptic, that all our intellectual arguments are ultimately resolvable into faith. Intuition resolves itself into the constitution of our nature, and [this] resolves itself into the will of God. To rely upon the faculties which our Creator has given us, is, in effect to rely upon the veracity of the Creator himself; and he that will believe nothing must rest content with being hopelessly ignorant of everything.

Reason and faith, then, are not rivals but partners in the intellectual process. Thornwell would say with the medieval scholastic, "We must believe in order to understand."[71]

A close reading of the preceding paragraph reveals a fundamental inconsistency which, as several modern scholars have shown, marred the philosophical position that orthodox theologians took in the antebellum era. While they virtually sanctified Sir Francis Bacon and advocated the Baconian method as a safeguard against unstructured speculation, they did not practice it. Or rather, they practiced it with a single exception so glaring as to call into question all they said in its behalf. John Adger said that among the last statements uttered by his old friend Thornwell was the one he had used so often in his classes. "You have stated your position—now prove it." To Adger, these words symbolized the Baconian orientation of Thornwell's mind. Opinions are useless without factual evidence derived from experience or careful induction. But what constituted "proof" for

---

[70]Ibid.

[71]Ibid.

Thornwell, or for orthodox theologians generally? Baconianism insists upon proof from experience and observation of nature. Metaphysics finds proof in reasoned argument. Thornwell granted the place of both processes, as we have seen, but added a third, which he placed in a position at least equal to these. This was the Word of an omnipotent and omniscient God. This "given," the Bible as the infallible word of God, circumscribed free inquiry for the orthodox Christian, and to this extent impinged upon his Baconianism. One evening Thornwell and his colleague Benjamin Palmer were locked in deep metaphysical dialogue when Thornwell suddenly interjected, "You know, Palmer, if there is but one passage of Scripture against us, our speculations must go to the winds."[72]

Thornwell, in company with rational Christian thinkers through the centuries, felt the need to build a rational proof of the existence of God as a foundation for his theology. Still, behind all of this sometimes tortured prose lay the "self-evident truth" of God. With most of these thinkers, the same rational process could lead beyond the assertion of God's existence to a description of His nature. Once established, these became implicit assumptions, which thus limited the Baconian methodology these men could employ. This point is made very succinctly, though exaggeratedly, by Herbert Hovenkamp. "Two things are quite clear about American religion and science in the 1820's and 1830's," he writes.

> First, Americans were very excited about something they called the 'empirical' or 'Baconian' method of acquiring factual knowledge, and many believed that this method was the only one a Christian could use. Secondly, for all the excitement, no one had a clear idea of how to go about using the method. 'Baconianism' was not really a tool; it was a symbol— something to use in the opening paragraph of an essay in order to show that one was on guard against rationalism, deism, speculative science, or anything else that might approach infidelity.

Having thus covered oneself, one could then proceed to "do Christian metaphysics in the same way it had been done for nearly two thousand years."[73]

---

[72]Palmer, 545. Palmer's *Thornwell* was published in 1875, and as a conservative he may, if only subconsciously, have used his mentor to defend his views.

[73]Hovenkamp, *Science in an Age of Reason,* 26-27. Drew Faust found that her circle of Old South intellectuals—Simms, Hammond, Holmes, and Tucker—preached Bacon without practicing him in their approach to history. Drew Faust, *A Sacred Circle; The Dilemma of the Intellectual in the Old South, 1840-1860* (Baltimore, 1978) 70-71, 84-86. Hovenkamp concedes that by 1850 Baconians were producing works that were less like medieval theology and more like natural science. Hovenkamp, 44.

Such intellectual game playing was no doubt common, but Hovenkamp obscures an important point when he concludes that antebellum theologians generally were merely hiding their closed minds behind a Baconian facade. The most significant thing about the widespread homage to Bacon and his method among the clergy was that it demonstrated the confidence they had in the veracity of revelation and its ultimate consistency with nature. Natural theology did begin to appear vulnerable toward the end of the antebellum period, as more thinkers supported Kant's view that we cannot deal with the unobservable in a scientific way, and as pre-Darwinian geology and biology made ever-more ominous suggestions about natural history. The full effects of these challenges would come after the Civil War. During the 1850s, especially in the South, the dominant orthodox clergy still retained enough confidence in natural theology to see science as an ally. Theologian-scientist Edward Hitchcock's career as professor of "natural theology and geology" and president of Amherst College indicates the "belief of the day that a good natural theologian is also a competent scientist."[74]

Yet to return to Thornwell, his lectures on metaphysics place him somewhat outside the mainstream of orthodox thought in terms of confidence in natural theology. He was less optimistic than many regarding man's ability to answer, through the Baconian method, any and all scientific questions. Here his Calvinism subdued his intellectual pride. Further, he was more willing than others to allow for the value of speculation and abstract rational thought in assisting and directing the course of scientific investigation. So on both of these counts, Thornwell was a less than wholehearted Baconian.[75]

Still, he seems to have been unable to resist the desire to defend the faith with the tools of science when he saw it being attacked from that quarter. In 1856, while editing the *Southern Quarterly Review,* he published an essay in that journal on "Miracles." It was a response to the attacks on the reliability of the biblical record where supernatural occurrences were concerned; and it employed, or attempted to employ, the methodology of science. That it fails to satisfy the modern mind may be readily admitted. Yet it reveals careful thought and a certain scientific perspective. Nothing is more repugnant to the mind of the modern skeptic than the bib-

---

[74]Hovenkamp, *Science in an Age of Reason,* 47.

[75]See Thornwell's "Lectures on Metaphysics."

lical accounts of miraculous events, Thornwell begins. Attempting to accommodate itself to the intellectual currents of the day, the Church has in some quarters engaged in various contortions on this subject, which amount to "the church making its Christ, and not Christ his church." The German theologian Friedrich Schleiermacher (1768-1834) exemplified this trend, seeking a Jesus who was "the archtype [*sic*] of perfect humanity," and whose superior knowledge of nature enabled him to do things that seemed miraculous. David Friedrich Strauss (1808-1874), another liberal theologian, contended that the New Testament was, in Thornwell's words, merely the "drapery in which a grand idea is represented," and that the idea may be accepted without the drapery.[76]

Thornwell's view of these rationalists was that they want "a religion which promises to satisfy the longings of their nature, without demanding an extraordinary faith, which meets their wants without repressing the freedom of speculation. . . . The divine with them is only the true, and the true is that which authenticates itself to [their] souls." They want, he contends, the impossible. Their faith is not the path to salvation. "We hope," he replies, "that religion can be reconciled with science upon a safer and easier plain than the sacrifice of either." The subject of miracles, he admits, is fraught with difficulty. Anticipating Mark Twain, he continues, "Suppose an unprincipled man of science should go among savages, and find that his attainments could give to him the distinction of being the great power of God, would God arrest his exhibitions, because they were deceiving and cheating the ignorant multitudes?" No, he answers. So we are right to be skeptical where the "unnatural" is concerned.[77]

Biblical miracles, he suggests, are of two kinds: those that "carry their credentials upon their face," and those that do not. The story of Jesus walking on water he places in the latter category. But "with a few trifling exceptions . . . we feel instinctively that they are of a character . . . which

---

[76]Thornwell, "Miracles," *Southern Quarterly Review,* n.s. 1 (August 1856): 347-82. This was reprinted in the *Southern Presbyterian Review* 10 (July 1857): 161-201. Such works were common productions of antebellum natural theology. See, for example, Edward Hitchcock, *The Religion of Geology and Its Connected Sciences* (Glasgow, 1851); idem, "Special Divine Interpositions in Nature," *Bibliotheca Sacra and Biblical Repository* 11 (1851): 776-800. Thornwell's essay was a review of three recent publications on the same subject. Quotations from it are on 345 and 346.

[77]Ibid., 346, 347, 348, 360.

render the supposition of secondary cause ridiculously absurd.'' In this category he puts the miracles of Jesus, the parting of the Red Sea, and the Manna from heaven. Regarding these, he finds ''no room for doubt.''

Turning from defense to the more-comfortable position of attack, he insists that it is ''incumbent upon the rationalists to show how God is precluded from a privilege, which, so far as we know, pertains to all other personal existences,'' that is, the act of communication, which is essentially what a miracle is. ''We are bound to believe, upon competent testimony, what is not *demonstrably impossible*.'' When competent and sincere witnesses testify to the occurrence of an event, we must, barring contradictory evidence, accept it. People with working senses saw Lazarus raised from the dead and testified to the fact. David Hume's unwillingness to accept this, his skepticism in general, is ''in fatal contradiction to the whole genius and spirit of the inductive philosophy.'' We must apply our sound faculties and accept what they report to be true. Otherwise the new or extraordinary would never be accepted. Certainly no one should presume to judge the reliability of widely believed accounts. ''To make a limited and uniform experience the measure of existence is to deny that experience itself is progressive, and to reduce all ages and generations to a heartless stagnation of science. . . . If Hume's laws were the laws of philosophy, where would have been the sciences of chemistry . . . electricity, geology . . . the Copernican theory of the heavens?'' The record being unfolded by geology reveals a God who not only created, says Thornwell, but intervened in ''successive periods.'' ''That science which at its early dawn was hailed as the handmaiden of infidelity and skepticism . . . has turned the whole strength of its resources against the fundamental principle of Rationalism. . . . The geologist begins with miracles, every epoch in his science repeats the number, and the whole earth is to his mind vocal with the name.''[78] Thornwell closed his essay in a burst of confident assertion.

> Future generations will wonder that in the nineteenth century men gravely disputed whether God could interpose, in the direct exercise of His power, in the world He has made. The miracle, a century hence, will be made as credible as any common fact. Let the earth be explored; let its physical history be traced, and a mighty voice will come to us, from the tombs of its

---

[78]Ibid., 361-62, 365, 366, 367, 370, 372, 373, 375.

perished races, testifying, in a thousand instances, to the miraculous hand of God. Geology and the Bible must kiss and embrace each other, and this youngest daughter of science, will be found, like the eastern magi, bringing her votive offerings to the cradle of the prince of peace. The earth can never turn traitor to its God, and its stones have already begun to cry out against those who attempt to extract from them a lesson of infidelity and atheism.[79]

Here, then, was one theologian who had found a middle way on epistemological questions, which enabled him to utilize natural theology as the harmonizer of science and Scripture. If the pursuit of knowledge could be conducted within the guidelines of the Thornwellian paradigm, the Christian faith and the Church that articulated its moral traditions need not fear the advance of science. That he remained apprehensive on this point was the result of the continued "misuse" of science, in his view. Thornwell would continue, often at the urging of others, to write and speak on the themes presented above.[80] But he would also grow increasingly cynical as to the social and moral impact of the new science and the theological liberalism that grew up in response to it in Europe and in the North. "Irreligion is now a religion," he told his seminary students.[81] "We shall have some desperate battles to fight with false brethren, before the enemy is subdued," he wrote a friend. "The world will be on their side. They will make the impression that they are very learned and profound; and that their opponents are equally ignorant and shallow, mistaking the spirit of bigotry for the spirit of religion. Reproaches of this sort . . . are part of the cross which attaches to discipleship in our day," he concluded.[82] As his conception of this struggle began to focus more clearly on the country's regional differences, Thornwell would soon look favorably upon the suggestion that the South should insulate itself, politically and ecclesiastically, from the outside world.

---

[79]Ibid., 382.

[80]George F. Holmes, the Virginia intellectual with whom Thornwell formed a friendship based on shared interests and views, urged him to continue his work on natural theology with a study on "The Divine Economy of the Universe." Holmes to Thornwell, 5 September 1856, Holmes Letterbook, Perkins Library, Duke University.

[81]Thornwell, "Inaugural Discourse," 582.

[82]Thornwell to Matthew J. Williams, 26 August 1850; quoted in Palmer, 344.

CHAPTER **5**

The Philosopher-
Theologian
and His World

John C. Calhoun is said to have remarked, after a long conversation with James Thornwell in Pendleton, South Carolina, in the summer of 1843, that he "expected to find Dr. Thornwell perfectly posted upon his own department of study; but when he came over into mine, I was not prepared for the thorough acquaintance he exhibited with all the topics that are generally familiar only to statesmen."[1] Calhoun should not have been so surprised, for a wide-ranging knowledge was not unusual among the liberally educated clergy of antebellum America. Indeed, one finds few topics of current interest unexplored in the manuscripts and publications of the leading clergy of that day. The cleric may have been dogmatic, as indeed many "broad-minded" people are, but his dogmatism was not based on ignorance. A thorough study of the Bible will bring one into contact with virtually all fields of learning. This connection between the Bible and government, invoked by Calhoun, can be seen in the following remark by Methodist minister-jurist-college president Augustus Baldwin Longstreet on, coincidentally, Calhoun's political philosophy.

I believe that he regarded the government of the children of Israel in the

---

[1]Benjamin M. Palmer, *The Life and Letters of James Henley Thornwell, D.D., LL.D.* (Richmond, 1875) 306. Palmer provides no source for this quotation.

wilderness [as] the most perfect that ever existed on earth. Be that as it may, he called my attention to it more than once as exactly the government ours ought to be. "There," he said, "each tribe had its own place on the march [and in the] camp, each managed its own concerns in its own way, neither interferred in the slightest degree, with the private affairs of another, nor did their common head interfere with any of them in any matters, save such as were of equal interest to all, but unmanageable by them as separate and distinct communities."[2]

With one eye firmly fixed on his theological foundations, Thornwell, along with many of his colleagues, ranged over the spectrum of nineteenth-century thought and formed opinions on the major issues of his day. Those opinions were, in a word, conservative.

One must be careful in using this label, since it is so widely and vaguely applied to public figures and to the general public mood in our day. In describing Thornwell, or Old South intellectuals in general, as conservative, one is talking about that particular species of conservatism associated with such thinkers as Chateaubriand, Burke, and de Maistre, which might be called genteel or aristocratic conservatism. It was, by mid-nineteenth century, increasingly reactionary in its view of society, harking back to a better time when the industrial revolution and the egalitarian philosophy had not yet produced their massive social consequences in Europe and the Northern states. "These are times of excitement and agitation," lamented the Presbyterian General Assembly of 1840. The nation seemed like a "boiling cauldron" to these conservative clerics.[3]

---

[2]Augustus Baldwin Longstreet, "Review of Governor Perry's Article on Calhoun," *Nineteenth Century Magazine* (January 1870): 622-23; quoted in John D. Wade, *Augustus Baldwin Longstreet* (New York, 1924) 60.

[3]"Narrative of the State of Religion," *Minutes of the General Assembly, A.D. 1840* (Philadelphia, 1841) 311. 1840 was the year of the "Log Cabin campaign" between William Henry Harrison and Martin Van Buren, which one historian has called "the most idiotic presidential contest in our history." Samuel Eliot Morrison, Henry Steele Commager, and William E. Leuchtenburg, *The Growth of the American Republic*, vol. 1 (New York, 1969) 516. François René de Chateaubriand (1768-1848), a French Roman Catholic who wrote in the romantic tradition, defended Christianity against the attacks of rationalists. He held that the Church had been the inspiration and bulwark of European civilization. Edmund Burke (1729-1797), an English statesman, is perhaps best known for his *Reflections on the Revolutions in France* (1790). He stressed the value of tradition and distrusted democracy. Joseph De Maistre (1753-1821) was a rationalist early in life, but turned reactionary during the French Revolution. He saw the Church as the safeguard of political stability.

This conservatism was the product of several characteristics: a skeptical view of human nature, inherited in part from Calvin and Hobbes; a desire for order, not just for its own sake but as a buffer between the present and the onrushing future; an organic concept of human society; a preference for personal relationships over institutional relationships; and a pervasive spiritual and moral orientation.

While this philosophy was in retreat from the eighteenth century on, it was enjoying a modest but significant renaissance in the mid-nineteenth century, both in Europe and America. Its most visible political exponent, Prince Metternich, had gone down with the revolutions of 1848; but that same movement had acted to confirm the fears of conservatives, and they accordingly increased their efforts. The resulting resurgence of conservative thought can be seen in the works of Thomas Carlyle, Benjamin Disraeli, Georg F. Hegel, and others. These writers were familiar to an American audience through periodicals being published on both sides of the Atlantic, and American conservatives such as George Fitzhugh recognized their debt to British and European thought. Fitzhugh was delighted by Carlyle's description of liberal government as "anarchy plus a street constable" and by his attacks on "misguided philanthropy." He even borrowed some of Carlyle's phrases, such as "Mammonism" and "slaves without masters."[4] Fitzhugh was reflecting the thought of Carlyle when he wrote a classic expression of conservatism, "Alas, poor human nature! It is ever grasping at truth, and hugging itself."[5]

Indeed, the European upheavals of 1848 seem to mark a watershed in American thought as well as that of Europe. A "volcano" had "burst upon the world," wrote George Howe of Columbia Seminary. Men who were already conservative became more so, while those who had been moderates in many cases moved to the right. Virginian Nathaniel Beverly Tucker wrote his South Carolina friend Gilmore Simms of his growing uneasiness. "Time was when I might have been less desperate, because I could have sought refuge under some emperor, or king. But all such refuges are broken up, and there is now no escape from the many-headed despotism

---

[4]Harvey Wish, *George Fitzhugh, Propagandist of the Old South* (Gloucester MA, 1962) 43-44, 71-75.

[5]Wish, *Fitzhugh*, viii. See also William Gilmore Simms on Carlyle, in *Southern Quarterly Review* 17 (1850): 509.

of numbers, but by a strong and bold stand on the banks of the Potomac."[6] The young Virginia liberal clergyman Moncure Conway noted with regret the growing conservative trend among his contemporaries. Worse, he said, it was Virginia's "most scholarly and philosophical men" who were rejecting Jeffersonianism and embracing slavery.[7] Literary Southerners were turning from criticism to the romanticizing of their region's ways, as illustrated by John Pendleton Kennedy's popular *Swallow Barn*. Gilmore Simms, much of whose earlier writing had been critical of the South, turned to romantic novels and used the *Southern Quarterly Review*, which he edited from 1849 to 1854, as a forum for criticism of the Northern and European reformist mind. He saw the social chaos of Europe as a warning for the American North, and traced this tendency ultimately to the Reign of Terror.[8] Scholars were turning to more overtly political topics and rejecting the thrust of modern thought, as in the essays of George F. Holmes.[9]

The Southern public reacted similarly to the events of the day, giving a cool reception to Hungarian patriot Louis Kossuth when he toured the United States in 1851. University of Virginia professor William Barton Rogers noted that this illustrated the growth of an automatic opposition to what was perceived as dangerous social and political experimentation. Given "the excitable character of the South, and its great admiration for eloquence and chivalrous daring, Kossuth is a person for whom, under other circumstances, an unbounded enthusiasm would be aroused," Rogers observed.[10]

Two observations might be made about this revival of conservatism. First, it was not a purely sectional phenomenon. Northerners like James Kirke Paulding were as much a part of it as were Fitzhugh, Tucker, and company. William R. Taylor calls Paulding "a Northern man with Southern Principles," but if he was this, he was not alone. Paulding's distress over the trends of his day are vividly portrayed in this commentary: "When

---

[6]Howe, "The Secondary and Collateral Influence of the Holy Scriptures," *Southern Presbyterian Review* 7 (July 1853): 113. Tucker to Simms, 14 February 1851; quoted in Henry Shanks, *The Secession Movement in Virginia* (Baltimore, 1934) 69.

[7]Moncure Daniel Conway, *Autobiography of Moncure Daniel Conway*, vol. 1 (Boston, 1894) 223-24.

[8]*Southern Quarterly Review*, n.s. 6 (July 1852): 235; n.s. 1 (April 1850): 228-29.

[9]See, for example, Holmes, "The Spirit of Positivism," MS, 1853, page 9, Holmes Papers, Library of Congress.

[10]Clement Eaton, *The Mind of the Old South*, rev. ed. (Baton Rouge, 1967) 234.

love of self becomes the ruling passion, and the golden calf the only divinity; when money is made the standard by which men are estimated, and held as the sole agent in the attainment of that happiness which is the common pursuit of all mankind; then will this majestic fabric of Freedom . . . crumble to pieces, and from its ruins will arise a hideous monster with Liberty in its mouth and Despotism in its heart."[11] Theodore D. Bozeman has shown that Northern clergymen, as well as Southern, were expressing conservative moralism during the antebellum era.[12]

The second observation is that in much of this conservative thought, there is a moral or spiritual tone that unites these thinkers in rejecting the materialist-rationalist view. As always, the writings of the clergy reflected this perspective. More significant, though, are the many examples of moral concerns coming from laymen, including some who were not particularly "religious." Gilmore Simms is a good example. While he frequently encouraged the diversification of the Southern economy as a prerequisite for building Southern nationalism, Simms bemoaned the harmful effects of industrialism on morals, warning that "all the railroads in the world can [not] carry one poor soul to heaven." He admitted that there was an ulterior motive behind much of his epic prose. Modern society needed the right kind of heroes, and he was holding up characters worthy of emulation. To the like-minded Beverly Tucker, he wrote that "the downward tendency of political and social moral[s] in this country has been so rapid and extreme that it is easy and justifiable to suspect any rascality of existing powers. Our sores are everywhere running to the surface."[13]

---

[11]William I. Paulding, *Literary Life of James Kirke Paulding* (New York, 1867) 347.

[12]Theodore D. Bozeman, "Inductive and Deductive Politics: Science and Society in Antebellum Presbyterian Thought," *Journal of American History* 64:3 (December 1977): 704-22.

[13]William R. Taylor, *Cavalier and Yankee; The Old South and the American National Character* (New York, 1957) 279; William Gilmore Simms, *The Partisan*, vol. 1 (New York, 1835) xii; *Southern Quarterly Review*, n.s. 1 (April 1850): 26-27; Simms to Beverly Tucker, 12 March 1851, in Mary C. Oliphant et al., eds., *Letters of William Gilmore Simms*, vol. 3 (Columbia, 1955) 98-99. The disgust that Simms and others felt with the low level of political morality in the South and nation would soon provide a part of the drive toward secession as a new beginning for the South. Beverly Tucker felt that "secession would remove the South from occasions of sin." Robert Brugger, "The Mind of the Old South: New Views," *Virginia Quarterly Review* 61 (Spring 1980): 29. Simms, in his pessimistic moments, called for secession and a purging war as the means for the South's deliverance. Simms to Beverly Tucker, 12 March 1851, *Simms Letters*, 3:98-99; Simms to James Hammond, 9 June 1851, ibid., 3:128.

When Simms learned that the younger brother of his friend James Hammond was considering running for public office, he tried to convince him not to taint himself. "There is no more magnanimity or patriotism in the State than there is vitality in an empty beer barrel," he wrote. "Close your nostrils when you hear of public virtue among public men, for there is a d—nable stench threatening."[14] Judge Longstreet shared this cynicism about politicians and expressed little hope that politics could rectify the human predicament. "Human laws . . . do not reach the seat of the disease they are designed to cure," he wrote.[15] John Pendleton Kennedy concurred with Simms's assessment of the current political leadership, describing the politicians he knew as "a miserable array of charlatans, and make-believe statesmen."[16]

To what source could this rampant immorality and amorality be traced? For the conservative mind, the answer often was the challenge to the traditional concept of society as an organism. Whether coming from the perspective of the scientist, such as Joseph LeConte (see ch. 3), or of the historian, such as Frederick Porcher or James Petigru (see ch. 3), or of the Christian theologian, the typical Southern conservative applied this organic view to human society and concluded that the reforming rationalism of the nineteenth century was amiss in its abandonment of organicism.[17]

Organicism provided its adherents with a perspective from which the difficult questions of morality and ethics could be answered with relative ease by suggesting that such questions depended upon the relationship one held with the other person or people involved. A good example of this view is Jasper Adams's *Elements of Moral Philosophy* (1837). Adams, an Epis-

---

[14]Simms to Marcus Hammond, 31 October 1851, *Simms Letters,* 3:148.

[15]Augustus B. Longstreet; quoted in John D. Wade, *Augustus Baldwin Longstreet,* 219-20. For another reference to this morality theme, see Paul Hamilton Hayne, "Ante-Bellum Charleston," *Southern Bivouac* n.s. 1 (October 1885): 257-58.

[16]Kennedy to Phillip C. Pendleton, 11 May 1859; quoted in Charles H. Bohner, *John Pendleton Kennedy: Gentleman from Baltimore* (Baltimore, 1961) 227. The theme of morality in late antebellum Southern writing is treated in Drew Faust, *A Sacred Circle; The Dilemma of the Intellectual in the Old South, 1840-1860* (Baltimore, 1978); Nicholas Olsberg, "A Government of Class and Race; William Henry Trescot and the South Carolina Chivalry, 1860-1865" (Ph.D. dissertation, University of South Carolina, 1972).

[17]Theodore Bozeman, "Joseph LeConte: Organic Science and a 'Sociology for the South,' " *Journal of Southern History* 39 (November 1973): 565-82.

copalian trained at Andover Seminary, was president of the College of Charleston from 1824 to 1836. Socially and politically conservative, he admired Edmund Burke and saw as a primary purpose of moral philosophy the determination of obligations in "the various situations and relations of life."[18] The key relationships that determined our duties, said Adams, were Creator and creature, ruler and ruled, husband and wife, parent and child, master and servant, wealthy and poor. If proof were needed that these were valid bases for a moral code, Adams simply noted that no community had ever existed without them.[19]

Fearful that the revolutions in Europe and the reform movement in the North were threatening to undermine this eminently rational divine plan, Thornwell and his fellow Old School Presbyterians sought a social philosophy that was both conservative in its goals and intellectually respectable to their own minds and the minds of the educated elite they addressed, North and South. The intellectual conflict of the nineteenth century began, for them, as a debate among the colleges and universities who espoused various theological positions; shifted to the Protestant denominational assemblies, culminating there with the sectional schisms in the Baptist and Methodist Churches and the Old School-New School schism in the Presbyterian Church; and finally moved to the arena of national politics, there culminating in the secession of the South. Throughout this process, orthodox theologians maintained, as one of them said, that "the conflict is not between the friends of progress . . . and of stagnation . . . but between the friends of different kinds and methods of progress."[20] "God is wiser than man," another insisted, and His "infinite wisdom and benevolence have devised and disclosed the way of human improvement."[21] What was the "way of human improvement" that God had disclosed? Thornwell answered: "All real improvement must begin from within." When a man is reborn spiritually, he begins to work as a subtle agent for betterment in society. In this way "the past and the future [will be] so imperceptibly blended

---

[18]Brooks Holifield, *The Gentlemen Theologians; American Theology in Southern Culture, 1795-1860* (Durham, 1978) 146.

[19]Ibid., 146-47.

[20]Lyman Atwater, "True Progress of Society," *Biblical Repertory and Princeton Review* 24 (January 1852): 19.

[21]Thomas Smyth, "National Righteousness," *Southern Presbyterian Review* 12 (April 1859): 34.

together that they should run together and coalesce without an absolute commencement or sudden termination.''[22]

Was this theological view developed in Thornwell's mind independently of the social forces of his day, or was it simply a convenient refuge against the social activism then emanating from the North, which threatened the South's status quo? To answer such a question with certainty, one would have to know Thornwell better than a distant perspective permits. However, a careful examination of Thornwell's life suggests that neither of these views is adequate. One may assume that from the time of his affiliation with the Presbyterian Church, if not before, he was deeply influenced by its social concepts. But the theological tradition of Presbyterianism is not monolithic. It was informed, first, by the thought of John Calvin and the reformed ministers of Geneva, and also by the Scottish and Westminster divines. The former tradition dealt substantially with questions of community morality and justice. The latter stressed the search for and elucidation of divine truths. For Thornwell, as for most Presbyterian clergymen of that day, the latter tradition was clearly the more popular model. It maintained the Calvinistic tradition of biblical exegesis, one scholar has noted, but lost its prophetic function regarding social justice.[23] With his theology shaped by this inward-looking theme, it was natural that Thornwell developed the pious, socially conservative outlook for which he is known—natural also that he became the leading advocate for the doctrine of the "spirituality of the church." But to suggest that he followed this path unthinkingly, or that his social thought was merely the result of conditioning, is to underestimate him.

Even as a young man Thornwell's idealism was checked by a skepticism concerning the more abstract philanthropy of reformers. While at Harvard in 1834, he had encountered the nascent transcendentalism of that

---

[22]Thornwell, in John B. Adger, ed., *Collected Writings of James Henley Thornwell*, vol. 2 (Richmond, 1871) 466, 601. An excellent study of the conservative thought of Old School Presbyterians in the antebellum era is Bozeman, "Inductive and Deductive Politics," 704-22. As Bozeman shows, the conservative views expressed by Thornwell were shared by his Northern colleagues. Charles Hodge of Princeton said much the same thing as Thornwell (above) in an article on slavery in 1836. Ibid., 712. Hodge, "Slavery," *Biblical Repertory and Princeton Review* 8 (April 1836): 268-305; see esp. 292.

[23]Robert N. Watkins, Jr., "The Forming of the Southern Presbyterian Minister: From Calvin to the American Civil War" (Ph.D. dissertation, Vanderbilt University, 1969).

era and analyzed his thoughts on it in a letter to his old friend Alexander Pegues.

> I am charmed with the notion of universal philanthropy . . . but then I find more real enjoyment . . . in the narrower circle of domestic affection and of private friendships. I am willing to grant that love to the species should be the mainspring of all our actions, [but] it is a sad misnomer to call an unfaithful friend or a cruel husband a genuine philanthropist. The man who is careless of his own household is hardly able to take care of the world. . . . He is the best philanthropist who is the truest friend, the most faithful husband, the most tender parent, and affectionate neighbor.[24]

Building on the twin bases of his Calvinism and modified Baconianism, Thornwell proceeded to the study of morals. His interest in this subject was, as I have shown, typical of his age. For Thornwell, questions of morality began with the fact of man's rational nature. God, in providing man with rational faculties, had enabled him to develop a *moral sense*. This term was used by some of the Scottish Realists as a more specific expression of what they generally called *Common Sense*. It was for them the universal faculty that elevated man above the level of the rest of creation.[25] Having this moral sense, man was capable of accepting responsibility for his behavior and, said Thornwell, for his opinions as well.[26] The function of the Bible in this regard was to aid in the development of ethical values by validating the conclusions to which a man's moral sense led him.

Here Baconianism, whatever its role in the study of science by the orthodox, played only a small part, for it was not left to the individual to search out the best moral code for himself. This was provided for him by his society, or in the case of the privileged few, by a course in moral philosophy. Along with instruction in the Evidences of Christianity, this course was ubiquitous in Old South colleges. In this course students learned philosophy, political theory, social decorum, religious values, and a sense of civic responsibility. Here, in short, was the heart of the process by which the

---

[24]Thornwell to Alexander Pegues, 11 September 1834, Thornwell Papers.

[25]Garry Wills, in his provocative study, *Inventing America; Jefferson's Declaration of Independence* (Garden City NY, 1978), suggests that moral sense was the quality Jefferson believed all men were equally endowed with, and hence ''created equal.''

[26]This was the central theme of his *Discourse on Truth* (New York, 1855). See esp. 456-59, 467, 502, 527.

values of Southern culture were passed on to each generation of leaders. The instructors in these courses were generally clergymen. In fact, one study of the moral philosophy courses taught at Southern colleges has identified only four instructors who were not trained for the ministry: Thomas Dew of William and Mary, George Tucker of the University of Virginia, David Swain of the University of North Carolina, and Francis Licber of the South Carolina College. These, admittedly, were notable exceptions.[27]

While Lieber was using his moral-philosophy course as a platform for views that Thornwell considered entirely too utilitarian, Thornwell presented what amounted to a continuing course on the same subject in his sermons to the students in Rutledge Chapel. Seven of these sermons were published in 1855 as *Discourses on Truth*. These sermons are the major source on Thornwell's morality, but can be augmented by his lectures in theology to the students at Columbia Seminary.[28] The sense of moral urgency that Thornwell brought to his consideration of late antebellum society is revealed in the preface to *Discourses on Truth*. "The times require such a discussion as that which is here attempted," he said.

These sermons show Thornwell as a consistent rationalist, even when dealing with religion and morals. His method is to explore with his audience various moral doctrines, expose their fallacies, and then present his own view. He is again careful, however, to caution against too great a confidence in reason. "It is one thing to say that reason is a law," he warned, "and another to say that it is a perfect law. In our present fallen condition, it is impossible to excogitate a standard of duty which shall be warped by none of our prejudices, distorted by none of our passions, and corrupted by none of our habits."[29] One cannot help wondering whether Thornwell ever reflected on this caveat in the heat of the secession winter or after. Yet having issued this note of caution, he proceeded to expound on morals without paying much heed to it. In the remarks excerpted above, he was clearly working on the rational sense of his young listeners, as Palmer tells us he generally did with his congregation.[30]

---

[27]Holifield, *The Gentlemen Theologians*, 128.

[28]See vol. 1 and the first part of vol. 2 of the *Collected Writings*.

[29]Thornwell, *Discourses on Truth* (New York, 1855) 17. Delivered in the chapel of the South Carolina College.

[30]Palmer, 547.

Typical of these essays on morality is a sermon Thornwell preached in February 1846 on Romans 14:12. "So then every one of us shall give account of himself to God" (King James Version). Noting that modern philosophy often holds that men should not be punished for their opinions because they are not responsible for them, Thornwell invokes Paul, who argued that men are responsible for their faith. Paul makes the nature and limits of that responsibility "the true ground of toleration," Thornwell adds. "Persecution never has arisen from the principle that men are responsible for their opinions, but from the principle that they are responsible to the *magistrate*. It is not responsibility but the object of that responsibility which has produced all the mischief." The Christian concept of the individual's responsibility to God obviates this problem of persecution. "We are not each other's masters. In the solemn interest of religion the Divine will is our sole law."

Without considering here the question of the scope of this "solemn interest of religion," Thornwell presses his argument further. If one accepts the popular philosophical view, man is not responsible at all. Therefore, he is not responsible for the idea that he has the right to persecute! But a sense of human responsibility before the ultimate magistrate prevents the abuse of power by the earthly magistrate and his minions. Thus, he concludes, these philosophers of irresponsibility leave toleration in a more precarious condition than they found it. Whence comes this idea that man is not responsible? Thornwell believed it derived from the view that belief was involuntary. Having no control over the evidences that are presented to him, the argument goes, a man has no responsibility for the beliefs to which these evidences lead him. But, says Thornwell, a man does not believe on this basis alone. His will and his moral sense are both factors in the process of discrimination that produces belief. Further, it is only a small step, he contends, from this view to that which frees a man from responsibility for his actions as well. Having adopted this position, one must argue for "good" behavior only on the pragmatic grounds that it produces happiness. Then punishment would be based on expediency, rather than the higher concept of distributive justice that a truly moral society employs. Where punishment is based on expediency, how can it be argued that it has become tyrannical? For where moral distinctions have been destroyed, "tyranny has lost its moral turpitude."[31]

---

[31]Thornwell, sermon MS, 1 February 1846, Thornwell Papers.

Having thus reasoned through to this conclusion, Thornwell turns to Scripture for its validation of humankind's sound morality. Scripture teaches, he concludes, that man is responsible for his faith, for his words, for his affections, and for his actions. Such responsibility, he reminds his young hearers in closing, is "the dignity and glory of our nature."[32]

It is interesting to compare this sermon with a lecture Thornwell gave to his Seminary class in theology several years later on the subject, "The Pollution and Guilt of Sin."[33] Here he returns to the theme of individual responsibility, but from a different perspective. He is now considering the proper attitude of the civil authorities toward behavior that undermines public morals. Responsibility before God does not, he implicitly assumes, preclude the citizen from responsibility before human laws. Again referring to modern environmental and behaviorist philosophy, he bemoans its impact in the area of public attitudes toward sin. "One of the worst signs of the times is the slender hold which the idea of punitive justice has on the public mind," he asserts. "Moral order cannot be preserved without it, and it is a fatal symptom that a nation is tending to anarchy when it becomes indifferent to the first principle of prosperity." Contrary to what was becoming the all-too-popular opinion, "Penal justice does not aim at the reformation of the offender, but it asserts the awful inviolability of the moral law by the terrible wretchedness with which it reacts upon the soul of the offender. It is the recoil of that law upon the person of him who had the audacity to resist it, and no surer sign of moral degeneracy can be found among a people than a sickly fastidiousness in relation to the demands of justice."[34]

In words that ring familiar to modern ears, Thornwell continues,

> Our people, at least in so far as it is represented by the prevalent opinions of our educated classes, no longer earnestly believe the *character* of sin and crime to be that which *deserves punishment*. Whoever gives his attention to the discussions of our representative assemblies concerning capital punishment, political crime, civil offense, and the like, will everywhere find this dissipation of the moral consciousness to be the fundamental fea-

---

[32]Ibid.

[33]Adger, *Collected Writings,* vol. 1, Lecture 15, 400-24. Parts of this sermon are startlingly like much of the "law and order" rhetoric of our day.

[34]Ibid., 1:411.

ture. No one is more sure of the applause of the majority than he who discovers some new means . . . of disarming justice, and of making the scoundrel and villain unpunishable before the law, and, where possible, before public opinion too.

Why has this attitude of tolerance become so prevalent? It is the product, Thornwell suggests, of determinist philosophy. "The actor is not the author of his act," the argument goes, "but the circumstances, or the bad education, or the deficiency in social arrangements. . . . Crime is misfortune, not guilt." Hence the violator of the law is to be treated, not punished. However fallacious this point of view was in Thornwell's opinion, its consequences were of greater concern to him than the deterministic philosophy itself. It produces "a decided moral skepticism, to which the moral law is only a matter of arbitrary invention and social agreement." A society that follows this deterministic concept of behavior will eventually lose its moral grounding and become heedless of the cry of its prophets. Europe, in Thornwell's view, was already well advanced along this disastrous course, and the North was showing signs of following its lead.[35]

Fearing the appeal that this deterministic philosophy might have, Thornwell, along with most orthodox moralists, rejected one of the two most popular texts on the subject—William Paley's *Principles of Moral and Political Philosophy* (1785). Paley was anathema to them because he focused his argument on the positive results of moral behavior—God's pleasure, man's heavenly reward, and the social benefits—and therefore made ethics an externally derived thing rather than the product of an internal moral sense. They saw in Paley no distinction between right and expediency. Utility, argued Thornwell, is not the criterion of moral behavior; duty is. Virtue derives not from the results of one's actions, but from the intent to obey the divine law.[36]

Reason, then, led man toward the divine law of morality, while careful study of the Scriptures and of authentic moral writings clarified and confirmed his moral sense. It was possible, therefore, even with his sinful na-

---

[35]Ibid., 1:412-13. For a modern conception of this idea from the perspective of social psychology, see Carl Menninger, *Whatever Became of Sin?* (New York, 1973).

[36]Thornwell, "Review of Paley's Moral Philosophy," esp. 24. The other popular text on moral philosophy was Francis Wayland's *Elements of Moral Science* (1835), which conformed more closely to Thornwell's views on the subject, but which was flawed, for Southerners, by Wayland's dislike of slavery.

ture, for man to understand and approximate moral behavior through intensive study and self-control. This, for Thornwell, was man's goal in his relationship with society.[37] However, for men to be able to pursue this arduous course, it was necessary to avoid certain social conditions that had the effect of subverting their efforts. Thornwell's social philosophy, in other words, was conditioned by his moral philosophy in that the kind of society he wanted was one in which men could most readily work toward moral improvement. It is hence ironic that in articulating his social philosophy, he placed himself in diametric opposition to people who were also working, from a different perspective, for just such a society.

Thornwell's social thought epitomized the moralistic conservatism of the mid-nineteenth century. He borrowed from conservative historians and scientists, including some that he knew well and with whom he worked closely in the cause of defending traditional values. His peculiar contribution was the blending of a strong theological focus with the interest in scholarship that his rational mind demanded, to produce a synthesis of conservative theology and sociology. Much of his social thought concentrated on the abolitionist attack on slavery because of that subject's immediacy for him and his region; but his response to that attack cannot be understood in isolation from his theology and social thought generally.

Thornwell expressed the essence of his conservative social thought in a letter to the South Carolina College Board of Trustees while he was president of the College. Describing conditions on the campus that were in need of change, he qualified his position in favor of modifying the school's policies with the note that "violent and radical changes, even where the change . . . is an improvement, are not desirable." Paraphrasing Shakespeare, he added, "It is better to make the best of what you have than to throw it away in the hope of getting something still better." Turning to the subject of student behavior, always a topic of concern on this, as on most antebellum campuses, the president exhorted, "Perpetual vigilance is the only guarantee of order."[38]

---

[37]Thornwell, *Discourses on Truth*, 454.

[38]Letter to the Board of Trustees, n.d., Thornwell Papers. It is interesting that later in the same letter Thornwell recommended a change that most would call radical: the reduction of the undergraduate program from four years to three, and the introduction of graduate programs in philosophy, science, and philology.

Here we see the twin pillars of Thornwell's social thought. On the one hand, he contended that human history was in the hands of God, whose wise plan was moving mankind forward at a pace slow enough to ensure stability as well as progress, and that man's proper response was to accept the status quo for now, while looking for signs of God's will regarding change. On the other hand, human institutions must protect the orderly functioning of society and guard against the forces of anarchy and radical change that would threaten the organic structure of society and undermine the divine plan for progress. Social evils did exist and would continue to exist until the millennium; but God was at work on them, and for man to ignore the divine light that guided him slowly and carefully forward would invite horrors far worse than anything that might presently disturb the reformer's conscience.[39]

As a young minister Thornwell was content to concern himself with the world within man. Consequently he seems to have avoided politics. Although he did express his opposition to the Nullifiers while a college student, he took no part in that contest. While this aloofness from public issues would eventually change, it was the natural position for one who insisted upon the doctrine of the spirituality of the church (see ch. 7).[40]

Was Thornwell inconsistent, even hypocritical, in eventually rejecting his long-held belief in the noninvolvement of the church and clergy in public affairs? He is certainly open to the charge, but in tracing his gradual arousal to public issues one sees him reacting rather than initiating. Indeed, he appears to have been forced by the social and political involvement of other religious leaders to choose between forfeiting to them the role of spokesmen for God and picking up the gauntlet for his orthodox and socially conservative views. It should not be surprising that a man of Thornwell's intellectual combativeness chose the latter course, as have the leaders of today's "new religious right" who have embraced the Republican party.

As a young minister concentrating on his pastoral duties and ecclesiastical business, he first became interested in the relationship between the church and public issues during the Old School-New School conflict in the

[39]Thornwell, "Address Delivered to the Euphradean and Clariosophic Societies of the South Carolina College, December 3, 1839," MS, Thornwell Papers; Thornwell, "Matthew 22:29," *Southern Presbyterian Review* 4 (April 1851): 527.

[40]Thornwell to Alexander Pegues, 2 February 1832; quoted in Palmer, 88-90.

Presbyterian Church in the late 1830s. The rationalism of the New School "made the prophets and apostles succumb to philosophy and impulse," he warned, and thus loosed the church from its traditional biblical moorings, opening up the possibility of radical theological and ecclesiastical innovation. This, he predicted, could lead to "serious disasters, not only to the religious, but likewise the political interests of the country." New School beliefs and values, in other words, could threaten slavery and the union.[41]

As long as Thornwell and his orthodox colleagues were able to employ the doctrine of the spirituality of the church as a shield against the activist views of reformers, the strictly Calvinist, Old School Presbyterian church remained largely outside the social ferment of mid-nineteenth-century America and, coincidentally, remained united North and South. His continued association with conservative Northern colleagues through the 1850s no doubt made it easier for Thornwell to remain a unionist until the sectional tensions began to reach the breaking point in the waning weeks of 1860. Until that time he would continue to work for a more moral society through his traditional pastoral role and to contribute to the Southern apologia from his theological perspective.

As with most nineteenth-century clergymen, Thornwell's social thought was heavily concerned with questions of personal and social morality. In a chapter entitled "The Moral Idea," Ernest Trice Thompson considers the high moral standards proclaimed, if not always followed, by the antebellum Presbyterians.[42] Prominent among their concerns were sabbath-breaking, drinking, dancing, novel reading, excessive materialism, adultery and fornication, theater going, card playing, profanity, dueling, and gambling. Thompson notes that questions on which the *Confession of Faith* offered little help received less attention. These included business ethics, stewardship of possessions, and the separation of married slaves.[43] The lit-

---

[41]Bruce Staiger, "Abolitionism and the Presbyterian Schism of 1837-1838," *Mississippi Valley Historical Review* 36 (1949): 393-94.

[42]Ernest T. Thompson, *Presbyterians in the South*, vol. 1 (Richmond, 1963) 305-22.

[43]Ibid., 314. On the dilemma of slave separations, see *Southern Presbyterian Review* 8:1 (July 1854): 15-17. For a thorough study of the social mores of antebellum Southern Presbyterians, see William D. Blanks, "Ideal and Practice: A Study of the Conception of the Christian Life Prevailing in the Presbyterian Churches of the Nineteenth Century" (Th.D. dissertation, Union Seminary, 1960). The first chapter of this study contrasts the laxity of today's Christian life-style with the strict moral code that prevailed a century ago.

erature of the antebellum Southern churches also reveals concern over the dangers of Northern reform fever, spiritualism ("rapping"), Catholicism, Unitarianism, and in fact virtually all denominations other than the one with which the author or the publication was affiliated.[44]

The records of individual churches may reveal more about the moral expectations of their clergy and membership than the public pronouncements of denominational leaders. Unfortunately, congregations varied widely in the care they took with record keeping, and denominations were not always as concerned with their archives as the historian would wish. Yet even partial records can suggest general attitudes toward specific kinds of behavior. One study of Southern Presbyterian attitudes on moral questions uses the records of sixty-one churches during the nineteenth century. Disciplinary actions were taken by these churches in fourteen categories of misbehavior, and the author breaks these cases down by decade, from 1800 to 1899. As his table shows, the number of cases rose steadily during the early and middle decades, and then declined after 1860 in most instances. The 1850s produced the largest number of cases of any decade. Of the total of 1,150 disciplinary actions taken by the sessions of these sixty-one churches, the most common offenses, in order, were intemperance, sexual misconduct, and nonattendance, which together accounted for some sixty-five percent of the cases; then followed profanity, dancing, fighting, business practices, slander, lying, attending the theater, sabbath-breaking, gambling, and nonspecified or miscellaneous.

If these figures can be taken as typical, nineteenth century Presbyterians could hardly be said to have engaged in massive disciplinary actions against their wayward members. The average church in this sample took such actions only nineteen times during the century and only five times during the peak decade of the 1850s. A closer look at the sessional minutes of one church, the First Presbyterian Church of Columbia, South Carolina, with which Thornwell was associated for most of his career, reveals that formal disciplinary action was taken in only a small percentage of the cases in which misconduct was reported and discussed by the Session. Far more common was the issuing of a "solemn warning." The Session was reluctant to go further, even at the urging of the minister, because it recognized

---

[44]See files of the *Southern Presbyterian, Central Presbyterian, Watchman and Observer.* Regarding novel reading, see *Central Presbyterian,* 28 February 1857. Regarding dueling, see *Southern Presbyterian,* 3 January 1857.

that ''it may be difficult to draw accurately the line of demarcation between the lawful and unlawful pleasures of the Christian.''[45] But the frequency with which matters of personal conduct were brought before this
Session indicates that the nineteenth-century church was more acutely
concerned with upholding the moral standards it proclaimed than its more-
tolerant twentieth-century offspring.

Thornwell's lecture notes indicate that he spent a good deal of time addressing his students on the subjects of character, personal habits, and the
love of material things. ''Among the worst habits,'' he warned his young
audience, ''are those of sensual indulgence—which are all intimately connected.'' His cautions against strong drink were practical. ''Such as are

TABLE 1*

CASES OF DISCIPLINE FOR 61 PRESBYTERIAN CHURCHES DURING THE NINETEENTH CENTURY											
	1800 1809	1810 1819	1820 1829	1830 1839	1840 1849	1850 1859	1860 1869	1870 1879	1880 1889	1890 1899	Total	%
Sex & Marriage	0	5	20	28	49	58	34	21	16	0	231	20.0
Non-attendance	0	1	15	20	51	60	23	23	3	0	196	17.0
Slander	0	1	4	10	14	11	0	0	0	0	40	3.5
Sabbath-breaking	0	0	1	8	3	6	1	2	0	0	21	1.8
Gambling	0	0	0	1	2	5	1	0	0	0	9	.7
Profanity	0	0	4	19	24	21	9	9	0	0	86	7.5
Intemperance	0	2	9	63	72	81	29	46	15	3	320	27.7
Theater	0	0	10	1	2	3	2	5	0	0	23	2.0
Dancing	0	0	1	4	6	15	12	39	2	2	81	7.0
Fighting	0	0	6	13	13	11	5	4	1	0	53	4.6
Theft	0	0	0	1	4	10	3	0	0	0	18	1.6
Lying	0	0	1	8	12	4	0	0	0	0	25	2.1
Business Practices	0	1	3	13	11	6	1	4	2	0	41	3.6
Non-specified and Miscellaneous	0	0	1	2	1	2	0	0	0	0	6	.5
Total	0	10	75	191	264	293	120	153	39	5	1150	
* Table found in William D. Blanks, ''Ideal and Practice,'' appendix.												

[45]''Minutes of the Session, First Presbyterian Church, Columbia, South Carolina, 1847-
1874,'' W.P.A. transcript, South Caroliniana Library. The quotation is from the December
1847 minutes.

ablest at the bottle are generally the weakest at the book."[46] True to his conservative nature, Thornwell put great emphasis upon the importance of habit in forming character. For him a virtuous man was one who was so by habit. Good habits, formed at an early age, will survive even if we become calloused with age, he maintained. To make this point, he drew an interesting analogy with the behavior of soldiers on the battlefield. "The veteran soldier is much readier in extending himself to the wounded than the novice—but is not so much affected by their suffering." This sounds strangely deterministic, coming from one so opposed to the utilitarian basis of modern morality.[47]

One habit that enjoyed increasing popularity in the nineteenth century was novel reading, a pastime that Thornwell, as a pious clergyman, decried. Novels, he suggested, "present us with themes calculated to arouse our feelings without offering opportunities for action." The reader becomes excited, but has no way of channeling that feeling positively. Furthermore, fiction sometimes holds up ignoble characters as admirable, and thus warps the values of impressionable minds. But his major objection to novels was that the time spent in reading them could, and should, be spent "in active intercourse with society, where experiences may be had which both serve our fellowmen and build character through good habits." Again contradicting his usual position on utilitarianism, he concluded that the morals of society were threatened by a "swarm" of "productions whose utility has not been duly investigated." "Shall there be placed into the hands of children books whose moral bearings are not fully understood? Let us rather listen to the voices of philanthropy and wisdom," he urged.[48]

Dancing was another activity that Thornwell, again in company with many of his colleagues, shunned. Though he may have mellowed on this

---

[46]MS notes on College lectures, Thornwell Papers. Notes on Lord Bacon's *Prima Philosophia*, Thornwell Papers.

[47]"Novels," MS essay by Thornwell, in Thornwell Papers.

[48]Ibid. Another Presbyterian clergyman, William F. Hutson, expressed similar views in a review of Benjamin Disraeli's novel *Tancreed, or the New Crusade* (Philadelphia, 1847). He typified the Presbyterian willingness to confront any and all competitors for the mind of man, and made no apology for the appearance of a fiction review in the religious press. But he added that he "would be willing to part with even Walter Scott, if the whole vile crew of French immorality, German dreams, and English namby pambyism could vanish with him." *Southern Presbyterian Review* 1:2 (September 1847): 57-58. Views similar to those of Thornwell and Hutson are expressed in "Novel Reading," *Central Presbyterian*, 28 February 1857.

subject later in life, as a youth he was adamantly against social dancing. Referring to a party he had been invited to while a student in Cambridge, Massachusetts, he wrote his friend Alexander Pegues, "I am rather afraid there will be dancing. If there should be, I most assuredly shall not go." He noted that Cicero shared his sentiments on the subject, seeing "neither rhyme nor reason in 'capering nimbly over a lady's chamber, to the lascivious pleasings of a lute.' I am an open and avowed enemy of the sport," he continued, "because I believe that it is an enemy to the best and most substantial interests of man." "It is an insult to God, who has made us beings of intellectual dignity." "Is it not a mere invention to kill time?"[49] Though this attitude seems harsh to twentieth-century minds, one should remember that with the exception of the Episcopalians, nineteenth-century Southern churchmen, and their Northern brethren as well, took a dim view of many, if not most, forms of entertainment now pursued without any qualms at all. A Columbia Episcopalian woman of the mid-nineteenth century commented upon the abstinence of the Presbyterians and noted that some of her fellow parishioners objected to their children marrying members of that church because a Presbyterian often acted as a "wet blanket" in the midst of the more socially active Episcopalians. "Gay society seems to have been relegated to the Episcopalians," she said, who alone "supported the race course, dancing master, and theater."[50]

In his own personal habits, Thornwell was far from ascetic. He enjoyed food, drink, cigars, and clothes, and insisted on the best quality that he could afford in all cases. Palmer recalled that he "always bought the best edition of books; wore clothing of the finest texture; was fond of fine horses; and smoked always the best brands."[51] In letters to close friends, Thornwell often alluded to his rather sumptuous habits, with no hint of apology. He was never accused of excess, however, and his abhorrence of any conduct that was demeaning naturally prevented him from placing

---

[49]Thornwell to Alexander Pegues, 18 September 1834; quoted in Palmer, 124. Palmer reveals the liberalizing of Presbyterian views on dancing by omitting from this letter Thornwell's most colorful criticism of dancing, that it was "fit only for the horned inhabitants of the subterranean regions" (ibid.).

[50]Sally Eleanor Taylor; quoted in Mary Fulton Green, "A Profile of Columbia in 1850," *South Carolina Historical Magazine* 70 (1969): 118.

[51]Palmer, 135.

himself in this position. On the subject of strong drink he was particularly adamant. In Palmer's words, he viewed drunkenness as

> in the single act a crime. It is a sin against the whole man, and against the whole law. It makes a man worse than a beast. . . . [D]runkenness, in its principle, is a conspiracy against the law of a refined civilization. It is marked by the predominance of the animal over the rational; and society is therefore called upon, for its own protection, to strike at an enemy that threatens the very citadel of refinement. [S]ince it affects the rights of others . . . the law should interpose, and deal with the drunkard as it deals with the minor, or with the maniac.

These views Thornwell expressed in an address to the State Temperance Convention on 4 July 1854. Yet strong as his feelings were on this subject, he opposed any official agency of the Presbyterian Church involving itself in the temperance movement.[52]

When invited to deliver a sermon to the South Carolina Legislature in December 1854, Thornwell took the opportunity to call for greater vigilance in the punishment of crime. "On this day, my brethren, have we not reason to apprehend that our land mourns on account of unpunished crime?" he wondered. "Does not the voice of innocent blood cry to us from the ground? Is not violence increasing in our borders? Is it not a fatal symptom . . . that secret weapons can be carried without branding their possessors as sons of Beliel? . . . This shocking practice . . . ought, in some way, to be rebuked. It is a stain upon us." Harking back to the Old Testament, he urged the state to "visit blood with blood" to curb the rise of crime.[53]

Clearly a man with so piercing a sense of human shortcomings and social ills, and with so little confidence in the capacity of human institutions to rectify these ills, was not in a position to join in the launching of a new nation. In fact Thornwell had labeled any such attempt in those unstable times "perilous in the extreme."[54] However, his work in the courts of the

---

[52]Ibid., 376-77. By the 1850s alcohol consumption, which had climbed to several gallons per capita (adult) in 1810, had fallen to about three gallons. Mark Lender and James Martin, *Drinking in America: A History* (New York, 1980).

[53]Thornwell, *Judgements, A Call to Repentance; A Sermon Preached by Appointment of the Legislature in the Hall of the House of Representatives, December 9, 1854* (Columbia, 1854) 22-23.

[54]Thornwell to Reverend Hooper, 8 March 1850, Thornwell Papers. See also Palmer, 477-78.

Presbyterian Church was gradually bringing Thornwell to a more careful consideration of questions that were essentially political, as he struggled—often in the minority and at times alone—against the forces of change in that denomination. First in the fight with the New School faction, and then even within the more homogeneous body that remained after the schism in 1837, he and his orthodox colleagues felt the pressure of the trend toward a more flexible theology and greater humanistic and social-welfare emphasis in the Church (as in society). As he continued to pursue his theological studies and to confirm more surely his orthodox Biblicism, Thornwell at times despaired of the liberal nineteenth century. Thus the necessity, to his mind, of fighting the battle wherever it could be fought. His church papers, esoteric though they seem to our minds, contained, in his words, "principles of the highest importance, in their application to both Church and State."[55]

Passionately interested in the political events of his time, and yet remaining outside the political arena, Thornwell watched and pondered, and turned to his religion for insight and solace. As the revolutions of 1848 began to unfold in Europe, he wrote to his friend and faculty colleague Matthew J. Williams:

> The present posture of the nations baffles the speculations of philosophers and statesmen. I turn from all carnal calculations to the sure word of prophecy; and as I believe that *the only safe guide* is to be found in the prophetic Scriptures, I have begun with increased zeal the study of a book, which has heretofore been to me, as it has been to the great majority of Christians, a sealed volume: the Apocalypse of John. That sublime document contains the history of the world, from Christ to the end of time; and though its figures are mystic, they are not hopelessly obscure. . . . We are upon the eve of great events; and watchfullness and prayer are the postures in which we should be found. God is riding on the whirlwind, and directing the storm; and out of the chaos and tumult of the nations, He will surely evolve His own grand purposes, and make the angry passions of men subservient to the scheme of His glorious providence.[56]

---

[55]Thornwell to Matthew J. Williams, 17 July 1848; quoted ibid., 310.
[56]Ibid.

CHAPTER 6

"The Calhoun of the Church"

It was not until the climactic months of 1860-1861 that the antebellum clergyman's deep concern for morality led him into the public arena. The conception of the church as a spiritual institution dictated that it restrict itself to preaching the Gospel and instructing its members in matters of personal piety and morality. Further, St. Paul's statement that the powers that be are ordained of God, and Jesus' admonition to "render unto Caesar the things that are Caesar's" led most ministers to conclude that political concerns were not within their jurisdiction. Seldom did a clergyman follow the path of Methodist Augustus Baldwin Longstreet, who wrote letters of advice to state and national politicians, including President James Polk, and commented publicly on political topics. In 1855 Longstreet published and signed an article supporting the Know-Nothing party, and his bellicose orations before the students of the South Carolina College led them to volunteer en masse for military service in 1861.[1]

More typical was the attitude expressed by Moses Hoge in an article entitled "What Do Christians Owe Their Country?" While urging Christians to support responsible (conservative?) candidates for office, Hoge cautioned that "the pious man should stand aloof from all the rancor of

---

[1] J. R. Scafadel, "The Letters of Augustus Baldwin Longstreet" (Ph.D. dissertation, University of South Carolina, 1976) 223, 229, 421.

party passions.''² Charleston Presbyterian Thomas Smyth told the readers of the *Southern Presbyterian Review* that religion and politics have an important, if somewhat delicate relationship. ''The connection between true religion and sound politics is very intimate,'' he wrote. ''The well-being of the one is the well-being of the other.'' ''To convert the pulpit into an instrument of political agitation is most certainly to invade its sacredness. . . . But to make it the means of instructing Christians in the Christianity of their political relations, is simply to accomplish one of the ends for which it was intended.''³

The position of Columbia Theological Seminary was that ''activities and utterances by a minister in the field of political and social theory should be clearly separated from his ministerial functions.'' The historian of the seminary states that this position was ''based on the doctrine of the separation between church and state'' and its purpose was ''to keep the church loyal to first things and not let it degenerate into a debating society.'' Yet through its Society of Missionary Inquiry, the seminary supported the Seamen's Bethel in Charleston, a ministry to sailors, as well as foreign missions, domestic missions, Bible and tract societies, temperance societies, and opposition to the African slave trade.⁴

So if the position of the Old South clergy regarding public affairs was not the activist involvement of modern liberal churchmen, neither was it the otherworldly detachment of the monk. There was, then as now, great diversity among the denominations, and even within them, in this regard.⁵ In the Old School Presbyterian Church, the question centered on whether the General Assembly should create and support agencies for social improvement, such as temperance societies.

---

²Moses Hoge, ''What Do Christians Owe Their Country?'' *Southern Religious Telegraph,* 13 April 1832; quoted in Blanks, ''Ideal and Practice: A Study of the Conception of the Christian Life Prevailing in the Presbyterian Churches of the Nineteenth Century'' (Th.D. dissertation, Union Seminary, 1960) 263.

³Thomas Smyth, ''National Righteousness,'' *Southern Presbyterian Review* 12 (April 1859): 25.

⁴Louis C. LaMotte, *Colored Light; The Story of the Influence of Columbia Theological Seminary, 1828-1936* (Richmond, 1937) 100-101.

⁵See John Bodo, *Protestant Clergy and Public Issues, 1812-1848* (Princeton, 1954); Elwyn A. Smith, *The Presbyterian Ministry in American Culture: A Study in Changing Concepts, 1700-1900* (Philadelphia, 1962); J. T. David, ''Presbyterians and the Sectional Conflict,'' *Southern Quarterly* (January 1970): 117-30.

Like most antebellum churchmen, James Thornwell held himself aloof from the public arena. While the man of God should not divorce himself from public life, he contended, he should avoid becoming identified with a party and shun the spotlight where politics are concerned. Like Longstreet, Thornwell supported the Know-Nothings, but he made this known only to his friends.[6] It was only late in his career, and with reluctance, that Thornwell violated this clerical rule of thumb by writing and speaking publicly on political questions. Still he was, in effect, rehearsing for this phase of his career almost from the moment he was ordained into the Presbyterian ministry in 1835. For Thornwell saw in the theological and ecclesiastical debates within his denomination issues of utmost urgency, not only to the Church, but to the nation and even modern civilization itself. He became involved in those debates early in his career; moreover, no man was a more familiar or respected figure in the annual General Assemblies of the Presbyterian Church in the twenty years before the Civil War. No less an adversary than Henry Ward Beecher conceded that "by common fame Dr. Thornwell was the most brilliant minister in the Old School Presbyterian Church, and the most brilliant debater in the General Assembly." "Whenever he was present in the Assembly, he was always the first person pointed out to a stranger."[7]

The theological and ideological tensions within antebellum American Presbyterianism are perhaps less familiar than those experienced by the Baptists and Methodists, both of whom divided along sectional lines in the 1840s over the issue of slavery.[8] American Presbyterians had united with their Congregationalist cousins in 1801, hoping that by cooperating rather than competing they could stem the rising tide of Arminianism on the frontier. But the marriage was unstable from the start; and by the 1830s the orthodox Calvinist, or Old School presbyteries were fearful that the more rapidly growing New School faction, with its liberal theology coming out of the New England seminaries, would destroy the traditional Reformed

---

[6]Thornwell to Alexander Pegues, 26 July 1855; quoted in Benjamin M. Palmer, *The Life and Letters of James Henley Thornwell, D.D., LL.D.* (Richmond, 1875) 478-79.

[7]Quoted in Paul L. Garber, *James Henley Thornwell, Presbyterian Defender of the Old South* (Richmond, 1943) 5.

[8]Donald G. Mathews, *Methodism and Slavery* (Princeton, 1965). John L. Eighmy, *Churches in Cultural Captivity; A History of the Social Attitudes of Southern Baptists* (Knoxville, 1972).

178 JAMES OSCAR FARMER, JR.

theology with its emphasis on human depravity and salvation by grace. In addition to this fundamental question of theological latitude, the Church confronted a question of constitutional law: was it permissible for Congregationalists to sit in the Courts (district and national assemblies) of the Presbyterian church? A third question involved church polity: should the benevolent work of the Church be conducted in cooperation with voluntary societies over which the Church had little or no control? And finally there was the by-now inescapable question of ethics: was slavery a sin?[9]

While it is necessary to state and examine these questions separately in order to understand the schism of 1837, one should note how intertwined they were. The rise of church "boards," as the benevolent societies were called, was the result of the growing influence of New England theology with its view that salvation was tied, to some degree, to good works. Further, since Congregationalism was generally "New School" in theology, the constitutional issue would determine the doctrinal emphasis of the Church. The issue of slavery was tied to the dispute over literal biblicism that was at the heart of the conflict between the Old and New Schools. In all of these matters the lines of division were not between North and South, but rather between New England and the West, on one hand, and the Mid-Atlantic and Southern regions, on the other. Yet the South was the only region in which there was virtually no division, with eastern Tennessee and Charleston being the only Southern areas having significant New School strength.[10]

Tensions within the Church had been simmering for many years when the General Assembly of 1836 heard the appeal by the Reverend Albert Barnes of Pennsylvania. He had been convicted by his synod of heretical views expressed in a published commentary on Paul's Letter to the Romans. The General Assembly reversed the decision of the synod, thus confirming the fears of the orthodox that the Church was embracing doctrinal laxity. Their anxiety is apparent in Benjamin Palmer's conclusion that "clearly, it was time to act, for each year saw the sound and evangelical

---

[9]Ernest T. Thompson, *Presbyterians in the South,* vol. 1 (Richmond, 1963) 350-51.

[10]Ibid., 358. The question of slavery's role in the schism is debated in Elwyn A. Smith, "The Role of the South in the Presbyterian Schism of 1837-1838," *Church History* 29 (1960): 44-63; and John McCardle, *The Idea of a Southern Nation: Southern Nationalists and Southern Nationalism, 1830-1860* (New York, 1979). Smith sees the slavery issue as of minor importance, and McCardle disagrees, as does Thompson.

portion of the Church drifting under the power of a majority becoming larger and larger by means the most unscrupulous."[11]

After being in the minority in the General Assembly for several years, the Old School delegates found themselves in the majority in 1837. Seeing in this an opportunity that might not come again, they repealed the Plan of Union, declared several New School synods to be no longer eligible for representation in the General Assembly, and thus split American Presbyterianism. Only in this way, they concluded, could the tradition of Calvinism be rescued from certain oblivion.[12] Thornwell, who had been ordained only two years earlier, was a delegate to this assembly, appearing for the first time. Though a very interested observer, he informed his wife that "I have not opened my mouth in the Assembly . . . except to give a vote." He left no doubt as to where he stood, however. He was "deeply grieved" at the "mutual recrimmination [sic]," but focused his feelings on the "unfairness" of the New School delegates, who seemed to him to be trying to appeal to the galleries. "The Lord has shown me, in the proceedings of this General Assembly," he added, "that there is no confidence to be placed in man; that the best of us are weak and erring mortals, who cannot see afar off." He rejoiced that the expulsion of the New School meant that the bitterness of this meeting would not be repeated. "One hour spent in the General Assembly would convince your mind that the two parties ought never to meet again in the same body," he told Nancy. "They are wide apart in spirit, principle, and doctrines." As painful as the process had been, "the Lord has opened up an unexpected door of deliverance to his people."[13]

The issue was far from settled, nonetheless. While a large majority of the presbyteries in the East and South accepted the action of the General Assembly, a few, including the Charleston Presbytery, denounced it as "unconstitutional." Their opposition was in part theological. Some ministers and members argued that Calvin had been excessive in his doctrine of salvation through grace. They held that man could come to God by an act of will, or, in the words of one South Carolina minister, "that faith precedes regeneration." As this clergyman explained, "If God has to plant

---

[11]Palmer, 206.

[12]Ibid., 207-208.

[13]Ibid., 212-13.

. . . salvation in a sinner's heart, to enable him to believe, . . . it must be impossible for God to condemn a man for unbelief, for no just law condemns . . . any person for not doing what he cannot do." This, of course, was the New School's view. All who held it, while living in areas dominated by the Old School, were now in something of a dilemma.[14]

Others opposed the schism on quite different grounds. "A Voice from South Carolina," writing in the *Southern Religious Telegraph*, saw ominous political ramifications in the Church's action.

> The last hold of the Southern States is the constitution. And when this is trampled under foot . . . our peculiar institutions, dear as life, *are annihilated.* . . . Let the principles involved in the doings of the late Assembly be carried out, and as a minority in the Assembly our rights, as Presbyterians and christians here, are held in suspense, at the mercy of non-slaveholding States. . . . The majority decide our fate. And who are the majority? Not abolitionists, to be sure, in the technical sense of the word; but *to a man anti-slavery.*

This Southern Presbyterian's New School views gave him a peculiar insight into the problems of the minority when the majority decides to exert its full power. By purging itself of its liberal elements, American Presbyterianism would avoid the sectional division that would soon befall the Methodists and Baptists. But it was striking a blow at the concept of pluralism that had enabled the creation of so diverse a nation as the United States, and that, for the South, was the only tenable basis for its continuance.[15]

It was this continuing controversy that brought Thornwell, then just shy of twenty-six, to the forefront of church politics. At the 1838 meeting of the Synod of South Carolina and Georgia, he introduced a paper endorsing the doctrines of the Old School. These excerpts summarize its contents: "[T]he guilt of Adam's first sin is imputed to all his posterity . . . so that

---

[14]Thompson, *Presbyterians in the South,* 1:358-61.

[15]*Southern Religious Telegraph,* 4 August 1837; quoted in Thompson, *Presbyterians in the South,* 1:401. This was also the view of Thomas Magruder, editor of the *Southern Christian Sentinel* and spokesman for the opponents of the schism in the Charleston Presbytery (ibid., 403). But Dr. Thomas Smyth of Charleston disagreed, saying that the vast majority of the Old School was opposed "to the doings of the abolitionists" (ibid., 402). See also C. Bruce Staigner, "Abolitionism and the Presbyterian Schism of 1837-1838," *Mississippi Valley Historical Review* 36 (1949-1950): 391-414.

they are born in a state of condemnation and depravity.'' ''The obedience and death of Christ constitute the alone [*sic*] ground of a sinner's acceptance before God.'' ''The inability to comply with the demands of the Divine law, to believe the Gospel, or to exercise any holy affections, is absolute and entire; so that regeneration is effected alone by the direct and immediate agency and power of God the Spirit.'' The paper was adopted by a vote of forty-nine to eight, with those voting in favor pledging that ''no contrary doctrine shall be taught in the [Columbia] Seminary, or in our pulpits.''[16]

To this thumbnail sketch of Thornwellian theology may be added a brief statement of his ecclesiastical beliefs. His colleague and close friend John Adger presented them as follows: ''(1) That the Scriptures are the only sufficient rule of faith and practice, and that in religion whatever is not commanded is forbidden. (2) That the main features of Presbyterian government are of Divine right. (3) That all presbyters have parity, not just ministers. [This refers to Thornwell's view that ruling elders hold equal rank with teaching elders, or ministers.] (4) That Deacons may be employed in upper as well as lower courts. [They may sit in the General Assembly and Synod as well as the Presbytery.] (5) That in mission work the church must act directly, through Executive Committees, and not through boards which can never meet [because their members are so widely dispersed]. (6) That the church is to have no connection with political or moral societies. (7) That Calvin's teachings regarding tithing, the Lord's Supper, and such matters must be upheld.'' It is important to bear in mind that this is not Thornwell's list, nor did he, as far as is known, ever reduce his ecclesiastical beliefs to such a form. But one detects in Adger's list something of the dogmatic tone that, as we have seen, enemy and friend alike attributed to Thornwell.[17]

For one as distressed as Thornwell was by the tendencies of modern life, a firm stand must be made wherever symptoms of these tendencies appeared. So for the rest of his life, he would make an issue of questions

---

[16]Palmer, 214-15; Thompson, *Presbyterians in the South,* 1:402-403. Six of the eight delegates voting ''no'' were from the Charleston Presbytery, which split the following year, with a slight majority of its congregations declaring themselves independent of the Presbyterian Church (ibid., 1:403).

[17]John B. Adger, ''Memorial of James Henley Thornwell,'' in *Memorial Volume of the Theological Seminary at Columbia, South Carolina* (Columbia, 1884) 192.

that, for others, were often too trivial to deserve concern. A divinely ordained plan was in danger of subversion, he had concluded. At first this threat manifested itself in the ecclesiastical disputes within his denomination. He met it with a vigor that many would see as excessive and a dedication to detail that many would see as pedantic. He might have pleaded guilty to this charge, for with all "true believers" he made no apology for zeal in the defense of truth. If the Presbyterian Church could be preserved as a bastion of orthodoxy in a world tilting toward heresies of all kinds, the fight would be well worth the effort. His published essay on the "Elder Question" is a case in point. Thornwell wrote his friend Matthew J. Williams that it dealt with "principles of the highest importance, in their application to both Church and State." "I am afraid," he continued, "that the tendency of things in this country, is to corrupt a *representative* into a *democratic* government, and to make the State the mere creature of popular caprice."[18]

The evil that was infecting the Church was simply an aspect of the evil he had detected in society at large. "Our whole system of operations [in the Presbyterian Church] gives an undue influence to money," he wrote his friend and colleague Robert J. Breckinridge. "Where money is the great *want, numbers* must be sought; and where an ambition for numbers prevails, doctrinal purity must be sacrificed. The root of the evil is in the *secular* spirit of our ecclesiastical institutions. What we want is a *spiritual* body."[19] So determined was Thornwell to preserve the doctrinal purity of Old School Presbyterianism that when the Charleston Union Presbytery,

---

[18]Thornwell to Matthew J. Williams, 17 July 1848, Thornwell Papers, South Caroliniana Library. Republicanism, which may be defined as the ideal of government by representatives who act in the public interest, was a powerful ideology in antebellum America, and perhaps nowhere more so than in South Carolina, where the eighteenth-century concept of "virtual representation" shaped the republican ideal in a peculiar way. Well into the nineteenth century, Palmetto State leaders clung to the notion of the free representative, who was morally pure because he followed his own light of reason rather than the whims of his constituents. Thornwell's mentor, Thomas Cooper, and his state's leading public figure, John C. Calhoun, both held this view. So for Thornwell political theory endorsed ecclesiastical theory. Kenneth S. Greenberg, "Representation and the Isolation of South Carolina, 1776-1860," *Journal of American History* 64:3 (December 1977): 723-43; Thomas Cooper, *Two Essays* (Columbia, 1826) 34; Richard K. Cralle, ed., *The Works of John C. Calhoun,* 6 vols. (New York, 1860-1863) 2:177-79.

[19]Thornwell to Robert J. Breckinridge, 24 July 1846; quoted in Palmer, 291.

which had been independent since 1838, sought readmission in 1852 to the Old School General Assembly, he objected. He and others were apprehensive as to "what the members of the Charleston Union Presbytery really do believe in regard to original sin—the nature and extent of the atonement, and the ability of man in his natural state."[20] Whether Thornwell was satisfied by the response to his concerns is not known, but the Synod of South Carolina voted fifty-six to seventeen to readmit the wayward congregations.[21]

The expulsion of the New School presbyteries in 1837-1838 had virtually eliminated the heterodox views associated with that faction; the members of the Old School were now nearly of one mind on the major issues facing American Christians in the mid-nineteenth century. Thornwell epitomized that mind. "My doctrines . . . are rapidly growing," he wrote to Nancy from the General Assembly of 1848, "and in a few years more they will be the predominant type of opinion in the Presbyterian Church."[22] Only a narrow conception of what constituted conformity prevented Thornwell from asserting that his doctrines were already predominant. By the time he wrote those words, he had been a delegate to five General Assemblies (1837, 1840, 1845, 1847, and 1848), played a major role in their

---

[20]*Minutes,* Synod of South Carolina, 1852, 13; quoted in Thompson, *Presbyterians in the South,* 1:422.

[21]Ibid. The ecclesiastical situation in Charleston in the 1830s and 1840s was complex and difficult to unravel. Thomas Smyth, pastor of the Second Presbyterian Church from 1830 to 1870, wrote that he and Reverend Benjamin Gildersleeve were the only defenders of the Old School in the city during the 1830s. His unpopularity on this account was compounded by the charge, made in the *Mercury* of 18 December 1838, that he was tainted with abolitionism. Smyth, who had been a Congregationalist earlier in life, found himself torn between the Old School theology and his desire for Presbyterian unity. Tensions were such that, by Smyth's account, several other Presbyterian preachers would barely speak to him. Still, his congregation rallied behind him, and he made some important converts in Daniel Ravenel, Judge Mitchell King, and Benjamin M. Palmer, pastor of the Congregational Church. Smyth differed with Thornwell on the "Elder Question" and the "Board Question" and was generally more concerned with evangelism than was Thornwell. He was a respected scholar, and his voluminous writings earned him an honorary doctorate in Divinity from Princeton in 1843. Thomas Smyth, *Autobiographical Notes, Letters and Reflections,* ed. Louisa Cheves Stoney (Charleston, 1914) 19-20, 165, 211-16, 227, 239.

[22]Thornwell to Nancy Thornwell, 29 May 1848, Anderson-Thornwell Papers, Southern Historical Collection.

deliberations and, at the age of thirty-four, had been the youngest man ever elected moderator of that body (in 1847).[23]

Indeed, for two decades no voice was more prominent in the debates of the General Assembly, and few if any pens were more active in the written arguments on theology and polity that filled the pages of the religious press. Thornwell's early adopted and long-maintained positions on the various issues before American Presbyterianism in those tense years were based upon his fundamental belief that "Christ has prescribed the model in conformity with which His people should be governed." With Robert J. Breckinridge, John B. Adger, and others, he advanced the doctrine known as *jure divino* Presbyterianism: the Scriptures set forth not only the doctrine, but also the polity of the church.[24] This viewpoint, while not endorsed unanimously by Southern Presbyterians, would disarm efforts to involve the Church in issues that would dilute its orthodoxy, and would, in all probability, have broken it along sectional lines. It served, in other words, the same function as the states' rights argument in Calhoun's politics: it preserved the union through providing a means by which damaging issues could be kept at arms-length. Thus the label "the Calhoun of the Church" was fitting.

Using this device—if the doctrine can be so described without impugning the integrity of those who subscribed to it—Thornwell and his allies developed effective, if not always successful, arguments on several issues: the "Boards question," the "Elder question," the question of who could call a pastor, the question of selling or renting pews, the question of the necessity of the office of deacon, the question of benevolent fund raising, the question of instrumental music in worship, and the question of the Church's position on slavery and other social or political issues. Thornwell was not equally active on all of these fronts; however, there was no question too small when it touched on the integrity of Old School Pres-

---

[23]Palmer, 211-13, 297-99. For an extended discussion of his place in the Church, see A. M. Fraser, "Thornwell as an Ecclesiologist," in *Centennial Addresses Commemorating the Birth of the Reverend James Henley Thornwell, D.D., LL.D.* (Spartanburg SC, 1913) 31-52. Among other examples of Thornwell's position, Fraser notes that when the General Assembly was facing a crisis in 1857 regarding its rules of discipline, the moderator chose Thornwell to chair a committee on revision of these rules (ibid., 33-34).

[24]Thompson, *Presbyterians in the South,* 1:518.

byterianism, a body whose behavior could affect the outcome of the great struggle in which modern civilization was engaged.[25]

The boards question involved the administration of the Church's mission work. The General Assembly created various boards and appointed their directors. The boards designated the missionaries or agencies to carry out the work and met annually to review the work. The time and hardships involved in travel meant that generally less than half of the members attended the meetings of the boards, which usually were held in Philadelphia. The only control the General Assembly exercised over these operations was its action on the annual reports of the boards. To many, this lack of control over the missionary efforts of the denomination was a serious but solvable problem. To Thornwell, the problem was not the abuses of this system, but the "essential evils of the system itself." Scripture required Church courts to control all church affairs. "The total silence of the Word of God in regard to such contrivances as Boards seals their condemnation," he wrote. His preference was to have domestic and foreign missions conducted by the presbyteries, which could have personal contact with the missionaries, know their theology, and contribute directly to their support.[26]

Opponents of Thornwell on the boards questions, including Thomas Smyth, took a "loose constructionist" view of the biblical guidelines. The debates on this issue are reminiscent of those between Hamilton and Jefferson on the Constitution. In Smyth's opinion, "That which the Church is required to do, she is empowered to do by all means not expressly forbidden [in Scripture]." Thornwell's reply warned of the return of doctrinal confusion against which the English Puritans had rebelled in the sixteenth and seventeenth centuries; and he added a more timely point: "Under the system of Boards, the churches in South Carolina may be supporting a man sent out by a Presbytery denouncing them as unchristian and hypocriti-

---

[25]See ch. 2, n. 1.

[26]Thornwell, "Argument against Church Boards," *Baltimore Literary and Religious Magazine*, 1841; reprinted in John B. Adger, ed., *Collected Writings of James Henley Thornwell*, vol. 4 (Richmond, 1871) 164. Palmer, ch. 16. Thompson, *Presbyterians in the South*, 1:365-76, 511-12. See also Thornwell, MS Lecture on Boards to Seminary Students, n.d., Thornwell Papers; Thornwell, "The General Assembly," *Southern Presbyterian Review* 1 (September 1847): 90.

cal—a Presbytery that would silence all their ministers and excommunicate all their members.''[27]

This debate climaxed in the General Assembly of 1860. Thornwell reiterated his position and proposed a compromise that would have given the assembly more direct supervision of missionary activity. Princeton's Charles Hodge, leading the other side, attacked the idea that Jesus had ordained a system of church government in detail, and that creating a new office was no more permitted than creating a new doctrine. Indeed, he coined a term for it, calling it ''hyper-hyper-hyper High Church Presbyterianism.'' Thornwell replied that Hodge's views amounted to ''no, no, No Presbyterianism, no, no, No Churchism!'' The assembly supported Hodge by a large majority on the principle involved, but did adopt a compromise along the lines proposed by Thornwell.[28]

His position had been voted down, but the effect of Thornwell's efforts, and those of his fellow supporters of *jure divino,* was to hold the Church to a fairly orthodox stance while the Southern presbyteries were still in it, and to provide a foundation for the even more orthodox position that the Confederate Presbyterian Church would assume in 1861. The same results were obtained on several other issues addressed by the Church in the late antebellum era. Regarding the ''Elder question,'' the 1843 General Assembly said that elders should not take part in the ordination of ministers by the laying on of hands, nor were they necessary to form a quorum at presbytery meetings. Thornwell concluded that these positions reduced the biblical status of elders and implied a more distinctive position for the clergy than the Bible gives them. He thus joined with Breckinridge, Adger, Robert L. Dabney, and others in opposing them.[29] Again resting his case on biblical ''strict constructionism,'' Thornwell joined with several others in opposing the growing use of instrumental music in Presbyterian worship. Although organs did not become common in Presbyterian churches

---

[27]Thomas Smyth, ''Argument for Church Boards,'' *Collected Writings of Thornwell,* 4:494, 504; Thornwell, ''Argument against Church Boards,'' ibid., 210, 214, 222. Thompson, *Presbyterians in the South,* 1:512.

[28]*Collected Writings of Thornwell,* 4:217-41, esp. 226-31; Thompson, *Presbyterians in the South,* 1:515-16.

[29]Palmer, ch. 18; Thompson, *Presbyterians in the South,* 1:516-18. Smyth, *Autobiographical Notes,* 209-301, contains several letters on this issue. See also Fraser, ''Thornwell as Ecclesiologist,'' 49-50.

until the end of the century, urban congregations were using them before the Civil War, and the General Assembly considered this a matter for each congregation to decide. For Thornwell, the lack of biblical sanction settled this question in the negative. Here he was joined by Breckinridge, Adger, Dabney, John Girardeau, and Thomas Peck.[30] Questions in which Thornwell did not play a conspicuous part included those involving the role of nonmembers who contributed to the church in the calling of a pastor, the selling and renting of church pews, and the duties of the office of deacon.[31]

But on two other issues he was unyielding: the Church's relation to slavery and its relation to secular humanitarian organizations. (A full discussion of his views on slavery will be found in chapter 7.) In 1818 the General Assembly had concluded that slavery was "utterly inconsistent with the law of God." By 1845, however, the peculiar institution had become, in Thornwell's words, "a purely civil relationship, with which the church, as such, has no right to interfere." The subject was laid to rest, at least officially, as a sectional issue within the Church, for the 1845 assembly affirmed Thornwell's statement "that the existence of domestic slavery is no bar to Christian communion." While there was some opposition to Thornwell's report on slavery, it was adopted in essence, and he felt confident that "abolitionism will be killed in the Presbyterian Church, at least for the present." The significance of this action was not lost on the members of the assembly, and Thornwell's speech in its defense made him "the object of general attention and curiosity. I have had compliments, which God grant may not injure my humility."[32]

Thornwell's prediction about the demise of the slavery issue in the Church would prove essentially accurate; some twelve years later a leading Southern Presbyterian paper wrote: "The statement of the Old School Assembly of 1845 on slavery has met with almost universal support in the Church, and has been the basis for the peace and harmony in our midst the last ten years, in spite of the public turmoil of this period."[33] Looking back on the period in 1875, Benjamin M. Palmer agreed that the statement on

---

[30]Thompson, *Presbyterians in the South,* 1:463, 528.

[31]Ibid., 1:519-22.

[32]La Motte, *Colored Light,* 127; Thornwell to Nancy Thornwell, 19 May 1845; quoted in Palmer, 286-87.

[33]*The Southern Presbyterian,* 7 February 1857, 2.

slavery had "formed the basis upon which the Church continued to stand until the disruption occasioned by the late civil war."[34] The question did not, of course, disappear. Shifting the ground to the Church's role regarding the treatment of slaves, opponents again raised the issue in 1847. Thornwell, who presided over this assembly, was concerned; and while he maintained his ground on the basic question of the Church's relationship to the institution, he would address the abuses so endemic to it in several essays during the 1850s. He favored, for example, repeal of the state laws against teaching slaves to read.[35]

Another indication of Thornwell's influence in the Church came in 1848, when the General Assembly gave unanimous consent to his resolution opposing any connection between the Church and secular humanitarian organizations such as temperance societies. This event established the concept of "the spirituality of the church," which would provide conservatives in general, and Southern Presbyterians in particular, with a strong argument against ecclesiastical involvement in political and social issues.[36]

Thornwell's position, which had been maturing for several years, was that the Church was God's creation and both its doctrine and its policy were prescribed in Scripture. The secular influences of modern life were contaminating this divinely ordained institution by introducing agencies for social welfare that were not biblical and thus had no place in any true church. "I am satisfied," he wrote to a colleague, "that there is a dangerous departure, in the present age of bustle, activity, and vainglorious enterprise, from the simplicity of the institutions which Christ has established for the legitimate action of the Church." No mere human invention was necessary to accomplish the divine purposes of the Church. Therefore, he held that "the entire system of voluntary societies and ecclesiastical Boards, for religious purposes is fundamentally wrong." While he faced opposition on these points, he was in good company, for "if I am singular, at the present day, in maintaining that the Bible is our *only* rule, and that where it is silent we have no right to speak, I have the consolation of knowing, that I stand on the same ground which was occupied by Calvin

---

[34]Palmer, 285.

[35]Thornwell to Robert Breckinridge, 20 October 1847; quoted in Palmer, 301.

[36]Ibid., 303.

. . . and the venerable Assembly of Divines at Westminster. I would particularly direct your attention to Calvin's 'Institutes,' Book IV, chapters 8th, 9th, 10th, and 11th.''[37] Referring specifically to temperance societies, he described them as ''secular enterprises, for temporal good, having no connection whatever with the kingdom of Christ.'' They were ''of great service to society,'' but the Church should not affiliate itself with them, or with any other such organization. Indeed it should have nothing at all to do with them ''as long as false principles are not promulgated, and wrong practices are not indulged.''[38] The Church's influences on society will be felt more strongly, if indirectly, through its generic impact than through any attempt to attack social problems directly through societal boards. If it did its proper job well, the Church would encourage people to ''act as a Christian should act'' in the responsibilities of life, by seeing to the education of their children, helping the needy, and setting good examples of citizenship in their communities. The Church, then, for Thornwell, *was* a social welfare agency in the truest sense and did not *need* such agencies to do its divinely ordained task.[39]

With the secession of the South and civil war, Thornwell abandoned the doctrine proclaiming the church's noninterference in political questions. But throughout the antebellum era he stood firm in it. When the General Assembly of 1859, meeting in Indianapolis, debated endorsing the African colonization of slaves, Thornwell's argument was unchanged: ''The church is exclusively a *spiritual* organization, and possesses only *spiritual* power.'' Her great strength lies in the fact that ''the only voice she utters is the Word of God. . . . The salt that is to save this country is the Church of Christ, a Church that does not mix with any political party, or any issue aside from her direct mission.'' Palmer, who was present, recalled this as the only time the decorum of the assembly was broken by applause, as delegates from North and South responded to the ''patriotism'' of Thornwell's remarks.[40]

Not all of Thornwell's ecclesiastical concerns were of a sectional nature. He was, with most American Protestants in the nineteenth century, a

---

[37]Thornwell to John Douglas, 4 August 1840; quoted ibid., 225.

[38]Fraser, ''Thornwell as Ecclesiologist,'' 42-43; Palmer, 303 (Palmer's paraphrase).

[39]Fraser, ''Thornwell as Ecclesiologist,'' 45-46. Thornwell to the Reverend John Douglas, 4 August 1840. Quoted in Palmer, 225-26; see also 303.

[40]Palmer, 435-37. Fraser, ''Thornwell as Ecclesiologist,'' 43-44.

violent opponent of Roman Catholicism. The General Assembly of 1845 listened with "breathless attention" [Thornwell's words] as he spoke for two hours in opposition to the validity of "Popish" baptism. After the debate the assembly sustained his view by a vote of one hundred seventy-four to six. When the *Princeton Journal* criticized this position, Thornwell called it "an apologist for Rome" and wrote a series of three articles in rebuttal.[41] His friend Breckinridge found Thornwell's articles too mild, but Thornwell replied that he wanted to show that it was not a "personal war."[42] Perhaps he was by now thinking better of some of his attacks on Bishop Patrick Lynch of Charleston, which took place in a printed exchange that could be characterized as a "personal war." The debate had begun in 1841, when an article by Thornwell on the Apocrypha was reprinted in a Charleston publication and drew a reply from Bishop Lynch. Thornwell rejoined the contest, and for the next few years the battle raged. Thornwell published his collected writings from this debate in 1845.[43]

He began his polemic with an explanation of the "severity of rebuke" that was necessary in "reproving error," and went on to characterize "popery" as "anti-Christian and dangerous—no better than Mahometanism [*sic*]." He rejected Bishop Lynch's defense of the Apocrypha as "ambiguous," and submitted that the testimony of the papacy on this subject was "entitled to no consideration." Thornwell went on to attack the doctrine of papal infallibility as ill founded, "conducive to licentiousness and immorality," and "the patron of Superstition and Will-worship." The remainder of his letters dealt with the history of this debate, which, for Thornwell, was weighted entirely in favor of his position.[44]

In these letters Thornwell is at his polemical best, or worst. He concedes that Bishop Lynch's arguments are covered with "a veil of affected politeness" that is rare in the writings of his "Royal Masters," the popes, who have "reduced fraud to a system, and lying to an art."[45] Reminding

---

[41]Thornwell to Nancy Thornwell, 19 May 1845; quoted in Palmer, 286.

[42]Thornwell to Breckinridge, 24 March 1846; quoted in Palmer, 290.

[43]Palmer, 226; Thornwell, *Arguments of Romanists from the Infallibility of the Church and the Testimony of the Fathers in Behalf of the Apocrypha, Discussed and Refuted* (New York, 1845).

[44]Thornwell, *Arguments of Romanists*, table of contents. Thornwell wrote twenty-nine letters to Lynch on this subject.

[45]Ibid., 9-10.

his readers of the use of torture and execution by Roman Catholics in the past, he calls freedom of thought and obedience to God "the only crimes which Rome cannot tolerate."[46] He even takes issue with Bishop Lynch's use of the name "Catholic Church," for "so far are you from being the Holy Catholic Church, that your right to be regarded as a church at all in any just or scriptural sense, is exceedingly questionable."[47] As to the harsh tone of Thornwell's attack, which Lynch had noted with sadness, he replied: "It is only among those who hardly admit the existence of such a thing as truth—who look upon all doctrines as equally involved in uncertainty and doubt . . . that a generous zeal is likely to be denounced as bigotry, a holy fervency of style mistaken for the inspiration of malice." Jesus, he added, was stern in his rebuke of the scribes and Pharisees.[48]

In his attacks on the Apocrypha, Thornwell dismisses the idea that the existence of a catalogue or list gives special status to any work that appears on that list, and suggests that the Apocrypha was adopted by the Council of Trent because the rest of the Bible contained nothing for which Martin Luther could be indicted. As for the council itself, he says that its most respected member, Cajetan, could not read Hebrew. "So much for the *learning* of these venerable men," he adds. He treats Lynch as belonging to the same class of unqualified authorities. Referring sarcastically to his adversary's "skill in the art of definitions," he adds, "[I] tremble to encounter so formidable an opponent."[49]

Turning to the doctrine of papal infallibility, Thornwell retreats not an inch from his aggressive stance. He rejects it on two grounds: since popes have contradicted popes, and two contradictions cannot be true, popes are therefore fallible; and since the bishop of Rome was not always infallible, he can never be so.[50] Lynch's argument in defense he finds totally unconvincing. "It may be adapted to children and idiots," he says, "but it is ill suited to bearded men. Perhaps one reason why you are so anxious to establish schools for Protestant children and erect asylums for Protestant orphans, while you suffer starving millions of your own flock to live by

---

46Ibid., 9.

47Ibid., 13.

48Ibid., 12.

49Ibid., 17-20, 21, 23, 25-26.

50Ibid., 78-83.

begging, and die in ignorance, is to be found in the secret conviction which you feel that your only hope of success is among those who cannot discriminate between legitimate reasoning and puerile sophisms."[51]

Throughout these letters Thornwell appears as the man of reason, insisting on the need for evidence to prove the truth of any assertion, and employing logic against Lynch's purportedly illogical arguments.[52] Here he is the modern—discovering the fallacies in the medieval metaphysics of Rome, and expressing confidence that his own position regarding the compatibility of religion and science was secure in light of the charges he brought against Roman Catholicism. "You have become involved in a maze of contradictions," he tells Lynch, "which can have no other effect than to draw upon you the pity and contempt of your readers." But "[c]onsistency cannot be expected from the advocates of a black and bloody superstition."[53]

The *Arguments of Romanists* provoked further rebuttal from Bishop Lynch and others, including Orestes Brownson, who wrote three articles reviewing it in the 1848 issues of his *Brownson's Quarterly*. Thornwell, ever the combatant, wanted to respond to these "feeble" pieces, noting that "the Papists may crow" if he remained silent. But, as he wrote Robert J. Breckinridge (who had urged him on), if he responded to every reviewer "who may take me in hand, I may make business enough for myself to occupy my whole time." Other concerns were pressing him by now, so he moved away from this field. He never softened his views on Catholicism, as his affiliation with the American party, or Know-Nothings, would show.[54]

Even as he opposed the monarchial structure of "Popery," Thornwell was equally opposed to the notion of the church as a democracy. It was partly the representative system of church government that had first attracted him to Presbyterianism when he came across a copy of the *Westminster Confession of Faith* as a college student. In his view, this system, when properly understood, achieved the ideal balance between monarchy and democracy. That the apostle Paul spoke of elders (presbyters in the

---

[51]Ibid., 72.

[52]Ibid., 213.

[53]Ibid., 58.

[54]Thornwell to Robert J. Breckinridge, 24 February 1849; quoted in Palmer, 329-31.

Greek) in several of his letters provided the biblical authority for this system.[55] But Thornwell's own concept of republicanism placed the elder in a special role, which explains his stand on the "elder question" mentioned above. For him, the elder was not merely a spokesman for those who elected him, but was to decide, as another Presbyterian clergyman put it, "in accordance with their best interests . . . as determined from his more advantageous point of observation." This, the writer reminds us, was the viewpoint of Burke and Pitt, and makes an elder analogous to a member of Parliament or Congress, except that he is also the "deputy of God." Paul admonished the early Christians to be obedient to their elders, or bishops (the terms were used interchangeably), and thus Thornwell saw the elder as an enlightened, rational leader, avoiding the capriciousness of the group while still being responsible to it. Obviously he saw Presbyterianism as a fine model for the United States and was thus disturbed by the democratizing tendencies in both state and church.[56]

The sectional tensions of the late antebellum years are well known, and the bloody climax toward which they drove the nation has often been regarded as virtually inevitable. Yet there were, down to the very eve of the war, institutions that managed to keep their intersectional bonds intact through compromise and emphasis upon tradition. The Old School Presbyterian Church was one of these, and the efforts of Thornwell and other Southern leaders in that body were in no small way responsible for this. "Never, perhaps, since the founding of this branch of Christ's kingdom upon the Western Continent, has there existed greater harmony in doctrine, in feeling, and in aims, than . . . now prevails in every part of our widely dispersed Churches, and people." So stated the General Assembly of 1854. While noting with regret shortcomings in the keeping of the Sabbath and the rise of the "worldly spirit" of materialism, the moderator rejoiced at the harmony that prevailed in spite of "the great diversity of views, and interests on other subjects that of necessity [exist] between different sections."[57]

---

[55]Thornwell, "Judgements . . . ." (Columbia, 1854) 17-19. First Timothy 5:17; Titus 1:5.

[56]Fraser, "Thornwell as Ecclesiologist," 38, 41. See n. 18.

[57]"A Narrative of the State of Religion in the Presbyterian Church in the United States, Adopted by the General Assembly, May, 1854, and Addressed to the Churches." Quoted in the *Southern Presbyterian*, 29 June 1854, 1.

Yet even within this bastion of orthodoxy there were signs of friction. Financial support for Princeton Seminary, the denomination's largest, was declining dramatically among the Southern churches. Union Theological Seminary was established in Richmond, along with Columbia Seminary in the South Carolina capitol and Danville Seminary in Kentucky, as alternative institutions for the training of Southern clergymen. Northern ministers and professors were finding it increasingly difficult to obtain Southern pastorates and faculty posts. Southern Presbyterians were imagining Henry Ward Beecher as all-too-typical of Northern Presbyterian preachers.[58] While all of this was the result of differing attitudes toward the general trends of the nineteenth century, a single issue did gain ascendancy. That single issue crystallized the mutual suspicion within the Church, as within the nation. John Adger spoke not just for the advocates of *jure divino* Presbyterianism, but for Southerners generally, when he defended slavery by saying that the Church "cannot make anything to be sinful which God himself has not in His holy word, forbidden." The Church, Adger continued, "has no legislative power, except as to the mere circumstances of time and place . . . which, from the nature of the case, scripture could not regulate. . . . All the power which the church has about laws is declarative and ministerial. Her officers declare, not their own will, but the Lord's and that only as he makes it known in the word."[59]

A society that was unwilling to order itself according to "the word," and further considered man's knowledge as progressive and God's revelation as evolutionary, was an unsafe environment for those whose images of both man and God were fixed in Reformation perspectives. Metaphysically, Southern thinkers were creating for themselves and their people a confederacy that excluded the nineteenth century. The Confederacy that Southern politicians would soon create was but the edifice, built to house that mind that had been its harbinger.

---

[58]Margaret Burr DesChamps, "Union or Disunion? South Atlantic Presbyterians and Southern Nationalism, 1820-1861," *Journal of Southern History* 20 (November 1954): 484-98. Alexander T. McGill, of Pennsylvania, was almost rejected as a faculty member at Columbia Seminary in 1851 because of his Northern roots (ibid., 487). See also Margaret DesChamps Moore, "A Northern Professor Winters in Columbia, 1852-1853," *South Carolina Historical Magazine* 60 (1959): 183-92.

[59]John Adger, *My Life and Times* (Richmond, 1899) 364-65.

CHAPTER **7**

The Southern Clergy and the Slavery Debate

"Southern slavery," wrote South Carolina College professor Maximilian LaBorde in 1856, "is regulated by law, the principle of humanity is infused into it, it is the slavery *of the Bible.*"[1] Historians of the Old South would generally agree that LaBorde was expressing what had become the dominant Southern position on this subject. But they are not in agreement as to the inner thoughts and feelings of those who spoke in slavery's defense. How sincerely was this position held? Did Southern whites—slaveholders and slaveless, religious and not—honestly regard slavery as LaBorde described it?

They wrote prolifically in defense of the institution on every ground they could find, especially the moral.[2] Yet modern historians have tended to discount these works for several reasons. First, they see human slavery as reprehensible on its face. Second, they have discovered that Southern whites had not always been as fond of the institution as they were on the eve of the Civil War. Indeed, the early abolitionist movement was as strong

---

[1]Columbia *Daily South Carolinian,* 3 May 1856; quoted in Daniel W. Hollis, *The University of South Carolina,* vol. 1 (Columbia, 1951) 183.

[2]William S. Jenkins, *Pro-Slavery Thought in the Old South* (Chapel Hill, 1935); Drew G. Faust, ed., *The Pro-Slavery Argument, 1830-1860* (Baton Rouge, 1981).

in the South as in the North.[3] Equally important, many nonabolitionist Southerners had been openly ambivalent about slavery before 1830, but their ambivalence either abated or became more hidden as time passed. The defenses that late antebellum Southerners provided for their institution were thus suspect, many have concluded, because they were so recently developed. Third, modern historians have questioned the sincerity of the defense because the slavery pictured in these apologias bears so little resemblance to the institution as it has been described in the voluminous literature on the subject produced during the last thirty years. In the hands of men like George Fitzhugh, William Gilmore Simms, Henry Hughes, Nathaniel Beverly Tucker, Daniel R. Hundley, or William J. Grayson, slavery often became a utopian social system and an ideal labor system.[4]

Some have seen the proslavery argument as a clear case of self-serving rhetoric. Calling it "specious," Ronald Lora has said that while the argument was complex, "after the Southern fear of the social consequences of abolition are [sic] considered, little of substance remains except economic motivation."[5] Others have suggested that the proslavery argument was an effort to escape the guilt Southern whites felt because of their regrettable association with a labor system so out of step with American values. In defending slavery, this view holds, Southern writers were addressing their neighbors, and even themselves, rather than the Northern antislavery forces. Unwilling, or perhaps unable, to confront the ugliness of a system

---

[3]William M. Boyd, "Southerners in the Anti-Slavery Movement, 1800-1830," *Phylon* 9 (1948): 153-63; Carl Degler, *The Other South: Southern Dissenters in the Nineteenth Century* (New York, 1975) chs. 2 and 3; Gordon E. Finnie, "The Antislavery Movement in the Upper South before 1840," *Journal of Southern History* 35 (1969): 319-42; Kenneth Stampp, "The Fate of the Southern Anti-Slavery Movement," *Journal of Negro History* 28 (1943): 10-22; idem, "The Southern Refutation of the Pro-Slavery Argument," *North Carolina Historical Review* 21 (1944): 35-45.

[4]George Fitzhugh, *Cannibals All! or Slaves without Masters* (1855); William Gilmore Simms, essay in E. N. Elliott, ed., *Cotton is King, and Pro-Slavery Arguments* (1860); Henry Hughes, *Treatise on Sociology* (1854); Nathaniel Beverly Tucker, *George Balcombe* (1836); William J. Grayson, *The Hireling and the Slave* (1856). For a provocative analysis of these and other works, which he says produced a "sustaining illusion," see William R. Taylor, *Cavalier and Yankee: The Old South and the American National Character* (New York, 1957) esp. ch. 7.

[5]Ronald Lora, *Conservative Minds in America* (Chicago, 1971) 40-41.

that was so fundamental to their way of life, they rationalized it into something they could defend.[6]

This is a difficult argument to refute, perhaps because it appeals to the mind of an age confronting its own guilt. The morally minded person of the late twentieth century is accustomed to guilt and may want to see it in others, even those who are removed in time. The argument is attractive also because the evidence is indeed there. The Southerner who felt a recurring sense of doubt, or even guilt, about slavery was not rare. No doubt at least some of the proslavery rhetoric was written as an exercise in self-persuasion and read in the hope of freedom from doubt. Some, like a Southern reviewer of Mississippian Henry Hughes's *Treatise on Sociology*, were disturbed by the Southern "habit" of admitting that slavery was "an evil in the abstract." This book, published in 1854, George Fitzhugh credits with helping to revolutionize Southern public opinion on slavery.[7]

The implication that just six years before the birth of the Confederacy large numbers of Southerners harbored deep doubts about their peculiar institution is indeed hard to escape. This implication is substantiated by the vitriolic tone of much of the proslavery writing and by the fact that the quantity of this writing increased steadily through the late antebellum era. Indeed, it has even been suggested that Eric Erikson's psychological concept of the "identity crisis" is an instructive way of analyzing the mind of the Old South. If individuals living in times of rapid, disorienting change experience and try to master such a crisis, perhaps societies do also. Could not late-twentieth-century America be a case in point?

For the Old South, Henry Hughes is an excellent example of the identity-crisis idea. As a youth of nineteen, he had thought it his chief aim in life "to unite the great powers of the earth in one Republic, to abolish slavery, and to reform the system of human laws and human society." Three years later he was still hopeful of abolition, "but not to the hurt of the

[6]Wilbur J. Cash, *The Mind of the South* (New York, 1941) 62-63, 85-89; Charles G. Sellers, Jr., ed., "The Travail of Slavery," in *The Southerner as American* (Chapel Hill, 1960) 40-71; William Freehling, *Prelude to Civil War; the Nullification Movement in South Carolina, 1816-1836* (New York, 1965) ch. 3; Ralph E. Morrow, "The Pro-Slavery Argument Revisited," *Mississippi Valley Historical Review* 48 (June 1961): 70-94.

[7]Ronald Takaki, *A Pro-Slavery Crusade: The Agitation to Reopen the African Slave Trade* (New York, 1971) 96-97.

South.''[8] He soon saw the futility of this plan, however, and turned to developing a theory of moral and humane master-slave relationships. The result was his *Treatise on Sociology*. William Gilmore Simms called it a profound and conclusive defense of slavery, which Hughes preferred to call Warranteeism.[9] He predicted that when his system was adopted in the South, the nation and the world would praise his region for solving the problems ''free'' societies are unable to solve.

But when the events of the late 1850s seemed to threaten the institution itself, Hughes lashed out at Northern critics. The African slave trade should be reopened, he argued, and though the newly arrived Africans will have to be identified for purposes of white safety and black socialization, this would be no problem.

> If necessary bloody letters may by State authority be branded on the negroes' cheeks or hips. Or if rampant free-labor philanthropy, fattening on its own abuses but sickening at ours, shall still fall into foaming convulsions at the horrors of our labor system, then, let us in healthy, cool and laughing defiance, identify by other means, the negroes and their children. Let us . . . in humorous contempt, in delightful and deliberate detestation of sanctimonious meddlers . . . mark them like hogs and brand them like beeves; let us slit their nostrils, let us pinch in their bleeding ears, . . . or with hot and salted irons, fry on their brows and breasts lasting letters. . . . Then let freedom shriek till her face is red, and her voice is cracked as her skull.[10]

When one realizes that as a boy, the author of these words had a close relationship with a family slave whom he called ''Uncle Alex,'' the extent of the abolitionist movement's impact on the Southern mind becomes clear.[11] It can also be argued that the ease, and in some cases even relief, with which Southerners accepted the end of slavery after the Civil War is an indication of their less-than-whole-hearted support of the institution.[12]

---

[8]Hughes Diary, 16 November 1848, 13 April 1851—in Takaki, *A Pro-Slavery Crusade*, 95, 96.

[9]Ibid., 96-98.

[10]''St. Henry'' in the Jackson *Semi-Weekly Mississippian*, 4 October 1859; quoted ibid., 84-85.

[11]Ibid., 87.

[12]James G. Randall and David Donald, *The Civil War and Reconstruction* (Lexington MA, 1969) 546-47.

Notwithstanding the above arguments, a close examination of the mind of the Old South points to the conclusion that uncertainty was not the prevailing sentiment for Southerners. To take the last point first, James Roark has concluded that planters as a whole found the readjustment of the Reconstruction period so frustrating precisely because of the strength of their commitment to slavery and to its wellspring, white supremacy.[13] That commitment was in large part the product of self-interest, heightened by what Steven Channing has called the ''memories and forebodings'' of Southern whites, slaveholders and non-slaveholders alike, which had been aroused by the abolitionist attacks and brought to a fever pitch by John Brown and the Republican party.[14] But it was also the result of a long period in which Southerners had examined their own society and that of the North and Europe and, in light of their racial attitudes, concluded that their way of life, slavery included, was preferable to any practical alternative.[15]

In this self-examination, the Calvinistic mind of Southerners played an important part. ''The slaveholders of the nineteenth century South did not wallow in guilt over their ownership of slaves,'' writes Eugene Genovese.

> They took their world for granted. Yet, many perceptive and knowledgeable historians have interpreted their behavior as guilt-ridden. In a sense, they have not been mistaken. The whites of the South inherited an Anglo-Saxon civilization based on religions that profoundly deepened whatever sense of guilt may be inherent in human experience. But for precisely that reason, the notion that slaveholders' relationship to their slaves can be understood as a function of guilt must be scouted. They felt guilt about everything. But everything in this respect equals nothing. Their guilt feelings ended, as they began, as a personal matter. And in no sense can their response to slavery be interpreted as a function of a pervasive and yet ultimately self-indulgent expression of this general sensibility.[16]

---

[13]James L. Roark, *Masters without Slaves; Southern Planters in the Civil War and Reconstruction* (New York, 1977) ch. 4.

[14]Steven Channing, *Crisis of Fear; Secession in South Carolina* (New York, 1970) chs. 1 and 2.

[15]An excellent discussion of this question is in Louis Rubin, *The Writer in the South* (Athens GA, 1972) 14-25.

[16]Eugene D. Genovese, *Roll, Jordan, Roll; The World the Slaves Made* (New York, 1972) 120.

What part did the South's religious leaders play in the debate over slavery? How did their position on this most vital question contribute to the prominence of theological matters in the region? Ministers shared with their white neighbors the apocalyptic vision of emancipation and added to the common racism of their society the view that God had ordained the Southern social system to prevail until such time as He might prepare the races for its modification. Daily contact with slaves gave many clergymen the assurance that they knew firsthand what the Northern critics of slavery could only see in the abstract. Northern churchmen who came South frequently found themselves taking the Southern view of the issue after observing the institution in practice. "My own views," wrote one, "which were once perhaps somewhat ultra—have been very much modified, not as some would suppose by a local prejudice but from a more expanded view of the subject. No logic can plead with the power of ocular demonstration."[17] Another visitor from the North, while not converted to belief in slavery, revealed feelings about the slaves themselves that were no different from those of most Southerners. Alexander McGill of Pennsylvania spent the 1853 spring term as a professor at Columbia Seminary. In a letter to his wife, who had remained at home, he called the servants who were assigned to him "lazy, lying and deceitful rascals. They know I don't whip; and neither do I pay; and they don't care whether I freeze or not."[18] As the March weather allowed more outings in Columbia, he commented in disgust on seeing "so many niggers" everywhere. Yet despite these feelings McGill was charmed by life in Columbia and gave much consideration to an offer to remain at the seminary. Presenting this possibility to his wife, he showed that he had pondered the South's dilemma. "Shall we [go] to the sunny South, and mix . . . with its institutions and its destiny?"[19]

---

[17]Zelotus Holmes to "Much Respected Cousin," 1 February 1840, Zelotus Holmes Papers, South Caroliniana Library. Holmes, an Ohio native, came to study at Columbia Seminary. He had been in Columbia about three months when this letter was written. He seems to have already developed the appreciation for empiricism that was so central to the Scottish philosophy taught by the Presbyterians.

[18]Alexander McGill to his wife, 18 January 1853; quoted in Margaret DesChamps Moore, "A Northern Professor Winters in Columbia, 1852-1853," *South Carolina Historical Magazine* 9 (1959): 186.

[19]McGill to his wife, 17 and 31 March 1853, ibid., 188, 191. McGill chose a position at Princeton instead (ibid., 191). That McGill was invited to teach in the South at this time was unusual, and he commented to his wife on the distrust of Northerners among the people of Columbia. "It was only because I was regarded as half a Southern man, that they sent for me," he said. McGill to his wife, 24 March 1853, ibid., 189.

It may be supposed that clergymen who owned slaves treated them somewhat better than slaveholders generally, but McGill made two comments to his wife which point out that ministers had the same difficulties with their servants as other masters and were likely to be just as insensitive. Noting that the servants of George Howe, a seminary colleague, were unmanageable, McGill called Howe "a poor master—a mixture of weak indulgence and particular strictness—magnificent in outlay one while, [*sic*] and pinching in parsimony another." Another colleague, whom McGill did not name, had "got negroes by marriage," and bought and sold them "without remorse, as it suits his interests and feelings."[20]

Presbyterians, while comprising only a small fraction of the Southern population (there were about 100,000 members of Presbyterian churches in the South in 1860), owned a disproportionate number of slaves.[21] A statement in 1849 by the Reverend James Smilie of Mississippi, saying that three-fourths of the Presbyterian Church members in the South owned slaves, is often cited, though it is considered excessive by some.[22] In any case, Presbyterians were at least as fully involved in slavery as any denomination and had to come to terms with the religious and moral questions that the institution raised. The way this was done illustrates that when theology clashes with the dominant ideology of a culture, theology is revised. This revision took place earlier in South Carolina than elsewhere in the South because the ideology which dominated that state was more pervasive and less ambiguous on this subject than was true elsewhere. By 1820 in South Carolina and by the 1840s throughout the South, contradictions between doctrine and practice had been eliminated; and by the mid-1850s the subject of Christianity and slavery was virtually closed as far as most Southerners were concerned.

When the English established their colony at Jamestown in 1607, the concept of one Christian owning another was abhorrent.[23] By 1860, how-

---

[20]Letters of 7 April and 3 February 1853; quoted ibid.

[21]Paul L. Garber, "A Centennial Appraisal of James Henley Thornwell," in Stuart C. Henry, ed., *A Miscellany of American Christianity; Essays in Honor of H. Shelton Smith* (Durham, 1963) 134; Lewis G. Vander Velde, *The Presbyterian Churches in the Federal Union, 1861-1869* (Cambridge MA, 1932) 4-7.

[22]Garber, "A Centennial Appraisal," 134-35.

[23]For a discussion of the development of English attitudes towards blacks and slavery, see Winthrop Jordan, *White over Black; American Attitudes toward the Negro, 1550-1812* (Chapel Hill, 1968).

ever, New Orleans Presbyterian minister Benjamin M. Palmer expressed a widely held belief when he told his congregation, "In this [slavery] struggle, we defend the cause of God and religion."[24] The pace of evolution from the former attitude to the latter varied from state to state and from individual to individual. Moreover, the process was not complete when the Civil War began; but by the 1840s most Southerners, whether church members or not, would have agreed with Palmer's statement. Christian theology, while it was helping to shape the ideology of the region, was being shaped—most moderns would say perverted—to accommodate the social and economic realities of Southern life.[25]

The experience of the Presbyterians in this regard was fairly typical. During the colonial and early national periods they indicated deep misgivings about slavery and took positions favoring its ultimate extinction, but by the 1830s they had made peace with it. Pioneers in Presbyterian missions to the slaves included Virginian Samuel Davies, who began preaching to them in 1756, and South Carolina's Henry Patillo.[26] Patillo saw emancipation as "an event that all the wisdom of America seems at present unequal to; but which divine providence will accomplish in due time."[27] Although he shared the widely held view that too much discussion of the subject would injure his denomination's growth, he contributed to that discussion in 1787 by publishing *The Plain Planter's Family Assistant,* a catechism aimed at destroying the idea of racial differences beyond "black skin and curled head." The two races, said Patillo, are essentially alike. "The one talks and lives as wickedly as the other." He asked his white reader, "What would you have been with his education, or what might he have been with yours?" He approved of slaves fleeing from tyrannical masters, but did not advocate immediate emancipation. In the pulpit he avoided the subject altogether, after once touching on it "with caution. It

---

[24]Walter B. Posey, *The Presbyterian Church in the Old Southwest, 1778-1838* (Richmond, 1952) 74.

[25]For general accounts of this process, see H. Shelton Smith, *In His Image but . . . Racism in Southern Religion, 1780-1910* (Durham, 1972); John L. Eighmy, *Churches in Cultural Captivity* (Knoxville, 1972); Donald G. Mathews, *Slavery and Methodism* (Princeton, 1965); idem, *Religion in the Old South* (Chicago, 1977).

[26]Andrew E. Murray, *Presbyterians and the Negro, a History* (Philadelphia, 1966) 10-11.

[27]Ibid.

offended some and pleased none: tho I mentioned it as a very distant object."[28] Another South Carolina Presbyterian who spoke publicly against slavery was Alexander Hewatt, pastor of the Scots (First) Presbyterian Church of Charleston from 1763 to 1775. Hewatt argued that "the inhabitants of Africa have the same faculties as those of Europe" and criticized slavery in his history of colonial South Carolina and Georgia, published in London in 1779.[29]

The subject of slavery naturally found its way into the courts of the Presbyterian church, North and South. At the 1794 meeting of the Presbytery of South Carolina, the Reverend W. C. Davis preached a sermon denouncing all Christians who owned slaves. He was answered by the Reverend Thomas Reese, a native of Pennsylvania and a pastor of three South Carolina congregations. According to one observer, his reply "met with the entire approbation of the Presbytery, and greatly mortified Davis."[30] Three South Carolina Presbyterian ministers—James Gilliland, Robert C. Wilson, and William Williamson—left the state in 1804 because their antislavery views had alienated their congregations. All three moved to Ohio.[31]

As men with such views left the state and region, and their less-bold sympathizers (whose number can only be guessed) chose silence, the subject was projected into the distant future. In 1800 the synod of the Carolinas received a request from other denominations to petition the state legislatures for a plan of gradual emancipation. The synod replied that it favored the goal, "yet, as it appears to us that matters are not yet matured for carrying it forward, especially in the Southern parts of our states," the effort should be postponed. Meanwhile, said the synod, Presbyterians should instruct their slaves and so prepare them for the day when emancipation "shall be contemplated by the legislatures of our Southern

---

[28]Margaret B. DesChamps, "Antislavery Presbyterians in the Carolina Piedmont," *Proceedings of the South Carolina Historical Association*, 1954, 6-13.

[29]Jordan, *White over Black*, 283; Alexander Hewatt, *An Historical Account of the Rise and Progress of the Colonies of South Carolina and Georgia* (London, 1779) 10-11, 347-55.

[30]George Howe, *History of the Presbyterian Church in South Carolina*, vol. 1 (Columbia, 1870) 638.

[31]William B. Sprague, *Annals of the American Pulpit*, vol. 4 (New York, 1858) 137; Ernest T. Thompson, *Presbyterians in the South*, vol. 1 (Richmond, 1963) 336.

States.''[32] Northern Presbyterians, though divided on the subject, were in general accord with this view. In 1810 the General Assembly reaffirmed that slavery was ''a violation of the law of God,'' but added, ''We cannot indeed urge that we should add a second injury to the first, by emancipating them in such a manner that they will be likely to destroy themselves and others.''[33]

Considering what was perhaps the most delicate point in the slavery debate, the Transylvania Presbytery of Kentucky in 1797 held a discussion that was summarized as follows. ''Is slavery a moral evil?'' ''Yes.'' ''Are all persons who hold slaves guilty of a moral evil?'' ''No.'' ''Who are not guilty of moral evil in holding slaves? Resolved that this question . . . is of so much importance that the consideration of it be put off till a future day.''[34] How Transylvania Presbytery resolved this question is not known; but Southerners of a later day would ask if slavery was a sin, and relying on the Bible, they would answer ''no.''

Ironically, as Presbyterian leaders were retreating from any fight on the status of blacks in America, the General Assembly made what has been called its strongest statement on the evils of the institution. In 1818 this body called slavery ''a gross violation of the most precious and sacred rights of human nature [and] utterly inconsistent with the law of God, which requires us to love our neighbors as ourselves.'' The assembly added that it was the duty of all Christians to work toward the removal of ''this blot on our holy religion.'' No requirements were made of those who owned slaves, however, and it seems clear that for South Carolinians at least, any such action would have been met with a deaf ear, or worse.[35] Having fired this salvo, the General Assembly fell silent on the subject until the New School faction directed its attention to abolitionism in the mid-1830s, precipitating the schism of 1837. By then even moderate Southern Presbyterians had come to agree with Virginia's John Holt Rice that further discussion of slavery on religious grounds would be counterproductive. The debate might be carried forward from an economic and political viewpoint, Rice suggested, but the Church should leave it alone.[36]

---

[32]Thompson, *Presbyterians in the South*, 1:327.

[33]Murray, *Presbyterians and the Negro*, 24-25.

[34]Ibid., 18.

[35]Thompson, *Presbyterians in the South*, 1:331.

[36]John Holt Rice to William Maxwell, 24 February 1827; quoted ibid., 339.

The combined effects of the Denmark Vesey plot, the Nat Turner rebellion, and the advent of Garrison's militant *Liberator* had presented the Southern churches with obstacles they could not overcome: aroused self-interest and fear. In such a climate, genuine desire to convert slaves to Christianity, a project challenging enough for any crusader, was fatally jeopardized by the churches' opposition to slavery. Add to this the aggressive sectarianism generated by the revivals of early-nineteenth-century America, which defined success in terms of the size of church membership, and confronting slavery head-on appeared unwise to the vast majority of Southern clerics. In addition, these revivals emphasized orthodox biblical literalism and thus prepared the ground for the next generation of Southern clergymen to develop a biblical defense of slavery that would attack Northern rationalism and liberalism. A leading historian of South Carolina said it succinctly many years ago. The Church, he wrote, "gave her support to human slavery lest she lose the power of doing good in a slave-holding society."[37]

Yet the accommodation was not made on the basis of a conscious choice between alternatives, as this statement suggests. It is doubtful that any Southern churchmen sat down and reasoned through their choices and selected the one calculated to do their careers and their cause the least harm. Instead, looking at life through the perspective that Southern culture had given them, they searched for meaning and for God's will in the unfolding events of their time. The failure of the evangelical attack on slavery made it difficult for churchmen who remained in the South to sustain the view that God favored abolition, and buttressed the view that the chief goal of Christianity in that time and place was people's spiritual elevation; their social levels were not to be the Church's responsibility. As Donald Mathews has put it, "The perception that worldly distinctions were false could and did give Evangelicals the power of the Holy Spirit but not the power to destroy those distinctions." Those Southern churchmen who remained troubled by slavery would shift their attention to the efforts of the American Colonization Society, or to the mission to the slaves. Hence their dis-

---

[37]David D. Wallace, *The Historical Background of Religion in South Carolina,* Annual Address before the Upper South Carolina (Methodists) Conference Historical Society, 14 November 1916 (published by the society) 28.

tinction would no longer be between slaveholder and nonslaveholder, but between bad and good masters.[38]

Though this transition probably would have occurred in any case, the post-1830 abolitionist movement hastened it and confirmed Southerners in it. There were at least two reasons for this. First, the abolitionists were outsiders, in whom Southerners detected a maddening self-righteousness and condescension. Second, while abolitionism was born out of Christianity, the abolitionists who attracted the most attention in the South were radicals whose religious orientation was so liberal and materialistic as to strike most Southerners as heretical if not atheistic. Thus it was a simple matter for Southern churchmen to conceive of the slavery debate as a struggle between pious Christian orthodoxy and the modern ideology they came to call rationalism, with the soul of American society at stake.

Thornwell showed his resentment of the Northern abolitionists in his Zion Church dedication sermon in 1850. "They pity us . . . they lament our lot—admit that our case is bad, desperately bad—but then we are not so much to be blamed. They curse us with their sympathies."[39] Virginian Robert Lewis Dabney held the same view. Recalling that before the abolitionists "began to meddle in our affairs," most Virginians had seen slavery as "injudicious," he held that the Old Dominion would have emancipated her slaves within twenty years if not for this outside interference.

> As it is, their unauthorized attempts to strike off the fetters of our slaves have but riveted them on the faster. Does this fact arise from the perversity of our natures? I believe that it does in part. We are less inclined to do that which we know to be our duty because persons, who have no right to interfere, demand it of us. But the change of public opinion in the South . . . doubtless arose partly from free discussion. We have investigated the subject, and we find emancipation more dangerous than we had before imagined. Who knows but that this uproar of the Abolitionists . . . may have been designed by Providence as a check upon our imprudent liberality. If

---

[38]Mathews, *Religion in the Old South*, 78-80.

[39]Thornwell, "Slavery and the Religious Instruction of the Coloured Population," *Southern Presbyterian Review* 4 (July 1850): 109. Donald Mathews sees this resentment as crucial in the hardening of Southern attitudes on the issues (*Religion in the Old South*, 155).

we had hastened on to give the slave his liberty at once, as I believe public sentiment was tending, we might have done [him] irreparable injury.[40]

Other clergymen considered the motives of the abolitionists and found them suspect. Was it true Christianity that led them to demand immediate emancipation, John Adger asked? Looking to historical accounts, he found that according to Adam Smith and Macaulay, the abolition of slavery in Europe occurred very slowly and was the result neither of "legislative regulation nor physical force." "What share Christianity had in effecting this abolition has been much disputed," he noted. Agreeing with those who had accorded it great influence, he continued, "it is curious . . . to see how exceedingly gradual was the process by which Christianity operated in the abolition of [European] slavery." Writers on both sides agree that Christianity coexisted with slavery for several centuries "without any great horror or irritation being expressed against it." In Adger's view Christianity had been "constantly producing such an effect upon society that when one thousand years had passed away, strict personal slavery had, in most parts of Europe, begun to disappear." From the vantage point of the century's end, Adger ventured that "the great and good school of slavery" had been civilizing the slaves, and that by 1865 "a good many pupils . . . were ready to be graduated." A century more might have fitted them all for freedom, he concluded.[41]

The hot breath of the abolitionists did not drive all Southern churchmen to defend slavery, no matter how orthodox their theology may have been. One exception to the general trend was Dr. Benjamin Mosby Smith. A professor at Union Theological Seminary, located in Virginia's black belt near Farmville, Smith was a slaveowner who was profoundly troubled by his position. After reading one of Frederick Law Olmstead's descriptions of slavery, he wrote in his diary in December 1858, "Oh what trouble, running sore, constant pressing weight, perpetual wearing, dripping, is this patriarchal institution! What miserable folly for men to cling to it as something heaven-descended. And here we find our children after us must

[40]Robert L. Dabney to G. Woodson Payne, 20 January 1840; quoted in Frank B. Lewis, "Robert Lewis Dabney; Southern Presbyterian Apologist" (Ph.D. dissertation, Duke University, 1946) 40.

[41]John Adger, *My Life and Times* (Richmond, 1899) 161-63. See also Adger, "The Christian Doctrine of Human Rights and Slavery," *Southern Presbyterian Review* 2 (1848): 582-83.

groan under the burden—our hands tied from freeing ourselves.'' Searching his own actions and feelings, he could only add, ''One's inconsistencies are amazing.'' The subject was on his mind ten days later, as he wrote: ''I am more and more perplexed about my negroes. I cannot just take them up and sell them though that would be clearly the best I could do for myself. I cannot free them. I cannot keep them with comfort . . . what would I not give to be freed from responsibility for these poor creatures. Oh, that I could know just what is right.''[42]

Intriguing as it is to speculate on how many Southerners shared Smith's anguish, it seems certain that they were a minority, if not as small a minority as the institution's defenders insisted. John Adger knew there had been many like Smith, but he noted with approval the ''complete revolution of sentiment'' on the subject, which he attributed to the work of the abolitionists. ''From a state of doubt and anxiety in regard to their position, that was very general among the religious and intelligent classes of the community, they pass, by a careful examination of the Scriptures, to a calm and quiet conviction that their slaveholding is not condemned by the Christian religion,'' wrote Adger.[43]

An ample number of clergymen were ready to lead this examination of the Scriptures, which they were confident would erase doubts and ease consciences in the South, and perhaps quiet the abolitionists, who used the Bible to support their views. One of the most aggressive was Methodist Augustus Baldwin Longstreet. In 1845 he published a series of ''Letters'' to a group of Northern clergymen whom Longstreet felt needed some basic Bible study. American Methodism had been ruptured the previous year by irreconcilable differences over the clergy's ownership of slaves. Could the schism be healed? Yes, wrote Longstreet, if you can convince us through Scripture that slavery is wrong and forbidden to Christians. But, he argued, you prefer to ''retreat behind the Declaration of Independence; or to throw up a breast work out of the long forsaken rubbish of the Social Compact; or to bewilder [your] pursuers in the mazes of metaphysical subtlety.'' ''Can you not immitate [sic] your great Master's example,'' he taunted, ''when Satan quoted scripture to him, can you not hear us calmly,

---

[42]Quoted from Francis R. Flournoy, *Benjamin Mosby Smith, 1811-1893* (Richmond, 1947) 74.

[43]John Adger, ''The Revival of the Slave Trade,'' *Southern Presbyterian Review* 11 (April 1858): 101-102.

and meet us with our own weapons?'' If the abolitionists could convince him that Paul, in his letter to Philemon, is not saying a slaveowner may be a good Christian, said Longstreet, ''I will instantly become your ally, and preach against slavery in my own land, if it costs me my head.''

Having the ''facts'' on his side, Longstreet could proceed in the tradition of Scottish Common Sense philosophy to compile the data and rationally present his argument. Focusing on Paul's letter, he cited several biblical scholars to establish the authenticity of the work. Next he cited twelve authorities to establish that the servant Onesimus was Philemon's slave, in the modern sense of that word. Onesimus had left Philemon ''for a season'' and Paul returned him to his master ''as a brother,'' but still as a servant as well. The institution of slavery was therefore not a barrier to Christian fellowship, nor was the church concerned with the institution per se, but with the souls of those who were tied together by it. If Paul loved Philemon, a slaveowner, should you abolitionists not love us, asked Longstreet? ''Yet look how you treated Bishop Andrew!''[44]

It is difficult to generalize about the road toward the endorsement of slavery traveled by thousands of Southern clergymen. One student has identified 123 ministers who wrote major proslavery tracts. He suggests that among the common denominators in this group was the influence of Federalist ideology through their education at Northern colleges (71) or Southern colleges staffed by Northern professors with Federalist biases (20).[45] Other common traits have been pointed out by Brooks Holifield and Anne Loveland, who emphasize the desire for more prestige and greater impact on their society, and the self-image as ''guardians of the religious and moral purity of the Southern people.''[46]

The biblical defense of slavery rose in conjunction with the secular defense; the two should not be considered as separate developments. Richard

---

[44]A. B. Longstreet, *Letters on . . . Philemon;* quoted in J. R. Scafadel, ''The Letters of Augustus Baldwin Longstreet'' (Ph.D. dissertation, University of South Carolina, 1976) 172-80, 220, 307.

[45]Larry Tise, ''Pro-Slavery Ideology: A Social and Intellectual History of the Defense of Slavery, 1790-1861'' (Ph.D. dissertation, University of North Carolina, 1974); quoted in Mathews, *Religion in the Old South,* 166.

[46]Brooks Holifield, *The Gentlemen Theologians; American Theology in Southern Culture, 1795-1860* (Durham, 1978) ch. 2; Anne C. Loveland, *Southern Evangelicals and the Social Order, 1800-1860* (Baton Rouge, 1980) ix-x.

Furman's *Exposition of the Views of the Baptists, Relative to the Coloured Population of the United States* is among the earliest statements of the views of his denomination, and Southern Christians generally, in slavery's defense.[47] Furman's apologia followed by only one year the pioneering "positive good" pronouncement of William and Mary professor Thomas R. Dew, in his *Review of the Debate in the Virginia Legislature of 1831 and 1832* (Richmond, 1832). Together these publications mark the early 1830s as the turning point in Southern attitudes toward slavery. It is significant that the mission to the slaves—a theoretical commitment of long-standing, but receiving very little attention at this time—was reactivated almost at the same instant. In fact, the religious defense of slavery and the mission to the slaves were two sides of the same coin—the development of a slaveholding ethic.[48] An eloquent statement of the slaveholding ethic is John Adger's justification of his work among the black population in and around Charleston:

> They belong to us. We also belong to them. They are divided out among us and mingled up with us, and we with them in a thousand ways. They live with us, eating from the same store-houses, drinking from the same fountains, dwelling in the same enclosures, forming parts of the same families. Our mothers confide us, when infants, to their arms, and sometimes to the very milk of their breasts. Their children [grow up with us] and then, either they stand weeping by our bedside, or we drop a tributary tear by theirs. . . . There they are—behold them. See them all around you, in these streets, in all these dwellings; a race distinct from us, brought in God's mysterious providence from a foreign land, and placed under our care, and made members of our households. They fill the humblest places in our state and society; they serve us, they give us their strength, yet they are not more truly ours than we are truly theirs.[49]

---

[47]Furman's *Exposition* was published in Charleston in 1833. Perhaps the best Baptist defense of slavery is Richard Fuller's extended debate with Francis Wayland, president of Brown University, published as *Domestic Slavery Considered as a Scriptural Institution* (New York, 1845). Fuller, a South Carolinian, and Wayland were both considered moderates in their regions. See Eighmy, *Churches in Cultural Captivity.*

[48]Charles C. Jones, *The Religious Instruction of the Negroes. A Sermon, Delivered before Associations of Planters in Liberty and McIntosh Counties, Georgia, by the Rev. Charles Colcock Jones, of Savannah* (Princeton, 1832); idem, *A Catechism for Colored Persons* (Charleston, 1834). Professor Jack P. Maddex, Jr., of the University of Oregon, is working on a study of the proslavery ethic as espoused by antebellum Presbyterians.

[49]Adger, *My Life and Times*, 167.

While many Southern churchmen were uncomfortable with the ''positive good'' notion of Dew and others, their reaction to abolitionism was by no means reticent. William S. Plumer, minister of Richmond's First Presbyterian Church, was typical. In calling abolitionism ''the most meddlesome, imprudent, reckless, fierce and wicked excitment [sic] I ever saw,'' he was publicly placing the Southern church in step with the region's general opinion and thus reassuring nervous masters as to the trustworthiness of their clergy. But in adding to this the opinion that abolitionism was crippling private and public efforts at ''ameliorating the character and condition of the poor slave,'' he was simply stating his sincere conviction.[50]

So it was that the Southern clergy moved simultaneously toward the rejection of abolitionism and the effort to convert heathen blacks and ameliorate their condition. The relationship between these movements was obvious, at least to some. Summarizing the state of religion in its region, the *Southern Presbyterian* suggested that ''the position taken by our church with reference to the much agitated subject of slavery, secures to us unlimited opportunities of access to master and slave, and lays us under heavy responsibilities before God and the world, not to neglect our duty to either.''[51] Robert Lewis Dabney put the notion of responsibility even more bluntly. ''To enjoy the advantages of the Bible argument in our favor,'' he wrote his brother, ''slave-holders will have to pay a price.''[52] The late antebellum religious press carried many articles on various aspects of the mission to the slaves; and the importance of amelioration in making slavery easily defendable, while not always explicit, was generally part of the argument in favor of the work.[53]

---

[50]*Southern Religious Telegraph,* 11 September 1835; quoted in Thompson, *Presbyterians in the South,* 1:344-45.

[51]*Southern Presbyterian,* 29 June 1854.

[52]Robert L. Dabney to his brother, 15 January 1851; quoted in Thomas C. Johnson, *Life and Letters of Robert Lewis Dabney,* 128-29.

[53]See ''Duties of Masters to Servants,'' *The Southern Presbyterian,* 29 November 1856, 1; ''Interesting Work among the Blacks,'' ibid., 2, describing twelve black professions of faith at the Hopewell Presbyterian Church; ''A Report on Slave Marriages,'' by a committee of the Charleston Baptist Association, Basil Manly, chairman, ibid., 3 January 1857,

Records of individual church evangelism among slaves are scarce. The First Presbyterian Church of Columbia paid a Mr. Ladsden two hundred dollars in 1860 for catechizing and preaching to "the negroes." His efforts evidently paid off, for church records show the following additions to the membership in 1860 and 1861:

14 servants and 4 free blacks, 27 June 1860
22 servants and 1 free black, 9 October 1860
4 servants and 2 free blacks, 3 January 1861
6 servants and 0 free blacks, 28 March 1861

A group of "coloured members" met with elder F. W. McMaster in March 1861 to express their pleasure with the work of Mr. Ladsden and to urge the session to retain him. The session acknowledged this information with pleasure.[54]

While the efforts of Southern whites to evangelize their black charges must be accounted small in comparison with what it would have been if they had taken Jesus' Great Commission seriously, this must be weighed against the obstacles of planter apathy and opposition to mission work, which were both subtle and overt. When Charleston Episcopalians and Presbyterians began construction on Zion Church for a black congregation in 1849, a mob gathered in December of that year, intent upon burning the partially completed structure. Only the timely diplomacy of James Louis Petigru saved this building. The following year, with the support of such

---

1-2; and an editorial on p. 2 supporting efforts to impose the Christian view of marriage among slaves; John B. Adger, *The Religious Instruction of the Colored Population. A Sermon, Preached by the Rev. John B. Adger, in the Second Presbyterian Church, Charleston, S.C., May 9th, 1847* (Charleston, 1847); "The Baptism of Servants," *Southern Presbyterian Review* 1 (June 1847): 63-102; "Duties of Masters," *Southern Presbyterian Review* 8 (October 1854): 266-83; "Religious Instruction of the Black Population," *Southern Presbyterian Review* 1 (December 1847): 89-120; H. N. McTyeire, "Plantation Life— Duties and Responsibilities," *DeBow's Review* 29 (September 1860): 361.

[54]Minutes of the First Presbyterian Church, Columbia, South Carolina, typescript, South Caroliniana Library. For additional information on the work of Presbyterians among slaves, see Adger, *My Life and Times*, ch. 7; George A. Blackmon, *The Life and Work of John L. Girardeau* (Columbia, 1916). John McLees Diary, South Caroliniana Library. Sources reveal only one black student at Columbia Theological Seminary before the Civil War. His name was Thomas Catto, and he became the pastor of a church in Washington, D.C. Thomas Smyth, *Autobiographical Notes, Letters and Reflections*, ed. Louisa Cheves Stoney (Charleston, 1914) 205.

public figures as Petigru and United States Senator Franklin H. Elmore, the church was completed.[55]

While the leading articulators of the slaveholding ethic were rarely satisfied with the effort to evangelize and improve the conduct of the slaves, they generally recognized that some progress was being made. George Fitzhugh expressed a widely held view when he wrote in the mid-1850s, "Our slaves are treated far better than they were forty years ago, because they have improved in mind and morals."[56] Yet whatever progress had been made was threatened by the continued importation of Africans into the Southern states. Although outlawed, as of 1808, by a clause of the United States Constitution, the African slave trade never completely disappeared until the Civil War, and attitudes toward it were far from universally negative. In fact, there was a movement in the 1850s to legally reopen the trade, so that slaveowning could become the common trait of Southern whites rather than the status symbol of the minority.[57] For opponents of the trade, a major argument was that it threatened the very improvement in master-slave relations on which they based, or hoped to base, their defense of the institution. Each generation of blacks was more civilized than the one before, they reasoned, and hence more subject to moral suasion and self-discipline. Thus the slaveholder could adopt "milder" methods of control. Newly arrived Africans could not be treated so paternally, and their demoralizing effect upon the other slaves could cause the system to revert to what one writer called its "pristine cruelty."[58] For James L. Petigru, the trade was the great shame of the South. To his friend John Belton O'Neal he wrote, "There is a proverb that says, that crimes should be punished, deeds of shame buried. Yet history must have its rights, and sorry I am that one of its pages will be defiled by recording the depravity of the present

---

[55]James P. Carson, *James Louis Petigru, the Union Man of South Carolina* (Washington, 1920) 280.

[56]Fitzhugh, *Sociology for the South,* 211; quoted in Harvey Wish, *George Fitzhugh, Propagandist of the Old South* (Gloucester MA, 1962) 110.

[57]Takaki, *A Pro-Slavery Crusade.*

[58]Ibid., 70. The writer was Fitzhugh, in *Sociology for the South,* 211. Fitzhugh would soon reverse his position. See Fitzhugh, "Wealth of the North and the South," *DeBow's Review* 23 (December 1857): 593, and "The Administration of the Slave Trade," ibid., 26 (1859): 145. His argument was that the Southern position must be consistent and if slavery is proper, so is the trade.

day, when the laws against kidnapping of Africans . . . cannot be enforced."[59]

No Southern clergyman was more outspoken in his criticism of the African slave trade than Charleston Presbyterian John Adger. A close friend of Thornwell, Adger spent several years as a missionary in Africa and Afghanistan, and was a leading advocate of the mission to the slaves in the American South. In addition to arguing the evil effects of the trade upon the master-slave relationship, he pointed out that it was the cause of tribal warfare in Africa and of "the involuntary separation of the negro from his relatives."[60] For Episcopal Bishop William Meade of the Diocese of Virginia, the Bible condemned the trade by forbidding "manstealing" and the church must do the same.[61] Yet both Adger and Meade defended slavery itself in almost the same breath.[62] For them, as for the Southern clergy generally, the institution was separate from the abuses that sinful men committed in practicing it. The abuses were wrong and to be condemned, but slavery itself was permissible.

Here is one way in which the religious leaders of the South differed, however slightly, from the stance taken by the region's defenders generally. Historians of the Old South have been correct in attributing to the clergy the role of apologists for slavery. By bringing biblical and philosophical arguments into the debate on slavery's side, they provided a valuable supplement to the more self-serving arguments of the planters and the more secular defenders. Yet they were also a distinct group within the family of proslavery men, for they did not agree totally with the view of their fellow combatants on the secular side. While the planters were glad to have the clergy join in the debate so long as their contribution was positive, they recognized that the views of the preachers were not always suitable for their cause.

It is well known that by the 1850s free and open discussion of slavery was not conducted in most of the South. The Presbyterian Synod of South Carolina decided against inviting a group of Irish Presbyterian ministers,

---

[59]Petigru to O'Neal, 1 January 1859; quoted in Takaki, *A Pro-Slavery Crusade*, 216.

[60]John B. Adger, "A Review of the Reports to the Legislature of South Carolina on the Revival of the Slave Trade," *Southern Presbyterian Review* 11 (October 1858): 113-15.

[61]Meade to Bishop Leonidas Polk, 10 December 1856; quoted in Takaki, *A Pro-Slavery Crusade*, 131.

[62]See nn. 60 and 61.

touring the country in 1859, to visit its churches and describe the revival currently underway in Ireland. The "well known tendency of these Irish brethren to protest against slavery" has been suggested as the reason for this inhospitality.[63] What is not so well known is that even at this late date, the views of the region's own orthodox clergy on some aspects of the issue were considered subversive of public confidence. It was rarely necessary to censor the writings of the clergy because they read the public mood and, in effect, censored themselves. In 1857, for example, the Reverend Thomas Smyth wrote William A. Hallock, secretary of the American Tract Society, that in his considered opinion neither John Adger's sermon, "The Religious Instruction of the Colored People," first preached in 1847, nor Thornwell's "Duties of Masters," preached at the dedication of the Zion Church in Charleston in 1850, "ought to be issued in the existing state of things." "We have concurred with you in this," Hallock answered, "assured that no [religious] publication bearing specifically on the subject of slavery in any of its aspects, can now be circulated at the South. What we have to say to sober anti-slavery men at the North is that we have done our best to find something that Christians at the South could approve, but in the present lamentable collisions it is impracticable."[64] Hallock's assumption was not strictly true, for the Southern press, both secular and religious, continued to publish essays on slavery to the end of the antebellum period and beyond. But insofar as sermons like those of Adger and Thornwell were concerned, he was correct. (See below.) In other words, the subject of slavery must have been treated positively in all its aspects, or the essay would be unacceptable.

The effort to develop a slaveholding ethic in conformity with the values of Christianity had met with failure, for the white South as a whole was more interested in defending the institution as it was than in reforming it and ameliorating the slave's condition. The effort at amelioration ran head-on into the attitude, expressed by George Fitzhugh, that in spite of any evils slavery may harbor, the region's public stance must be always to defend it and never to acknowledge any of its faults.[65]

---

[63]F. D. Jones and W. H. Wells, eds., *History of the Presbyterian Church in South Carolina since 1850* (Columbia, 1926) 48-49.

[64]Smyth, *Autobiographical Notes,* 278-79.

[65]Fitzhugh admitted that he saw "great evils in slavery," but thought it best not to speak candidly in his *Sociology for the South.* Fitzhugh to George F. Holmes, 11 April 1855; quoted in Wish, *George Fitzhugh,* 111.

In the face of such immovable resistance, the position of the Southern clergy could hardly have been other than what it was. Against the criticisms from the outside world stood their own innate conservatism, their orthodox Biblicism, their benevolent wish to convert the slave to Christianity and to ameliorate his condition—while ameliorating their racism at the same time. Two aspects of their position on slavery are revealing, however. First, the slavery they defended was slavery "at its best." If we can admit that there were gradations of master-slave relationships in the Old South, surely the institution's defenders thought in terms of the most humane examples of slavery. It was an ideal, not the reality, that they were defending. Had the events of 1860-1861 not intervened, their efforts to develop a slaveholding ethic might in time have been seen as more realistic responses to the abolitionists than the uncompromising stance of the leading secular defenders of slavery. But in another sense it was they who were unrealistic: they refused to see slavery as it was. The ideal they defended could hardly have been the result of the inductive investigation they championed in the name of Lord Bacon. Their position on the slavery issue reveals more clearly than anything else the intellectual inconsistency of these "Baconians." They pleaded with the abolitionists to approach the issue inductively, but they came no closer to that method than did their enemies.

To the subject of slavery, James Henley Thornwell brought the same rational mind and orthodox theology that shaped his thought on every other question. Thus it is not surprising that his treatment of the issue so epitomized the views of the Southern pulpit that he became virtually the spokesman for the Southern church on this crucial sectional issue. His staunch support of the Union throughout the antebellum era forced him to look for common ground in the midst of the polarizing emotionalism that drove the more radical spokesmen of both North and South. As early as 1831, when he was not yet nineteen, he wrote disparagingly of those fellow Southerners who allowed their emotions to dominate their reason where slavery was concerned. As rumors flew in the wake of Nat Turner's rebellion in Virginia, he noted, "Frightened men trust to their imagination for their facts, instead of their memories." Bringing his academic studies to bear on the topic, he added, "Our good old metaphysical vocabulary teaches us that memory is the record of facts; the new vocabulary of fear teaches us that the imagination is." He confessed that he had "thought much on the subject," but was "not satisfied yet." Then he recalled "the beautiful passage in Shakespeare's 'Tempest,' where Prospero compares his brother to one 'Who having unto truth, by telling it/Made such a sinner of his memory/To credit his own lie.' " The brother had told a lie so often that he came to believe it. This, said the young Thornwell, was the case with those "sons of terror" who "circulate the most outrageous rumors for serious truth." Showing insight beyond his years, he concluded, "I know that many censure them as the propagators of malicious falsehoods; but they should be pittied [*sic*] as the dupes of their fears. But enough of this *black* subject."[66] At least until the closing weeks of 1860, Thornwell managed to avoid the emotionalism and susceptibility to rumor that he had decried as the era of sectional tension was being born.

The rationality that Thornwell so admired in others and so carefully cultivated in himself was sorely strained as he followed the course of the abolitionist movement during the 1830s and 1840s. His college training, so steeped in Common Sense philosophy, had taught him to suspect conclusions not arrived at inductively and especially to spurn all fanaticism and unscientific social criticism. Whatever his private scruples about slavery, he recoiled in horror from the image of a world operating according to the beliefs of those passionate perfectionists. "Revolutions are always dangerous," he wrote in an undated manuscript expressing his views on slavery. "Long established institutions cannot be destroyed without countless hazards and [except where duty demands it] innovation ought always to be avoided." The question then reduced itself to whether duty demanded the end of slavery. After studying the question from secular as well as religious viewpoints, Thornwell concluded that it did not. Slavery was for him a rational way of organizing the society of the American South; moreover, it was "distinctly recognized by Moses" and "not inconsistent with the principles of Christianity." Having reached these conclusions, he pronounced himself "decidedly opposed" to the abolitionists.

The strength of his reaction to abolitionism is perhaps nowhere better seen than in an entry Thornwell made in his journal during his tour of England in May 1841. The twenty-nine-year-old College professor had been traveling with an Englishman who, their conversation revealed, was an abolitionist. To Thornwell, "He was a perfect fanatic on the subject of slavery, though profoundly ignorant of it. . . . Whenever you find it,

---

[66]Thornwell to Alexander H. Pegues, 7 October 1831; quoted in Benjamin M. Palmer, *Life and Letters of James Henley Thornwell, D.D., LL.D.* (Richmond, 1875) 85-86.

abolitionism is a species of madness. It is a hot, boiling, furious fanaticism, destroying all energy of mind and symmetry of character and leaving
its unfortunate victim like the [?] oak, a spectacle of pity and of dread.''
Enlarging his thought, Thornwell expressed a view that he was to develop
fully in the coming years. ''Abolitionism,'' he added, ''is only a single
aspect—a special direction of an absorbing mania—a particular form of a
general spirit of madness and fanaticism. Socialism, *teetotalism,* perfec-
tionism are all symptoms of the same great disease. The agitations of modern times, the convulsions of church and state [are] the elements which have
produced this monstrous gangrine [*sic*] of society.'' Returning once more
to his English opponent, he added, ''I profoundly pity him.'' Whether this
was a sincere remark we cannot know, but pity might well have been
Thornwell's reaction, given his negative interpretation of abolitionism.
''They no doubt deceive themselves that this strange excitement [under]
which they labour is the genuine spirit of benevolence. . . . [But] their philanthropy always evaporates [when there is] no opportunity of creating an
excitement. When they have *freed* the slave, he may sob in beggary and
wretchedness and they will never lift a finger to relieve him.'' ''Feeling
free from sin themselves they can cast a stone at their erring brethren without compunction or remorse.''[67]

By the mid-1840s Thornwell's thoughts on slavery were focusing on
the question of the Church's role in the controversy. By this time his Calvinism was clearly evident in such published essays as *A Tract on the Doctrines of Election and Reprobation* and *The Vanity and Glory of Man,* and
his views on the slavery issue were strongly influenced by his theology. In
1845, the year the Methodist and Baptist Churches of the United States split
into Northern and Southern bodies over the slavery issue, the Old School
Presbyterian General Assembly adopted by a vote of 168 to 13 a report
which, in the words of Benjamin Palmer, was ''so temperate and well
guarded, that it put to rest, to a considerable degree, the hurtful agitation
on that subject, and formed the basis upon which the Church continued to
stand until the . . . Civil War.''[68] By his own account, Thornwell was

---

[67]''Slavery,'' undated MS in Thornwell Papers. Thornwell Journal, May 1841, ibid.

[68]Thornwell, *A Tract on the Doctrines of Election and Reprobation* (Columbia, 1840);
*The Vanity and Glory of Man. A Sermon Preached in the Chapel of the South Carolina
College, October 9, 1842* (Columbia, 1842). See also *The Necessity of Atonement. A Sermon Preached in the Chapel of the South Carolina College on the First Day of December,
1844* (Columbia, 1845). Palmer, 285.

largely responsible for this report. To his wife Nancy he wrote, "Though not a member of the committee [charged with preparing the report] I have been consulted on the subject, and have drawn up a paper, which I think the Committee and the Assembly will substantially adopt, and if they do, abolitionism will be killed in the Presbyterian Church, at least for the present."[69]

The essence of this report was that "the Church of Christ is a spiritual body. . . . She cannot legislate where Christ has not legislated. . . . The question, therefore, which this Assembly is called upon to decide, is this: Do the Scriptures teach that the holding of slaves, without regard to circumstances, is a sin, the renunciation of which should be made a condition for membership in the Church of Christ?" The report answered that since Christ and His Apostles did not bar slaveholders from communion, the Church can not. Furthermore, though ameliorating the conditions of slaves and even removing "slavery from our country" may be desirable, "these objects . . . can never be secured by ecclesiastical legislation," nor by the rantings of the abolitionists, which "tend only to perpetuate and aggravate" the supposed evil.[70] Southern Presbyterians would take comfort in this statement and thus feel little of the anxiety that led their Methodist and Baptist neighbors to sever ties with their Northern brethren.[71]

This concept, that the Church "cannot legislate where Christ has not legislated," might be interpreted as a bar to all social involvement by Christians who ascribe to it, but Thornwell and most of his colleagues were not so otherworldly as that. They had some difficulty determining where to draw the line between proper and improper church action regarding social institutions and ills; however, few of them took the extreme position regarding the separation of church and state. As noted, Southern churchmen tried to develop a slaveholding ethic that would inspire their society and so ameliorate the condition of the slave. Thornwell joined in this effort, expressing deep concern about the "abuses" and "evils" present in the institution, and calling the South Carolina law against teaching slaves to read "disgraceful."[72] In an article in the newly launched *Southern Pres-*

---

[69]Thornwell to Nancy Thornwell, 19 May 1845, in Palmer, 286.

[70]Thompson, *Presbyterians in the South,* 1:530-31.

[71]Ibid.

[72]Thornwell to Robert J. Breckinridge, 20 October 1847; quoted in Palmer, 301.

byterian Review in 1847, he explored the subject of slave conversion and salvation, and called on masters to minister to their slaves by providing them access to sound preaching.[73] Such religious instruction would not only nourish their souls; it would also lead them to be more obedient and more self-disciplined, thus enabling the master to adjust his management methods toward a more humane philosophy. With his condition thus ameliorated, the slave would in turn find it easier to identify his interests with those of his master.[74]

By 1850, then, Thornwell had resolved his own position regarding slavery and was ready to provide a strong voice of conservative orthodoxy in the decade ahead. The white people of the South, he would argue, were refining their peculiar institution and ameliorating the condition of their slaves. Yet the stridency of the abolitionists threatened to strain the relationship of the South and the Union to the breaking point. Supporters of slavery were to articulate their position persuasively and continue to minister to their slaves as fellow creatures of a loving God, so that they could stand with the forces of reason and the divine will.

On 26 May 1850, as sectional tensions were being inflamed by the debate on California's petition for statehood, an event of little fanfare but substantial symbolic significance took place in Charleston. Zion Church, also called Anson Street Church, was dedicated. It had been built by white Presbyterians and Episcopalians to house a black congregation. Considering the opposition to this enterprise and the Northern attack on slavery, it was decided to combine the dedication with a presentation of the views of the South's religious community on slavery. "Accordingly, the congregation that assembled . . . was composed exclusively of white people."[75] Having just arrived in the city to take the pulpit of the new Glebe Street Presbyterian Church, James Thornwell was asked to preach the dedicatory sermon.[76] He took as his text Colossians 4:1, "Masters, give unto your servants that which is just and equal, knowing that ye also have a

---

[73]Thornwell, "Baptism of Servants," *Southern Presbyterian Review* 1 (June 1847): 63-102.

[74]Ibid. See also Thornwell's published review of John B. Adger's sermon on the mission to the slaves, *A Review of Rev. J. B. Adger's Sermon on the Religious Instruction of the Colored Population* (Charleston, 1847).

[75]Adger, *My Life and Times*, 178.

[76]Palmer, 347.

master in heaven.'' It is significant that, of the many biblical references he
could have chosen, Thornwell selected one that, while implicitly sanctioning the existence of slavery, focuses on the duties of the masters.[77] He
began by reminding his audience of the ''insane fury of [abolitionist] philanthropy'' that threatened the ''utter ruin of this vast imperial Republic.''
How should Southerners respond? What better response could be offered,
he suggested, than the construction of the building they had gathered to
dedicate?[78] This, Thornwell maintained, was a far better way of meeting
the abolitionists than embracing the doctrine of separate creation and asserting that the black man is a fit subject for slavery because he is not human. ''We are not ashamed to call him our *brother*,'' he insisted.[79]

The minority status of the South, which held values that the rest of
Western culture considered anachronistic, was creating great tensions and
strains for the region's people. Appreciating this, Thornwell raised questions that many in the room must have asked themselves: Can we be right
when so many are against us? Is God shaping events toward eventual defeat? Too firm a Calvinist to claim sure knowledge of God's will and plan,
Thornwell nonetheless asserted that there was biblical justification for the
South's position; in fact, the extent of her opposition might have been part
of the divine plan. ''God has not permitted such a remarkable phenomenon
as the unanimity of the civilized world in its execration of slavery to take
place without design,'' he assured his listeners. The strength and fury of
the enemy have ''been ordered for wise and beneficient results; and [even-
tually it will be seen] that a real progress has been made in the practical
solution of the problems which have produced the collision.'' What difficulties lie ahead for the South, he cautioned, ''no human sagacity can
forsee,'' but ''truth must triumph . . . and if our institutions are indeed
consistent with righteousness and truth, we can calmly . . . watch the storm
which is beating furiously against us, without terror or dismay. . . . If our
principles are true, the world must come to them.''[80]

---

[77]An expanded version of the sermon was published in pamphlet form on *The Rights
and Duties of Masters* . . . (Charleston, 1850) and in the *Southern Presbyterian Review* as
''Slavery and the Religious Instruction of the Colored Population,'' 4 (July 1850): 105-41.
It may also be found in John B. Adger, ed., *Collected Writings of James Henley Thornwell*,
vol. 4 (Richmond, 1871) 398-427.

[78]Adger, *Collected Writings*, 398, 401.

[79]Ibid., 403.

[80]Ibid., 404.

What were these principles? They were the same principles that were under attack by liberalism everywhere. We are living in a day when fundamental questions are being explored and are "shaking thrones to their centers," Thornwell reminded his audience.

> The agitations which are convulsing the kingdoms of Europe [the revolutions of 1848-1849], the mad speculations of philosophers, the excesses of unchecked democracy, are working out some of the most difficult problems of political and social science; and when the tumult shall have subsided, and reason resumed her ascendency, it will be found that the very principles upon which we have been accustomed to justify Southern Slavery are the principles of regulated liberty; that in defending this institution we have really been upholding the civil interests of mankind, . . . that we have been supporting representative, republican government against the despotism of the masses on the one hand, and the supremacy of a single will on the other.

Seeing the struggle from this larger perspective, Thornwell asserted that the "parties in this conflict are not merely Abolitionists and Slaveholders; they are Atheists, Socialists, Communists, Red Republicans, Jacobins on the one side, and the friends of order and regulated freedom on the other."[81]

In analyzing the institution of slavery, Thornwell continued, it is important to distinguish between the abstract view of one who reflects upon it from afar and the actual relationships that form its essence. First, slavery must be understood in the context of The Fall, as "part of the curse which sin has introduced into the world."[82] Admitting that slavery would not exist in a perfect world, Thornwell saw no impediment to defending its existence in an imperfect one.[83] Properly understood, slavery is not the dehumanizing institution the abolitionists describe. Defining the institution in William Paley's words as "the obligation to labor for another, determined by the Providence of God, independently of the provisions of a contract," Thornwell insisted that the master holds the right to the labor,

---

[81]Ibid., 404-405.

[82]Jones and Wells, *The Presbyterian Church in South Carolina*, 62.

[83]Adger, *Collected Writings*, 4:431, 460-61. Charles C. Bishop has noted that in Thornwell's view the ultimate aim of Providence must be to abolish slavery. Whether this means before or after the millennium is not clear. Bishop, "The Pro-Slavery Argument Reconsidered: James Henley Thornwell, Millennial Abolitionist," *South Carolina Historical Magazine* 73 (January 1972): 18-26; see 20.

but not the man. No labor is truly voluntary, but the slave may give his labor as freely as, or more so than, the "free" laborer. The determining factor is not his legal status, but his moral character, which is the source of his motivation. In our system of slavery (as it ought to be practiced, he might have added), "the ideas of personal rights and personal responsibility pervade the whole system. It is a relation of man to man [which] Christian knowledge softens. . . . Jesus Christ, in binding his subjects to God, binds them more closely to each other in the ties of confidence, fidelity and love."[84]

The modern mind is uncomfortable with slavery, Thornwell suggested, because it is confused by its love of the concept of freedom. No one, he insisted, is free in the way that word is loosely used today. To be free in this sense is to be lost. No person, subject to the onus of Adam's fall, is capable of enjoying such an existence. True freedom for such a creature is

> that which is the end and glory of man, the only freedom which the pen of inspiration has commended. It is . . . the liberty wherein Christ has made us free. It consists essentially in the dominion of rectitude, in the emancipation of the will from the power of sin, the release of the affections from the attractions of earth, the exemption of the understanding from the deceits and prejudices of error. It is a freedom . . . enjoyed by the martyr at the stake, a slave in his chains, a prisoner in his dungeon, as well as the king upon his throne.
>
> [I]t is precisely the assertion of this freedom . . . which the Apostle enjoins upon slaves when he exhorts them to obey their masters . . . and to do their work as in the eye of God. To obey, under the influence of these motives, is to be a slave no longer.[85]

Having thus placed the master-slave relationship in the context of his theology, Thornwell moved to confront some of the thorny questions raised by the abolitionists. Is slavery sinful in that it strips the slave of some rights that belong to the condition of humanity? On this question both sides in the debate have been guilty of excess, he admitted. The one has minimized

---

[84]Adger, *Collected Writings*, 407, 413, 416. *Southern Presbyterian Review* 4 (July 1850): 121-22.

[85]Adger, *Collected Writings*, 418. The psychologist Erich Fromm developed a similar view of the delusion of freedom in the modern mind. Fromm, *Escape from Freedom* (New York, 1941).

the value of freedom, while the other has exaggerated the extent of human rights. For Thornwell this question was better put, Is slavery compatible with the Gospel? In one sense the answer was no. The "perfection of the race," he conceded, is the design of Christianity, and when this is achieved, slavery must end. "This is only asserting," he added, "that there will be no bondage in heaven. If Adam had never sinned, and brought death into the world, the bondage of man to man would never have been instituted. . . . In *this* sense slavery is inconsistent with the gospel, *viz.*, that it contemplates a state of things, an existing economy, which it is the design of the gospel to remove."[86] "Slavery," he asserted, "is a part of the curse which sin has introduced into the world, and stands in the same general relation to Christianity as poverty, sickness, disease or death. . . . It springs, not from the nature of man as man, nor from the nature of society as such, but from the nature of man as sinful and the nature of society as disordered." We cannot picture slavery in a perfect world, nor can we imagine "hospitals and beggars." That slavery is "not absolutely a good, a blessing, the most strenuous defender of slavery ought not to permit himself to deny." But the Gospel does not propose "to make our earth a heaven. Here is where the philanthropists mistake."

For Thornwell the real question was, Is slavery incompatible with the goals of the Christian life in this fallen society? He answered no, because slavery does not pose insurmountable obstacles to the practice of Christian duty. That it presents opportunities for sin is clear, but this is no argument against it, any more than against any social arrangement. The essence of the abolitionist argument, he concluded, is that the slave cannot engage in all human activities and is therefore denied his rights as a human. But when carried to its logical conclusion, he maintained, "This argument would condemn every arrangement of society which did not secure to all its members an absolute equality of position; it is the very spirit of socialism and communism." Implicit in this view is the organic concept of society and the notion of "relation" discussed in chapter 3. For Thornwell, as for most Southern thinkers of his day, human rights could not "be treated as a fixed and invariable quantity. Dependent as they are upon our duties, which, in turn, are dependent on our circumstances, they fluctuate with the gradations and progress of society." The slave thus has rights, but the rights of

---

[86]Adger, *Collected Writings,* 419.

the citizen are not among them. Furthermore, these rights are not, he argued, essential to humanity or they would belong to women and children.[87]

Turning to another question raised by the abolitionists, he asked whether slavery was inconsistent with the progress of society. Again the answer was no, since "the feet are as indispensable to the head as the head to the feet." If all of its elements follow the principle of duty, society will be like a healthy body "in which all the limbs and organs perform their appropriate functions without collision or tumult."[88]

More difficult, it seems, was the objection that slavery was inconsistent with the golden rule. Jesus taught that men should love their neighbors as they love themselves. To the abolitionists, enslaving a man could not be consistent with this admonition. Lincoln put this point most effectively when he wrote, "As I would not *be* a slave, so I would not *own* a slave."[89] Thornwell's response to this argument was that if this ideal were followed literally, "the judge could not condemn the criminal, nor the executioner behead him; the rich man could not claim his possessions nor the poor learn patience from their sufferings." For Thornwell, the true meaning of the golden rule was "the inculcation of justice from the motive of love. . . . [I]n the case of slavery, [the rule requires] that we should treat our slaves as we should feel that we had a right to be treated if we were slaves ourselves."[90]

Finally, Thornwell admonished his audience that a slaveowning society has a moral obligation to protect its slaves by law against brutality in its many forms. This, he implied, includes protecting the slave's access to information that he needs in order to nourish his soul and accept salvation. Masters, in other words, must give their slaves "free access to the instructions and institutions of the gospel." Even "the meanest slave," he reminded them, "has within him a soul of priceless value." And it was, after all, the soul in which Thornwell was ultimately interested. "Our design in giving them the gospel," he assured his white audience, "is not to civilize

---

[87]Ibid., 420-22.

[88]Ibid., 423.

[89]Steven B. Oates, *With Malice toward None: The Life of Abraham Lincoln* (New York, 1977) 136.

[90]Adger, *Collected Writings,* 425-27.

them—not to change their social condition—not to exalt them into citizens or freemen—it is to save them.''[91]

This sermon—though neither his first nor last on the subject, nor perhaps his most eloquent—expresses what Thornwell and many other Southern clergymen saw as the crux of their region's dilemma. Its text goes to the heart of the slaveholding ethic as Thornwell understood it, and his selection of it indicates the role he was increasingly choosing to play in the slavery debate. For slavery to be fully worthy of defense, more was needed than the citing of biblical passages that, in Southern minds, substantiated the argument that the institution was divinely ordained. Having recognized that slavery, like all human institutions, was corruptible, the South's leading evangelicals directed their efforts toward making the institution as faithful to the Christian model as human frailty would permit. For Thornwell, the easiest analogy for this was the family; and he, like many others, used this analogy repeatedly in preaching to both races.[92] The notion of African slaves as members of the master's family is a difficult one for modern students of the Old South to accept, as it was for the abolitionists in Thornwell's day. There seems to be a paradox involved in the analogy between the master-slave relationship and the family relationship. Would a parent enslave his child? Would a master accept a mere slave as a family member? It is dangerous to generalize on this problem, but for Thornwell the relationship followed naturally from his theology, as did everything else in his social philosophy.

One historian of Old South Presbyterianism has suggested that the chief source for this family analogy was the *Larger Catechism*, question 129, which asks what things are required of superiors in their relationship with inferiors. The answer reads, in part, ''to love, pray for, and bless their in-

---

[91]Thornwell, *The Rights and Duties of Masters. A Sermon Preached at the Dedication of a Church Erected in Charleston, South Carolina, for the Benefit and Instruction of the Coloured Population* (Charleston, 1850) 50-51.

[92]See, for example, his article, ''Duties of Masters,'' 270, and ''The Baptism of Servants,'' 101-102. In ''Duties of Masters,'' he states that the master-servant relationship is ''to be regarded as belonging to the family, coming under the same policy and benevolent discipline, regulating other family relationships.'' Thornwell once wrote to an unknown correspondent, urging him to include his slaves in family Bible reading and prayers. Thornwell to [?], 10 October 1851, in Simon Cratz Autograph Collection, The Historical Society of Pennsylvania; cited in Margaret DesChamps, ''The Presbyterian Church in the South Atlantic States, 1801-1861'' (Ph.D. dissertation, Emory University, 1952) 55.

feriors; to instruct, counsel, and admonish them . . . providing for them all things necessary for the soul and body,'' and to set a good example.[93] This notion of superior and inferior members of society, or the concept of relation, as it has been called, was central to Thornwell's understanding of all social arrangements, particularly that of slavery. The paradox of the slave as a family member is present also in his racism and universalism. That Thornwell was a racist should come as no surprise. It is difficult to measure the intensity of his racism, but his letters reveal no significant difference from the prevailing Southern view of the black man. He may have gone beyond the normal Southern attitude, for on one occasion he seems to have insisted on a white nurse for his children.[94] Thornwell was not entirely typical of Southern whites, in that he spent his adult life in Columbia, in an academic and ecclesiastical environment, and experienced plantation life only in the summers when his family visited the Witherspoon plantation near Lancaster. Yet he had sufficient contact with blacks, both as the child of an overseer on a Marlboro District plantation, and in later life, to have developed some of the same ambiguous feelings toward them as did Southern whites in general.

To these feelings he added his theological concept of universalism, which, if he was able to synthesize it with his racism, mitigated the latter attitude to a substantial degree. He understood the doctrine of Original Sin to imply the generic unity of man, with Adam as the representative of all mankind. ''The human race is not an aggregate of separate and independent atoms,'' he lectured his Columbia Seminary class, ''but constitutes an organic whole, with a common life springing from a common ground. There is a unity in the whole species; there is a point in which all the individuals meet, and through which they are all modified and conditioned. Society exerts even a more powerful influence upon the individual than the individual upon society, and every community impresses its own peculiar type upon the individuals who are born into it.'' ''This,'' he argued, ''is the secret of the peculiarities of national character. There was one type

---

[93]William D. Blanks, ''Ideal and Practice; a Study of the Conception of the Christian Life Prevailing in the Presbyterian Church of the South during the Nineteenth Century'' (Ph.D. dissertation, Union Seminary, 1960) 100. Blanks concludes from the ''number and tenor of the articles urging [conversion and amelioration] as a duty'' that this ideal was poorly met by masters (ibid., 109).

[94]John Adger to Thornwell, 26 April 1848, Thornwell Papers.

among the Greeks, another among the Asiatics, and still another among the Romans. The Englishman is easily distinguished from the Frenchman, the Chinese from the European, and the Negro from all. In the same way, there is a type of life common to the entire race in which a deeper ground of unity is recognized than that which attaches to national associations or the narrower ties of kindred and blood. There is in a man what we may call a common nature." Elsewhere he wrote that the sons of Adam "are one race, one blood, one body—an unity, not . . . answering to the definition of a genus or a species, but an unity founded in the relations of individual beings."[95]

In another seminary lecture he returned to this theme from another perspective. Discussing the question, Is heathenism a misfortune or a crime? Thornwell rejected the view that the pagan worshipers are pleasing God with their rituals. The sincerity of religion is not its most important aspect, he argued. We tend to minimize the "crime" of the pagan, because we "lose sight of the fact that the heathen are men like ourselves, rational, moral, religious; that they have a nature in all respects like ours—the same primitive cognitions, the same laws of belief, the same conscience in its fundamental commands, and the same instinct for personal communion and worship. Their constitution, as spiritual, responsible beings, in no respect differs from our own. . . . To the bar of reason they are certainly responsible."[96] Such was the nature of Thornwell's mind on the subject of race: a complex and, to the modern mind, contradictory set of beliefs that, while leading him to condone slavery, led him also to insist on the imposition of the slaveholding ethic, even as it allowed him to sincerely rebuke the abolitionists for their misunderstanding of the master-slave relationship.

What sort of master was Thornwell to the slaves he and Nancy inherited from his father-in-law? The evidence, though slim, suggests that he typified the tenderhearted masters who predominated among the Southern clergy.[97] The Witherspoon plantation near Lancaster—which Thornwell named Dryburgh Abbey, after the Scottish estate where Sir Walter Scott

---

[95]Adger, *Collected Writings*, 1:349-50; Thornwell, review of Baird, *Elohim Revealed,* ibid., 552. Other examples of this universalism are in his essay, "The Necessity and Nature of Christianity," ibid., 2:64, and his Theology Lecture #2, ibid., 1:99-100.

[96]Ibid., 1:99-100.

[97]Loveland, *Southern Evangelicals and the Social Order*, ch. 2.

was buried—was not very productive and, says Palmer, "was never of much pecuniary benefit to him. He was an easy and indulgent master and it is doubtful if his slaves made their own support." Thornwell seems to have practiced what he preached about ministering to the slaves. He led services for them himself at times, though he generally paid other ministers, including a Methodist named Cauthen, to hold regular services for his slaves.[98] A family member later recalled that the Thornwells "felt a sacred responsibility . . . for training their immortal souls, as well as clothing and feeding [them]." "Dr. T. never could brag on his crops for he would not allow his servants to hurt themselves working and if the plantation supported them he was satisfied." Long after his death former slaves from Columbia and Lancaster would visit Nancy and reminisce about the old days.[99] As for the instruction these slaves received, one may assume that "Amanda" was typical. On 3 October 1849 she was received on profession of faith as a member of the First Presbyterian Church of Columbia "after a full and more than usually satisfactory examination into the grounds of her faith and hope."[100]

Further development of a slaveholding ethic depended, in Thornwell's view, upon maintaining the ban on the African slave trade. This was so because of the nearly universal revulsion, not only of Northerners but of Southerners as well, against the trade, and also because of its effects upon slavery. Writing to his friend and colleague John Adger of Charleston, Thornwell said that both his "judgment" and his "feelings" were "decidedly opposed to the slave trade, in every respect in which the subject can be viewed." "In the first place, It would change the whole character of the institution, as it exists among us. It is now domestic and patriarchal; the slave has all the family associations, and family pride, of the master. He is born in the house, and bred with the children [of the master]. The sentiments which spring from this circumstance, in the master and the slave, soften all the *asperities* of the relation, and secure obedience as a sort of filial respect. This *humanizing element would be lost,* the moment we cease

---

[98]Thornwell to Matthew J. Williams, 17 July 1850; quoted in Palmer, 341; also see 342-43; unsigned and undated manuscript in Thornwell Papers, by a niece of Nancy Thornwell, evidently written in the 1890s.

[99]MS by Nancy Thornwell's niece. She mentions "Elsie, Eliza, Isaac, [and] Charles."

[100]Minutes of the First Presbyterian Church, South Caroliniana Library, Columbia, South Carolina.

to rear our slaves, and rely on a foreign market.'' He added that a sudden influx of Africans would make the institution dangerous, since many of them ''are accustomed to command, to war and to cruelty, and none of [them] have been accustomed to work.'' ''We should have to resort to a standing army, as they do in the West Indies, to keep our plantations in order.'' Even if these objections could be answered, he concluded, the trade would be repulsive on its face, since it would encourage ''wars and seditions in Africa,'' and would make the crime of ''manstealing'' into a lucrative and common enterprise.[101]

Thornwell, like so many Southerners of his generation, was a man of conflicting loyalties. He saw himself first as a man of God, then as an American and a citizen of his native South Carolina. Just where the balance between these last two loyalties would eventually be was something he hoped never to learn. Until the last weeks of 1860, he was a Unionist who clung to the hope that sectional issues could be resolved without destroying the nation that he saw as God's modern Israel.[102]

Yet his love for his state was hardly less than that for his nation, and his confidence that its way of life more closely approximated the Christian ideal than that of the Northern states naturally led him to defend his region and its institutions. By the 1850s he had already charted a course in church circles of insisting on the need for biblical authenticity as the test of any church action, and it was natural for him to treat the issue of the church's stand on slavery in the same way. He continued to press the victory that he had helped win for the Southern wing of Old School Presbyterianism in 1845, when the General Assembly had determined to speak only on subjects about which the Bible was clear, and thus to avoid any criticism of slavery. (See chapter 6.) For Thornwell and his fellow Southern Presbyterians, their church, which after the 1840s was the only national evangelical body still united North and South (unless one includes the

---

[101]Thornwell to John Adger, 10 December 1856; quoted in Palmer, 422-23. These arguments were largely incorporated into an article Adger wrote on the subject about a year later. See ''A Review of the Reports to the Legislature of South Carolina on the Revival of the Slave Trade,'' *Southern Presbyterian Review* 9 (April 1858): 100-35.

[102]Thornwell saw the agitation of radicals in both sections as aimed ''at the destruction of the Government and the subversion of religion'' (Palmer, 574). Palmer writes that Thornwell ''glorified in the American name,'' for it was with ''unspeakable pain'' that he cut his ties with the Union (ibid., 468).

Episcopalian church among the evangelical denominations), could remain one body only so long as it continued its neutral stand on the slavery issue. To this goal he dedicated himself throughout the final antebellum decade.

In 1851 the Synod of South Carolina named Thornwell chairman of a committee charged with presenting a statement on slavery. The report, which was published as a pamphlet and as an article in the *Southern Presbyterian Review,* stated that the church "is not, as we fear too many are disposed to regard it, a moral institute of universal good, whose business is to wage war upon every form of human ill, whether social, civil, political or moral, and to patronize every expedient which a romantic benevolence may suggest as likely to contribute to human comfort, or to mitigate the inconveniences of life." All "anomalies of our fallen state" such as poverty, insanity, lawlessness, intemperance, gambling, and lust, while not outside the scope of the Christian's concern as an individual, were outside the sphere of the church. The report insisted that the Bible formed the boundaries of the church's vision and action. "Beyond the Bible she can never go, and apart from the Bible she can never speak. She has a *creed,* but no *opinions.*" Since the Bible sanctions slavery, then, the position of the church is clear. "Slavery as a political question is one in regard to which communities and States may honestly differ. But as a *moral* question, the Bible has settled it."[103] In both sanctioning slavery and holding that the slave was a human soul in need of salvation, the Bible gave the church its charge: to minister to the slave, while avoiding any interference with his legal condition. What God in His providence might eventually do regarding the slave's lot, man could not know.[104]

While other Southern clergymen, including Thornwell's protégé, Benjamin Morgan Palmer, would go beyond this statement of church neutrality on slavery, Thornwell remained consistent to the end, maintaining his view that the church could not speak where the Bible was silent. In his *Address to All the Churches of Jesus Christ throughout the Earth,* written in December 1861 for the newly born Presbyterian Church of the Confederacy, he reiterated his position that "in our ecclesiastical capacity, we are neither the friends nor the foes of slavery. . . . We have no right, as a

[103]Adger, *Collected Writings,* 4:382-84; 388.

[104]Bishop, "The Pro-Slavery Argument Reconsidered," 18-26.

Church, to enjoin it as a duty, or to condemn it as a sin. Our business is with the duties which spring from the relation [of master and slave]." [105]

In trying to assess the influence of Thornwell, and the clergy generally, upon the Southern conception of slavery and upon its defense, one is faced with a situation where there is a large and persuasive body of circumstantial evidence, but no real proof. As discussed (see chapter 1), the clergy held a highly influential position in the society of the Old South. As articulators of the religious ideology of that society, they were looked upon as the champions of decency and order in a crass and often violent world. While their position on the slavery issue has been described as merely a reiteration of the argument that Southern white self-interest dictated, Thornwell and his colleagues were clearly trying to shape, as well as to defend, the institution. [106] Their success may be measured by examining the statements of Southern laymen on slavery and comparing these writings with the main themes in the sermons, articles in the religious press, and church pronouncements on the issue. Ample illustrations can be found of the parallels between the two. [107]

If such comparisons are far from conclusive proof of the idea that the clergy was shaping the views of the Southern population generally on slavery, they do at least suggest that for the secular Southerner, slavery could be most effectively defended against the essentially moralistic attacks of the abolitionists by employing the weapons of the clergy—weapons highly respected throughout the nation in the mid-nineteenth century and peculiarly suited to rebut the attack. Perhaps more persuasive is the suggestion of Eugene Genovese and others that slavery was showing signs of the humanizing impact of the slaveholding ethic, which the clergy had promoted. There may have been a circular pattern here, between the expression of a Christian ideal for its own sake, and the concomitant desire to make the reality of slavery meet the ideal that was being expressed in its defense.

---

[105]*Minutes of the General Assembly of the Presbyterian Church in the Confederate States of America* (August, 1861) 55-56.

[106]Doralyn Hickey, "Benjamin Morgan Palmer: Churchman of the Old South" (Ph.D. dissertation, Duke University, 1962). Hickey concludes that Palmer's views on slavery "can be called expedient" (186).

[107]Drew Faust, ed., *The Ideology of Slavery: Proslavery Thought in the Antebellum South, 1830-1860* (Baton Rouge, 1982). William S. Jenkins, *Pro-Slavery Thought in the Old South* (Chapel Hill, 1935). Tise, "Proslavery Ideology."

Thornwell and others saw, it seems, that the effectiveness of the defense depended upon the moral integrity of the argument being advanced in slavery's defense. What they seem not to have realized is that for those who were opposed to slavery on principle, and thus opposed to its expansion into the American West, no amount of amelioration of the institution would matter. Thus the Southern clergy's efforts in this regard were futile in terms of their desired effect upon the course of national politics, and ultimately upon the future of slavery itself.

CHAPTER 8

Toward
Secession and War:
The Southern Church
and the Climax
of Sectional Antipathy

As the decade of the 1850s neared its end, the people of the South experienced both a "crisis of fear" and a rising tide of righteous self-confidence. Their mood ranged from paranoia over slave revolts and carping criticism of their leaders to exultant anticipation of their long-awaited vindication. The Southern clergy, while its ultimate concern may have been with more lofty matters, provided in its pulpit rhetoric and essays a moral girding for conflict that would carry the Southern people into secession, nationhood, and war in an almost sublime state.[1]

Southern intellectuals responded to the rise of Southern nationalism in a variety of ways. On the one hand, there was, even for these more rational minds, a heady and at times euphoric sense of a new nation's emergence. In some, this took a bellicose form, as with Mississippian Henry Hughes's

---

[1]Steven A. Channing, *Crisis of Fear; Secession in South Carolina* (New York, 1970); James W. Silver, *Confederate Morale and Church Propaganda* (New York, 1957).

suggestion to Southern mothers as to the proper rearing of the young who would carry the fight. "Let all such as [are] slapt slap back," he urged. Let them "have flags for wrappers, powder boxes for saddles, drums for rattles, and for common playthings, pistols . . . ramrods and scabbards." "Let them play most with the rod that they may long for the rifle, and most with the scabbard that they may prize the sword."[2] Though few matched Hughes's cockiness, many shared the same confidence in the Southern way of life that Virginia's George Fitzhugh expressed in an article in *DeBow's Review* in 1860. "Our seceding states best understand and practice the art of government," he wrote. "A master race necessarily improves upon itself, and practices as severe a drill as it subjects its inferiors to. . . . The gentlemen of the South are better horsemen, better marksmen, have more physical strength and activity, and can endure more fatigue than their slaves. Besides, they have the lofty sentiments and high morals of a master race, that would render them unconquerable."[3]

Others despaired at the prospect of a revolution led by unworthy men. Wrote James Hammond, the "South has *prostituted* herself all at once to every sort of adventurer—Cuban fillibusters [*sic*], slave trade felons, and political asperants [*sic*] of the basest and *silliest* order. Who would have thought it? I am ashamed of her."[4] Seeing the base level of much of the secessionist movement, Hammond warned his friend Gilmore Simms not to think it the product of "Virtue," or "inspired *Intellect*. It is the insanity of one-idea *Enthusiasts . . .* whose unbridled ambition knows no check of knowledge of conscience."[5] Maryland's literary giant, John Pendleton Kennedy, writing during the Democratic-party convention of 1860, referred to politicians as "those glass-eyed, scurvy fellows."[6] Virginian

---

[2]"St. Henry" in the Jackson, Mississippi, *Semi-Weekly Mississippian,* 4 October 1859; quoted in Ronald Takaki, *A Pro-Slavery Crusade: The Agitation to Reopen the African Slave Trade* (New York, 1971) 95.

[3]George Fitzhugh, "Frederick the Great, by Thomas Carlyle," *DeBow's Review* 29 (1860): 155.

[4]James H. Hammond to William Gilmore Simms, 22 April 1859, in Hammond Papers, Library of Congress; quoted in Drew Faust, "A Sacred Circle: The Social Role of the Intellectual in the Old South, 1840-1860" (Ph.D. dissertation, University of Pennsylvania, 1975) 315.

[5]Hammond to Simms, 22 April 1859, Hammond Papers.

[6]Kennedy to Mrs. Henry Duncan, 27 May 1860, Kennedy Papers, Peabody Institute, Baltimore.

George William Bagby echoed this view from the nation's capitol. "What is to become of the country, Heaven only knows. There is no longer a party to be trusted—indeed there is none in existence. There is no man, nor any set of men, who enjoy the confidence of the nation. We have no truly great men!"[7] William Gilmore Simms touched a note familiar among intellectuals when he wrote bitingly that "it is not the Yankee race alone that needs purging and scourging. We too need punishing to destroy the packed jury, the old family systems, the logrolling and the corruption everywhere."[8]

Those who dissented from the prevailing view naturally felt even more unhappy about the direction in which the region was moving. James Louis Petigru shared the low regard for the current leadership of his state. Thanking Edward Everett of Massachusetts for a copy of his biography of Washington, he added that reading it reminded him of the mediocrity of today's leaders, whose ambitions so outstripped their ability. As for his assessment of the current situation, "My own countrymen here in South Carolina are distempered to a degree that makes them to a calm and impartial observer real objects of pity."[9] Petigru, who knew how it felt to be alone, complained to University of North Carolina President David Swain, "The most deplorable part of our case here is the total absence of a minority and the general contempt for consequences—what hope is there for the human race when there is no minority?"[10]

[7]George W. Bagby in *The Crescent*, 26 February 1859; quoted in J. L. King, *Dr. George William Bagby: A Study in Virginia Literature, 1850-1880* (New York, 1927) 58.

[8]William Gilmore Simms to James Hammond, 18 November 1861, in Mary C. Oliphant et al., eds., *Letters of William Gilmore Simms*, vol. 4 (Columbia, 1955) 355. Mary Boykin Chesnut expressed similar views. See C. Vann Woodward, ed., *Mary Chesnut's Civil War* (New Haven, 1981) 6-7. Others close to the seats of power shared this cynicism. Ralph Elliott, the son of South Carolina planter William Elliott and a member of the state legislature, wrote his mother in December 1860, "I can see nothing but anarchy and confusion staring us in the face. No man appears to have the slightest confidence in more than one other man beside himself." Ralph Elliott to "Mama," 10 December 1860, Elliott-Gonzales Papers, Southern Historical Collection. William Elliott wrote to Ralph sometime that fall, "I look in vain for the men who are fit for the crisis" (ibid).

[9]James Louis Petigru to Edward Everett, 28 October 1860; quoted in James P. Carson, *James Louis Petigru, Union Man of South Carolina* (Washington, 1920) 359-60.

[10]Petigru to David Swain, 4 March 1861; quoted in Clement Eaton, *Freedom of Thought in the Old South* (Durham, 1940) 386. The repressive atmosphere in Columbia was noted by William Campbell Preston, former United States senator and president of the South Carolina College. The South Carolina capitol had become "a focus of slave traders, disunionists and lynching societies which possess it entirely," he wrote, and described the city as being under "a reign of terror." Preston to Waddy Thompson, 27 January 1860; quoted in Channing, *Crisis of Fear*, 30.

Petigru is, of course, a special case, standing so conspicuously alone that he might be called the exception that proves the rule regarding South Carolina opinion. But his views are surely no less instructive because of this. By November 1860 he had concluded that the Union would be ruptured and wrote poignantly to his daughter, "The Constitution is only two months older than I. My life will probably be prolonged until I am older than it is."[11] His opposition to the course his state was pursuing was sharpened by his view of its leaders' minds. "The South Carolina men show by their precipitancy that they are afraid to trust the second thought of even their own people," he told his sister.[12] The lack of dissent was again on his mind while he was in Columbia in early December. "All are galloping down the same road and every one striving to be ahead," he wrote. "More jealousy among the members [of the legislature] and more mutual distrust I have never seen." Even conservative men, including his old friend Frederick A. Porcher, had "not escaped the contagion. Even he, the host of Henry Clay, is ready to cut the tie."[13] As events proceeded at a bewildering pace, Petigru told a Northern correspondent, "We are here in such a disturbed condition that the things that are going to happen in a week are as uncertain as if they belonged to a distant future."[14]

Others, taking stock of the South's alienation from the rest of modern society and sensing the future, experienced moments of total resignation. Robert W. Barnwell had observed many years earlier that "our institutions

---

[11]Petigru to Susan Petigru King, 10 November 1860; quoted in Carson, *James Louis Petigru*, 361.

[12]Petigru to his sister Jane, 13 November 1860; quoted ibid., 362. Two weeks later he noted the "prevalence of fear among them that are rushing into an unnecessary and untried danger," and lamented that his kinsman James Johnston Pettigrew was "full of fight" (to Jane, 27 November 1860; quoted ibid., 362).

[13]Petigru to Jane, 6 December 1860; quoted ibid., 362-63. His letters of December and January continued in the same vein (ibid., 363-69). To Edward Everett he reported that "the bitterness of spirit with which I witness the downfall of my country, is only qualified by wonder and astonishment, [at] the apathy and carelessness that mark the behavior of men otherwise respectable." Petigru to Everett, 20 January 1861; quoted ibid., 367. One can only wonder at the names of the men he was referring to, and one may also wonder if behind what Petigru saw as apathy and carelessness were ambiguous minds and breaking hearts.

[14]Petigru to R. C. Winthrop, 25 February 1861; quoted ibid., 369.

arc doomed, and the Southern civilization must go out in blood."[15] Barnwell's fatalism was echoed on the eve of secession by another South Carolinian, Frederick Porcher. "It may be that slavery is doomed," he concluded. "Be it so. Everything happens for the best. All that we ask is that it may perish manfully."[16] Though not so pessimistic about its ultimate outcome, South Carolina College President Augustus Baldwin Longstreet told the graduates in December 1859 that they were already engulfed in "a Revolution from which there was no escape."[17]

But these feelings of *que será será* were in most cases balanced by a sense of confidence in the South's position, which, while it may strike us as irrational, was a strong and growing aspect of Southern thought in the 1850s. Cotton was gradually rising in price during the decade, and Senator Hammond spoke for many when he called it "King." Perhaps equally important was the overriding sense of moral rectitude, which a half century of evangelical religious piety had instilled in the region. Ironically, James Louis Petigru referred to both of these factors in a March 1861 letter. The new Confederacy, he asserted, "is formed on principles that are hollow, on the shallow conceit that all nations will pay tribute to King Cotton." Mentioning the "surprising unanimity" of opinion in support of the new government, he added, "None are so full of this newborn zeal as the clergy, including in this term the preachers of every denomination from the Roman Catholics to the Baptists."[18]

Not all of the region's thinkers were caught up in the excitement of political events. While the national Democratic party was holding its convention in Charleston in May 1860, a group of scientists pursued their intellectual interests in a meeting of the Cheraw Lyceum, where they heard the Reverend Moses Ashley Curtis of North Carolina discourse on "The Pleasures and Advantages of a Study of Nature and Natural History."[19] But more typical was the situation in Columbia's First Presbyterian Church,

---

[15]Robert Barnwell to Robert Barnwell Rhett, 19 February 1845; quoted in Channing, *Crisis of Fear,* 62. The two men were cousins.

[16]William S. Elliott to Mrs. William Elliott, 1860; quoted ibid., 62.

[17]Address of Augustus Baldwin Longstreet, Charleston *Courier,* 13 December 1859; quoted ibid., 93.

[18]Petigru to William Carson, his grandson, 2 March 1861; quoted in Carson, *James Louis Petigru,* 370-71.

[19]Moses Ashley Curtis Papers, Southern Historical Collection.

where the session, which had been meeting weekly for many years, found itself too occupied with current political developments to continue this schedule. Its minutes show only six meetings between October 1860 and April 1861.[20] The journal of South Carolina planter-botanist Henry William Ravenel reveals the current preoccupation with politics of one who was essentially a private man. Ravenel sensed the seductive appeal of power on both sides and looked hopefully to the dawn of a new, more moral social order. As he watched the sabre-rattling in the spring of 1861, Ravenel noted in his journal,

> What a commentary does this spectacle afford upon the boasted civilization of the nineteenth century! It is too sad a proof that with all the progress made in the *Arts* and *Sciences*—with all the writings of learned men upon *Civil Liberty,* and *Political Rights*—upon *Moral* and *Intellectual Philosophy*—with all the great modern *improvements* in *manufactures* and *material prosperity,* mankind are [*sic*] no better now than at any previous time—the evil natural passions of our fallen state are just as prominent and as easily brought into exercise as in those earlier times that we, in our self-sufficiency[,] have called the *dark ages.* Nations like individuals become arrogant with power, and Might becomes Right. Egypt, Babylon, Ninevah, Persia, Rome have all learned the lesson, but we cannot profit by their example. We are working out our destiny, Deo duce.[21]

Despite these concerns, when he compared the virtues of Northern and Southern society, Ravenel had little difficulty concluding that his region, though imperfect, was superior. "Our bulwark of strength in the South," he wrote, "lies in our consciousness of rectitude in the sight of God and of man."[22] As the war began, Ravenel, a devout Christian, searched his soul. "Ever remembering my profession as a Christian," he confided to his journal, "I do not desire to separate my religious from my patriotic duties." He found them "not incompatible with each other, but perfectly consistent and harmonious. Looking all these duties and obligations steadfastly in the face, in the light of conscience, with my present convictions

---

[20]Minutes of the Session of the First Presbyterian Church, Columbia, South Carolina, typescript, South Caroliniana Library. There is no mention of political developments in these minutes.

[21]Henry William Ravenel Journal, 1 May 1861, South Caroliniana Library.

[22]Ibid., 27 March 1861.

of right, I would cheerfully go forth as a Christian Soldier to do battle for my Country." Again recognizing the danger of putting faith in human perception, he added, "May God enlighten us all and keep us on the path of Duty."[23]

Where this "path of Duty" led was a matter of some confusion among Southerners. The Nashville, Tennessee, *Union and American* urged the border slave states to assume "the glorious and Christian mission of peacemakers."[24] Others envisioned a crusade that would free the South at once from evils both external and internal, creating a society more closely attuned than any other to the divine will and the natural order.[25]

That this latter vision came to dominate the mind of the Deep South was due in no small way to the influence of the region's clergy. That influence was long-standing and pervasive, and it was hardly abating on the eve of secession, for the last of the "great awakenings" of the nineteenth century occurred in the South in 1858.[26] Like most knowledgeable Southerners, the leading clergy followed events closely in the final months of the antebellum era. Their private papers indicate that, while they may have differed on the question of their own role in these crucial days, they were no less "political" than anyone else.[27] A few, such as Methodist Augustus Baldwin Longstreet, threw themselves unreservedly into political affairs,

---

[23]Ibid., 15 June 1861. Poor health prevented Ravenel, then forty-seven, from enlisting.

[24]*Union and American*, 11 November 1860; quoted in Avery Craven, *The Growth of Southern Nationalism, 1848-1861* (Baton Rouge, 1953) 350.

[25]William Gilmore Simms to James Lawson, 20 November 1860, in Oliphant, *Letters of Simms*, 4:268-69. Simms to Jacob Bockee, 12 December 1860, ibid., 287-305.

[26]White, *Southern Presbyterian Leaders*, 303.

[27]The Basil Manly Papers, Southern Historical Collection. The letters of late 1860 and early 1861, by both Basil Manly, Sr. and his son Basil, Jr., both Baptist ministers, are full of politics. The same is true of the papers of James Henley Thornwell, South Caroliniana Library; Benjamin M. Palmer, Perkins Library, Duke University; Leonidas Polk, Southern Historical Collection. See also John Adger, *My Life and Times* (Richmond, 1899) 327-50; Thomas Smyth, *Autobiographical Notes, Letters and Reflections,* ed. Louisa Cheves Stoney (Charleston, 1914) 547-676; John A. Broadus, *Memoir of James Petigru Boyce* (Louisville, 1893) 183-97; John D. Wade, *Augustus Baldwin Longstreet* (New York, 1924) 339-51; George M. Smith, *Life and Letters of James Osgood Andrew, Bishop of the Methodist Episcopal Church, South* (Nashville, 1883) 473. See also Lewis M. Purifoy, "The Southern Methodist Church and the Pro-Slavery Argument," *Journal of Southern History* 32 (May 1966): 325-41. One Southern Presbyterian minister who seems to have had little interest in the crisis was John McLees. See his diary, 1860-1861, South Caroliniana Library.

seeing no virtue in clerical aloofness. Indeed, Longstreet had been unburdening himself of political opinions and advice long before the final collision. (See chapter 6.) In early December 1860, he was responding to newspaper accounts that said the politicians were the only South Carolinians who wanted secession. On the contrary, wrote President Longstreet, the movement "is the result of a universal outburst of indignation on the part of the people, at Lincoln's election." "Sirs, you never saw anything like it; I never saw anything like it; the world never saw anything like it." He added the opinion that three-fifths of the Southern people were for secession, "because everybody knows what Black Republicanism is. . . . What is there to consult about, to debate about?"[28]

After rejoicing at the secession of South Carolina and the other cotton states, Longstreet had a surprising change of mood. "Early spring of 1861 found the Judge in Charleston, appalled over the approach of the holocaust which up to that moment he had done nothing but further," writes his biographer.[29] Changing direction in mid-crisis, he produced a pamphlet entitled *Shall South Carolina Begin the War?* In it he urged the "authorities and people of South Carolina to put aside passion [which is] the poorest accompaniment to reason and argument." If war comes, it will be fought between "the bright and gallant sons of South Carolina and [Republican] hirelings. Woe to the people who bring on such a conflict but from dire necessity." He went on to argue that patience would bring the state and the South all that was demanded, without war. Secession, for Longstreet, was justified—war was not.[30] Yet when the war began, he threw himself heart and soul into the cause, visiting the scenes of action around Charleston and proposing a scheme for destroying Federal ships lying offshore. He was greatly disappointed when Robert E. Lee, then commanding Confederate troops in Charleston, dismissed the plan as too dangerous.[31] He offered his services as a chaplain to the governor of his native Georgia and

---

[28]Augustus Baldwin Longstreet to Editors of the *Richmond Enquirer*, 6 December 1860; quoted in William Scafadel, "The Letters of Augustus Baldwin Longstreet" (Ph.D. dissertation, University of South Carolina). Longstreet was president of the South Carolina College from 1857 to 1861.

[29]Wade, *Augustus Baldwin Longstreet*, 339.

[30]Ibid., 339-40.

[31]It involved Longstreet and a few former students at the College, disguised as blacks, boarding a Yankee ship and placing explosives aboard (ibid., 344).

was named to the largely honorary post of chaplain to the Georgia Militia. He spent the early period of the war at his Mississippi home with his wife and daughter, then moved to Columbus, Georgia, where he acted as self-appointed adviser to his brother, General James Longstreet, and his son-in-law, Lucius Quintus Cincinnatus Lamar.[32]

Longstreet was not typical, of course. Other clergymen observed events in fascination from the cloistered environment of their parishes and seminaries, but avoided direct involvement. From the Baptist Seminary in Greenville, South Carolina, where he was a professor, Basil Manly, Jr. wrote regularly to his parents in Montgomery, Alabama, during the secession winter. The letters are full of events and speculations about what the future holds. "Is it not clear," Manly suggested, "that 'Union' has become . . . a mere *juggling term*—just as 'Liberty, Equality and Fraternity' were with the bloody and treacherous Red Republicans upon whose steps [the Northern leaders] seem to be so rapidly following?" He complained that the [New York?] *World,* to which he subscribed, had become a "Republican paper," but he planned to continue reading it as a way "to keep watch upon the rascals." He called William Seward "that arch-demagogue" and rebuked Northern poet Bayard Taylor for his "sinful scoff at prayer" in the poem "A Prayer Meeting in a Storm," which depicted President James Buchanan as a ship's captain calling the crew to prayer as the ship is tossed by a storm. Touching a note he would repeat several times, Manly needlessly reminded his father that "we must look to the hills, from whence cometh our help. God . . . looks down upon the storm, and . . . amid all the wild waters and howling winds, he [can] discern the little company. . . . [He will] deliver the souls who put their trust in him."[33]

Like so many other Southerners, in and out of the pulpit, the younger Manly had confidence in the moral strength of the South. "They—the Yankees—are stronger than we—and can whip us, if they have a mind to—but we can stand a good deal of whipping—and the more they whip us—the more [they] won't conquer us," he wrote his parents.[34] Every day's news and rumors gave him greater reason to endorse Southern national-

---

[32]Ibid., 344-50.

[33]Basil Manly, Jr. to Basil Manly, Sr., 29 December 1860, Manly Papers, Southern Historical Collection.

[34]Basil Manly, Jr. to his parents, 8 January 1861, ibid.

ism. Regarding the idea reportedly being discussed in the North, to liberate and arm the blacks in the South in the event of war, he wrote, "Alongside this incendiary scheme, the arming of Indians, which Lord North was almost annihilated for proposing, [would have] been a mild and humane measure." With such things as this being said, he added, "I see not how any man can now debate 'which side to choose.' "[35] By mid-February he was reporting that "the times furnish so much exciting reading in the daily news as to take up nearly all my spare time." He added, "It is clear that we live in *historic times*—and if we do not *now* inform ourselves of the cause [?] of current events it is hard to say when we ought." Though caught up in the pace of events, he concluded that "on the whole, as I can't do anything anyway, it is perhaps as well to take it patiently."[36] As February 1861 drew to an end, Manly saw "no possibility, scarcely, of avoiding war." He speculated that the "ill-timed prudence" of the border states in delaying their decisions to secede would "probably cost many lives," since their quick action would have forced the Union to accept secession without a fight. Admitting that he could not see where events were carrying the American people, he concluded, "The whole is in the hands of God. It may be a cup of wrath for our sins, . . . but he knows how to use it, and when to desist—though he slay me, yet will I trust him." He added that the Greek word for "trust" means "to flee to," or "to take refuge in," and he advocated just this stance.[37]

The excitement of events in Washington, Montgomery, and Charleston contrasted with the routine of daily life in Greenville, and Manly noted, "So quiet and orderly is everything that you wouldn't know, unless the papers told you, that we are in the midst of a revolution." Lincoln's inaugural address struck him as having "all the softness and purring of a cat, and yet you can't help seeing the claws." He wondered what he and others in need of them would do for books, now that their chief source, New York, seemed about to be closed off. We will have to "read what we have, I suppose," he wrote, "just as I have been doing with my old clothes." As the new political landscape became clearer, he observed that the caliber of men being chosen for high office was no better than had been the case before. Spoilsmen were everywhere, and "some of the delegates to the Alabama

---

[35]Manly to his parents, 22 January 1861, ibid.

[36]Manly to his parents, 12, 15, 16 February 1861 (one letter), ibid.

[37]Manly to his parents, 23 February 1861, ibid.

Convention are specimens of this class of animal, in remarkable perfection."[38] But the season of political turmoil was not without its blessings, as he found in the experience of his Greenville church. For "amid all the war excitements, there is a very promising state of religious feelings in the church. The prayer meeting on Tuesday night was so fully attended" that meetings were held on the next two afternoons as well. "It is curious that there have been a number of revivals in Va. amid all the political excitement which is kindled there," he reported. Much reassured by these developments, he concluded, "The Lord makes us a holy people, and we should find that all is well."[39] Manly remained fully committed to the Confederate cause and offered to serve as a chaplain if needed. His later letters to his parents continued full of news and opinions, and occasionally noted with disappointment the flagging zeal of some of his neighbors in upper South Carolina. But his public role was slight.[40]

Among the denominations of Southern Christianity, the group least inclined to support a separate Southern nation was the Presbyterians. They alone among the evangelical churches remained united with their Northern brethren, although the schism of the Old and New Schools in 1837 has been equated by some with the North-South splits in the Baptist and Methodist Churches. Further, the Presbyterian clergy members of the Atlantic South were overwhelmingly conservative Whigs in politics. A leading student of antebellum Presbyterianism in this region has noted that she "has not found a single instance of a Presbyterian in Virginia, Georgia or North Carolina mentioning in diary or letter adherence to any political party except the Whig, or the Know Nothing which was formed [from it]." South Carolina, the other state of this region, was unique in that after the 1830s it was solidly Democratic. "The Presbyterian clergy are Whigs," wrote a Mississippian, "not because they are aristocrats but because they are opposed to radicalism, and in favor of conservatism."[41] South Carolina Presbyte-

---

[38]Manly to his parents, 8 March 1861, ibid.

[39]Manly to his mother, 10 April 1861, ibid.

[40]Manly to his parents, 22, 31 May; 14 June 1861, ibid.

[41]Margaret B. DesChamps, "Union or Disunion? South Atlantic Presbyterians and Southern Nationalism, 1820-1861," *Journal of Southern History* 20 (November 1954): 492. For a fuller exploration of this topic, see her dissertation, "The Presbyterian Church in the South Atlantic States, 1801-1861" (Emory University, 1952). Jackson, Mississippi, *Southron*, 15 October 1845; quoted in Margaret DesChamps Moore, "Religion in Mississippi in 1860," *The Journal of Mississippi History* 22 (1960): 235.

rians tended to side with the Unionists in the Nullification controversy; and in the crisis of 1850 most Southern Presbyterians supported the Union also, including most South Carolinians. As North Carolinian Robert H. Morrison put it, ''The people who are worth consulting look on this [secession] agitation as foolish, wicked, and abominable.''[42]

In general, this attitude prevailed throughout the 1850s. Indeed, it was not until the election of Lincoln that the Presbyterians joined the clamor for secession.[43] In this regard James Thornwell was entirely typical. Despite the influence of Thomas Cooper, he early indicated a strong attachment for the Union, opposing nullification in an essay he submitted to the *Southern Whig* and signed ''Clio.''[44] Yet his opposition to the radical states' rights doctrine did not issue from any lack of devotion to his native region or state. In fact, even while supporting the Union, he bemoaned the death of the *Southern Review,* his favorite publication, as an embarrassment to the South, ''a blot on our character.''[45] These two statements would continue to characterize Thornwell's position regarding the South and the Union until the Republican victory in the election of 1860. He loved them both. And despite his unhappy experience as a student in the Boston area, he developed a certain admiration for the Northeastern manner. ''I love the Yankees since I met a few Englishmen,'' he noted in his journal during his European trip in 1841. He went on to praise the Northerner's inquisitive and communicative nature, and to compare him to the Athenian in his eager pursuit of the new. The Englishman, on the other hand, ''thinks it would detract from [his] dignity to *learn.*''[46]

The infectious appeal of manifest destiny increased the young Thornwell's patriotic feelings when he visited the West in 1845. On the train returning from Cincinnati to Baltimore after attending the General Assembly, he wrote to Nancy, ''The more I reflect upon the subject, the more I am satisfied that the mission of our Republic will not be accomplished, until

---

[42]William W. Freehling, *Prelude to Civil War; The Nullification Controversy in South Carolina, 1816-1836* (New York, 1965) 224; DesChamps, ''Union or Disunion?'' 492-93.

[43]Henry S. Stroupe, ''The Religious Press in the South Atlantic States, 1802-1865'' (Ph.D. dissertation, Duke University, 1942) 281-321.

[44]Thornwell to Alexander Pegues, 19 April 1832; quoted in Benjamin M. Palmer, *Life and Letters of James Henley Thornwell, D.D., LL.D.* (Richmond, 1875) 93.

[45]Thornwell to Alexander Pegues, 29 April 1832; quoted ibid., 93-94.

[46]Thornwell Journal, May 1841, Thornwell Papers, South Caroliniana Library.

we embrace in our Union the whole of the North American continent.'' A strong supporter of Texas annexation, he added, ''It would be better for this country, and for the interests of the human race, to give up New England [if she tries to block the annexation] than to abandon any new territory.'' ''I go for Texas; I should like also to have California; we must hold on to Oregon, if we have to do it at the point of the bayonet; and I would be glad even to get Mexico itself.'' He was beginning to anticipate the strength of sectional tension and to consider the South's options for the future. ''If the Yankees feel disposed to leave us, let them go; but the West and the South can never be separated. There is at work in this land a Yankee spirit, and an American spirit; and the latter must triumph.'' He added that since most Northerners and Westerners are not abolitionists, the South, by behaving prudently, could kill this movement.[47]

When California's petition for statehood led to the Congressional Compromise of 1850 and in turn to the secession movement of 1850-1851 in South Carolina, Thornwell remained steadfast in his Unionism. ''The prospect of disunion is one which I cannot contemplate without absolute horror,'' he wrote a colleague. He listed three grounds for his concern. First, ''A peaceful dissolution is utterly impossible. There are so many sources of discord and controversy: the division of the army, the navy, the territories; so that, however disposed we might be to an amicable separation, the settlement of these points would inevitably, and that very soon, engender a war. And a war between the States of this confederacy would, in my opinion, be the bloodiest, most ferocious, and cruel, in the annals of history.'' But even if the separation could be accomplished peacefully, he was concerned on a second count. As a conservative, he feared the disruption of traditional political and social forms, and ''the attempt to construct other governments, the formation of new constitutions, in this age of tumults, agitation, and excitement, when socialism, communism, and a rabid mobocracy seem everywhere to be in the ascendant, will lead to the most dangerous experiments, the most disasterous [sic] schemes.'' Finally, Thornwell's conception of the United States as a chosen nation had led him to view the country's political future and God's historical purposes as virtually inseparable. ''The interests of the Savior's kingdom are too intimately connected with the permanence and prosperity of this great con-

---

[47]Thornwell to Nancy Thornwell, 14 June 1845; quoted in Palmer, 287-88.

federacy, to allow any disciple to be a calm spectator of passing scenes.'' The prospect of chaos was so fearful, he concluded, that "I cannot dwell upon the subject. May the Lord mercifully turn the tide.''[48]

When John C. Calhoun, whom many in South Carolina regarded as the state's and the South's indispensable champion, died in the midst of the 1850 crisis, Thornwell took the occasion to meditate on God's inscrutable plan. "Never in the annals of our confederacy has there been a more critical period than this," he told the students of the South Carolina College who had gathered in Rutledge Chapel on 21 April. He repeated the concerns he had shared with his friends. To suppose that disunion could be achieved "without cruel, bloody, ferocious war, terminating in a hatred more intense than any" ever known, is to ignore "all the lessons of history; and to suppose that in the present state of the world . . . amid this chaos of opinion, which has cursed the recent revolutions of Europe—we could [form a new government] without danger, is to arrogate a wisdom to ourselves which the progress of events, in some sections of our land—shows we are not entitled.''[49]

Turning to his vision of America's role in the divine plan, he assured his young audience that the United States was destined to dominate the whole of Western civilization, and perhaps the world. "We stand, indeed, in reference to free institutions and the progress of civilization, in the momentous capacity of the federal representatives of the human race." But the fulfillment of this destiny "depends upon Union as well as Progression. Our glory is departed—the spell is broken—whenever we become divided among ourselves." One can hardly imagine a Northern speaker rising to greater heights of American civil religion than this lover of the South. "The liberty of the world is at stake," he assured the students. "The

---

[48]Thornwell to Dr. [John De Berniere] Hooper, 8 March 1850; quoted in Palmer, 477-78. He expressed the same views in a letter to John Adger on the same day. See Adger, *My Life and Times,* 202. These fears of radical change in the wake of secession were at the heart of much of the Unionist movement in South Carolina throughout the 1850s. See, for example, the letters of William Elliott to his son Ralph and other members of his family, in the Elliott-Gonzales Papers, Southern Historical Collection. Thornwell was much relieved, in the winter of 1860-1861, to find these fears unwarranted, as his state held to its "law and order" mood. Thornwell to Reverend John Leighton Wilson, 7 January 1861; quoted in Palmer, 486-87.

[49]Thornwell, *Thoughts Suited to the Present Crisis; A Sermon on the Occasion of the Death of the Hon. John C. Calhoun . . . April 21, 1850* (Columbia, 1850) 4-5.

American Congress is now deliberating upon the civil destinies of mankind.'' But equally ''the interests of religion are deeply at stake. Here Protestant Christianity is ascendant, and stretches its missionary arm across the globe—we can not interrupt this divine task with civil strife.''[50]

Turning to the man whose death was being commemorated, he summarized Calhoun's life and recognized his greatness, but called on the state and her people to place their trust not in the greatness of their leaders, but in God. As he had done so many times before, he urged the students to recognize their obligation to serve as God's agents in the careers and lives that lay ahead of them. ''The state is a school in which the Deity is conducting a great process of education,'' he concluded, adding his hope that South Carolina would learn well the lessons of that day.[51]

The nation's troubles were on his mind again in July 1850, when President Zachary Taylor died. He told his good friend Matthew J. Williams, mathematics professor at the College, that ''it seems God is giving us warning after warning, line upon line, and precept upon precept. Every good man should be found constantly wrestling at the throne of grace for our bleeding and distracted country,'' he added, for only repentance can save us from ''the just consequences of our national sins. . . . The subject is constantly in my thoughts and in my prayers, and there is nothing I would not do, or suffer, to promote the peace of our beloved country.''[52]

Thornwell gave his views to a wider audience in an essay published in the January 1851 *Southern Presbyterian Review*. Taking his cue from five sermons by conservative Northern Presbyterians, he lauded ''Christian efforts to arrest an agitation which aims alike at the destruction of the Government and the subversion of religion.''[53] It was, he said, the people of the North who held the future of the Union in their hands, for they would determine whether the federal structure of the Constitution would be upheld, ''or whether the Southern States shall be driven, in vindication of their rights, their honour, and their safety, to organize a distinct Govern-

---

[50]Ibid., 6-7.

[51]Ibid., 31.

[52]Thornwell to Matthew J. Williams, 17 July 1850; quoted in Palmer, 342. For further indications of Presbyterian Unionism in 1850, see Benjamin M. Palmer to Thornwell, 10 September 1850, Anderson-Thornwell Papers, Southern Historical Collection.

[53]Thornwell, ''Critical Notice,'' in Palmer, 573-80. The quotation is on 574.

ment for themselves." All that was needed was for the national government to avoid taking sides on the subject of slavery and its expansion. Alluding to Senator William H. Seward's assertion of a "higher law" during the debates on the Omnibus Bill the previous year, Thornwell wrote, "We cheerfully concede that there is a higher law than that of man, and that, when human legislation contravenes the authority of God, it should not be permitted to bind the conscience." If slavery were a sin, "it would be the duty of the Northern states, entertaining this opinion, to dissolve the Union themselves" rather than remain parties to a contract that is a "snare to their conscience." However, since under the original terms of the contract the North possesses no power over the South, "their consciences should not be pressed for not doing what have they no right to do." Therefore, Thornwell "affectionately" urged his "Northern brethren" to "cherish the Constitution of our fathers."[54]

Thornwell then reiterated his threefold concern about the dangers of secession, emphasizing the "lofty mission" of the United States and warning that "ours will be no common punishment" if, instead of carrying out this mission, "we exhaust our resources, and waste our advantages, in biting and devouring each other." If the Union perishes, he added, "we freely confess that our tears shall bedew its grave; and our hopes for liberty and man be buried with it."[55] How could the crisis be resolved? Thornwell had a message for each section in this regard. The people of the North must recognize that "to love the Union is to love the Constitution" and see to it that it is obeyed. The people of the South should seek first to "restore the Constitution to its supremacy. We do not think that it is wisdom suddenly to destroy a government, because it has been perverted." "What surgeon would amputate a limb until he was convinced that it was the last resort?" As for the impulsive stance of his own state, Thornwell was blunt. "Singlehanded secession, which is understood to be the aim of measures now in progress, however it might be justified in a crisis in which the Federal Government had become openly pledged to the extinction of slavery, under the present circumstances of our country, is recommended by not a single consideration that we are able to discover, of wisdom, pa-

---

[54]Ibid., 574-75. The logical dilemma here, between conscience and authority, is made more difficult for Thornwell, it would seem, because of his notion that the state is a divine creation.

[55]Ibid., 576.

triotism, or honour.''[56] ''There may be great boldness in the enterprise,'' he admitted, ''but it should be remembered, as Lord Bacon has well expressed it, that boldness is blind; wherefore it is ill in counsel, but good in execution.'' But should his native state pursue its bold course, Thornwell left no doubt where he would be found. ''We are not only in the State, but of the State, and we have no thought but that of sharing her fortunes.'' ''[W]e are linked to South Carolina for weal or for woe.''[57]

The ''great subject of the day'' continued to distress Thornwell in the spring of 1851, and he found the support of colleagues like Robert J. Breckinridge of Kentucky ''very cheering to my heart.'' Breckinridge had written to praise his essay (above), and Thornwell responded that ''such sentiments as those I have ventured to express are anything but popular.'' He added that he saw the ''finger of the Lord'' in every step of the nation's history and could not imagine the country being ''permitted to make shipwreck of our glorious inheritance.'' Yet South Carolina seemed to him bent upon secession. ''Men from whom one would have expected better things, are fanning the flame, and urging the people on to the most desperate measures.'' ''You can not imagine how the matter preys upon my spirits. It is the unceasing burden of my prayers.''[58]

In 1852 Thornwell ventured into New England, in his newly acquired capacity as South Carolina College president, to observe the administrative and instructional methods at Harvard and Yale. At Cambridge he was very courteously received by President Jared Sparks and former President Edward Everett, and was invited to sit on the stage during the commencement exercises. Although he reported to his wife that ''the exercises of the young men were not equal to those we have at our own College,'' he was most impressed with the proceedings and with his reception. The stimulating atmosphere of Harvard enchanted him, and he was particularly taken with Mr. Everett. ''He is what you would call a *finished man*,'' he told Nancy. ''We have no other such man in America.'' ''You can not imagine

---

[56]Ibid., 577-78. If Thornwell looked back on these words during the crisis of 1860-1861, he must have felt pleased to have been consistent in his actions of that time with the principle he had enunciated ten years earlier.

[57]Ibid., 579-80.

[58]Thornwell to Robert J. Breckinridge, 28 March 1851; quoted in Palmer, 477. Another example of support from like-minded Southerners is a letter from John D. Hooper, 23 February 1853, Thornwell Papers.

how attractive this place is to me," he added, though he hastened to note that the prevalence of Unitarianism saddened him. "I have really had scruples about associating with them as I have done. But it must be confessed that Boston is a great city. There are things about it that make you proud of it as an American city." "There is none of the littleness that you meet with in other parts of New England."[59] While in Boston he tried to find a friend who operated a spinal clinic. He was about to give up on his search when a Dr. Cotton came to his rescue, taking him in his buggy and showing him the sights of the city in the process. Describing this experience to Nancy, he asked, "Now, can South Carolina beat that?"[60]

While in Cambridge Thornwell was asked to help judge the student orations, and accepted. He also spoke at one of the dinners held in conjunction with commencement, and while no record of his remarks has survived, he did note that following his speech and one by John S. Preston, the brother of Senator William Campbell Preston, "There were three hearty cheers given to South Carolina."[61]

Leaving Cambridge after a one-week visit, he traveled to New Haven, where he was received with equal hospitality by the men of Yale. "I was never more kindly treated than I have been here," he wrote Nancy.[62] He became "acquainted with most of the literary men of the place," and presented an address to the alumni that was, in his words, "remarkably well received." In this speech, the text of which has survived, Thornwell was clearly seeking to rub salve on the sectional wounds, as well as to address the relative merits of various philosophies of education. While boasting "in no vain spirit" about the sons of his alma mater, Legare, McDuffie, and Preston, he took the opportunity to express South Carolina's gratitude to Yale "for the part she took in fashioning a man" whose name "cannot be pronounced in Carolina without the profoundest emotion . . . and as that name is one in which we have a common interest, permit me, without any reference to any type of political opinions, . . . to give as a sentiment: 'The

---

[59]Thornwell to Nancy Thornwell, 21 July 1852; quoted in Palmer, 360-61. Both Everett and Sparks were leading intellectuals of the day; each had served as editor of the *North American Review*. Thornwell had been "absolutely charmed" with Everett when he was a student at Harvard in 1834 (ibid., 121).

[60]Thornwell to Nancy Thornwell, 24 July 1852; quoted ibid., 362-63.

[61]Thornwell to Matthew J. Williams, 24 July 1852; quoted ibid., 364.

[62]Thornwell to Nancy Thornwell, 30 July 1852; quoted ibid., 365.

Memory of John C. Calhoun.' '' If some in the audience had taken this as inflammatory, he calmed them by adding, ''I rejoice that in letters, as in religion, there is neither North nor South, East nor West.''[63]

Thornwell's deep distress over the future of the Union is probably the explanation for his joining the American, or Know-Nothing party in the mid-1850s. As Palmer put it, ''His attachment to the Federal Union was yet so strong that he gave his adhesion to almost any organization that held out the least promise of preserving it.'' Perhaps there is nothing suprising in this, given both his fears regarding secession and his religious bigotry, for the Know-Nothings were strongly anti-Roman Catholic. But one sees here an indication of Thornwell's political naiveté. His old friend Alexander Pegues, while refusing to believe that ''you could countenance such a movement,'' suggested to him that he was more responsible ''than you are aware'' for the rise of Know-Nothingism in South Carolina, because of his vituperative exchange of letters with Father Patrick Lynch of Charleston.[64] Thornwell responded that while he was glad to hear his friend was ''alive and kicking'' (Pegues had been ill with yellow fever), ''I could wish, however, that you would kick against something more worthy of being kicked than the American party. You know that I always was perverse in politics.'' ''My heresies in these respects might have prepared you for finding me in the ranks of the only organization which, in my judgment, can save the country from impending ruin.'' He added that he agreed with the party's principles ''so far as its principles are known,'' and he offered the hope that the South would support the party in the coming election, so that ''the Republic may be saved.''[65] Pegues, then living in Mississippi, responded that in the West the Know-Nothing movement had reached ''a maturity not to be found elsewhere.'' ''Could you have seen and known what *I* have,'' he added, ''your views would certainly have been different from what they are. Without going farther I say that since its introduction into our community there has been a most alarming degeneracy in public morals.'' It seemed to Pegues that ''every black leg gambler and every midnight assassin in this country is a member of that secret order.''

[63]Ibid., 366-68.

[64]Alexander H. Pegues to Thornwell, 26 June 1855, Thornwell Papers, South Caroliniana Library.

[65]Thornwell to Alexander Pegues, 26 July 1855; quoted in Palmer, 479.

He added that Judge A. B. Longstreet, who was then president of the University of Mississippi, had preached against the party and had been ridiculed for it.[66]

In 1856, in the wake of Senator Charles Sumner's "Crime against Kansas" speech and Preston Brooks's caning of Sumner, and with the nascent Republican party endorsing "free soil" and nominating John C. Fremont for president, Thornwell was more anxious than ever. "The prospects of the country fill me with sadness," he wrote his new literary friend, George Frederick Holmes of Virginia, in October. "The future is very dark. The North seems to be mad, and the South blind." Now editing the *Southern Quarterly Review,* he asked Holmes's help in securing an article on the political situation that was done in "a manly, patriotic, statesman-like, philosophical style." "I have no whim of entrusting this subject to a hotspur," he added.[67]

The Democratic victory in 1856 and the Dred Scott decision provided small comfort at best to Southern conservatives, for events in Kansas continued to stir the political pot. And when the aborted slave-insurrection scheme of John Brown evoked sympathy from some Northern quarters, Thornwell's seminary colleague George Howe spoke for this group. We have never seriously considered the dissolution of the Union, he wrote, "but how can we live together in this perpetual conflict?"[68] Yet throughout this period Thornwell's relationship to politics remained that of an interested observer. He was busier than ever with the threefold occupation of preaching, editing, and writing for the *Southern Quarterly Review,* and teaching theology at the Columbia Seminary. He also continued to write for the *Southern Presbyterian Review* and published his *Discourses on Truth,* a collection of sermons preached to his South Carolina College students, in 1855.

Thornwell's health, never robust, declined during these years, and in the summer of 1860 he traveled to Britain and Europe in the hope of re-

[66]Alexander Pegues to Thornwell, 25 September 1855, Thornwell Papers, South Caroliniana Library. No response to this letter has been found, and it is not known whether Thornwell revised his views on the Know-Nothing party.

[67]Thornwell to George Frederick Holmes, 9 October 1856, Holmes Papers, Perkins Library, Duke University.

[68]George Howe, "The Raid of John Brown, and the Progress of Abolition," *Southern Presbyterian Review* 12:4 (January 1860): 812.

storing some of his lost strength. This was an inspiring experience for Thornwell, who visited many of the sites, in England, Scotland, and on the Continent, where religious history had been made. He was thrilled to stand on the ''hallowed ground'' where Calvin and Knox had stood, and to see the Swiss Alps. He was also pleased to discover that he was ''not wholly unknown to the clergy of Scotland.'' But absence from his homeland only amplified his patriotic feelings, and he wrote to his old mentor, General Gillespie, ''America, after all, is the country for me; it is the country in which man is himself.''[69] ''There is no land like our own,'' he wrote Nancy from Switzerland in August, ''and if we can have the grace to deal justly and honestly with one another, and hold together as a people, the time is at hand when the distinction of being an American will be as proud and glorious as it ever was to be a citizen of Rome.''[70]

It must have been a shock, then, to see the intensity of the Southern nationalism that greeted him on his return to South Carolina in September. His health was much better, but his spirits fell as he realized the depth of antipathy toward the North that so many South Carolinians had developed during his absence.[71] He would later confide to Benjamin Palmer that he had come home determined to propose the gradual emancipation of the slaves as a means of removing the most emotionally charged issue separating the sections. ''But when I got home,'' he recalled, ''I found it was too late, the die was cast.''[72]

Thornwell needed only a few weeks, at most, to make his decision to support South Carolina. It is difficult to picture him being swept along by the tide that was carrying South Carolina so heedlessly toward secession. Indeed, Palmer takes pains to show that, despite Thornwell's love for the Union, he had for at least two years held that the Union he loved was a federation that respected the peculiarities of its members. It was not, as Lincoln's election would characterize it for so many Southerners, a centralized democracy in which the will of a majority section could be im-

---

[69]Thornwell to James Gillespie, 21 July and 25 August 1860, Thornwell Papers, South Caroliniana Library. See also his letters to Nancy, 18 June; 15, 20, 25, 29 August 1860, in Palmer, 450-64.

[70]Thornwell to Nancy, 15 August 1860; quoted ibid., 457.

[71]See Channing, *Crisis of Fear,* ch. 7.

[72]Palmer, 482-83. Palmer says that Thornwell told him this in 1861.

posed on an exotic minority. In any case, Thornwell had said that he would go with his state, come what may. But how vigorously would he support it? How intimate would be the connection between this churchman and his people's political choice?

In addition to their aversion to the radical action of secession, Presbyterians were deterred from involvement in the movement by the doctrine of the spirituality of the church. While this concept would become a cornerstone of Presbyterian orthodoxy after the Civil War, there is considerable debate as to how strong it was before 1860. Clearly, it was not followed during the secession winter and the war years, when leading Southern Presbyterians formed the vanguard of support for the Confederacy. Whether these men were breaking with a strong tradition is the controversial question. According to one authority, "Official discussion of political questions by the clergy had had relatively little place in the South prior to the outbreak of the war between the sections. It had developed no Beechers, no Parkers, . . . to disseminate political fads through the medium of their sacred office." In particular, he adds, Old School Presbyterians had been noted for their "studious avoidance of meddling with the subject of slavery."[73] The leading authority on Southern Presbyterians points out that the men who supported church involvement in defense of Southern rights were aware of their break with ecclesiastical tradition and felt the need to explain it. Border-state Presbyterians, he notes, held to the doctrine longer than their cotton-states brethren—waiting until their states had seceded before endorsing the move, or denouncing secession only after their states had chosen to remain in the Union.[74]

However, it is clear that the doctrine of the spirituality of the church was not consistently applied by Old South Presbyterians. Some of them

---

[73]Thomas C. Johnson, *Life and Letters of Benjamin Morgan Palmer* (Richmond, 1906) 236-37.

[74]Ernest T. Thompson, *Presbyterians in the South*, vol. 1 (Richmond, 1863) 558-60. Thompson cites South Carolinian John Adger as one who explained his synod's endorsement of clerical pronouncements on politics by saying that sacred rights were involved. Robert Lewis Dabney of Virginia was typical of border-state Presbyterians who endorsed Southern independence only after their state had seceded, while Kentucky's Robert J. Breckinridge, a close friend of Thornwell, illustrates the other reaction. Breckinridge wrote a vigorous pro-union article for the *Danville Quarterly Review* and was elected chairman of the 1864 Republican national convention. For the position of Northern clergymen, see James H. Moorhead, *American Apocalypse: Yankee Protestants and the Civil War, 1860-1869* (New Haven, 1978).

took issue with it, at least implicitly, in recognizing social justice as a legitimate goal of the church. Charlestonian Thomas Smyth saw the church gradually hastening the millennium by its improvement of human behavior.[75] John Adger, a close friend of Smyth, revealed a flaw in the doctrine when he addressed the subject of foreign missions. To Adger, one object of the missionary was "to effect a change in the character, life and manners of the people to whom he came." He contrasted this with the role of the "minister at home," who "must carefully conform to his congregation, for many of their ideas and customs are good and right." Adger was saying that the role of the church depends on whether it approves of the mores of the people to whom it ministers. Where error is noted, the church should confront it and try to change it; but where the church basically approves of the values and customs of its audience, it should remain silent. Southern Presbyterians developed the view that it was right for the church to speak against unacceptable behavior when it was clear that such behavior was condemned by Scripture (as in the case of cannibalism or polygamy), but not in cases where the Bible failed to attack the behavior (as in the case of slavery). Thus Thornwell could denounce the abuse of alcohol and the desecration of the Sabbath while defending slavery.[76] Indeed, Old South Presbyterians at one time or another involved themselves in practically every social concern, and at least one historian has concluded that the doctrine of the spirituality of the church was "merely a protective posture during the slavery controversy."[77]

In the most thorough recent study of this question, a leading scholar of Southern religion agrees with this assessment. Before Reconstruction, argues Jack P. Maddex, Southern Presbyterians were theocrats in their view of the church's social role. While upholding the separation of church and state "in the elementary sense that there should be no established church," they "considered Christianity the national religion and (with a certain amount of reserve) expressed 'Christian' views of public policy from their

---

[75]J. William Flynn, ed., *Complete Works of Thomas Smyth, D.D.* (Columbia, 1910) 3:2; 10:490, 495.

[76]Adger, *My Life and Times,* 144.

[77]Brooks Holifield, *The Gentlemen Theologians; American Theology in Southern Culture, 1795-1860* (Durham, 1978) 154.

pulpits.''[78] Thomas Smyth, for example, wrote that the ''connection between true religion and sound politics is very intimate.'' And Benjamin M. Palmer declared that religion ''does not *exclude*, but rather . . . *embraces*, all the social relations of man.'' At the end of the antebellum era, the *Central Presbyterian* of Richmond editorialized, ''That religion ought to be carried into politics . . . has always been held among us.'' Nor were such statements empty rhetoric. Presbyterian ministers spoke out on such issues as the establishment of public schools and the teaching of religion in them, Sunday mail delivery, the Mexican War, reform in mental asylums and prisons, and dueling.[79] Maddex finds the slavery issue no exception in terms of Southern willingness to address it from the pulpit. As discussed (chapter 7), Thornwell led the General Assembly of 1845 in its adoption of a statement declaring slavery to be no bar to Christian communion. His protégé Palmer declared that slavery was ''in its origin a question of morals and religion.''[80] While he recognizes that Thornwell, with Robert J. Breckinridge, led in the establishment of a *jure divino* school of church polity that permitted no action on any matter unless the Bible sanctioned it, Maddex argues that this ''did not greatly constrict the church's scope, because Thornwell by inference found biblical mandates on a wide range of topics.''[81]

How, then, did Thornwell get this ''undeserved reputation as champion of an apolitical church''? Maddex traces it to a ''chance incident at the 1859 Old School General Assembly. A proposal to endorse the American Colonization Society program seemed sure of adoption, to Thornwell's chagrin. [Benjamin] Palmer suggested to him the idea of an

---

[78]Jack P. Maddex, ''From Theocracy to Spirituality: The Southern Presbyterian Reversal on Church and State,'' *Journal of Presbyterian History* 54 (Winter 1976): 438-57. These quotations are on page 439. In this statement Maddex is agreeing with the conclusion of John R. Bodo in *The Protestant Clergy and Public Issues, 1812-1848* (Princeton, 1954) 3-60.

[79]Thompson, *Presbyterians in the South*, 1:258-64, 471-88, 492, 494-98; *Southern Presbyterian Review* 3 (July 1849): 74-121; (October 1849): 169-200; Flynn, *Smyth's Complete Works*, 5:351-77; *Southern Presbyterian Review* 3 (October 1849): 324; 4 (July 1850): 78-97; 5 (July 1851): 255; 7 (October 1853): 207-209; (January 1854) 403-46; 10 (April 1857): 126-37.

[80]Maddex, ''From Theocracy to Spirituality,'' 440.

[81]Ibid., 441. See John B. Adger, ed., *Collected Writings of James Henley Thornwell*, vol. 4 (Richmond, 1871) 255-59, 292.

ecclesiological objection. Hastily, Thornwell *improvised* [my emphasis] an argument that the church should have 'nothing to do with the voluntary associations of men for various civil and social purposes that were outside of her pale' because unwarranted by scripture."[82] In his account of this episode, Palmer recalled alerting Thornwell to the opportunity "to urge your views as to the spiritual function of the Church." Thornwell then presented his concept of the church as "exclusively a spiritual organization" having "no mission to care for the things, or to become entangled with the kingdoms and policy, of this world. To this view," he continued, "the church has been steadily coming up" and has been steadily rising in the sight of the world as a result.[83] Did Thornwell mean to be taken literally when he opposed church statements on "the kingdoms and policy of this world"? Maddex says no, and asserts that his Southern followers "understood that he was not opposing church pronouncements on political issues of moral concern."[84] Thornwell himself saw logical difficulties in his position, yet justified it as a way of avoiding division within the church.[85]

One should not dismiss his *jure divino* concept lightly, however. It was a view he had been tending toward for some time, and it was perfectly consistent with his social philosophy. It was also a doctrine that was widely attractive among Presbyterians North and South. The unanimous election of Benjamin M. Palmer to a professorship at Princeton Seminary by the General Assembly of 1860 is inexplicable outside of the context of the "spirituality of the church." This action and the robust singing of "Blest Be the Tie That Binds" as the closing hymn at this assembly serve as graphic reminders of the ability of Old School Presbyterians to overcome (because their doctrine led them largely to ignore) sectional issues.[86] But Calvinistic

---

[82]Maddex, "From Theocracy to Spirituality," 441-42.

[83]Palmer, 436.

[84]Maddex, "From Theocracy to Spirituality," 441. *The North Carolina Presbyterian*, 19 May 1860, 2. He sees Palmer's synopsis of the General Assembly as a clarification of Thornwell's position, asserting that the church should condemn immoral policies. See *Southern Presbyterian Review* 12 (October 1859) 598.

[85]*Central Presbyterian*, 11 July 1859, 2; cited by Maddex, "From Theocracy to Spirituality," 441.

[86]Thompson, *Presbyterians in the South*, 1:552-53. Palmer did not assume the chair at Princeton. For an approving comment on the lack of sectional tension within Old School Presbyterianism, see the *Presbyterial Critic*, October 1855, 441-42.

theology includes a strong theocratic concept: John Calvin was surely no supporter of the separation of church and state during his years as virtual ruler of Geneva. One may wonder how Thornwell, and Presbyterians generally, would have behaved had they been in a position to impose their values on a government, as Calvin was. Thomas Jefferson, early America's foremost opponent of established churches, called the Presbyterians "the most tyranical [sic] and ambitious sect" in Virginia, and warned that they "would tolerate no rival, if they had power."[87] Thornwell never had the opportunity to dictate his religious and moral views to a government, though his support of the Confederacy was at least partly the result of his assumption, or at least his hope, that the new nation would reflect those views.[88]

As the news of Lincoln's election swept across the South in November 1860, the reaction of church spokesmen was mixed. The *Southern Presbyterian* of Charleston announced, "The deed is done. . . . The South cannot continue to endure the perturbations and harrassments [sic] of the past." Further north, in the border slave states, most Presbyterians, while depressed by the Republican victory, saw no justification in it for precipitous action. James M. Brown spoke for most Virginia Presbyterian ministers when he wrote, "I did think we owed it to the Union to stand by it, and see whether during the next four years, we could scatter the Black Republican Party, and settle our strifes." The (Fayetteville) *North Carolina Presbyterian* typified the "wait and see" attitude of the border states, endorsing secession only after the firing on Fort Sumter.[89] On the whole, border-state Presbyterians were much less willing to plunge into the polit-

---

[87]DesChamps, "The Presbyterian Church," 27. In his book, *The Spirituality of the Church: A Distinctive Doctrine of the Presbyterian Church, U.S.* (Richmond, 1961), Ernest T. Thompson calls the doctrine an "ultimate strangeness" to the Calvinistic heritage.

[88]"The Reverend Dr. Thornwell's Memorial on the Recognition of Christianity in the [Confederate] Constitution," *Southern Presbyterian Review* 16 (July 1863): 77-87.

[89]*Southern Presbyterian*, 9 November 1860. James W. Brown to Francis McFarland, 17 May 1861; quoted in DesChamps, "Union or Disunion?" 496. See also James W. Silver, *Confederate Morale and Church Propaganda* (Tuscaloosa AL, 1957) 13-20. *North Carolina Presbyterian*, 20 April 1861; quoted in DesChamps, 497. These border-state Presbyterian periodicals urged caution during the winter of 1860-1861: *Central Presbyterian*, Richmond; *North Carolina Presbyterian*, Raleigh; *Presbyterian Herald*, Louisville; *Christian Observer*, published in Philadelphia but pro-South. In addition, the New Orleans *True Witness and Sentinel* took a moderate stand, while the *Southern Presbyterian Review* of Columbia supported South Carolina's action. Thompson, *Presbyterians in the South*, 1:554-55.

ical arena than their Deep South colleagues.[90] But for those with any inclination to address political questions, an appropriate setting was provided by the national day of fasting and humiliation called for on Sunday, 21 November. In sermons preached from pulpits throughout the South, they sought to interpret the political crisis theologically.[91]

Mitchell Snay provides an enlightening analysis of the Fast Day Sermons' role in focusing and explaining to the people of the South the national crisis of 1860-1861.[92] After noting the importance of religion in Southern culture and the power of its pulpit rhetoric, Snay analyzes the form and content of some forty sermons. Arguing that rhetoric "imposes structure and meaning on the world, giving form to problems and thereby implicitly suggesting solutions," he suggests that the Fast Day Sermons can shed light on "the deepest values of southern society on the eve of the war."[93] Snay notes that these sermons are reminiscent of the jeremiad style of Puritan New England, and concludes that for the men who preached them, and presumably for their audiences as well, secession was "an act of purification from a sinful society."[94]

Snay finds a common structure in most of the sermons: (1) Acknowledgment of a providential design in human affairs. (2) The conception of the nation as having a relationship with God, just as an individual does. (3) The conclusion that God blesses and punishes nations based on the collective behavior of their people. (4) Recognition of the sin of America. (5) Characterization of this sin as the neglect and perversion of religion. (6) Designation of the main sinner as New England, and the secondary sinner as the Southern slaveowner. (7) Proposal of the solution: secede to avoid further contamination, and then reform Southern society.[95]

Thornwell's Fast Day Sermon conforms to the structure of most of these sermons. It was fittingly titled "Our National Sins." If, as he believed,

---

[90]Virginia's Robert Lewis Dabney was typical. Silver, *Confederate Morale,* 20.

[91]*Fast Day Sermons, or The Pulpit on the State of the Country, 1860-1861* (New York, 1861).

[92]A paper introducing this study, entitled "Religion, Rhetoric and the Growth of Southern Nationalism," was presented by Mr. Snay at the 1981 Citadel Conference on the South and commented on by this author.

[93]Snay paper, in possession of the writer, 2-3.

[94]Ibid., 3. See also Sacvan Berkovitch, *The American Jeremiad* (Madison WI, 1978).

[95]Snay paper, passim.

the state is a "moral institute, responsible to God, and existing for moral and spiritual ends, it is certainly capable of sin," he assured his audience.[96] Therefore, the state should do as the sinful individual should: look to God. "As the individual, in coming to God, must believe that He is, and that He is the rewarder of them that diligently search Him, so the State must be impressed with a profound sense of His all-pervading providence, and of its responsibility to Him, as the moral ruler of the world."[97]

Both sections were guilty of sin, in Thornwell's view. Egocentric sectionalism was too prevalent in both the North and the South. But the people of the North, and especially New England, were guilty of the more fundamental sin of pride, which had led them to assume work that rightfully belonged to God—the resolving of fundamental social conflicts. It was their haughty interference with providence's shaping of Southern institutions that had provoked the Southern people to some excesses of their own. Now that a party opposed to slavery had been elected to power, the security of the South was threatened, he added. But equally important was the threat posed by the popular Northern ideology to the cause of Christianity itself. With such prospects before it, Thornwell concluded, the South must secede and form a new confederacy even though "our path to victory may be through a baptism of blood."[98]

So effective was the Fast Day as a vehicle for propaganda, says James Silver, that Jefferson Davis proclaimed nine such days, and the Confederate Congress, state legislatures, and religious bodies proclaimed so many more that strict compliance with them "might have saved enough food to feed Lee's hungry army."[99] Though Fast Days doubtlessly were effective propaganda devices, Silver is perhaps too cynical in describing them as such. The frequency with which the Southern establishment, spiritual and political, proclaimed such days, is simply a measure of religion's place in this society. Thomas Smyth expressed views similar to Thornwell's in his

---

[96]*Fast Day Sermons*, 22-24.

[97]Ibid., 28.

[98]Ibid., 28, 41. The phrase "baptism of blood" would become a common one in the religious lexicon of the Confederacy. See Charles R. Wilson, *Baptized in Blood; The Religion of the Lost Cause, 1865-1920* (Athens GA, 1980) 4.

[99]Silver, *Confederate Morale*, 15.

Fast Day sermon, ''The Sin and Curse, or the Union, the True Source of Disunion, and Our Duty in the Present Crisis.''[100] Other Presbyterian ministers who preached Fast Day sermons and shared similar views with their congregations include William C. Dana of Charleston, Robert K. Porter of Waynesboro, Georgia, Benjamin Palmer of New Orleans, and John Adger of Charleston.[101]

The most famous, and probably the most extreme of these sermons, was Palmer's. His pulpit, in the First Presbyterian Church of New Orleans, was perhaps the most prestigious Presbyterian post in the South, and his words were reproduced far and wide. The New Orleans *Daily Delta* alone published thirty thousand copies. He began his sermon with an explanation of its blatant political content. He said, ''I have never intermeddled with political questions,'' but ''at so solemn a juncture . . . it is not lawful to be still. Whosoever may have influence to shape political opinion, at such a time must lend it or prove faithless to a trust as solemn as any to be accounted for at the bar of God.''[102] Calling slavery a ''Divine Trust,'' Palmer said that the South had a duty to preserve and perpetuate it in the name of ''self-preservation,'' for the good of ''the slaves themselves'' and for the advancement of ''the uncivilized world.'' Lincoln, he warned, would do all he could ''to arrest the tendency to make slavery national and perpetual.'' Under such conditions secession was the will of God. ''Paradoxical as it may seem,'' he asserted, ''if there be any way to save, or reconstruct the union of our forefathers it is this.''[103] One of his contem-

---

[100]J. William Flynn, ed., *The Complete Works of Rev. Thomas Smyth, D.D.*, 10 vols. (Columbia, 1908–1912) 7:537-61.

[101]William C. Dana, *A Sermon Delivered in the Central Presbyterian Church, Charleston, South Carolina, November 21, 1860* (Charleston, 1860). Robert K. Porter, *Christian Duty in the Present Crisis; The Substance of a Sermon Delivered in the Presbyterian Church in Waynesboro, Georgia* (Savannah, 1860). Johnson, *Palmer*, 206-22. Robert L. Stanton, *The Church and the Rebellion* (New York, 1864) 161-63. For a unionist Fast Day Sermon, see Dabney's ''The Christian's Best Motive for Patriotism,'' *Fast Day Sermons*, 81-97. See also Haskell Monroe, ''Southern Presbyterians and the Secession Crisis,'' *Civil War History* 6 (December 1960): 351-60.

[102]Louis C. LaMotte, *Colored Light; The Story of the Influence of Columbia Theological Seminary, 1828-1936* (Richmond, 1937) 131; Johnson, *Palmer*, 206.

[103]LaMotte, *Colored Light,* 131; Johnson, *Palmer*, 206.

poraries would later credit Palmer with doing more than "any other non-combatant in the South to promote rebellion."[104]

Others, if less strident, were generally in accord with Palmer. James W. Silver concludes that the vast majority of Southern clergy supported, or at least accepted, secession. The chief difference was between those who were ready to leave the Union on the basis of Lincoln's victory and those who waited until the firing on Fort Sumter and Lincoln's call for troops. In this split, one sees a striking parallel with the division of the South generally, as churchmen adopted the views of their state's political leadership. Some South Carolina Presbyterians were ready to take an advanced position even before their state's politicians had acted. On 20 November the Synod of South Carolina heard a resolution calling on it "to sever all connection with the Northern portion of the General Assembly." A faction led by John Adger succeeded in having the resolution tabled, arguing that any such move must originate in church sessions, move to the Presbyteries, and then to the synod. He further suggested that such action should not precede a decision by the state. Adger returned with a resolution, which was adopted by the synod, stating that "from our brethren of the whole church annually assembled [the General Assembly] we have received nothing but justice and courtesy." Adger added, however, his confident feeling that "the God whose truth we represent in this conflict will be with us."[105]

In December 1860 all eyes were on South Carolina as it convened a convention to consider response to Lincoln's election. As events moved quickly to the climax of secession, contemplative men from throughout the country searched for some means to stem the tide. His writings and travels had given Thornwell a wide reputation for intelligence and moderation; hence his mail that month contained several urgent inquiries from friends and acquaintances. A New Yorker wrote to ask Thornwell's reading of South Carolina's mood and probable course of action.[106] A business as-

---

[104]Avery Craven, *The Growth of Southern Nationalism*, 374. Palmer's sermon is in *Fast Day Sermons*, 57-80. In light of his emphasis on the slavery issue in this sermon, it is interesting that in his biography of Thornwell, Palmer wrote that this issue "never was more than the *occasion* of the war, either North or South. It was the mere rallying cry on both sides" (Palmer, 482). Henry A. White noted that Palmer "had made a careful study of all the facts and all the moral and legal principles involved in the great sectional debate" (*Southern Presbyterian Leaders*, 366).

[105]LaMotte, *Colored Light*, 132-33.

[106]Dr. Joseph P. Logan to Thornwell, 7 December 1860, Thornwell Papers.

sociate and family friend, also from New York, wrote to assure Thornwell that most Northerners were sympathetic to the South in its dilemma, and urged him to work and pray for reconciliation.[107] A Virginian only slightly acquainted with Thornwell, but taking the liberty that he felt the emergency warranted, wrote to ask him to use his influence to prevent an attack on the Charleston forts. "The collision will drench the Continent in blood, as well as stain the honor of Carolina," he warned, but your influence, "I am perfectly sure, *would* have weight." "I beg you as a friend of humanity, to use all your influence."[108] Presbyterian ministers who corresponded regularly with Thornwell asked for whatever assurance his views could provide as, in the words of one of them, South Carolina was "cut loose from her moorings, and the rest of the world!"[109]

Thornwell's responses are testimony to his agreement with South Carolina's position. Granting that "our affairs of state look threatening," he added, "but I believe that we have done right. I do not see any other course that was left to us. I am heart and head with the State in her move. But it is a time for the people of God to abound in prayer. The Lord alone can guide us to a haven of safety."[110] His own greatest fear, that secession would unleash the mob spirit of democracy and lead to radical change, proved unwarranted, and he exulted in the fraternal atmosphere created by the almost unanimous commitment to the cause. "The *whole State* is *like a family,* in which the members vie with each other in their zeal to promote the common good," he wrote one colleague. It is a blessing "to see how thoroughly law and order reign, in the midst of an intense and radical revolution." He predicted that South Carolina would not allow the reinforcement of Fort Sumter and would take it if it were not relinquished soon. "We do not want war," he wrote, "but we shall not decline the appeal to arms, if the North forces it upon us."[111]

---

[107]Robert Carter to Thornwell, 18 December 1860, ibid. Carter added, "There are few indeed with whom I have spent more delightful hours than with you."

[108]John H. Bocock to Thornwell, 22 December 1860, ibid. Bocock was writing from Georgetown, D.C.

[109]John Douglas to Thornwell, 25 December 1860, ibid.

[110]Thornwell to John Douglas, 31 December 1860; quoted in Palmer, 486.

[111]Thornwell to the Reverend John Leighton Wilson, 7 January 1861; quoted ibid., 486-87. Note his positive response to conditions Petigru deplored.

Having concluded that his state was acting properly, Thornwell did not hesitate to play a public role in the drama he had earlier sought to avert. He delivered the prayer at the opening session of the state legislature in January 1861, requesting divine guidance in the formation of the new nation and asking God to "protect us from the power of every adversary."[112] He also wrote an essay on secession for the January 1861 issue of the *Southern Presbyterian Review*. Entitled "On the State of the Country," it was evidently inspired by an article with the same title by Princeton Seminary's Charles Hodge.[113] Thornwell's article was also produced in pamphlet form, for distribution to an audience that would not see it in the *Review*. Chancellor Job Johnston of Newberry would later tell Palmer that he "took up the article by Dr. Thornwell with great trepidation, fearing that a divine would make a muddle of the question; but I found in it a model state paper."[114]

The essay was intended to explain the action of South Carolina and the other cotton states, and to advocate that both North and South adjust to the new realities peacefully. Secession's justification was presumed, Thornwell argued, in the unanimous vote of "a noble body" of men, for the Secession Convention was composed of South Carolina's finest figures. "It embraced the wisdom, moderation and integrity of the bench, the learning and prudence of the bar, and the eloquence and piety of the pulpit." It bore comparison with the "immortal Parliament of England, which taught the nations of the earth that resistance to tyrants is obedience to God." It reflected the mind of a people "who feel, in their inmost souls, that they have been deeply and flagrantly wronged." Some had accused the South of mercenary motives. Thornwell acknowledged that there were some such men in his region, but insisted that "we know the people of the

---

[112]Ibid., 511.

[113]The renowned botanist Asa Gray of Harvard sent a copy of Hodge's article to Henry William Ravenel, and Ravenel wrote a response to it in a letter to Gray. Ravenel Journal, 6 March 1861, South Caroliniana Library. Hodge had argued that there is no right of secession. *Southern Presbyterian Review* 13 (January 1861): 860-89. Portions of the essay survive in Thornwell's papers at the University of South Carolina. The January 1861 issue of the *Southern Presbyterian Review* contained two other articles by Thornwell: "National Sins" (his Fast Day Sermon) and "The Princeton Review and Presbyterianism" (a reply to an essay by Charles Hodge). See *Southern Presbyterian Review* 13:4 (January 1861): 649-89, 757-811.

[114]Palmer, 487.

South; and we can confidently affirm that . . . they would have preferred poverty, with honour, to the gain of the whole world by the loss of their integrity.'' The rosy future that was being painted for the new Confederacy was, he said, not the motive for its creation, but rather an afterthought that had occurred to some as they contemplated the results of secession for the Southern economy. He predicted, accurately, that the Confederacy would not legalize the African slave trade as some were expecting.[115]

The real cause of the secession movement, said Thornwell, was ''the profound conviction that the Constitution, in its relations to slavery, has been virtually repealed.'' ''The election of Lincoln, when properly interpreted, is nothing more or less than a proposition to the South to consent to a Government, fundamentally different upon the question of slavery, from that which our fathers established.'' This being the case, ''secession becomes not only a right, but a bounden duty.'' Thornwell then recounted the history of the Constitutional Convention, stressing the impossibility of slaveowning states' consent to a contract that threatened their property. The Constitution created a government that was ''neither pro nor anti slavery,'' he concluded. Further, justice requires that ''we of the South have the same right to our opinions as the people of the North. They appear as true to us as theirs appear to them. We are honest and sincere in forming and maintaining them.'' When two such regions unite to form a government, can one be expected to ''renounce doctrines which we believe have come down to us from the earliest ages, and have the sanction of the oracles of God?'' ''The thing is absurd.''[116]

Thornwell suggested that the North would not stand for the reverse of the situation now facing the South; that is, congressional statutes denying the admission of new states that outlawed slavery. ''What would they think if the South had taken such extravagant ground as this? What would they have done, if the South had taken advantage of a numerical majority, to legislate them and their institutions forever out of the common territory? Would they have *submitted?*'' ''We know that they would not.'' ''Let them give the same measure to others which they expect from others.'' To the argument that the Free Soil movement treats the Southerner and Northerner equally (since both may bear to a territory the same forms of prop-

---

[115]Ibid., 591-95.
[116]Ibid., 595-97.

erty), Thornwell responded with a statement that reveals just how intimately he conceived the relationship of the South and slavery to be. This argument can be reduced, he said, to the notion that "if the Southern man will consent to become as a Northern man, and renounce what distinguishes him as a *Southern* man, he may go into the territories. But if he insists upon remaining a *Southern* man, he must stay at home." "To exclude slaveholding, is, therefore, to exclude the South."[117]

Looking at the prospects presented by the Republican victory, Thornwell conceded that there was no immediate likelihood of an "attempt to interfere, by legislation, with our property on our own soil." Yet the Northern people generally regarded slavery as "a calamity, an affliction, a misfortune . . . and a drawback upon the prosperity and glory of the country. They pity the South [returning to a theme he had touched on ten years earlier in his Zion Church address] as caught in the folds of a serpent." Thinking along these lines, the North had come to assume that its ideology was to dominate the nation's future course. "The North is the thinking power, the soul of the Government." "The North becomes the United States, the South a subject province." This was "a state of things not to be borne. A free people can never consent to their own degradation." But what of the longer-range prospect? The very existence of slavery was threatened, for "you may destroy the oak as effectually by girdling it as by cutting it down." Surrounded by hostility, the institution would wither and die. " 'Like the scorpion girt by fire,' it will plunge its fangs into its own body, and perish." "The triumph of the principles which Mr. Lincoln is pledged to carry out, is the death-knell of slavery."[118]

One may wonder why Thornwell, having been willing to support gradual emancipation six months earlier, would now see this prospect as one so horrible as to warrant risking war. The answer may lie in his vision of the manner in which slavery would be brought down. One could not expect, he contended, that the leaders of Northern opinion would be content with their recent victory. They will turn next to the Constitution itself, to harmonize it with their own principles. The fugitive-slave clause will be expunged, and the result will be to encourage slaves to run away (or worse), first in the border states and later throughout the South. Indeed, the Re-

---

[117]Ibid., 598, 602.

[118]Ibid., 602-605.

publicans have already sensed their victory, he noted. ''They boast that they have laid a mine which must ultimately explode in our utter ruin. They are singing songs of victory in advance.'' Rather than wait for the consummation, ''Let us crush the serpent in the egg.''[119]

Turning to the future of the independent South, Thornwell granted the painful loss that the break with the Union entailed, but argued that the real change resulting from the separation would be minimal. The new confederacy would be a viable nation, with its various state constitutions unaffected by secession. Law would remain supreme and order would be preserved as before. Relations with the United States could be friendly and a mutual foreign policy could be drawn, to the benefit of both nations. The profound questions that have wrecked the Union could be more successfully addressed after the division, for ''two Governments upon this continent may work out the problem of human liberty more successfully than one.'' The new state of affairs would be more natural and stable, for ''are two homogeneous Unions not stronger than one that is heterogeneous?'' Thornwell had by now put aside his earlier concept of the destiny of America being, as Daniel Webster had argued, one of the inseparability of liberty and union. The only substantive difference he now saw was that ''the sections, separately, will not be as formidable to foreign powers as before. That is all. But each section [note the use of the now-anachronistic term] will be strong enough to protect itself, and both together can save this continent for republicanism for ever.''[120]

In closing, Thornwell appealed to the people of the North to accept the ''defensive'' actions of the South. Recalling the common heritage and the ties that could remain strong despite political separation, he urged the North to recognize the new realities. What, he asked, could the North gain by war? ''Suppose they should conquer us, what will they do with us? How will they hold us in subjection?'' ''They will have the wolf by the ears.'' But the South will never be conquered, he insisted. A long and bitter war would be followed by a return to the conditions that precipitated the present crisis, but with the difference that the sections ''would have learned to hate each other with an intensity of hatred equalled only in hell.'' ''Two great people united under one Government differ upon a question of vital im-

---

[119]Ibid., 605.

[120]Ibid., 607-608.

portance to one,'' he concluded. ''Neither can conscientiously give way.'' ''Let us part in peace; . . . and let the Lord bless us both.''[121]

If the letters Thornwell received during the secession winter are any indication, reaction to ''The State of the Country'' was substantial and, for Southerners, positive. Judge Mitchell King of Charleston called it ''matchless'' and said he read it with ''emotions which I am sure I could not find words to describe.'' King was too ill to play a role in public affairs, but, as he assured Thornwell, ''I have read with great interest every defense of the South which I have been able to procure. I have seen nothing else that has given me a tithe of the satisfaction which I have received from your productions.'' (The plural refers to Thornwell's Fast Day Sermon as well.) King gave Thornwell ''profound personal thanks'' for the article and predicted that ''posterity will point to it and venerate the memory of its author.'' On behalf of several of his friends, he asked permission to reprint it ''and give it the widest circulation in our powers.'' The letter is signed ''With highest respect.''[122] From Savannah, Robert N. Gourdin wrote to request copies of the essay so ''that I may send some to the North and to Europe. This article is a calm, truthful and Philosophical statement of the causes which have led to the crisis,'' he added, and ''the country is deeply indebted to you for this paper.'' He asked for fifty ''or even one hundred'' copies, and insisted on paying for them.[123]

Northerners as well as Southerners were interested in the article. Seth Bliss, secretary of the American Tract Society in New York, told Thornwell of the ''great gratification and entire satisfaction I have felt in reading your clear and very able exposition of the Constitution and defense of the

---

[121]Ibid., 608-609. In addition to this essay, Thornwell wrote at least one, and according to Palmer probably several, short piece on secession for the newspapers. There is no record of the dates or the papers in which such ''fugitive articles'' appeared. A fragment of one of these appears on pages 489-90 of Palmer's biography; it contains essentially the same points as the essay discussed above. In it he concludes that only the separation of the sections can secure true peace. Earlier he had said it would certainly produce war, and he would soon return to this view.

[122]Mitchell King to Thornwell, 9 February 1861, Thornwell Papers.

[123]Robert N. Gourdin to Thornwell, 13 February 1861, ibid. Gourdin was a college classmate and mentions in his letter remembering Thornwell from those long-ago days. Another letter praising ''The State of the Country'' was from Reverend Philip H. Thompson, of Memphis, a former student of Thornwell. Thompson to Thornwell, 8 February 1861, ibid.

justice of the claims of the Southern states to equality under the great organic Law of our Government.'' He asked permission for his society to reprint the article for Northern distribution.[124] Bliss was also impressed by Thornwell's Fast Day Sermon, and persuaded Appleton's Publishing Company to reprint it. Five thousand copies of the sermon were also printed by an association in New Haven, Connecticut, for distribution in that state. To Bliss, and like-minded men of the North, the views of such respected Southerners as Thornwell, Albert Taylor Bledsoe, and Horace [?] Stringfellow, if presented widely throughout the North, could do much to ''heal this split.''[125] Nathan Lord, president of Dartmouth college, wrote Thornwell regarding ''The State of the Country'': ''It is refreshing to have the difficult questions now at issue taken . . . out of the sphere of political and technical discussion—a sphere of shadows and chimeras, into that of a higher morality.'' He asked for two or three copies, saying that he could ''use them to good effect,'' and closed with assurance of ''my great respect.''[126]

In lending his respected name and his powers of debate to the Southern cause, Thornwell made a contribution that, while it is difficult to measure, was clearly significant in clarifying for other Southerners the grounds on which they were being asked to stand and confirming in their minds the legitimacy and morality of their cause. This is not to say that had he and other leading clergymen withheld their support, the Southern position would have been different; but without the Fast Day Sermons and essays such as ''The State of the Country,'' the righteous spirit that drove the Confederacy in its early years could not have been so strong. Perhaps comparing the effect of these efforts with that of Thomas Paine's *Common Sense* would

---

[124]Seth Bliss to Thornwell, 9 February 1861, ibid. The article was reprinted as *Hear the South! The State of the Country: An Article Republished from the* Southern Presbyterian Review *by James Henley Thornwell* (New York, 1861).

[125]Seth Bliss to Thomas Smyth, 13 March 1861; quoted in Smyth, *Autobiographical Notes,* 598, 600.

[126]Nathan Lord to Thornwell, 13 February 1861, Thornwell Papers. Lord, an orthodox Congregationalist clergyman, was a defender of slavery who admitted blacks to Dartmouth. *Appleton's Cyclopedia of American Biography,* vol. 4 (New York, 1887-1900) 25. Other letters expressing approval of Thornwell's views came from J. B. Smith of Spencerport, near Rochester, New York, on 5 March 1861, and from Samuel J. Harrington, of Ridge, Texas, on 24 March 1861—Thornwell Papers.

be exaggerating their importance, but they did play something of the same role as mobilizers of opinion at a critical moment.

Thornwell's impact on Northern opinion is even more difficult to gauge; however, the letters he received from the North demonstrate that a considerable body of conservative religious opinion existed there, which, together with the commercial interests centered in New York, might have been able to exert a calming effect on Northern policy. Ironically, if essays like Thornwell's had been given a chance to work their way, they might have induced the new administration to look more closely at the possibility of compromise. One must remember, though, that while Thornwell (and other Southern conservatives) may have sounded like the epitome of reason and restraint, he advocated the taking of Fort Sumter if the Union refused to abandon it, and stood ready to sanction battle if "Southern rights" were not respected.[127]

With the surrender of Fort Sumter and President Lincoln's call for troops, the states of the upper South reluctantly broke with the Union, and their clergy followed the politicians' lead. Virginia's Robert Lewis Dabney, who had decried the secession of South Carolina, calling her a "little impudent vixen" who had "forfeited the righteous strength of our position" and forced his state "to shield her from the chastisement she so condignly deserves," now embraced the vision of a godly Confederacy and became a chaplain in the Confederate army.[128] Ministers throughout the South invoked God's blessing on the young men who marched off to war, and assured them and their families of God's favor. "Blessed be the Lord my strength, which teacheth my hands to war, and my fingers to fight," read Benjamin Palmer to the New Orleans "Crescent Rifles" who assembled in his church in late May. As their battle flags stood against the walls of his sanctuary, he told them that they embarked on a struggle "between religion and atheism."[129] He told the members of another unit about to

---

[127]For another Southern minister's statement on the crisis, aimed at the North, see Thomas Smyth, "An Appeal to the Conscience of the Christian, Conservative Bible-Loving Men and Women of the North," *New York Journal of Commerce,* 1 March 1861. Smyth quickly abandoned his attitude of peacemaker after what he called the "glorious victory" at Fort Sumter, which was for him proof of God's protection of the South. See Smyth, "The Battle of Fort Sumter," *Southern Presbyterian Review* 14:3 (October 1861): 370, 381.

[128]Robert L. Dabney to his mother, 28 December 1860, and to Moses Hoge, 4 January 1861, quoted in DesChamps, "Union or Disunion?" 496, and in Silver, *Confederate Morale,* 20.

[129]Psalm 144:1; Johnson, *Palmer,* 237-38; LaMotte, *Colored Light,* 134.

board a train for Virginia that history had recorded no war "that is holier than this in which you have embarked." It was "a war of religion against blind and bloody fanaticism." Not to oppose the North, he informed them, would mean yielding to "a despotism which will put its iron heel upon all that the human heart can hold dear." Asking God to bless their flag, he sent them off with the prayer that "the Lord of hosts [will] be around about you as a wall of fire, and shield your head in the day of battle!"[130]

Christian pacificism had never been a strong force in Southern thought, and Palmer was performing what most Southerners saw as a fitting and proper function of the clergy. Indeed, other ministers who failed to show sufficient zeal for the Confederate cause found their congregations hostile, with the same being true in the North as well. William Swan Plumer resigned under pressure from Western Theological Seminary when he refused to lead a prayer for victory of Union troops.[131] Addressing the first graduating class of The Citadel in 1847, Thomas Smyth had examined the Christian's relationship to war and the role of the soldier. He told the cadets that God had instituted government and the right of self-defense. It was therefore clear that governments may defend themselves against enemies both within and without with God's blessing. The profession of soldier, he added, is neither condemned nor forbidden to a Christian in the New Testament. Christ's mission on earth was to bring peace, so the role of the soldier may be necessary, but he must be a gentleman, a patriot, and a Christian.[132] Seeing no violation of this doctrine in their course of action in 1861, most Southerners could have endorsed Smyth's message and ap

---

[130]Johnson, *Palmer*, 238-39.

[131]LaMotte, *Colored Light*, 144.

[132]Thomas Smyth, *The Relations of Christianity to War: and the Portraiture of a Christian Soldier. A Discourse Delivered on Occasion of the First Commencement of the Citadel Academy* (Charleston, 1847). A reviewer in the *Southern Presbyterian Review* praised the address and noted its timeliness "in these days of Peace Societies and sickly Philanthropy" (*Southern Presbyterian Review* 1 [June 1847]: 170-71). For another statement in support of national military action, see "The Mexican War Reviewed on Christian Principle," *Southern Presbyterian Review* 3 (July 1849): 74-124. William D. Blanks has concluded that pacifism was never a significant force among nineteenth-century Southern Presbyterians, and notes that the 1862 General Assembly of the Presbyterian Church in the Confederate States of America recognized "the right of the State to claim the services of any or all of her citizens in this time of her need." Blanks, "Ideal and Practice; a Study of the Conception of the Christian Life Prevailing in the Presbyterian Churches of the South during the Nineteenth Century" (Th.D. dissertation, Union Theological Seminary of Virginia, 1960) 264-66.

plied it easily to the conflict then looming before them. Smyth himself reiterated and elaborated on these views in an essay in the summer of 1861.[133]

The prevalence of views such as these probably predetermined the outcome of the 1861 General Assembly of Old School Presbyterians. Tensions, theological and sectional, had always been present, if muted, in the meetings of this body, and only the tacit agreement to respect the "spirituality of the church" had kept them from rising to the surface. Even old friends and fellow conservatives such as Thornwell and Robert J. Breckinridge had begun to feel the effects of these tensions, as a letter from Breckinridge to Thornwell some eighteen months earlier revealed.[134] In this letter Breckinridge is admitting to some concern over the rivalry between Danville (Kentucky) Seminary, where he taught, and Columbia, and trying to soothe Thornwell's frustrations on this account. The two had fought together in many ecclesiastical battles, but the sectional crisis found them on opposing sides.

Spring of 1861 found Thornwell in poor health once again, and he took a leave from his duties in Columbia to seek the restorative powers of Glenn Springs in western South Carolina. Thus he could not attend the meeting in May of the General Assembly, which was held in Philadelphia.[135] The fullest account of Thornwell's health during 1861 is in his letter of 19 November 1861 to General James Gillespie. Here he writes, "On the 15th of January I took to my bed, from which I hardly arose until about the 1st of April. My system was utterly broken down, and broken down, as the doctor said, in consequence of excessive work. About the 1st of April I began to amend [*sic*]; and had the folly to go down to Charleston, where I took an affliction of the bowels, that kept me prostrate during the whole summer. I had no energy for anything, except to pray for my country and the Church." After mentioning his visits to the springs and to the home of his son-in-law in Lincoln County, North Carolina, he reported his return to Columbia and the Seminary. "I am still improving, but my right lung is still feeble, and my bowels are in a great measure toneless."[136] He prob-

[133]Thomas Smyth, "The War of the South Vindicated, and the War of the North Condemned," in *Complete Works*, 7:563-698.

[134]Robert J. Breckinridge to Thornwell, 3 January 1860, Thornwell Papers.

[135]Palmer, 490-91.

[136]Ibid., 497-98.

ably would not have attended the General Assembly anyway, for South Carolina, along with Georgia, Alabama, North Carolina, and Arkansas sent no delegates. In a letter addressed to the assembly, he explained that illness and "other issues, much more pressing and much more solemn," kept him away. Indicating that he viewed the events of the previous months as irrevocable, he beseeched God's blessing upon their deliberations—"that he may restore harmony and good will between your country and mine." When this was read to the assembly, said the Philadelphia press, the last line evoked "great laughter."[137]

Writing toward the end of the Reconstruction era, Palmer regarded this assembly as a "splendid opportunity . . . of demonstrating the purely spiritual character of the Church." But "the golden vision was not to be realized," for the assembly ignored the "statute in our code" that bars church courts from "intermeddling with civil affairs."[138] It is a matter of controversy just how radical a break with tradition this was. But the 1861 assembly adopted a resolution offered by Dr. Gardiner Spring of New York, which declared the obligation of Presbyterians "to promote and perpetuate, so far as in us lies, the integrity of these United States, and to strengthen and uphold the Federal government in the exercise of all its functions." A milder resolution had been offered in opposition to this one by Charles Hodge. It pointed to the break with the tradition of avoiding secular politics and called it "unjust and cruel" to force Southern Presbyterians "to choose between allegiance to their States and allegiance to the Church." The vote by which the Spring Resolution was adopted was 156 to 64.[139]

This action became the rationale for the ecclesiological secession of Southern Presbyterians in the following months. Yet as John Adger recognized, that secession would have come in any case, for Presbyterians in the Confederate states were too firmly committed to the cause of their new nation to remain affiliated with their Northern brethren. Adger expressed this view when he wrote, in the summer of 1861, that no church "can properly perform its spiritual functions within the limits of two distinct na-

---

[137]LaMotte, *Colored Light*, 133; Lewis G. Vander Velde, *The Presbyterian Churches in the Federal Union, 1861-1869* (Cambridge MA, 1932) 45.

[138]Palmer, 501.

[139]Ibid.; Thompson, *Presbyterians in the South*, 1:564-65; LaMotte, *Colored Light*, 134. Palmer gives the vote as 154 to 66.

tions."[140] Thornwell's reaction to the Spring Resolution was predictable. "It has not only directed us to render unto Caesar the things that are Caesar's," he complained, "but it has assumed the right to adjudicate betwixt the claims of rival Caesars, and to say which is entitled to allegiance." On a more practical level, he noted the impossibility of Christian unity in a body "one half of whom believe that the other half ought to be hanged" and who denounce each other as "rebels" and "Tyrants."[141]

It has been noted that in professing their loyalty to the Confederacy, the Southern church bodies were guilty of the same violation of the "spirituality of the church" as the Spring Resolution. "In the excitement of the times," writes one scholar, it would be surprising to find them discerning this irony.[142] But some of them did recognize the departure and addressed themselves to it. John Adger asked the readers of the *Southern Presbyterian Review* how they could expect things to be otherwise in this unprecedented moment. With the noise of battle in its ears, how could the Church be expected to keep its attention on "routine and red tape," he asked. Warming to his topic, Adger continued, "It seems to us to be the absurdest possible notion of our Church Government, that the Confession of Faith forbids the Church Court from speaking out for justice and right and peace in such a case as this. The very idea casts ridicule, yes reproach, upon the Assembly, as a body of reverend recluses in white cravats and black coats, too sanctimoniously busy with their own holy or unholy pursuits . . . to turn an ear for one moment to the cry of a bleeding country." Adger, for one, was caught up in the compelling spirit of the time, in much the same way as Northern clerics had been compelled to take a stand on the issue of slavery. Those who had denounced others for bringing political and social issues into religious councils, or debasing religion by involving it directly

---

[140]John Adger, "The General Assembly of 1861," *Southern Presbyterian Review* 14 (July 1861): 343. Adger was, of course, ignoring the Roman Catholic Church in his statement. Episcopalians North and South would also demonstrate the possibility of functioning as one body despite divided political loyalties during the war. Palmer called the Spring Resolution the "equivalent to an act of expulsion." Palmer, 502. It is indicative of the unanimity of feeling among Southern Presbyterians that the forty-seven presbyteries bounded by the eleven Confederate states all, acting independently, dissolved their connection with the General Assembly during the summer and fall of 1861. Palmer, 502.

[141]John B. Adger, ed., *Collected Writings of James Henley Thornwell*, vol. 4 (Richmond, 1871) 439, 442.

[142]Thompson, *Presbyterians in the South*, 1:571.

in politics, were now experiencing the same intensity of emotion that had driven their antislavery brethren to action.[143]

Thornwell was careful in the resolution he drafted and presented to the Synod of South Carolina in November 1861 to obey the letter, if not the spirit, of the doctrine of the "spirituality of the Church." While the resolution pledged allegiance "to the Government of the Confederate States, as long as South Carolina remains in the number," and referred to the Confederacy as embodying "the only hope of constitutional liberty on this continent," it described the body adopting it as "the ministers and elders composing this Synod, not in their ecclesiastical capacity as a court of Jesus Christ, but in their private capacity, as a convention of Christian gentlemen."[144] Despite this disclaimer, the resolution was included in the minutes of the synod by "a singular clerical error," as Palmer explained it. It was later deleted by order of the Southern General Assembly of 1862, in order that the records of the Church should be free of any taint of political action.[145]

While poor health continued to keep Thornwell on the sidelines through the summer, he watched and thought about proceeding events and began to look to the formation of a new General Assembly. He announced his support for a special session of his presbytery to send delegates to a meeting at which plans would be made to form a General Assembly of the Confederate Presbyterian churches. Quick action was needed on this matter, he felt, so that potentially disruptive issues would not have time to take shape.[146]

By fall he was back in Columbia, somewhat restored to health, teaching at the seminary and helping to run the *Southern Presbyterian* newspaper during the absence of its editor, Abner Porter. He wrote several editorials, dealing in large measure with church politics, and produced a

---

[143]John Adger in *Southern Presbyterian Review,* July 1861; quoted in LaMotte, *Colored Light,* 135.

[144]Palmer, 509-10.

[145]Ibid., 510.

[146]Regarding his health, see Stephen Elliott to Thornwell, 10 June 1861, Thornwell Papers, and F. P. Mullally to Thornwell, 5 August 1861, ibid. Regarding his concern for quick action in forming a new assembly, see Thornwell to Mullally, 10 July 1861; quoted in Palmer, 593-94, and Thornwell to Abner Porter, editor of the *Southern Presbyterian* newspaper, n.d.; quoted in Palmer, 594-95.

piece for the *Southern Presbyterian Review*. He had abandoned preaching by this point and would return to the pulpit only rarely in the ten months left to him.[147] While he was not involved directly in public affairs, Thornwell's stature as a public figure led others to seek him out for council as the war heated up. Robert W. Barnwell, a former president of the South Carolina College, and an old friend, wrote from Beaufort, which was soon to fall to Federal invaders, inviting Thornwell to "share a few weeks" with him before he went to Richmond at the end of November. "I would like very much to have some long talks with you," he wrote. While expecting a visit from the enemy, he added, "we keep cool and resolute." The bickering in the press and the lack of solidarity among the Southern public generally distressed Barnwell, but "God has kept us," he concluded.[148]

The formation of the Presbyterian Church in the Confederate States of America, on 4 December 1861, in Augusta, Georgia, was a fitting climax to Thornwell's career. Though still weak, he attended the first General Assembly of the new church and was a leading force in its deliberations.[149] While the bulk of the assembly's time was taken in the formation of committees, agencies, and boards that would carry on the work of the new church, the most dramatic event in the week-long meeting was the reading and adoption of Thornwell's "Address to All the Churches of Jesus Christ throughout the Earth." This document presented the rationale for the body's separation from the Presbyterian Church in the United States of America, and it has been considered by one Thornwell scholar as the best expression of his thought.[150]

---

[147]Thornwell to Robert Anderson, 14 October 1861, Anderson-Thornwell Papers, Southern Historical Collection. Thornwell, "The Personality of God, as Affecting Science and Religion," *Southern Presbyterian Review* 14 (October 1861): 450-72. Palmer, 497.

[148]Robert W. Barnwell to Thornwell, 30 October 1861, Thornwell Papers. Thornwell did not go to Beaufort, but when the Port Royal area fell in November, the Barnwells came to stay with the Thornwells in Columbia. Thornwell to James Gillespie, 19 November 1861; quoted in Palmer, 497-98. In this letter he told Gillespie that his poor health was the result of "the profound interest I have taken in public affairs." Barnwell, an old friend, had preceded Thornwell as president of the South Carolina College and would soon become a member of the Confederate Senate.

[149]Palmer writes that the ailing Thornwell was "of course, one of [the assembly's] guiding spirits; and the papers which gave the largest character to this Assembly emanated from his pen, and were marked with the ability of his very best productions" (504).

[150]Paul L. Garber, "A Centennial Appraisal of James Henley Thornwell," in Stuart C. Henry, ed., *A Miscellany of American Christianity; Essays in Honor of H. Shelton Smith* (Durham NC, 1963) 95-137. The statement of Thornwell's "Address to All the Churches" is on page 100. The full text of the "Address" is in *Collected Writings*, 4:446-64.

The "Address" is divided into three parts. In the first Thornwell described the church and the state as "planets moving in different orbits," and argued that neither has "the right to usurp the jurisdiction of the other." In listing the separate natures and functions of the two, he explained, "When State makes wicked laws, Church can make humble petition." Only by the willingness of the Old School Assembly to respect this doctrine have American Presbyterians remained united during the last decades, he insisted. Unfortunately, the 1861 assembly's violation of it has forced the Southern synods to their present course. Had this assembly followed the traditional path, separation "might have been deferred for years to come," but, "like Pilate [it] obeyed the clamour of the multitude, and, though acting in the name of Jesus . . . kissed the sceptre and bowed the knee to the mandates of Northern frenzy." Southern Presbyterians were "grateful to God," he added, "that . . . we have never mixed the issues of this world with the weightier matters that properly belong to us as citizens of the kingdom of God."[151]

Next Thornwell recognized the more practical reason for the separation. Historically, he noted, "in all Protestant countries, church organizations have followed national lines." This is healthy since "it stimulates holy rivalry and zeal." In the present case separation from the Northern Church would better enable the South to pursue the principles that that Church once stood for, he added. "We have resolved . . . to realize its grand idea in the country, and under the Government, where God has cast our lot." Alexander Stephens and others had said the same thing in justifying the South's political separation from the Union. Thornwell candidly added, however, that the "one difference which so radically and fundamentally distinguishes the North and the South" was slavery. Begging the world's Christians to hear him objectively, he presented the position of the Southern Church on this issue. Our attitude toward it, he said, must be dictated by the Bible. Only if slavery is a sin may the church preach against it, and the Bible does not say that it is. We have denounced the abuses that the institution permits, but slavery itself is a state matter. Further, he argued, its drawbacks must be balanced against the fact that it has brought many Africans to us who "have been made heir to the heavenly inheritance." As to the concept of human rights, he asserted that they exist "not in a fixed, but a fluctuating quantity." "The truth is, the education of the

---

[151]Garber, "A Centennial Appraisal," 101-104.

human races for liberty and virtue is a vast providential scheme, and God assigns to every man, by a wise and holy decree, the precise place he is to occupy in the great moral school of humanity.''[152]

The final section of the ''Address'' asserts that the new assembly, while having aims ''common to all Christian churches,'' is ''not ashamed to confess that we are intensely Presbyterian.'' It concludes, ''We devoutly pray that the whole catholic Church . . . may speedily be stirred up to give the Lord no rest until He establish and make Jerusalem a praise in the earth.'' Despite the trauma that had led to this moment, there is no note of sadness or bitterness in the ''Address.'' The providential hand was at work, these men believed, and this was not the occasion for anything but gratitude.[153]

Thornwell also drafted a ''Farewell Letter'' to the Northern Church, in hopes that the new assembly would approve sending it as a gesture of good will. He also proposed sending a memorial to the Confederate Congress asking that the new nation's constitution include an article recognizing Christianity. Vigorous opposition to both measures led Thornwell and other supporters to withdraw them in the interest of harmony. A draft of the letter to the Northern Church, which was never officially presented to the Southern Assembly, repeated the main points of the ''Address to All the Churches'' and added one more: failure to disassociate themselves from the Northern body would seriously hamper the efforts of Southern Presbyterians to evangelize the slaves.[154]

The solemn adoption of Thornwell's ''Address to All the Churches'' was a fitting climax to his career, which later Southern Presbyterians would acknowledge as the cornerstone of their denomination. ''[T]o him, probably more than to any other single individual, our Church owes most of what is distinctive in her principles and her polity,'' said one.[155] One might add that Thornwell, as much as any other individual, expressed the ide-

---

[152]Ibid., 104-106.

[153]Ibid., 106-107.

[154]Palmer, 507, 509. For a summary of the Augusta meeting of the Southern General Assembly, see *The Assembly Reporter* (Augusta, 1861), reprinted as a special edition of the *Southern Presbyterian*, 1862.

[155]Garber, ''A Centennial Appraisal,'' 107, quoting President William McPheeters of Columbia Seminary, in 1901.

ology of the Old South, which was so much an amalgam of the political, sociological, and theological thought that his mind encompassed.

Thornwell did not live long enough to suffer the pain and doubt that battlefield reverses and final defeat would bring. Nonetheless, he saw enough deprivation and suffering, and sensed clearly enough the growing might of the Union, to experience the soul-searching that would temper the exuberance of so many Southerners before the war was over. While he had argued earlier that secession was the only way to achieve true peace, Thornwell admitted in November 1861, "I always thought war would be the consequence [of secession] but I preferred war to ignominious submission." He was not dismayed by the course of events following Fort Sumter, for he felt the final result was certain. "The hopes of liberty on this continent are centered in our success," he added.[156]

April of 1862 found the *Southern Presbyterian* daunted, but still optimistic. We must, it wrote, try to determine if our cause is God's cause. If it is, we need not worry. Asserting that the South was fighting for liberty in a war it had not caused and that God's purpose in bringing the slaves to America was yet to be worked out, the paper concluded that "our cause is safe if we truly put it into his hands."[157] Three weeks later Thornwell wrote to his old friend James Gillespie, "I feel an abiding confidence that we shall yet win the day—our people are beginning at last to wake up—they are rising in the right spirit all over the land."[158] It was this "right spirit" that provided his hope, for by this time Thornwell was deeply concerned over the lack of moral fervor on the part of the South's people. The selfless spirit that had inspired him during the secession winter and erased his fears of social chaos was declining all too rapidly, so he addressed his last literary effort, "Our Danger and Our Duty," to this critical shortcoming. Painting a horrible picture of the fate that awaited the South and its people if the Union armies prevailed, and adding that the hopes of humankind would be equally dashed, he sought to stir renewed zeal and selflessness in the Southern heart. Unless we want to see our land and homes become

---

[156]Thornwell to James Gillespie, 19 November 1861; quoted in Palmer, 497-98.

[157]*Southern Presbyterian*, 19 April 1862, 2. Possibly by Thornwell. An excellent example of the private expression of doubt as to the divine will is Henry William Ravenel's Journal, 18 March 1862. He wonders if "God has deserted us," or is "only teaching us through chastising," Ravenel Journal, South Caroliniana Library.

[158]Thornwell to James Gillespie, 8 May 1862, Thornwell Papers.

the prey of "Northern vandals," we must rise to "deeds of daring befitting the momentous crisis." God will not give us victory if our faith and dedication are unworthy. We say we prize liberty, "but liberty is the companion of virtue, intelligence and public spirit." "Let our spirit be loftier than that of the pagan Greek, and we can succeed in making every pass a Thermopylae, every strait a Salamis, and every plain a Marathon. We can conquer, and we *must*."[159]

Death spared Thornwell the ordeal of watching the "spirit of faction" and the "spirit of avarice and plunder" that had already shown themselves when he wrote these lines, but one can see in this essay a will that would have called for continued fighting, by any means at hand, rather than surrender. Along with pecuniary and political selfishness, he decried the laziness and the "fastidious notions of military etiquette" that were hindering the Confederate effort. If rifles are scarce, he wrote, we should take up "pikes, and axes, and tomahawks." If we cannot hold the open field, "we must prepare ourselves for a guerilla war."[160]

Personal tragedy added to Thornwell's anxiety about the Confederacy's future. In May his son Gillespie, who despite being underage had enlisted with his father's approval, was wounded in the Peninsula campaign in Virginia.[161] The trip to Virginia to bring the boy home for convalescence weakened Thornwell, and in June he left Columbia for Wilson's Springs, North Carolina, and then proceeded to his son-in-law Robert Anderson's home in Lincoln County, North Carolina. Letters to Nancy reveal that medicine was relieving the symptoms of his dysentery, but producing no cure. Further, his homesickness, his concern over Gillespie's wound, and the critical battle for Richmond weighed heavily on him.[162] After coming to Charlotte to see Gillespie as he returned to service in Hampton's Legion in mid-July, Thornwell's health collapsed and he took to what would become his deathbed, at the home of William E. White, of Charlotte. Two weeks later, on 1 August, after a steady decline and several spells of de-

---

[159]Manuscript draft of the essay published as *Our Danger and Our Duty*, Thornwell Papers. The published text is in Palmer, 581-90.

[160]Palmer, 585-86.

[161]Thornwell to James Gillespie, 8 May 1862; quoted ibid., 515.

[162]Thornwell to Nancy Thornwell, 26, 28 June, and 6 July 1862; quoted ibid., 517-19.

liriousness, he died quietly in the presence of his wife and his old friend John Adger.

After a funeral service at Columbia's First Presbyterian Church, conducted by Adger with the assistance of Columbia Seminary colleague George Howe, his body was buried in Elmwood cemetery.[163] He was not yet fifty years old. While he had written much, he had produced neither a systematic statement of his theology, nor a full treatment of his studies and thought in philosophy. He had endorsed the establishment of the Perkins Chair in Natural Science and Revealed Religion at Columbia Seminary in 1861, and approved the appointment of James Woodrow, a Ph.D. in science from Heidelberg University, to fill the position. It is tantalizing to think of him confronting the intellectual and spiritual crisis that Professor Woodrow thrust upon Southern Presbyterianism with his writings on Darwin in the 1870s. It is equally tantalizing to imagine him coming to terms with the outcome of the war and with Reconstruction. But it is also fitting that Thornwell remains for us a man of the Old South, fixed in that world of which he was so totally a product and so prominent a part.

[163]Ibid., 521-25.

EPILOGUE

When Mary Gaillard heard the news of the fall of Fort Sumter she was overwhelmed. "Then," she wrote, "came the flooding tide in gushing streams from my pent-up heart and I felt how good God was. At sunrise I got up and took my Bible [and read] in the 12 and 13 verses of one chapter in Nahum, 'I have afflicted thee, but thou shall be afflicted no more. For *now* I will break his yoke off thee, and burst thy bonds in sunder.' "[1] Such statements reveal the cathartic effect the outbreak of war had on those who had lived with the tensions of the sectional crisis for a decade or more. But the ironies of these statements overwhelm the modern reader and seem to mock their authors, for the afflictions of the past would soon seem small indeed to Mrs. Gaillard and her neighbors. The yoke that would soon be fastened on them was heavier by far than any they had borne before. Knowing this, it is difficult to get past the ironies such words suggest, to examine and explain them. This task is made more difficult for those who cannot view defenders of slavery as sincerely religious people, or for whom the writings of antebellum Southerners are largely self-righteous delusions.

It is important to understand that expressions such as Mrs. Gaillard's were a natural consequence of the peculiar religiopolitical climate of the late antebellum South. Perhaps in no other culture has a particular form of religious expression been so prevalent and so influential as has orthodox Protestantism in the American South. Lacking the religious pluralism that produced the more tolerant and increasingly secular societies of the North and West, the South did not develop a strong tradition of church-state separation. The absence of this tradition was never more apparent, and significant, than in the mid-nineteenth century, when a series of revivals and

---

[1] R. Nicholas Olsberg, "A Government of Class and Race; William Henry Trescot and the South Carolina Chivalry, 1860-1865" (Ph.D. dissertation, University of South Carolina, 1972) 201.

a self-conscious alienation from the outside world produced an intense orthodoxy.

This orthodoxy helped to shape the style of the antebellum clergy, who in turn helped to shape the self-image of their communities.

> When the religious, political, moral, and social spheres of society merge, that convergence evokes a style of ministerial leadership that can prosper only in this rare climate. Under these conditions the ministry is not forced to be prophetic, calling for social reformation, nor is it called to be evangelistic, urging personal transformation. The minister, rather, has the privilege of functioning as sage: the one who stands *in* culture, not over against it; the one who confirms what is wise in life and calls for mastery of it.[2]

The mid-nineteenth century was the classic age of the preacher-sage in the South.

The message of these sages, of whom James Thornwell was perhaps the quintessential example, was that Christianity was a reasonable faith as well as revealed truth, and that the Southern way of life was as close as man in his fallen state was likely to come to the Christian way of life. The justification of slavery, while the most notorious of their efforts, was logically consistent with their biblical literalism and their general inclination to explain and justify cultural realities. However, the sages did not stop with their confirmation of what was: they called for greater piety and honesty in everyday life, and for control of passions—under the rule of Christian love and reason—in everyday relationships, including that of master and slave. While never fully satisfied with the results of his efforts, the typical Old South clergyman often came to feel that his society had attained a religious ideal unmatched elsewhere. His parishioners, who heard and read his message regularly, reflected it in their ethos and actions. Indeed, so strong was their conviction in this regard that the clergy and its lay supporters would lead in the development of the Lost Cause myth after the war, with its attempt to maintain the Confederacy as a metaphysical presence in postbellum Southern life.[3]

---

[2]Thomas G. Long, ''Preaching,'' in Samuel S. Hill, ed., *The Encyclopedia of Religion in the South* (Macon, 1984) 593.

[3]See Charles R. Wilson, *Baptized in Blood; The Religion of the Lost Cause, 1865-1920* (Athens, 1980).

Viewed in this context, the words and actions—both confident and cautious—of Southerners during the war become more understandable. "For some wise purpose, now unrevealed to us," wrote one, "God has permitted us to become involved in a most iniquitous war, the iniquity being all on the side of the Northern portion of this country."[4] Others were less certain. "It appears to us," wrote the editor of the *Southern Presbyterian*, "that the present troubles between the North and the South should be viewed by religious men as in part the punishment of the sins of the whole people during long years of national prosperity and forgetfulness of God." The South had shared fully in this, he continued. Drunkenness, profanity, violence, Sabbath-breaking, parental irresponsibility, and the cheating of Indians had no doubt aroused God's anger. Equally bad was the willingness of Southerners to take full credit for their early battle successes. "Our danger," the editor warned, "lies in the boastfulness our victories have produced, and our willingness to trust in our arms for success. To expect divine blessing on our efforts, we must look constantly to God as the source of our strength, and we must take more seriously the responsibility He has given us to care for our slaves." The Confederate Constitution's acknowledgment of God was to this writer a good sign on the first account, and abundant crops during the war's first summer suggested divine favor. As for the second matter, that of Southerners' obligation to their slaves, the severing of national ties afforded a new opportunity to evangelize them, and this Christian duty must not be shirked.[5]

Such a mixture of hope and caution would continue in the religious press for the duration of the war, since the Confederacy had been spiritually fortified as had few warring nations before or since. The sectional tensions of the previous generation, highlighted by the slavery debate, had clarified the Southern point of view and thus produced a high level of confidence and optimism within the region. But this point of view had also mitigated the very confidence with which the Confederacy approached the war. For the cornerstone of the Southern ethos was its evangelical piety. Southerners who had imbibed the traditional Christian values of their region had the biblical admonition "pride goeth before the fall" always before them. Indeed, it was their willingness to grant God His place and accept for them-

---

[4] *The Southern Presbyterian* (Columbia), 27 July 1861.

[5] Ibid., 13 July, 10 August, 12 October 1861.

selves the humble station of fallen creatures that formed the basis of their optimism. In so doing, they saw themselves as defenders of the most profound truth and the North and modern society in general as entrapped in profound error. Surely, then, God would not desert them in their hour of desperate need, if only they remained faithful to Him.

But He had a rival—the god of Southern nationalism. Paradoxically, when Southerners fled from the modern liberal image of autonomous, laissez-faire man, cut loose from tradition to drift in dangerous waters with rationalism as his only oar, they sought security in that very nationalism which was becoming one of the chief deities of modern man. Could this nationalism remain only the means to the greater end of escaping the dangers they saw before them? Or would it become the end in itself and thus threaten to undo them? This fear led the Southern clergy continually to caution against the idolatry and pride of nationalism, while embracing the Confederacy with a fervor surpassed by few parishioners.[6]

In a sense they were merely being true to their tradition, for it is typical of Protestant thought to swing between fretful soul-searching and self-righteous damnation of outsiders. For Thornwell the Calvinistic suspicion of human institutions was always mitigated by a powerful tendency to identify with institutions of which he was a part. These included the Presbyterian Church, the United States, South Carolina, and slavery.[7] The conflict inherent in such loyalties would be resolved only with great pain. He opposed secession until Lincoln's victory, yet he stated in the midst of the first secession movement, 1850-1851, "We are not only in the State, but of the State, and we have no thought but that of sharing her fortunes."[8] Ten years later, in his essay "Our Danger and Our Duty," he warned of the disasters that would befall mankind in the wake of a Union victory and asserted that while great accomplishments were within reach of the new

[6]To further complicate matters, some have argued that it was the doctrines of John Calvin and his followers that gave birth to the very evils antebellum Southerners were combating. "Geneva," wrote George Fitzhugh, "was the birthplace of the modern *isms*, modern infidelity, anarchy, and military despotism." Harvey Wish, *George Fitzhugh: Propagandist of the Old South* (Baton Rouge, 1943) 226.

[7]Thornwell's "great capacity to identify with communities and institutions and to become their spokesman" has been noted by Professor John H. Leith of Union Seminary (VA) in a paper, "James Henley Thornwell and the Shaping of the Reformed Tradition in the South" (in the possession of the author).

[8]Thornwell, "Critical Notices," in Palmer, 579.

Confederacy, ''no nation ever yet achieved anything great, that did not regard itself as the instrument of Providence.''[9] Such regard should lead Southerners to remove from their midst ''whatever is offensive to a holy God.'' But it could, despite Thornwell's warning, make them vulnerable to the ultimate pride of thinking their cause divine.[10]

So the metaphysical confederacy was a creature of paradox. Resting on a foundation of piety, it structured a self-image that could easily lead to arrogance. Claiming allegiance to a philosophy of organicism, tradition, deference, and faith, it appealed for its defense to rationality, science, and sociology. And when it felt threatened by alien values, it insulated itself through that radical rationalist act, the construction of a new state. It is intriguing to ponder the dilemmas that such a paradoxical base ultimately would have produced in the new Southern nation had they not been short-circuited by the exigencies of war.

---

[9]Thornwell, ''Our Danger and Our Duty,'' ibid., 582, 583, 585, 586.
[10]Ibid., 586-87.

INDEX

Abolitionism: Southern religious view of, 102, 206-11; Southern response to, 24, 25

Adams, Jasper, and organicism, 158-59

Adger, John B., 34; and abolitionism, 207-208; compares Thornwell to Calvin, 126; critic of African slave trade, 214; and General Assembly of 1861, 275-76; and *jure divino* Presbyterianism, 184, 194; slaveholding ethic, 210; and spirituality of the Church, 257; on Thornwell's combativeness, 68

African slave trade, opposition to reopening of, 213-14

Agassiz, Louis, 100-101, teacher of Joseph LeConte, 105

Ambiguity of the Southern mind, 27-30

Ancient Greece: George Fitzhugh finds kindred spirit in Aristotle, 112-13; Old South identification with, 112

Anderson, James, religious perspective on sectional crisis, 11

Anthropology, American School of, 86

Aristotle: admired by Southern thinkers, 112-13; Thornwell and, 144

Bachman, John, 14; as naturalist, 85, 99-102

Baconianism, 88, 91-99; James Woodrow and, 120-21; pervasiveness of in nineteenth century, 92; Thornwell and, 135, 138-52

Bagby, George W., associates secession and religion, 11

Bancroft, George: admirer of Thornwell, 62-63; as historian, 115

Barnwell, Robert W., as example of Southern gentry, 26

Beecher, Henry Ward, admirer of Thornwell, 62-63, 177

Berkeley, George, 93

Bible and slavery, 231

Biology and Christianity, 99-102

Boards question, in Presbyterian Church, 184-86

Bozeman, Theodore D., 77

Breckinridge, Robert J., 34; and *jure divino* Presbyterianism, 184

Brugger, Robert J., 7

Brumby, Richard T., uses geology to support Christian view, 118

Calhoun, John C.: attitude of Southern thinkers toward, 39; as disciple of Jefferson, 24; political philosophy illustrated in *Exodus*, 3-4, 15; and Thornwell, 62, 153

Calvin, John, as theocrat, 260

Calvinism, 6, 53, 160

Cash, Wilbur J., 15, 18

Cash-Sellers school of Southern history, 2-3

Catholicism, Thornwell as opponent of, 190-92

Channing, Steven, 16

Charleston, South Carolina: clubs, 31; New School strength among Presbyterians, 178, 179-80

Chesnut, Mary Boykin, 19; as historian, 115

Church membership, growth of, 12

Clergy, Southern: friendships among, 34; impact of Common Sense upon, 98; influence on secular leaders, 14; interest in science, 83-87; number, in 1850, 12; and politics, 175-78; reinforcement of region's values, 9, 11, 13, 235; and Southern nationalism, 239, 241, 242-48, 285-89

Coles, Robert, on feelings of shame among Southerners, 29

Columbia, South Carolina, intellectual community in, 107

Columbia Theological Seminary: Chair in Natural Science and Revealed Religion,